Politics in Georgia

Second Edition

Politics in Georgia

Second Edition

Arnold Fleischmann and Carol Pierannunzi

The University of Georgia Press | Athens and London

© 1997, 2007 by the University of Georgia Press
Athens, Georgia 30602
All rights reserved
Set in 10.5/14 Minion by Newgen
Printed and bound by Thomson-Shore

The paper in this book meets the guidelines for
permanence and durability of the Committee on
Production Guidelines for Book Longevity of the
Council on Library Resources.

Printed in the United States of America

11   10   09   08   07   C   5   4   3   2   1
11   10   09   08   07   P   5   4   3   2   1

Library of Congress Cataloging-in-Publication Data

Fleischmann, Arnold.
Politics in Georgia / Arnold Fleischmann and Carol Pierannunzi.
— 2. ed.
         p.   cm.
Includes bibliographical references and index.
ISBN-13: 978-0-8203-2906-2 (hardcover : alk. paper)
ISBN-10: 0-8203-2906-1 (hardcover : alk. paper)
ISBN-13: 978-0-8203-2907-9 (softcover : alk. paper)
ISBN-10: 0-8203-2907-X (softcover : alk. paper)
1. Georgia—Politics and government. I. Pierannunzi, Carol.
II. Title.
JK4316.F54 2007
320.4758—dc22   2007015454

British Library Cataloging-in-Publication Data available

To Phillip and John

CONTENTS

ACKNOWLEDGMENTS

Preparation of the second edition of *Politics in Georgia* was a much greater task than we first envisioned. In working through the first edition, we discovered that we wanted to cover new issues and deal with some topics in different ways. As a result, the second edition took more time coming to press than we had hoped but is, we believe, better organized and more informative—and certainly longer. Plus, we had enough time to include the 2006 elections.

As is always the case in preparing a manuscript for publication, we have been assisted by a large number of helpful colleagues and associates. We are grateful to Dave Sjoquist and Charlotte Steeh of the Georgia State Poll, James Bason of the Georgia Poll, and Rich Clarke of the Peach State Poll for their contributions to the sections on public opinion. Thanks to Steve Anthony for helpful comments on the general direction of the second edition. We owe special thanks to students and former students Gio Diaz, Justin Freeborn, Chris Goodman, Wendy Gross, Maggie Heim, Brad Klaus, Bill McClure, Alicia Newberry, and Micah Savage for their help in tracking down data and formatting tables. Thanks to Sherry Williams at the Burruss Institute of Public Service of KSU for preparing and formatting text. Thanks also to Mark Patterson for assistance with maps. At the University of Georgia Press, thanks to Karen Orchard, Nancy Grayson, Jennifer Reichlin, and Ellen Goldlust-Gingrich for their helpful comments and stewardship of the manuscript.

Finally, an especially heartfelt thanks for the support of our families: Phillip Evans, John Hutcheson, and children Christine, John, and Anna Rose.

We are grateful that we have their encouragement in this and all other endeavors.

As we said in the first edition, it would be great to blame those named here for the shortcomings of this text, but it would be more fair to blame each other. What else are coauthors for, now that we have known each other for twenty years? We hope that readers find the second edition an informative and analytical guide to the always entertaining, often frustrating world of Georgia politics.

INTRODUCTION

Much has changed since the first edition of *Politics in Georgia* was published in 1997, yet much about Georgia politics has remained the same. In the introduction to the first edition, the major historical changes that we stressed were government restructuring, the declining influence of rural areas, the growing clout of blacks and the Republican Party, and a proliferation of interest groups. The continuing patterns that we highlighted were racial conflict, the political influence of business, limited regulation of campaigns, and low voter turnout. Outside the political realm, we emphasized Georgia's rapid population and economic growth along with its poor showing on social indicators such as poverty and educational achievement.

In some ways, we got it right in pointing out these trends to readers. Then again, we did not anticipate or might have downplayed other developments. Beyond the general growth in population was the huge increase in immigrants to Georgia. While suburbs continued to grow, they became more diverse, especially in metropolitan Atlanta. For its part, the city of Atlanta surprised many by increasing its population by more than twenty thousand during the 1990s and continued to grow during the early years of the new century. Perhaps more startling was the city's changing racial makeup: the percentage of African Americans dropped from 67 percent in 1990 to 61 percent in 2000 and continues to decline.

On the political front in 1997, Zell Miller was Georgia's Democratic governor, the state's two U.S. senators were Democrat Max Cleland and Republican Paul Coverdell, and Democrats controlled both houses of Georgia's legislature, where Sonny Perdue had been elected the previous November as a Democratic state senator from Bonaire. How times have changed. By 2005, Republicans controlled Georgia's legislature and Perdue had become Georgia's first Republican governor since Reconstruction. Some observers even wonder if rural white Democrats will become extinct.

Readers should not rush, however, to think of Georgia as the epitome of a Republican "red" state pitted against the Democratic "blue" states. Rather, Georgia might be "purple." The state has a large number of citizens identified as moderates. With the exception of Zell Miller's 58.2 percent in his 2000 reelection to the U.S. Senate, every winner for governor and U.S. Senate between 1994 and 2002—whether Democrat or Republican—was elected with less than 53 percent of the vote. On the flip side, Democrats seem to have given up on Georgia in presidential elections. Thus, we believe that Georgia politics remains in a state of flux.

Perhaps even more than in 1997, Georgia's political system deserves book-length treatment. One obvious reason is the state's economic and social status. The 2000 census placed Georgia as the ninth-most-populous state, with fifteen electoral votes in the 2004 presidential election. Twenty of the nation's one hundred fastest-growing counties between 2000 and 2003 were in Georgia, and Georgia's economy is also among the largest of the states.

As we indicated in the first edition, Georgia politics is interesting because of the tensions that exist between change and tradition. That statement may be even more true now. In addition to the trends we highlighted in 1997, the most obvious changes to watch in the near future are Georgia's growing ethnic diversity, including in suburban areas; the composition of the two major political parties; government services and finances, especially with Republican control of state government; and responses to growing concerns regarding education, transportation, and environmental quality. Change does not occur in a vacuum, of course. It is unlikely that new developments in Georgia politics will be divorced from the state's history of racial conflict, its traditional brand of conservatism, or the national government's growing role in policy areas such as education.

The Approach of the Book

This book draws on a wide range of scholarly work, popular accounts, and public documents to assist several audiences. On a somewhat practical level, it assists teachers, students, officials, and journalists in their work. Similarly, it can provide information that helps citizens—both natives and newcomers— understand and participate in the political process. A comprehensive volume also is valuable to researchers. First, it provides a wide-ranging overview of the state rather than just examining elections, some aspect of the legislative process, the actions of interest groups, or other specialized topics that have appeared in scholarly research. Second, a book such as this one permits useful comparisons of states, especially by researchers interested in the many changes that have occurred in the South. Finally and most pragmatically, a book on Georgia politics based on the widest possible range of published studies and government documents can be a valuable reference tool.

To appeal to all of these audiences, we have tried to avoid two extremes. First, this is not one of those tracts that bog down readers in jargon and obscure theoretical arguments. Second, this is also not one of those books that simply present names, dates, and other "facts" to digest. Rather, we seek to help readers understand how and why Georgia's political system functions the way that it does; evaluate existing politics and practices; and consider alternatives for the future. Such analysis requires more than a snapshot of the state today; it demands careful comparisons.

This book utilizes three important types of comparisons. First, it compares Georgia to the federal government. Second, it contrasts Georgia with the other forty-nine states. The third type of comparison might be considered more parochial—it involves comparing Georgia to itself over time. Examining how Georgia has changed or stayed the same is important for judging the present and considering alternatives for the future. Together, these three types of comparisons identify important similarities and differences.

The Organization of the Book

The first edition of *Politics in Georgia* was well received, and we have made some changes to accommodate the needs of scholars, teachers, students, and interested citizens. The most visible is the greater use of maps, figures, and tables. Readers of the first edition will also notice some changes in organization, especially in terms of covering elections, public opinion, and political parties. As with most works today, we have also relied more heavily on Web-based information sources.

The first two chapters set the context for examining Georgia's governmental institutions, political participation, and public policies. Chapter 1 examines American federalism, while chapter 2 provides an overview of

Georgia's history, population, and economy. These topics are followed in chapter 3 by an analysis of Georgia's constitutional development, including the impact of the federal courts on rights and liberties in Georgia.

This edition has expanded coverage of political behavior to three chapters. A new chapter 4 examines public opinion in Georgia, including attitudes on key issues and evaluations of officials. More widespread use of polling has increased the information available about the views of Georgia residents, and the will of the public remains a key factor in determining support for candidates, policies, and programs. Chapter 5 examines voting and elections. Chapter 6 analyzes political parties and interest groups, two major players in elections and policy making.

Four chapters cover Georgia's political institutions. One chapter is devoted to each of the three branches established in the Georgia Constitution. These three chapters feature frequent comparisons to the structure of government at the national level and in the other forty-nine states. We also place special emphasis on peculiar features such as the statewide election of certain department heads. Chapter 10 examines local government, which is not mentioned anywhere in the U.S. Constitution but remains a significant provider of public services in Georgia and the other states.

Chapter 11 closes out the book with an analysis of public policies in Georgia. The first edition devoted most of its coverage of policy to state taxing and spending. This edition expands and updates that coverage while adding more extensive discussion of additional types of policy, including education, the environment, public safety, transportation, economic development, and social welfare. The chapter concludes with a few thoughts about the future of Georgia politics.

Politics in Georgia

Second Edition

CHAPTER 1

States and Local Governments in the Federal System

Americans often take their political system for granted. Indeed, they might not appreciate how innovative the Framers of the Constitution were in establishing federalism, a unique invention that gives certain powers to the national government, others to the states, and some to both. Such an arrangement differs greatly from that in a unitary political system, as in Great Britain, where the national government possesses all authority and decides what powers and responsibilities lesser governments should have. This system also contrasts with a confederation, where independent states turn over limited powers to a larger government, as was tried in the United States in the 1780s and the former Soviet Union and Yugoslavia in the early 1990s. Even in 2005–2006, debates over federalism under Iraq's new constitution illustrate the struggles over national, regional, and local governance.

The dynamic character of American federalism has been instrumental in Georgia's political development, permitting Georgia to develop certain political institutions and practices that differed from those in the other states. Conversely, the federal government has used its authority to bring about significant changes in Georgia.

The Nature of Intergovernmental Relations

American federalism is a dynamic rather than fixed set of relationships. The U.S. Constitution mentions only the state and national governments, allowing the states to establish and control local governments. Given the diversity among different governments in the system, it should not be surprising that the distribution of power among the three levels of government has been a constant source of debate. Indeed, governments in the United States are linked to one another by regulation, cooperation, and competition.

Regulation

The key elements in the federal government's ability to regulate subnational governments are the supremacy clause, the enumerated powers, the elastic clause, and the Fourteenth Amendment of the U.S. Constitution. The supremacy clause (Article 6) declares that the Constitution and federal law are the "supreme law of the land." The federal government's power extends to the enumerated powers granted to Congress in Article 1—a long list that includes taxing and spending, regulating interstate commerce, establishing a postal system, declaring war, and many others. Most critically, the federal government's authority has expanded over the years as a consequence of the elastic clause, which allows Congress to enact laws "necessary and proper" for carrying out its enumerated powers. The practical meaning of that phrase has often proved a source of conflict. In the 1960s, for example, Congress used its power to regulate interstate commerce to prohibit segregated public facilities such as bus depots and motels. Finally, the Fourteenth Amendment requires the states to guarantee "due process of law" and the "equal protection of the laws." In practice, this has meant that the U.S. Constitution, particularly the Bill of Rights, provides minimum protections for all Americans that states cannot violate, although each state can grant its citizens more rights.

Below the national level, states have substantial power to regulate local governments. State constitutions and laws specify how local governments are created, what powers they have, how they can raise and spend money, the procedures for conducting their business, and a host of related requirements. Local officials often complain about state mandates—that is, standards and procedures imposed by the states, generally without state money to help meet the requirements (see chapter 10).

Cooperation

Governments also cooperate with one another to achieve goals. Many social welfare programs, for example, have been established and supervised by the federal government, administered by the states, and funded by all three levels of government. The federal government often coerces the cooperation of state and local governments by making money available only under certain conditions. For example, the federal government does not set speed limits but responded to the energy crises of the 1970s by giving highway funds only to states adopting a fifty-five-mile-per-hour limit. Similar action occurred regarding the drinking age and seat belt usage laws adopted by states. Thus, states have a choice in such matters, but failing to do what the federal government wants can cost tens of millions of dollars in federal money.

States work with lower-level governments in a wide array of fields through funding, technical assistance, training, and the like. For example, in 2000, direct state spending for elementary and secondary education was slightly higher than the amount spent by local school systems.[1] The states outspent local governments again in 2003. In that year, of the more than $440 billion in revenues allocated to elementary and secondary education in the United States, 8 percent came from federal sources, 48 percent came from state sources, and the remaining 44 percent came from local sources.[2] Like the federal government, the states use grants to push local governments in certain policy directions. More in the spirit of voluntary cooperation are efforts by local governments to share costs or resources, as when governments jointly build an airport or develop a landfill or when one government purchases services from another.[3]

Competition

Relations among governments also are characterized by competition, which can sometimes become very heated. An example of competition between levels is the federal government's efforts to restrict use of lands that it owns: states might see the same land as a source of economic growth and revenue if it were used for mining, logging, grazing, or recreation. Perhaps more common is competition among governments at the same level. The classic example may be officials using services, tax breaks, amenities, and other incentives to convince businesses to invest in one state rather than another. Local governments also compete for businesses by offering reductions or elimination of property taxes, sales tax breaks, water and sewer and other utilities at low cost, and other incentives.[4] For example, several states courted BMW before the company decided in 1992 to build an automobile factory in South Carolina. The selection of Georgia as the site for a Kia assembly plant in 2006 also illustrates this point. Similar actions occur at the local level, where cities and counties compete for a company's operations, as when United Parcel Service sought land for its new headquarters when leaving Connecticut for metropolitan Atlanta.

State and local governments have remained important players in the evolution of American federalism. The remainder of this chapter establishes a context for examining Georgia's government and politics by describing the scope of subnational government and by analyzing state and local responses to recent economic, social, and political changes.

The Scope of Subnational Government

The United States has more than 87,000 subnational governments—quite an array of states, counties, cities, villages, towns, school districts, and special districts. From 1952 to 2002, the total number of county governments remained relatively stable, at slightly over 3,000, but the total number of school districts declined significantly, from 67,355 to 13,522. During the same fifty-year period, 2,624 new municipal governments and 696 townships were created. The greatest percentage increase in governments occurred among special districts, which numbered only 12,340 in 1952 but grew to 35,356 by 2002.[5] Most special districts (91 percent) are empowered to provide a single service, such as hospitals, ports, or public transportation.

Despite receiving limited attention from many Americans, these governments are quite impressive in their size and activities. State spending in 2002 totaled $1.1 trillion, and local governments spent just over $1 trillion. During that year, federal government outlays totaled $2 trillion. For some activities, such as education and corrections, states and localities account for almost all direct expenditures. In 2002, state and local governments spent nearly $913 billion on education, more than 40 percent of all their expenditures, while the federal government spent a comparatively small $70.5 billion on education, including training and employment programs (see table 1.1).[6]

Table 1.1. Governmental Finances, Fiscal Year 2002

	Federal	State	Local
Revenue ($ billions)	$1,853	$1,180	$1,068
Sources			
Social Security Taxes	37.8%		
Individual Income Taxes	46.3%	17.6%	1.7%
Corporate Income Taxes	8.0%	2.7%	3.3%
Sales Taxes		21.9%	5.8%
Property Taxes		0.9%	23.7%
Other Taxes		3.1%	1.5%
Charges/Fees		15.5%	21.1%
Motor Vehicle Licenses		1.2%	0.1%
Intergovernmental Revenue		25.9%	35.2%
Other	7.9%*	11.2%	7.6%
Expenditures ($ billions)	$2,399,800	$1,186,108	$1,070,081
Functions			
Intergovernmental Relations	14.4%	29.5%	1.0%
Education	3.9%	12.8%	41.2%
Public Welfare	1.4%	18.6%	3.5%
Health and Hospitals	5.5%	5.3%	7.0%
Public Safety			
(Police, Fire, Corrections)		4.5%	9.0%
Highways/Transportation	2.8%	5.6%	3.8%
Natural Resources	0.9%	1.7%	2.8%
Sewage and Sanitation	N/A	0.3%	4.0%
Interest on General Debt	9.5%	2.6%	5.0%
Other Expenditures	61.6%	19.1%	22.7%

*May include revenues from fees and other taxes.

N/A = Not applicable.

Sources: Compiled by the authors from U.S. Census Bureau, *State and Local Government Finances, 2002 Census of Governments* (http://www.census.gov/govs/www/estimate02.html); U.S. Census Bureau, *State and Local Government Finances, 2002–03* (estimate03.html); and *Budget of the United States Government: Historical Tables Fiscal Year 2005* (http://www.gpoaccess.gov/usbudget/fy05/hist.html).

The scope of subnational government is impressive beyond the sheer dollars involved. In 2004, these governments employed 15.8 million workers; the federal government, by contrast, had 2.7 million civilian employees.[7] In addition to its broad scope, subnational government in the United States is characterized by great diversity. States and localities vary significantly from one another as well as from the federal government in organization, in the services they provide, in how they make and implement policies, in how they obtain and spend money, in how their citizens participate in politics, and in how they interact with other governments.

Recent Changes Affecting Subnational Governments

Change might be the hallmark of subnational government. The past three decades have confronted state and local officials with dramatic economic, social, and political challenges. These officials have responded with a wide array of policy innovations but also face a range of worsening and new problems in the twenty-first century.

Economic Changes

Subnational governments have had to deal with both overall shifts in the U.S. economy and changes in local conditions. The most pronounced change in the structure of the U.S. economy has been the shift from manufacturing to services. In 1980, the nation's 21.9 million manufacturing jobs accounted for 22 percent of all employment. The number of manufacturing jobs dropped 1.4 million by 1995 but represented just 16 percent of total employment. By 2004, only 16.5 million manufacturing jobs remained, a loss of more than 25 percent in just over twenty-five years. Similarly, agriculture lost 1.1 million workers between 1980 and 2004. During the same period, employment grew more than 98 percent in personal and business services, communications, transportation, finance, insurance, and real estate (40 million new jobs) and accounted for approximately 59 percent of all paid employees in the United States.[8] Projections for 2002–2012 showed the most rapid employment growth in software publishing (5.3 percent annually), with 4 percent annual increases in several other industries, including care facilities for the elderly. On the flip side, employment in apparel manufacturing was expected to drop

12 percent per year, with several other leather and textile industries experiencing job losses of more than 6 percent annually.[9]

Economic change is uneven, however—it does not occur everywhere in the same way or at the same rate. For example, the North lagged behind the national growth rate during the 1970s and experienced severe problems during the recession of 1981–1982. Resource-rich states in the Southwest and West, conversely, experienced more rapid growth in the 1970s, while the eight states in the South Atlantic region, which includes Georgia, grew slightly faster than the nation as a whole. By the mid-1980s, the New England economy had rebounded and was expanding faster than any other region, only to drop into a severe recession by the end of the decade. The nation as a whole generally enjoyed economic prosperity during the 1990s, but states experienced uneven growth. For example, the U.S. economy expanded 69.2 percent between 1990 and 2000. Georgia's economy did even better, growing 108 percent over that period, a higher rate of economic expansion than occurred in all five of Georgia's neighboring states. Several states in the West achieved even higher growth than Georgia. Other states were not as fortunate, however. West Virginia, Vermont, Kansas, North Dakota, New York, and other states that had relied for many years on manufacturing, mining, and agriculture grew more slowly than the nation as a whole during the 1990s.[10]

Similar patterns of uneven development have occurred at the local level. Rural areas have faced continuing changes in agriculture. The number of farms, their total acreage, and their value have experienced swings since the 1970s and dropped during the 1980s and early 1990s. Perhaps most unsettling have been shifts in the value of farms. Between 1997 and 2002, the number of farms dropped by almost ninety thousand. Even with a loss of acreage, the size of the average U.S. farm increased slightly.[11] The manufacturing sector in rural America also experienced trouble, in large part because its low-wage, low-skill industries face a high level of competition around the world. The instability of natural resource industries also poses problems for the future of rural areas.

Within metropolitan areas, many suburbs faced dramatic growth, especially in consumer services, with some suburban governments having difficulty providing services rapidly enough to keep up with new development and residents.[12] Central cities faced the other extreme: loss of businesses, aging infrastructure, and deteriorating services. Many central cities saw declines in their manufacturing bases, which had been the traditional means by which unskilled workers entered the economy. The shift to services and real estate speculation in the 1980s was associated with wild swings in the vacancy rates for office buildings. Many observers were surprised that the boom of the 1990s extended to cities, particularly those with jobs for immigrants and the young and educated people sometimes called the creative class.[13]

Social Changes

Subnational governments have also had to cope with problems related to population shifts, family structure, education, and poverty. During the mid-1970s, the media, public officials, and scholars focused on dramatic growth in the Sunbelt and the equally striking decline in the Frostbelt. When combined with births and deaths, migration produced widely varying growth rates among the states. Every state in the Northeast and Midwest except Vermont and New Hampshire grew more slowly than the nation as a whole during the 1980s; Iowa, North Dakota, and West Virginia lost population. Between 1990 and 2000, all twenty-two states in these two regions grew more slowly than the national rate of 13.1 percent, in large part because more people moved away than moved to those states. These trends have continued, with Nevada's population growing by 66 percent between 1990 and 2000. Another eleven states—all in the West and South and including Georgia—expanded by at least 20 percent during the decade.[14] The 2000 census noted shifts in the population but also indicated a growing number of Latino/Hispanic immigrants, especially in the South and Southwest. Latinos and Hispanics now represent a greater proportion of the population than do African Americans.

Growth also varied widely at the local level. Metropolitan areas have continued to gain residents since 1960, both in absolute numbers and as a percentage of the nation's population. In 2000, 80 percent of all Americans lived in metropolitan areas. Within metropolitan areas, central cities and suburbs frequently experienced sharply different population changes. In parts of the West, cities and suburbs alike have boomed. In some parts of the Northeast and Midwest, both cities and their suburbs have witnessed population losses during the past two decades. Smaller cities tied to manufacturing and agriculture have also faced decline.[15]

In Georgia, the city of Macon had a population of more than 122,000 in 1970, when its metropolitan area had 206,342 residents. By 2000, Macon's population had dropped by 25,000, but the metropolitan area had expanded to include a population of 322,549. Still, the boom of the 1990s revitalized many cities. For example, Atlanta's population approached 500,000 in 1970 but then shrank by more than 100,000 residents during the subsequent twenty years. A startling reversal occurred during the 1990s, however, when the city added 20,000 residents to reach a population of 416,474—almost the same as the 1980 census—and has since continued to add several thousand people annually. Perhaps most significantly for local politics, the white and Hispanic percentages of the city's population have risen, as have the income levels of the city's residents. Moreover, newer arrivals generally tend to be younger and less likely to include children within their households.[16] These patterns create a paradox: as many states and communities are struggling with population losses, others have had to confront rapid growth, including the costs of congestion, pollution, and similar problems.

Subnational governments have also faced challenges linked to education and poverty. U.S. schools have been criticized widely even though levels of educational attainment have risen, dropout rates generally have declined, and students are working more with computers. Complaints have arisen about the quality of high school and college graduates (especially in comparison to those produced by other nations), the decline in college admissions scores, the ways schools are organized, the preparation of teachers, and a myriad of other ills.[17] Many state and local leaders also complain about the additional regulations and costs they have borne since 2002, when Congress passed the No Child Left Behind Act. All of these concerns have weighed heavily on state and community leaders in general and perhaps especially on local school boards.

While noticeable progress in attacking poverty has been achieved, both the number and percentage of Americans living in poverty have risen since 2001. The poverty level remained below 15 percent from 1980 to 1993, when it rose to 15.1 percent (39.3 million people). The country then emerged from a recession and saw a decline to 31.6 million people in poverty (11.3 percent) by 2000. In 2003, almost 36 million Americans lived in poverty (12.5 percent). Poverty levels also differ by area, ranging from roughly 5 percent in New Hampshire to more than 16 percent in Mississippi, Louisiana, and the District of Columbia.[18] Methods for dealing with poverty have changed over time, particularly since Congress passed welfare reforms in 1996 that shifted more responsibility to the states. Moreover, the concentration of the

poor, including the homeless, in central cities poses special problems for local leaders. The aftermath of Hurricanes Katrina and Rita during the summer of 2005 highlighted the plight of many poor citizens concentrated in
older neighborhoods. When coupled with economic trends and segregation,
uneven social conditions have severely challenged state and local governments, taxpayers, social service agencies, schools, employers, and other
organizations.

Political Changes

Political developments have also had major effects on subnational governments. Especially notable are changes in federal policy, geographical shifts in
political power, and transformations in the groups and issues affecting state
and local politics.

Changes in the national government's role during the past generation have
reshaped American federalism. During the 1960s and 1970s, the federal government began providing substantial sums of money to lower-level governments to deal with their problems as well as with national concerns.[19] State
and local governments also benefited indirectly from subsidies provided by
federal tax laws. Beginning with Presidents Lyndon Johnson and Richard
Nixon, new programs and funds were added to a system of federal grants-in-
aid that had been devoted largely to highways and public assistance. Aid to
state and local governments grew from $10.9 billion in 1965 to $20.2 billion
in 1969, $68.4 billion in 1977, and $91.5 billion in 1980. Such grants came to
occupy an increasing share of both federal spending and state and local government budgets, raising the issue of whether the national government was
coercing or bribing lower-level governments to adopt particular policies.

Like funding levels, the purposes and structure of federal grant programs
have changed over time. Programs adopted during the Johnson years relied
heavily on categorical grants, which are for narrow purposes and maximize
the discretion of federal agencies dispensing the money. In contrast, the
Nixon administration emphasized revenue sharing and block grants, which
are given for broad purposes, use mathematical formulas to dispense funds,
and increase the discretion of state and local officials in using federal money.
Few changes occurred under Presidents Gerald Ford and Jimmy Carter
other than efforts to use federal funds to stimulate private investment.

The grant-in-aid system changed again during the 1980s. President Ronald
Reagan's administration proposed a "new federalism" to shift a wide range of

joint federal-state programs entirely to one level of government or the other. Although the more dramatic elements of this agenda were not enacted, in large part because of strong opposition from state and local officials, changes occurred nevertheless. After growing at double-digit rates during the 1970s, federal grants either increased less than 10 percent or declined every year during the 1980s. Several programs were terminated, including the General Revenue Sharing program begun under President Nixon and the Urban Development Action Grants initiated by President Carter. When inflation is factored in, federal grants from 1981 to 1990 dropped below their 1980 levels. Most notable perhaps was the fact that federal grants slipped from 25.8 percent of state and local revenues in 1980 to 18.2 percent by President Reagan's last year in office. Similarly, the majority of federal grant money since the mid-1980s has gone to individuals rather than governments or other organizations. Overall, federal grants to local governments have increased since 1989, and in 2001, federal money accounted for just under one-fourth of all local spending.[20]

Grant levels rose between 9 and 12 percent annually under Presidents George H. W. Bush and Bill Clinton. Especially after the Republicans took control in 1995, Congress increasingly emphasized turning over programs to the states and granting them greater flexibility. Proponents of this approach argued that the states know their needs better than the national government and can tailor programs accordingly. Critics were concerned about variation in eligibility and benefits among the states, particularly the degree to which some people would be cut off from programs that currently provide services.

Congress and the president also worked to "privatize" government enterprises (sell them to the private sector or contract them out to private businesses).[21] Critics attacked a whole range of federal subsidy programs for raising prices to consumers, supporting well-off businesses, and increasing the federal deficit. One major target was federal support for agriculture, including the peanut industry, on which Georgia depends heavily.[22]

Recent debates about whether the states or the federal government should forge policy are not necessarily based on ideology. Conservatives, who are traditionally aligned with states' rights, may argue for federal intervention, as with the 2004 debate on a ban against gay marriage. Liberals may prefer that states have the final say in some policy areas where federal jurisdiction might result in an undesirable outcome. In most cases, the federal government will attach aid to compliance with standards rather than specifying particular state action. For example, President Clinton set a strict standard for laws regarding driving under the influence of alcohol: states that failed to adhere to these standards would lose federal highway funds. President George W. Bush's No Child Left Behind law also imposed severe penalties in educational funding for states that did not comply.

Following the 2001 terrorist attacks on the World Trade Center and the Pentagon, the political environment shifted, with implications for federalism. Concern for safety gave the federal government opportunities to consolidate and coordinate law enforcement, a policy area that had previously been left largely to the states. Security concerns also provided the states with a new source of intergovernmental revenue, as funding for training became available though the 2003 Homeland Security bill.

Political power also has shifted geographically between and within states. The federal census, conducted every ten years, is used to reapportion the 435 seats in the U.S. House of Representatives among the fifty states. Today's political map looks vastly different from the one that existed following World War II. In 1952, the Northeast and Midwest accounted for 57 percent of the seats in the House of Representatives, whose largest delegations were from New York (43 seats), Pennsylvania and California (30 each), Illinois (25), Ohio (23), and Texas (22). By 1972, the North had 53 percent of the House seats, and California had the largest House delegation (43 seats, compared to 39 for New York, 25 for Pennsylvania, 24 for Texas and Illinois, and 23 for Ohio).

Recent population trends have accelerated the geographical shift in political power. The reapportionment of the House of Representatives is related to the balance of power within the Electoral College, which chooses the president. Each state has as many electoral votes as it has members in the House and Senate combined, and virtually every state awards its votes on a winner-take-all basis. Following the 2000 census, the state of New York lost twelve electoral votes, while California, Texas, and Florida gained a total of thirty-six. In general, the trend from 1990 to 2000 was a loss of electoral votes in the Northeast and Midwest coupled with gains in the South and West. Despite this overall trend, some southern states (Mississippi, Alabama, and Louisiana) lost seats, and some New England states (New Hampshire, Vermont, Rhode Island, and Maine) remained constant. Georgia, the fourth-fastest-growing state, moved from thirteen to fifteen electoral votes following the 2000 census.

Although no region has a majority, the South's 189 electoral votes are the most of any region.[23] From the mid–nineteenth century until the 1960s, the region voted solidly for Democratic candidates at all levels. However, Republican presidential candidates have enjoyed growing support in the South since 1964 and have had a near lock on the region since the 1980s. What has become the solidly Republican South in presidential elections has given the GOP a leg up in the race for the White House. Indeed, the presidency may be the Republicans' election to lose based on how the party does in other regions. Moreover, conservative voters and convention delegates in the South have been extremely important to conservative control of the Republican Party.[24]

Similar changes have occurred within many states. Prior to the mid-1960s, some legislatures had not been reapportioned in several decades, rural areas were substantially overrepresented, the population of legislative districts varied widely, and a minority of voters in every state could elect a majority in each house of the legislature, including twenty chambers where the majority of seats could be controlled by less than 25 percent of the state's population.[25] These patterns eroded in the face of population and political changes, however. Federal court decisions beginning in the early 1960s forced state legislatures to create districts with equal population, a policy that benefited suburban areas as they grew more rapidly than cities. The federal Voting Rights Act of 1965 created great pressure to improve the chances of minority candidates by drawing districts with large numbers of minority residents. These changes combined to create large numbers of districts in rapidly expanding suburbs, which were often white, affluent, and ripe territory for the Republican Party, as in the suburban rings around Atlanta, Savannah, and Augusta. Moreover, with half the nation's voters living in suburbs, such areas have strategic importance for presidential and statewide races.[26]

Dramatic changes in representation also occurred at the local level, where citizens and federal officials applying the Voting Rights Act pressed for the replacement of at-large city councils and county commissions with members elected from districts.[27] Critics claimed that at-large systems were biased against minorities in white-majority areas because electing candidates city- or countywide meant that whites would usually win because voters tended to vote along racial lines. Observers also argued that minorities generally live in segregated neighborhoods that could be represented by members of their own group under a district election system. During the 1970s, attempts to adopt district representation took place in more than half of the southern cities with populations of ten thousand or more and black populations of at least 15 percent. These efforts included referenda, petition and discussion campaigns, decisions by city councils or state legislatures, and legal action. Noteworthy legal conflicts over at-large elections and minority representation occurred in cities such as Richmond, Mobile, San Antonio, Houston, and Dallas.

In the late 1980s, 60 percent of American cities still had at-large councils, but this system of representation was most common in suburbs with fewer than one hundred thousand residents and in rural communities. In contrast, more than 70 percent of cities with populations of one hundred thousand or more elected at least part of their council by district. Electoral gains from district elections may be more extensive for blacks than Hispanics. People with lower incomes and less education are more likely to serve on councils chosen by district. Council members from poorer districts are more likely to become ombudsmen for constituents, although district councils may be more factionalized.

States and localities also face different interest groups and issues than was the case a few decades ago. One study of interest groups identified three trends at the state level since the 1960s: (1) significantly more groups trying to influence state government; (2) a broader range of interest groups, including those devoted to a single issue, social issues, and the public interest; and (3) more intensive and sophisticated lobbying. Some shifts occurred in political influence, with state employee associations, portions of the health care industry, environmentalists, and senior citizens gaining power in most states. Education interests (especially teachers), local governments, and business remain the dominant interests in state capitols, however. The growing importance of interest groups has also shown up in the rapid expansion of political action committees and their campaign contributions.[28]

At the local level, business interests and public employees still exert strong political influence. Business groups have become especially active since the 1980s in promoting local economic development, either on their own or with government cooperation. Neighborhood organizations, another new force in local politics since the 1970s, often go up against developers on zoning and other land-use issues. In built-up communities, these groups also work to maintain neighborhood amenities, to improve public safety, and to provide related public services.[29]

In terms of issues, states and localities have devoted significant attention during the past two decades to environmental problems, taxing and spending crises, economic development, education, crime, and governmental reform. States have also been forced to deal with social welfare programs. These are not new problems, but each has presented state and local officials with severe policy dilemmas.

State and Local Responses to Recent Changes

What have the nation's subnational governments done in the wake of the economic, social, and political developments of the past generation? Perhaps the simplest way to answer this question is to note that while state and local governments do not always get much media attention, they have produced significant policy and organizational changes. Indeed, they resemble only in part the way they appeared at the end of World War II or even at the start of the 1960s.

Economic Policies

State and local governments responded in several ways to the simultaneous inflation and unemployment of the 1970s; the recessions of the 1980s, of the early 1990s, and following the 2001 terrorist attacks; and the shift to global markets.[30] Subnational governments' first efforts in economic development policy began with industrial recruitment efforts in the 1930s. In the 1980s, state and local governments focused on retaining existing firms and creating an economic environment for expansion of private industries. The third wave, during the 1990s, focused on the political structure in which private firms operate. Policies during this period promoted public-private partnerships on the local level. During all of these phases, local strategies included major infrastructure improvements; tax breaks; loans and loan guarantees; land, building, and property improvements; job training; advertising and other promotional activities; and a variety of other initiatives.[31]

These waves of economic development activity are ironic in two ways. First, it is unclear to what extent these efforts actually influence businesses' decisions. Second, the impact of these policies diminishes as more and more governments try the same thing. Subnational governments also weathered economic hard times and the tax revolt that began in the late 1970s by developing new revenue sources, including a wide range of user fees, and relying more on the private sector, nonprofit agencies, and charities to provide services.

States and localities also devised several ways to deal with major side effects of the economy—pollution and congestion. The federal government has regulated management of air and water quality, but subnational governments have been leaders in dealing with solid waste. Problems still remain, though, in dealing with hazardous waste management. A number of policies have addressed traffic, erosion, and other problems related to rapid development, including statewide growth-management policies as well as local measures to preserve open space, limit the rate of development, control solid waste, and plan better for the future.[32]

Social Policies

States (and, to a lesser extent, local governments) have adopted a wide range of education, criminal justice, and welfare policies in response to social changes, which are often described in crisis terms. In 2003, subnational governments spent more than $411 billion on elementary and secondary education plus more than $156 billion on higher education. With public dissatisfaction growing, state officials adopted curriculum changes and stiffer graduation requirements for students as well as higher pay and standards for teachers. Controversies still exist, however, regarding the amount of schooling American children receive, the methods for financing public education, and families' degree of choice in selecting children's schools.[33]

State officials have responded to public concerns about crime with tougher and less variable sentences, more jail cells, and additional law enforcement personnel. These actions have been complicated by the federal courts, which increasingly have regulated prison conditions. As one might expect, these changes have affected spending. States allocated 4.2 percent of their direct general expenditures to corrections in 2002, compared to 2.6 percent in 1980.[34] Related state and local spending adds to these totals, and the costs of the criminal justice system seem likely to continue to rise rapidly.

All three levels of government are involved in social welfare programs. The federal government's main roles have been providing funds and regulating the actions of lower-level governments. States are important not only because of the funds they spend but also because they often determine who is eligible for programs and the amount of benefits people will receive. Local governments are required to help pay for welfare programs in several states and are usually responsible for delivering services to clients. In 2002, spending on social welfare, health, and hospitals totaled almost $426 billion and accounted for 25 percent of state and local governments' direct general expenditures.[35]

The controversy over social welfare programs deals with the number of clients, the length of time people receive benefits, and the effects of such programs on work incentives and the development of an underclass in the United States. Rising numbers of undocumented immigrants have further fueled this controversy. States have responded to criticism by tightening eligibility, limiting or cutting benefit levels, and imposing work requirements on program recipients. Some critics have argued that the federal government should take over or more closely regulate social welfare programs so that recipients do not get different benefits in different states. Yet with support from the Clinton administration and active encouragement by the Republican Congress elected in 1994, states received more leeway to experiment with social welfare programs.[36] It is doubtful, however, that state control of programs translates automatically into better management.[37] Several states, including Georgia, have begun to engage in policy debates that may lead to a refusal to offer public health services and even public education to residents who have illegally entered the United States.

Governmental Changes

Subnational governments have also modified the ways that they operate. As governors came under pressure to exert leadership during the past generation, states have changed the office in several ways. Unlike forty years ago, almost all governors have four-year terms, are elected in nonpresidential years, and have greater power over the budget and bureaucracy. Many states have matched the restructuring of the governorship with changes in the bureaucracy. Most states have tried to upgrade management practices and employees' professionalism. States have decentralized some activities to the regional and local levels and have turned over some functions to the private and nonprofit sectors. Still, state employment grew from 3.8 million in 1980 to 5 million in 2003, while local governments expanded payrolls from 9.6 million to 13.6 million workers. Importantly, however, 45 percent of these

18.6 million state and local workers are in education.[38] Some observers do not view this expansion positively, in part because this increase occurred while the federal government imposed greater requirements on state and local governments.

Economic, social, and political pressures have also affected local governments. One obvious change over the years involves the number and types of governments, including a huge reduction in the number of school districts and dramatic growth in the number of special districts (see chapter 10). Changes in the number and activities of local governments are controlled by the states, which are not known for dealing with local and regional issues in a very comprehensive manner.[39]

Local governments have also sought innovative ways to deal with problems. In many communities, government managers have received more discretion and can be rewarded like their counterparts in the private sector. Work rules have become more flexible, and contracting out to private organizations has become more common. Many local governments have also forged partnerships with businesses. Together, these developments are designed to make the public sector more entrepreneurial in serving local residents, both as consumers of services and as taxpayers.[40]

Change, Stability, and Subnational Governments

The U.S. federal system has witnessed dramatic changes over the past generation. Recent changes in international and national politics suggest that state and local governments may become even more important. Yet certain characteristics of subnational government in the United States have remained quite stable. Government structure, as reflected in state constitutions and city charters, has changed little. The Republicans and Democrats are the only two viable political parties, although their fortunes have shifted in various places and their influence is increasingly challenged by interest groups. Money still plays a powerful role in elections and policy making. Unlike members of Congress, those elected to state and local offices are generally not professional politicians and have limited staff and compensation for doing their jobs. Race and ethnicity still polarize citizens. Finally, much of state and local politics involves location—where to put highways or public buildings, which services get provided in different areas, where to draw the boundaries of cities or legislative districts, how to zone specific pieces of property, and many similar issues.

Georgia has not been immune to these developments during the past thirty years. The state has a long history of uneven development, however, which is typified by rural poverty and tensions between North and South Georgia. Politically, new groups have arisen, the political parties have become more competitive, and the national government has brought about significant changes in Georgia—often through the courts. In the end, V. O. Key Jr.'s description of rural whites' political control of Georgia in the late 1940s would not hold today, but it remains a base from which modern Georgia has developed.[41]

The Setting for Contemporary Georgia Politics

A variety of factors influence Georgia's political institutions and practices. As with any other state, understanding politics today requires considering the historical, social, and economic factors that have shaped the state's politics.[1]

The Historical Setting

Georgia's political development has not always been smooth; in fact, sometimes it has been downright tumultuous. A brief overview of seven periods demonstrates that a variety of events in Georgia history still affect the state's political culture and institutions.

European Settlement and the Colonial Period

The Creek and Cherokee nations inhabited much of what is now Georgia before the advance of European settlers in the sixteenth and seventeenth centuries.[2] Names of major rivers reflect the native presence: Chattahoochee, Etowah, Ogeechee, Ocmulgee. For a time, Spain, France, and England all claimed Georgia, although no country had any permanent settlement in the region. Not until 1727 did the English, following the philanthropic philosophies of James Oglethorpe, begin to muster the resources necessary to control the area. Georgia's original charter, proposed in 1730, called for set-tlement of the lands between the Savannah and Altamaha Rivers. Trustees were to govern the colony as a refuge for those suffering religious persecu-tion at home and as a source of relief for hardworking, unemployed, and even indebted Englishmen, who would provide economic well-being for the Crown while creating new lives for themselves. The trustees, headed by Oglethorpe, were prominent men in English society who were not permitted to own property in Georgia and to whom the king granted wide powers.

Because of an overwhelming number of applicants, the trustees seldom had to pick settlers who were debtors or societal outcasts. In fact, most were tradesmen and small businessmen. In 1732, approximately 120 set-tlers left England and landed at the site of what is now Savannah, for which Oglethorpe laid out plans. Although Oglethorpe opposed slavery, the prac-tice was introduced to the colony as early as the 1750s, prompting the devel-opment of plantation-like settlements rather than the smaller farms envi-sioned by the charter.

Georgia subsequently grew steadily. The first land cession by the Creeks was followed by many more as English settlements spread westward orga-nized around churches or parishes. Georgia under Crown rule remained much as it had under the trustees. The Commons House of Assembly, com-posed of nineteen men who owned at least five hundred acres of land each, enacted laws within royal limitations and with the approval of an upper house of twelve men appointed directly by the king. To vote for the members of the Commons House, male citizens of the colony had to show that they owned at least fifty acres of land.

The governor had royal authority to dissolve the legislature or overrule the judicial decisions made by the upper house. Georgia's colonial governors were primarily concerned with three major policies: military defense of the colony, negotiations with Native Americans, and border disputes with neigh-boring colonies, British or otherwise. After the 1763 Treaty of Paris ended Britain's war with France and Spain, Georgia's borders became better defined and less prone to attack from European competitors.

Georgia during the American Revolution

Discontent with British rule existed throughout the colonies in the 1770s.[3] Yet Georgia probably had fewer reasons than the other colonies to separate from England. The state depended on the British for most manufactured goods and profited from exporting raw materials to England. In response to what were deemed unfair acts by the British government, a group of citizens met in Savannah to protest Parliament's actions. The Council of Safety, as it came to be called, was the first organized protest against British rule in Georgia. This first government by Georgians preceded the Declaration of Independence by six months and was widely accepted by the newly declared free citizens of the state. Legislative power was vested in a provincial congress composed of representatives from each parish. The president of this body served as the executive, and courts were established. Thus, Georgia's first self-government incorporated the idea of three branches of government.[4]

With the news of the signing of the Declaration of Independence, Georgia adopted a new constitution in 1777 that provided for three branches of government, guaranteed religious freedom, and established the first eight counties as local jurisdictions. Problems arose quickly as powerful men struggled to fill the vacuum left by the toppled colonial government. To assure citizen support for the new state, British loyalists were declared to be traitors, were expelled from Georgia, and had their property confiscated. Political parties developed, mostly as factions within the Whig Party. Disharmony among the Whigs complicated the ability to govern and to fight the war. Even after the successful end of the war, factionalism within the Whig Party prompted new action on the part of the state to establish an effective government.

The Post-Revolutionary Years

After the war, the Articles of Confederation created the national government, which exerted little influence on the individual states.[5] The legislature was the dominant force in state government, whose major actions dealt with land cessions from the Indians, the migration of British settlers from Florida (which had been returned to Spain in the Treaty of Paris), and the sale of confiscated Tory property. The fledgling court system remained in the process of self-definition. Local government was established around counties, which were created by the state legislature and gradually assumed responsibility for roads, the poor, and local elections.

After the Articles of Confederation failed, Georgia adopted a new 1789 state constitution modeled after the U.S. Constitution. The Georgia Constitution provided for a bicameral legislature and a single executive. Georgia also laid claim to a vast western landholding and attempted to sell this land to the national government in exchange for badly needed revenues. Congress refused, however, and eventually forced the state to give up this territory with little or no compensation.

Georgia's leaders following the war differed substantially from its leaders during previous periods. Royal governors and trustees were wealthy, educated men—generally lawyers—selected by the king after distinguished careers as servants to the Crown. Following the war, Georgia's political leadership was likely to be drawn from the militia and had little training in government. Many of these individuals were illiterate, had been born in frontier country, and had few material goods. The new state constitution reflected this political emergence, and the aristocratic notions of the royal governors gave way in rapid order to the new concept of government by the "common man." Georgia's extensive landholdings were the basis for the most notorious political scandal of the time, the Yazoo Land Deal. The legislature contracted with land speculators for the sale of a tract of western land approximately the size of the current state of Georgia. Following charges of bribery, the legislature eventually passed laws to repeal the sale, but much of the land had been resold, and the matter eventually had to be settled in the federal courts. The Yazoo land fraud stirred many Georgians to the point of violence, and the incident prompted the drafting of a new state constitution with the expressed purpose of voiding the sale of any western lands by the state.

A second major event in Georgia during the post–Revolutionary War years was the invention of the cotton gin, which replaced the manual separation of cottonseed from the lint of the cotton plant.[6] This innovation, at a time when much of the Piedmont section of the state was being settled, prompted the development of larger farms devoted to cotton. Profits from these larger plantations made slavery more profitable, since owners could now clean cotton as quickly as it was picked. The westward movement of the white population also led to increased demand for land from Indian territory.[7] Larger cities were built around merchandising rather than manufacturing, as Georgia exported large quantities of lumber, cotton, and other local resources. Transportation posed a problem for manufacturers, although matters improved with the development of railroads in the 1830s. Banks were chartered during this period, and the state flourished economically.

Social and Political Life in Pre–Civil War Georgia

In the years preceding the Civil War, Georgians established a political culture and social order that came to represent a "southern way of life." Glorified today by oversimplification and the passage of time, this lifestyle implied a leisurely way of living on quiet, stately plantations. In fact, the vast majority of Georgians did not enjoy such a relaxed lifestyle.[8]

About thirty-five hundred white Georgians owned more than thirty slaves each. While only a few whites lived on plantations, many blacks did. The quality of life for slaves was determined by the length of time as slaves, their skills as craftspersons, or their work within white households. Despite laws prohibiting the education of slaves, many were highly trained in crafts, and many were leased out by their owners. Most white Georgians were subsistence farmers for whom life was not easy and religion was the focus of most social occasions.

Antebellum political life was defined by a splintering within the Democratic-Republican Party between the followers of two men, John Clark and George Troup, who opposed each other in Georgia's 1819 gubernatorial race. Although the legislature elected Clark by a narrow margin, the bitter factionalism based on the personalities of these two men continued, and Troup became governor four years later.

A major political crisis occurred when the Cherokees declared themselves an independent nation and sought negotiations with the federal government. U.S. President James Monroe agreed that the Cherokees could not be forced to sell their lands to the state and refused Troup's requests for federal troops to remove the Indians from their lands. Troup later hotly protested a treaty between the Creeks and the federal government involving lands within Georgia, declaring that the federal government had overstepped its authority by making a treaty without the approval of the state and calling out the Georgia militia to enforce his will to have the Indian land surveyed. Federal officials did not wish to pursue the Indian matter as far as violence and eventually interceded by paying the Indians for their land. Troup's strong defiance of the federal government won a powerful political victory for the ideals of states' rights.

The Troup faction eventually became more organized as the States' Rights Party. Troup served two terms as governor and then returned to his old seat in the U.S. Senate. Most Clark supporters joined the less radical Union Party.

As early as 1832, discussions of states' rights led to strong language favoring nullification of federal law, especially on issues regarding protective tariffs, which the South bitterly opposed. Yet Georgia was often less likely to radicalize these arguments into discussions of secession than was more polarized South Carolina. Georgia's political parties during this period were less defined by individuals and became more crystallized around ideology. Regionalism was beginning to develop among the southern states, which had little in common with the more industrialized North. States' rights were important to citizens who felt that the government in Washington threatened their way of life, prosperity, and autonomy.

The Civil War and Reconstruction

The Georgia Whig Party evolved from the old Troup and States' Rights Parties. It was affiliated with the national Whig Party, received most of its support from more established areas of the state, and was especially supported by those Georgians who owned slaves. Although the party did not represent the antitariff views of the States' Rights Party, its membership retained the ideology of states' rights. The Georgia Democrats, most of them former Clark-Unionists, also advocated states' rights but did so more in the context of southern regionalism. They quickly found an eloquent spokesman in John C. Calhoun of South Carolina. As Calhoun's rhetoric became more radical in the years immediately preceding the Civil War, Georgia Democrats also became radicalized. Acceptance of new states into the Union and national debate over the Missouri Compromise, which admitted some states as slave states and others as free, sharpened public opinion in Georgia.

Although Georgia was more moderate than some other southern states, in part because of its economic prosperity, states' rights constituted an integral part of the local political culture. The nomination and election of Lincoln were more than even the state's moderates could bear, and the legislature quickly voted appropriations for an enlarged state militia. The governor, Joseph Brown, moved Georgia quickly toward war, and the state seceded on January 2, 1861. The Confederate Constitution was adopted in March of that year, and a new state constitution was quickly drafted to reflect these changes.[9]

Governor Brown's lack of loyalty to a centralized war effort and his strict adherence to a states' rights philosophy undermined the military efforts of southern generals. Brown believed that conscription of soldiers by the Confederacy was unconstitutional, and his resistance to allowing Georgia's militia to defend other southern states proved problematic. He opposed the use of private property for the common war effort, martial law in Atlanta in 1862, and the military use of the railroads. Nevertheless, Brown was highly popular and was elected governor for four terms. Georgia was well represented within the Confederate government as well: Georgian Alexander Stephens served as vice president of the Confederacy.

The war stimulated industry in Georgia as the northern blockade forced Georgians to produce goods that had previously been imported. Despite this expansion, manufacturing failed to keep up with demand during the war years. Construction of railroads also accelerated, although many rail lines were destroyed as military targets. Many other infrastructure developments in the state also were destroyed during the Civil War's final days.

The state government established under the Confederacy was declared void at the end of the war, and the first military governor of the Reconstruction period called for a convention to establish a new government.[10] Delegates met at Milledgeville in 1865 and repealed the ordinance of secession, abolished slavery, drafted a new constitution, and repudiated state debt. Although elections were set for the following November, only those men who had not participated in the war or who were willing to take an oath of allegiance to the Union were permitted to vote.[11] Congress declared that the state delegates must not only repeal the acts of secession but declare them void. Moreover, Congress required that the state ratify the Thirteenth and Fourteenth Amendments to the Constitution before being readmitted into the Union. Until then, Georgia was occupied as a captured wartime territory.

Not until 1868, when a new state constitution was written and the state capital had moved to Atlanta, did Georgia's legislature comply with the federal conditions for readmission to the Union. Bitter political fighting followed as Georgia refused to recognize black elected officials in the state legislature and Congress refused to seat elected officials from the state. Black politicians elected during the early years of Reconstruction were never permitted to govern effectively and gradually lost office. Black voters were also rare and were often terrorized or coerced into voting for particular candidates. Thus, neither black officials nor black voters constituted significant political forces within the state during that time.

A highly organized group within the Democratic Party known as the Bourbon faction sprang up after the war to control the electorate and produced one-party politics in the state. Despite intraparty differences, the Democrats maintained their political stronghold for decades based on the general view that Republicans were northerners and outsiders. Bourbon Democrats based much of their appeal on the "southern way of life," a phrase that came to stand for states' rights and segregation.

The state slowly changed economically as well during this period.[12] Georgia was largely agricultural before and after the war. While most blacks had been slaves before the war and were unemployed after the war, large plantations still required the labor that slaves had provided. Tenant farming or sharecropping became common practices during these years. Tenant farmers, who leased land on which to live and grew crops in exchange for a portion of the harvest, replaced slaves as labor on large plantations. Most blacks and poor whites quickly found that they had no other way to make a living.

Railroads were gradually rebuilt, and the state itself became involved in the railroad construction industry. Northern investors, or "carpetbagger merchants," created a commodity market in the cities of Georgia, with Atlanta especially benefiting from this investment. Cotton and cotton milling remained important to the state's economy. Mining, along with fertilizer and lumber production, grew as an important source of economic recovery. However, Georgia's poverty relative to other states was worse in 1900 than it had been in 1860. Although manufacturing increased, the slower rate of development within the state caused it to lag even further behind other states, with many citizens still struggling with conditions of poverty.

1880–1945

The cycle of rural poverty in Georgia was well established in the early 1900s. Merchants provided farmers with credit against the upcoming harvest. Sharecroppers would often go into debt to feed their families until harvest. Because this often represented a substantial risk to merchants, interest rates were high. One or two bad crop years could condemn a farmer to lifelong debt. Because landowners and merchants were entitled to shares of the harvest, many good harvests would be necessary before sharecroppers could free themselves from debt. A drop in cotton prices before World War I and then again immediately after the war made life in rural Georgia even more difficult.[13]

Life in Georgia improved in some ways during this period, however.[14] Colleges were established and public education was expanded, although black and white students did not attend the same schools. In 1911, high schools became a part of the state's educational system, although many private high schools had been established before that date. As might be expected, white schools were uniformly superior to schools for black children, and even as late as the 1960s, some school districts did not provide high school education for minorities. More fortunate blacks were educated in several private black colleges founded in Atlanta. Most blacks worked as farm laborers, although a few owned and farmed their own land. Black women who worked outside the home were most often employed as domestic help in white households.

Women also took more active roles in public life. Conveniences such as canned foods and mass-produced clothing provided extra leisure time for many women. Child labor and the prison convict leasing system were important social issues of the day, and many of Georgia's reform advocates were women.

The financial and social plight of blacks and whites, especially those in rural areas, prompted the first real attempt at breaking the Democratic Party's stranglehold on the state. Because Georgia had remained essentially a one-party state since Reconstruction, real political contests were held not at the time of the general election but earlier, during the selection of the party's nominees for office. Prior to 1898, these nominees were selected by the party membership at conventions, but the introduction of the statewide primary election provided for more grassroots support for candidates. Black and white farmers, if united as a voting bloc, could control the nomination process under the primary system. A young attorney, Thomas E. Watson, sold himself as champion of these farmers, and a political movement based on agrarian political empowerment grew up around this dynamic young man.[15]

The Georgia Populists stood for low-interest loans for farmers and a graduated income tax. They were unique in that the party encouraged blacks to vote with whites on the basis of common interest in improved economic conditions. Georgia Democrats responded by calling up images of the destruction of white society as a consequence of the intermingling of the races. Democrats continued to attempt to intimidate blacks so that they would not vote or would vote for the party's candidates. Although the Populist movement secured some seats in the legislature, Watson lost a bid for a congressional seat. Populists achieved more success in later elections, as economic woes prompted more whites to vote for Populist candidates. However, to attract more white voters, Watson and his followers moved away from their biracial rhetoric, and Watson eventually called for the total disenfranchisement of black voters.

Watson was something of an enigma. At various points in his career, he campaigned for black votes, became staunchly anti-Catholic and anti-Jew, defended Bolsheviks in Russia, opposed Georgia's convict leasing system, and rallied behind the causes of Eugene Debs and other socialists. Watson's life was as tumultuous as the political times in which he lived. The Watson candidacies and brief rise of Populists in Georgia illustrated the deep divisions within the Democratic Party even though the Populists made few political gains in the state. The decline of Populism may best be attributed to the adoption of Populist values by the Democratic Party.

During the first decades of the 1900s, conflicts in Georgia politics were based on personalities within the Democratic Party, lower taxes, rural issues, and most of all, white supremacy.[16] Several people stand out as leaders of Georgia politics during this era. Perhaps the most influential was Richard Russell, who served in the state legislature, became governor in 1931, and was elected to the U.S. Senate in 1932, serving until his death in 1971.[17] Another important political figure was Eugene Talmadge, who served as governor in 1933–1937 and 1941–1943; he also ran unsuccessfully for the U.S. Senate in 1936 and 1938. Talmadge became almost dictatorial as governor, calling out the state militia to enforce his executive orders when other branches of government opposed his policies. Ellis Arnall was also a strong leader and perhaps the most progressive force in state politics prior to World War II. He reorganized the state Board of Regents that oversaw public colleges and universities, brought about simplification of the state constitution (which had been amended more than three hundred times since its last revision), and called for Georgia to adhere more strictly to the Fourteenth Amendment by allowing blacks to vote in greater numbers.

Georgia politics during the years of segregation was based on appeals to rural voters because Democratic candidates for statewide offices were chosen in primaries based on county-unit votes, which were comparable to the electoral votes used to elect a U.S. president. The system was used to select party nominees beginning in 1876 and became part of state law with the

Neill Primary Act of 1917. Under this process, each county received twice as many unit votes as it had seats in the Georgia House of Representatives, and candidates needed a plurality of unit—not popular—votes to win a primary. Since the Constitution of 1868, House seats had been assigned to counties using a three/two/one formula. Beginning in 1920, the eight largest counties in population had three representatives, the next thirty largest had two seats, and the remainder had one representative. Thus, Fulton County, which cast more than 6,000 popular votes in 1940, had six unit votes; Quitman and Chattahoochee Counties, each of which had fewer than 225 votes cast in that year, had 2 unit votes. With a county's unit votes awarded on a winner-take-all basis, candidates devoted great attention to rural counties, which accounted for nearly 60 percent of unit votes. In 1946, for example, Talmadge finished second in the gubernatorial primary to James Carmichael by about 16,000 votes, yet Carmichael lost the nomination to Talmadge, 242 unit votes to 146.[18]

World War II and the Subsequent Years

World War II ushered in significant changes for Georgia.[19] Military bases became an important part of the state's economy, and employment gradually shifted from farming to manufacturing, including textiles, aircraft production, food processing, and lumber. The development of Georgia's cities accelerated, especially in Atlanta, where growth was aided during the 1960s by the progressive policies of mayor Ivan Allen.[20]

Political changes also occurred. At the close of World War II, white supremacy was strong in Georgia, and all candidates sought the support of only white voters, with many openly aligning themselves with the Ku Klux Klan.[21] Jim Crow laws, which separated whites and blacks in most public and social settings, were rigidly enforced. Northern black soldiers stationed at Georgia's military bases often found such social stratification unbearable, and many were arrested for failure to observe the system. Action at the national level, including decisions by the U.S. Supreme Court, eventually prompted change in Georgia, but the civil rights movement relied heavily on support from outside the state and stimulated a backlash of "massive resistance."[22]

As the national movement toward integration gained momentum, the Georgia General Assembly produced an amazing array of legislation to prevent integration within the state.[23] At one point, the state suspended all aid to any integrated school and authorized direct payments to parents of children who attended segregated private schools. To prevent blacks from attending college in the state, requirements for admission were set to include letters of recommendation from two graduates of the institution to which a student was applying. Because most of these institutions had never had black students, they would have difficulty obtaining such letters. Federal courts declared most of these actions unconstitutional, but segregation largely remained in place until the 1964 Civil Rights Act and continued in many respects long after that date. Atlanta's black population was eventually empowered by the fact that white families, many fearing integration of the schools, left the city for the suburbs, and the city attained a black majority. The first black mayor, Maynard Jackson, was elected in 1973, and most of Atlanta's subsequent mayoral candidates have been black.

In recent decades, the federal courts have had a substantial impact on Georgia's political landscape. In *Fortson v. Toombs* (1965), the court ruled that reapportionment for the election of the General Assembly must be made on the basis of the population of the state, with districts having roughly the same number of residents, rather than by county or other political boundaries.[24] After four earlier challenges had failed, the U.S. Supreme Court finally struck down the county-unit system in *Gray v. Sanders* (1963), ruling that the system violated the Fourteenth Amendment's "equal protection" guarantee by malapportioning votes.[25] *Wesberry v. Sanders* (1964) also led to the redrawing of congressional districts in the state.[26]

The adoption of the Voting Rights Act of 1965 gave the federal government a direct role in the conduct of elections, particularly the power to object to districts thought to dilute the voting power of minority groups. Following the 1990 census, the U.S. Department of Justice objected to congressional redistricting by the state legislature. After two unsuccessful attempts to redraw districts, state lawmakers finally satisfied the guidelines established by the federal government to protect minority voting strength in the 1992 elections.[27] Ironically, those districts were ruled unconstitutional in 1995 because race was a "predominant factor" used in drawing the district lines.[28] Similar debates emerged following the 2000 census. District lines drawn by the state legislature were challenged on a number of grounds in federal court, and the Georgia General Assembly redrew the districts after partisan majorities had shifted to the Republicans. At that time, Republicans tried unsuccessfully to retract the federal lawsuit challenging districts in the state. As late as 2006,

Georgians continued to fight over the drawing of district lines as a result of the 2000 census.[29]

Politics at the statewide level experienced significant change in the thirty years after World War II, although Georgia remained a one-party state. One incident in particular indicates the degree to which personalities rather than partisan differences once dominated the political agenda. In 1946, Eugene Talmadge made a bid to regain the governor's office after an absence of four years. Since the primary was determined by the number of county-unit votes, Talmadge aligned himself strongly with the interests of the more numerous rural counties, which responded well to his good-old-boy image and emphasis on white supremacy and the "southern way of life." Talmadge won the gubernatorial primary and general election, while M. E. Thompson ran a successful campaign to be Georgia's first lieutenant governor. However, Talmadge's health was failing, and many voters in the general election wrote in the name of his son, Herman.

When the elder Talmadge died before taking office, controversy arose about who should succeed him under the 1945 Constitution. Thompson, the lieutenant-governor-elect, believed that he was legally the next governor. Ellis Arnall, the incumbent governor, refused to relinquish the office until Thompson was sworn in. Herman Talmadge argued that the General Assembly should elect a governor from the two candidates with the highest write-in totals. After maneuvering by the supporters of the various candidates, the legislature elected Herman Talmadge on January 15, 1947. The anti-Talmadge forces did not relent: Thompson continued to assert his claim to the governorship after being sworn in as lieutenant governor. The Georgia Supreme Court finally resolved the dispute on March 17, when it decided that Thompson was governor, but Herman Talmadge won the office a year later in a special election.[30]

Perhaps the most far-reaching change in Georgia politics has been the slow dissolution of the one-party system. This process has produced more competitive races for governor, prompted the election of Republican candidates for Congress and for the governor's office, and increased the number of Republican members in the General Assembly. In 2004, for the first time, the Republicans gained control of the Georgia House, having achieved a majority in the Georgia Senate two years earlier. Moreover, Republican presidential candidates have done well in Georgia in recent elections, and many local officials are aligning themselves with the Republican Party.[31] The overall composition of the General Assembly has changed in ways other than party.

Since 2000, members' levels of education and the numbers of minority and female members have risen. Despite these changes, however, the state legislature remains more conservative on most issues than the state's population as a whole.[32]

The Social and Cultural Setting

Urbanization and Migration

In recent decades, Georgia has become overwhelmingly urban, with most of its growth concentrated in the northern half of the state. The federal government has long tracked urbanization by examining metropolitan areas that develop around a core city or cities of at least fifty thousand people. Just 56 percent of Georgians lived in metropolitan areas in 1960, but that number grew to 67.7 percent in 1992 and 81.1 percent in 2002. The area considered metropolitan Atlanta has expanded dramatically. For the 1970 census, the metropolitan area was considered to be just five counties: Clayton, Cobb, DeKalb, Fulton, and Gwinnett. With the area's mushrooming growth, the number of counties considered part of metropolitan Atlanta expanded to eighteen in 1990, twenty in 2000, and twenty-eight as of 2003. In 2004, more than 4.7 million people lived in metropolitan Atlanta. Another 1.7 million people lived in the established metropolitan areas of Albany, Athens, Macon, Columbus, and Augusta. In response to Georgia's continued urban development, the federal government has designated additional metropolitan areas since the 2000 census, including Brunswick, Dalton, Hinesville–Fort Stewart, Rome, Valdosta, and Warner Robbins. In 2000, the federal Office of Management and Budget created the category of "micropolitan area" to designate smaller regional centers with populations between ten thousand and fifty thousand. In Georgia, this category includes Dublin, LaGrange, Milledgeville, Toccoa, and Waycross, among others.[33]

Georgia's rapid growth has not occurred evenly around the state. Population losses have occurred over many years in some areas: 53 counties, particularly in South Georgia, had fewer residents in 1990 than they did in 1930. During the booming 1990s, when Georgia's population expanded 26 percent, 8 counties experienced declines and another 42 grew by less than 10 percent. Between 2000 and 2005, when Georgia was estimated to have added nine hundred thousand people, 32 of the state's 159 counties lost population. However, three-fourths of these "declining" counties already had fewer than twenty thousand residents in 2000.[34] Such shifts have economic ramifications and are politically important for drawing legislative and congressional districts, securing benefits for specific areas, and targeting statewide election campaigns.

A number of factors have influenced this urban growth, including technologies that made farming less labor-intensive and caused the loss of many unskilled farm jobs, the development of manufacturing and the more recent growth in the service sector, availability of services in urban areas, expanded interstate and international export of Georgia's products, and the wider availability of transportation, especially airlines and railroads.

While farming remained important to the state's economy, many residents left farms for more lucrative jobs in urban areas. Between 1949 and 1969, the number of farming families in Georgia fell from 222,000 to approximately 47,000. In 1930, a majority of the state's black citizens lived on farms, but by 1970 few black families remained on Georgia farms.[35] As tenant farming and sharecropping became less available, blacks moved to the cities to find jobs, but economic conditions for black families still lagged significantly behind those of whites. Many blacks left the state to find employment in northern cities, and not until the 1970s did the number of blacks leaving Georgia fall below the number moving to the state.

As more black residents began to enter Georgia cities, white reluctance to integrate and political maneuvering to avoid it prompted heated discussion in Washington. Politicians from other regions who favored rapid social change in the South during the 1950s and 1960s were angered by the Georgia General Assembly's actions. Richard Russell, Georgia's senior U.S. senator, became so irritated by the federal government's insistence on integration that he presented several unsuccessful plans to "solve" the threats that he saw to the South. Arguing that the black population should be dispersed equally among the states, he proposed a bill to relocate black southerners to northern states, providing fifteen hundred dollars to each black resident who chose to move. Russell also later attempted to allocate funds to relocate southern blacks to Africa.[36]

When the federal courts began to strike down laws that separated the races, whites in Georgia began to move as well. Perhaps the most invasive action taken by the federal government was the integration of public schools. Although several actions by the Georgia General Assembly were struck down as unconstitutional, white parents moved to different school districts or sent their children to private academies that did not admit blacks. From 1963 to 1970, white enrollment in the city of Atlanta's public schools dropped by half. While the ratio of blacks to whites during the 1963–1964 school year was approximately even, Atlanta's public schools had twice as many blacks as whites by 1970. White enrollment declined each subsequent year, with the result that few whites eventually remained in the school system.[37]

The widespread "white flight" to the suburbs was not unique to Georgia. This move was subsidized and even encouraged by the federal government's tax break for mortgage interest and the increased availability of mortgages facilitated by the Veterans Administration and Federal Housing Administration. The interstate highway system, which gave suburban whites easy access to job opportunities within cities, also provided those who could afford automobiles with an incentive to move to the suburbs. Since many suburban areas do not want mass transportation, highways are often jammed during rush hours with autos carrying a single passenger each. Several central cities in Georgia are now predominantly black. Atlanta's black majority has elected black mayors since 1973, and most of the city's governing elite has been black for the past thirty years, although that could change if the city's racial and ethnic mix continues to include more whites and Hispanics. Savannah also has elected many black public officials, including a mayor in 1995.

More recent patterns of migration have produced population shifts within urban areas. Many younger, more affluent, and smaller households are moving back into central cities. Frustrations with commuting from the suburbs, the unique architectural styles of older homes, and proximity to cultural and social sites have drawn many residents back to the cities. Savannah and Atlanta residents have restored in-town properties originally built in the 1800s or earlier. This process of gentrification has increased demand for such homes, driven prices up, and moved some housing stock beyond the reach of lower-income residents. In 2006, residents of the city of Atlanta became concerned about the degree to which neighborhood culture was being changed by gentrification. In some instances, houses purchased for more than three hundred thousand dollars have been torn down to create space for large estate-like homes that tower over neighborhoods of smaller homes.[38]

Interstate migration patterns have also affected Georgia's population. During the 1930s, 1940s, and 1950s, when more people left Georgia than moved to the state, population increased because the number of births greatly exceeded deaths. Starting with the 1960s, however, the number of people moving to

Georgia was higher than the total leaving. As older, more industrialized areas in the northeastern section of the nation have recently declined, southern metropolitan areas including Atlanta, Savannah, Augusta, and Columbus have experienced overall population and economic growth. From 2000 to 2005, population growth for the nation overall was 5.3 percent. Population growth in Georgia during that period, however, reached 10.8 percent, fourth highest among the states. Hispanic populations in particular are expected to grow dramatically in the state. In 2000, Georgia had the fastest-growing Hispanic population of any state, and when compared with other municipalities, Atlanta's Latino growth was outpaced only by Nashville. Estimates for 2004 indicate that 11 percent of Georgia's population did not speak English.[39]

Thus, Georgia's population in the early twenty-first century is relatively "new" and mobile. Almost two-thirds of Georgia's residents in 1990 were born in the state; by 2004, that figure had dropped to 58 percent, including 250,000 who had lived in another state in the previous year. In metropolitan Atlanta, the figure was only 39 percent. In 2004, just over one-third of the state's housing stock had been built in 1990 or later. Fully 17.5 percent of the state's households did not live in the same residence in 2003 and 2004, although 22.3 percent were living in a residence they had occupied prior to 1990. Substantial population movements, especially from outside the South, affect politics as people come to Georgia with varying experiences and views regarding political parties, taxes, public services, and similar matters. Such high levels of mobility can also undermine community and neighborhood stability.

Current Population

The 2000 census counted Georgia's population at almost 8.2 million, an increase of 1.7 million from 1990. Of this growth, 45.4 percent resulted from natural increase (the difference between births and deaths within the state), 40.2 percent came from migration from other states, and the remaining 14.4 percent resulted from migration from outside the United States. In 2004, Georgia had an estimated population of 8,581,489 (see table 2.1). The state ranks as the ninth-largest in terms of population and is the fourth-fastest-growing.[40]

Georgia's population is becoming more diverse racially and ethnically. Data for 2004 indicate that the state's population was 64 percent white,

Table 2.1. Georgia and U.S. Population Profiles

	Georgia	United States
Population, 2004	8,581,489	285,691,501
Rank in Terms of Population	9	N/A
Change, 1980–1990	*18.6%*	*9.8%*
Change, 1990–2000	*26.4%*	*13.1%*
Change, 2000–2003	*6.1%*	*3.3%*
Rank in Terms of Rate of Growth	4	N/A
Projected Population, 2015	9,492,500	310,131,500
Race and Ethnicity, 2004		
White	63.6%	75.6%
Black	28.7%	12.2%
Other	7.6%	12.2%
Hispanic*	6.7%	14.2%
Age, 2004		
19 and under	29.3%	27.9%
20–44	38.4%	35.6%
45–64	23.1%	24.5%
65 and over	9.2%	12.0%
Median (years)	*34.0*	*36.2*
Education Levels, 2004[†]		
Not a High School Graduate	19.0%	16.1%
High School Graduate	29.7%	29.5%
Some College	19.9%	20.3%
Associate's Degree	5.8%	7.1%
Bachelor's Degree	17.0%	17.2%
Advanced Degree	8.6%	9.9%
Personal Income per Capita, 2004	$22,791	$24,020
Rank	22	N/A
Persons below Poverty Level, 2004	14.8%	10.1%
Rank	13	N/A

* Persons of Hispanic origin can be of any race.

[†] As a percentage of population 25 years and older.

N/A = Not applicable.

Source: U.S. Census Bureau, *Fact Sheet: Georgia,* available with annual updates as part of the American Community Survey (http://factfinder.census.gov/home/saff/main.html?_lang=en).

29 percent black, and 7 percent other races. Hispanics, who can be any race, constituted almost 7 percent of Georgia's residents (see table 2.1). Concentrations of various groups appear to exist in different parts of the state. For example, Hall County's Hispanic population is estimated to be almost 24 percent of its total, while Quitman County had only 16 Hispanic residents. Five counties reported fewer than 150 black citizens living within their boundaries, but eleven counties had black majorities.[41]

Table 2.1 points out other noteworthy patterns. Georgia's population is relatively young, with 29 percent of all citizens age nineteen or under. Female residents slightly outnumbered males. Recent statistics indicate that females are more likely than ever to be heads of households in Georgia, a trend that appears nationwide as well and may also indicate lower standards of living, as many female-headed households fall below the poverty line. In 2004, Georgia ranked thirteenth among the states in lowest per capita income. Still, Georgia's average number of persons per household dropped from 3.58 in 1960 to 2.65, and the proportion of persons living below the poverty line fell from more than 15 percent during the 1990s.[42]

Georgia's education levels remain somewhat low. While 25.6 percent of those age twenty-five or older in 2004 had earned bachelor's or advanced college degrees, 19 percent had not completed high school. The comparable national figures are 27.1 and 16.1 percent, respectively. Georgia has made noticeable gains over the past generation, however. According to the 1960 census, 49.7 percent of Georgians (and 39.6 percent of all Americans) age twenty-five or older had no high school training at all. The 1960 education levels for Georgia blacks were especially low: a median of 6.1 years of schooling, compared to 10.3 for whites.[43]

The Economic Setting

At the end of World War II, Georgia remained largely agricultural. Rural areas also depended heavily on textiles, the state's largest manufacturing industry. Moreover, prior to the 1970s, Georgia had few nationally prominent firms. Today, Georgia has become a key player in the service sector and in the world economy (see table 2.2). Although agriculture continues to comprise an important sector of the economy, farming, forestry, and fishing accounted for just 1 percent of the gross state product (a measure of the state's output of goods and services) in 2004. Service industries were the largest

Table 2.2. Georgia and U.S. Economic Profiles

	Georgia	United States
Gross State/National Product, 2004 ($ billion)	$343	$11,665
Average Annual Growth Rate, 1997–2003	3.2%	3.0%
Rank in 2003	20	N/A
Rank in 2004	21	N/A
Change, 2003–2004	4.5%	4.3%
Leading Components of Gross State/ National Product, 2004		
Manufacturing	13.9%	12.4%
Services	22.9%	24.5%
Finance, Insurance, Real Estate	17.5%	20.1%
Government	12.9%	11.6%
Transportation, Public Utilities	5.8%	4.8%
Farms, Forestry, Fisheries	1.0%	1.0%
New Business Incorporations	29,547	580,900
Change, 2003–2004	22.0%	4.9%
Business Failures, 2004	27,835	576,200
Change, 2003–2004	7.5%	0.7%
Unemployment Rate	7.3%	7.2%
Nonfarm Employment, September 2005	3,944,500	133,604,400
Manufacturing	11.2%	10.7%
Trade, Transportation, Public Utilities	20.9%	19.3%
Services	23.9%	25.6%
Finance, Insurance, Real Estate	5.6%	6.1%
Government	16.5%	16.3%

N/A = Not applicable.

Sources: Bureau of Economic Analysis (http://www.bea.gov); Bureau of Labor Statistics (http://stats.bls.gov); U.S. Small Business Administration (http://www.sba.gov/advo/research/profiles/05ga.pdf; and /05us.pdf).

source of employment that year, with 23 percent of the total. The sectors likely to grow the slowest or lose workers by 2010 are concentrated in agriculture and manufacturing, jobs that have provided an important entry to the workforce for those with limited education.[44]

Contrary to earlier patterns, Georgia now appears to be gaining economically relative both to other states in the region and to the nation as a whole. Georgia now stands as a premier Sunbelt economy. In 2004, Georgia was home to sixteen of the nation's five hundred largest companies as listed in *Fortune* magazine. In 2002, foreign firms owned 1,571 Georgia facilities and employed nearly 125,000 workers. In 2003, international capital investment in the state totaled $18 million. Georgia firms exported more than $20 billion worth of goods and services in 2005, with 23.5 percent of the total going to Canada. The next three countries—Mexico, Japan, and the United Kingdom—accounted for less than 7 percent of the total.[45] All of these changes mean that an expanded variety of economic interests that are national and even global in scale can place great demands on Georgia's political system at both the state and local levels. Indeed, some observers have expressed concern when companies in other states and countries acquire Georgia firms, as has occurred in the cases of several banks, Turner Broadcasting, Scientific-Atlanta, Georgia-Pacific, and BellSouth.[46] Despite questions about the loyalty of firms headquartered outside Georgia, city and state leaders continue attempts to attract investment from other states and nations.

The Importance of Context

When V. O. Key Jr. published *Southern Politics in State and Nation* in 1949, he subtitled his chapter on Georgia's political leadership "The Rule of the Rustics." The state, he argued, was dominated by powerful whites who controlled the belt of heavily black counties running through the middle of the state. Key went on to analyze the virtual absence of a Republican Party in Georgia, a Democratic Party split into two factions by the candidacies of Eugene Talmadge, limited participation in elections, conflicts between the state's cities and rural areas, support for conservative policies by Georgians in Congress, and an enduring politics of race. Yet Key saw change occurring in the South: "Its rate of evolution may seem glacial, but fundamental shifts in the conditions underlying its politics are taking place. All these changes drive toward

a political system more completely in accord with the national ideas of constitutional morality."[47]

In comparison to the conditions and "glacial" shifts Key witnessed in the
1940s, Georgia politics in the early twenty-first century may seem revolutionary. Many changes can be attributed to the kinds of political, social, and
economic trends described in chapter 1. Federal court decisions and legislation have influenced citizen behavior and attitudes, reduced the power
of rural areas in the Georgia legislature, eliminated government-enforced
segregation of businesses and government facilities, helped to diversify the
state and local government workforce, and removed barriers that prevented
blacks from registering, voting, and running for public office.

Population changes also have reshaped the Georgia that Key knew. Population shifts have helped the Republican Party develop a solid base, first in
suburban and later in rural areas, as the demographic makeup of the two
political parties has changed since the 1960s.[48] In 2002 statewide races, Republicans chalked up their first modern gubernatorial victory, having already achieved success in statewide races for U.S. Senate, Public Service
Commission, school superintendent, and insurance commissioner. After the
2004 election, Republicans gained the majority in the Georgia House and
increased their majority in the state Senate to thirty-four seats (a jump of
twenty-seven seats since 1983). Georgia Republicans have been elected to the
U.S. House of Representatives since the 1960s. They gained control of both
U.S. Senate seats with the election of Saxby Chambliss in 2002 and Johnny
Isakson two years later.

Population changes have had other effects, increasing residential segregation as well as animosity between cities and suburbs. Growing and declining
areas of the state often see themselves as competing with one another. Dramatic growth in some communities and neighborhoods also has given rise
to groups fighting development. New interests such as Latinos, seniors, gays
and lesbians, religious groups, and the disabled have become more organized and politically active. Policy debates are increasingly concerned with
social trends regarding family structure, educational achievement, crime,
and similar matters.

Economic changes also have had significant impacts on Georgia. The
state's leading industries and occupations are unlike what they were a generation ago. Investment capital is more mobile—less rooted to specific

places—than during earlier periods. All of these changes have placed great pressure on the political system to promote growth, although the types and location of development can be fiercely controversial.

The 2006 Elections

In 2006, 36 states, including Georgia, held gubernatorial elections. Of those, 22 governorships had been held by Republicans and 14 by Democrats. Democrats kept all of the states they had previously held and took 6 additional states. In addition, the Democratic Party regained control of the U.S. House and Senate in an election where President George W. Bush's policies toward Iraq were a central issue. But despite the national trend, Republicans in Georgia won many statewide and district elections.[49]

Sonny Perdue's reelection to the governor's office by 58 percent of the popular vote was an affirmation of the Republican Party's dominance in the state. In addition to Perdue, Georgia elected its first Republican lieutenant governor, Casey Cagle. Democrats were reelected to the offices of Attorney General, Labor Commissioner, and Agriculture Commissioner, but a Republican won the open position of Secretary of State, which had been held by a Democrat. Moreover, Republicans held onto majorities in both chambers of the Georgia General Assembly, increasing their numbers by two in the House. Of Georgia's 13 U.S. congressional districts, seven elected Reublicans (all incumbents). Two of Georgia's Democratic congressional incumbents, John Barrow and Jim Marshall, barely edged out Republican challengers.[50]

Georgia has displayed some clear patterns of partisan voting in recent elections. Democrats fare better within cities, and Republicans maintain their strongholds in suburban areas. Blacks tend to vote loyally for the Democratic Party. The rural and southern portions of the state largely maintain traditionally conservative voting patterns.

More of the Same?

Georgia has changed in many ways, but traditions and underlying conditions still make adaptation to change quite difficult. Despite improvement and local variation, the state trails most of the nation in education, poverty relief, and similar indicators. Perhaps the greatest political constant is racial conflict. Georgia has ended the widespread violence familiar to Key in the 1940s, but a wide variety of individuals, organizations, and government agencies have regularly handled disputes using random attacks, protests, and lawsuits. Conflicts have boiled up over election procedures and symbols such as the state flag. Moreover, the political parties have taken on a racial tinge in terms of membership, with almost all blacks voting for the Democrats and the Republican Party becoming overwhelmingly white. Ironically, these identities are the opposite of what existed before the mid-1960s, when southern Democrats staunchly defended racial segregation.

Georgia politics also seems to have sustained its image of devoting significant attention to parochial interests.[51] Many state boards, including those for higher education and transportation, have seats assigned to specific regions. Similarly, the Georgia General Assembly considers numerous bills dealing with matters that local officials would handle in many states. Certain aspects of political participation in Georgia—especially voting—still fare poorly when compared to other states. When Key examined voter turnout from 1920 to 1946, the share of Georgians of voting age who participated in general elections and most Democratic primaries hovered at or below 20 percent. Such low turnouts do not result simply from segregation: turnout among white voting-age Georgians in Democratic primaries for governor averaged 30 percent.[52] During the 1980s, fewer than 65 percent of all Georgians old enough to vote were registered, compared with roughly 70 percent nationally. Just 29 percent of Georgians age eighteen or older voted in the 1994 congressional elections, the nation's second-lowest rate. In the 1996 presidential election, 42 percent of voting-age Georgians voted; only four states had lower turnout.[53] The 2004 presidential race included the highest turnout in history nationwide in terms of absolute numbers: Democrat John Kerry received more votes than any other presidential candidate prior to 2004 but still lost to George W. Bush by 3 million votes. Georgia turnout was remarkably high that year as well, with 78 percent of the state's 4.2 million registered voters going to the polls.[54]

One form of political participation that remains high but is often viewed negatively is the involvement of interest groups in Georgia politics. More than fifty years ago, Key complained about the influence of Atlanta money in elections.[55] Until the 1990s, the state imposed no limits on the amount of money that individuals and most corporations could donate to candidates for state and local office and had virtually no regulation of lobbyists even though more than eleven hundred registered during the 1992 session of the Georgia General Assembly, double the number a decade earlier. By mid-2006, the Georgia State Ethics Commission reported 1,405 lobbyists. Because many contracted their services to multiple clients and lobbied at both state and local levels of government, these lobbyists represented 5,939 different organizations, agencies, companies, and groups.[56] Critics have complained about the benefits that interest groups provide to legislators (such as trips, preferential deals, and campaign contributions) as well as the limited reporting required of lobbyists and others trying to influence the legislature or bureaucracy.[57]

It is difficult to say how much Georgia now resembles the rest of the nation. Economically, the state has moved well past its isolated position at the end of World War II to become an integral player in the changing world economy. Socially, Georgia's population has grown dramatically; it also has become more educated, urban, and diverse. Politically, much has changed since V. O. Key's time and even since the 1960s. The dynamics of the American federal system almost guarantee change. Yet some characteristics are so pervasive, some traditions and institutions so powerful, and some conflicts so deep-seated that certain aspects of life in Georgia have changed little.

Georgia's Constitution

This chapter examines Georgia's current constitution, compares it to its nine predecessors and other state constitutions, and explains its connection to the U.S. Constitution. Constitutions are important because they establish the basic rules of the game for any political system. They specify the authority of government, distribute power among participants in the political system, and establish fundamental procedures for conducting public business and protecting rights.

Just as drawing up or changing the rules can affect the outcome of a game, the particulars of constitutions can help determine who wins or loses politically. For this reason, constitutions should be thought of as political documents. This especially holds true for state constitutions, which often include matters that seem like policy decisions better made by passing laws, as with Georgia's lottery. Yet putting such decisions in constitutions makes it harder for opponents to repeal or modify them. No matter what is in state constitutions, however, they cannot be at odds with provisions of the U.S. Constitution.

The U.S. Constitution: The Ultimate Authority

The U.S. Constitution has endured longer than any other document as a basis for government, in large part because of its broad but flexible grants of power and its reinterpretation in response to changing conditions. It is also difficult to amend. Article 1 of the Constitution specifically lists powers to be given to the federal government. Such "enumerated" powers can be adapted to new situations through the so-called elastic clause (Article 1, Section 8), which permits Congress to do whatever it considers "necessary and proper" to carry out the powers listed elsewhere in the document. The elastic clause has allowed a broad interpretation of the federal government's powers within limits established by the courts. Article 6 reinforces the idea of a powerful national government by declaring that the Constitution and federal law are the "supreme law of the land."

Under the Articles of Confederation, which were in force from 1781 to 1789, the national government had only those powers that the states agreed to give it. This caused major problems—especially with interstate commerce, taxation, war debt, and the military—and led to the drafting of the present U.S. Constitution to replace the Articles. Concern over the powers reserved to the states caused great debate during ratification of the Constitution. Alexander Hamilton and James Madison argued (in *The Federalist* nos. 17 and 45, respectively) that the national government would be highly dependent on the states. Madison claimed that state governments would be closer to the people and that many more people would be employed by government at this level. In addition, Madison asserted that with the Senate elected by the state legislatures and the president chosen by the Electoral College, concerns regarding the lack of states' rights were unfounded. Moreover, he argued, political culture within the states would provide a common bond for the citizens of each state that would overshadow the power of the federal government in the minds of the populace. Drawing on the ideals of the feudal system, Hamilton noted that people often had stronger loyalty to feudal lords than to a nation's king. He argued that states and localities, like feudal estates, would be closer to the people and that the people would respond to them rather than to the federal government. The Tenth Amendment to the U.S. Constitution addresses concerns that states would have too little authority by declaring that all powers not given to the federal government are "reserved for the states" or the people.

Madison and Hamilton, of course, could not have anticipated the degree to which people now move among states or imagined the impact of mass communication. Still, their views provide an understanding of what was expected of the states. Most people anticipated that national supremacy would have little effect on government operations within states. However, the elastic clause has allowed federal intervention into state affairs. For example, states traditionally have governed transportation, but federal highway funding has been withheld in instances where states failed to adhere to federal mandates regarding speed limits or the legal drinking age. Thus, the U.S. Constitution represents the ultimate authority: states may not pass legislation or implement policy that contradicts the Constitution. However, states often adopt laws to test the limits of decisions made by the federal government—for example, in attempts to restrict abortion practices following *Roe v. Wade* (1973) and related cases.[1]

States adopt constitutions as frameworks for governance. Many state constitutions are modeled after the U.S. Constitution, although most are much more detailed and restrictive. State constitutions do not include implied powers such as those in the U.S. Constitution, although states are presumed to possess "police power"—that is, the ability to promote public health, safety, morals, and general welfare. The police power is generally considered among the reserved powers of the states mentioned in the Tenth Amendment to the U.S. Constitution, but states often delegate this authority to local governments.[2]

Unlike the U.S. Constitution, which has fewer than nine thousand words and has been amended only twenty-seven times since 1789, state constitutions are long and are frequently amended or replaced (see table 3.1). The states vary widely in the manner in which they amend their constitutions and the detail within each of the documents. Many states have had only one constitution: Massachusetts's constitution, for example, has endured since 1780. Georgia has had ten constitutions, second only to Louisiana, and only Rhode Island has a newer constitution than Georgia's current document, which took effect in 1983.

Politics and State Constitutions

Unlike the U.S. Constitution, most state constitutions include a wide range of very specific policies. Of course, legislatures normally enact policies by passing laws. Why clutter up state constitutions rather than limiting them to more fundamental issues? At least three reasons stand out: efforts to gain political advantage, state court decisions, and the requirements of the national government. The Georgia Constitution has numerous examples of these processes.

Table 3.1. State Constitutions as of January 1, 2005

State	Number of Constitutions	Estimated Number of Words	Number of Amendments
Alabama	6	340,136	766
Alaska	1	15,988	29
Arizona	1	28,876	136
Arkansas	5	59,500	91
California	2	54,645	513
Colorado	1	74,522	145
Connecticut	4	17,256	29
Delaware	4	19,000	138*
Florida	6	51,456	104
Georgia	**10**	**39,526**	**63**
Hawaii	1	20,774	104
Idaho	1	24,232	117
Illinois	4	16,510	11
Indiana	2	10,379	46
Iowa	2	12,616	52
Kansas	1	12,296	92
Kentucky	4	23,911	41
Louisiana	11	54,112	129
Maine	1	16,276	169
Maryland	4	46,600	218
Massachusetts	1	36,700	120
Michigan	4	34,659	25
Minnesota	1	11,547	118
Mississippi	4	24,323	123
Missouri	4	42,600	105
Montana	2	13,145	30
Nebraska	2	20,048	222
Nevada	1	31,377	132
New Hampshire	2	9,200	143
New Jersey	3	22,956	36
New Mexico	1	27,200	151
New York	4	51,700	216
North Carolina	3	16,532	34
North Dakota	1	19,130	145

(continued)

Table 3.1. Continued

State	Number of Constitutions	Estimated Number of Words	Number of Amendments
Ohio	2	48,521	161
Oklahoma	1	74,075	171
Oregon	1	54,083	238
Pennsylvania	5	27,711	30
Rhode Island	3	10,908	8
South Carolina	7	22,300	485
South Dakota	1	27,675	212
Tennessee	3	13,300	36
Texas	5	90,000	432
Utah	1	11,000	106
Vermont	3	10,286	53
Virginia	6	21,319	40
Washington	1	33,564	95
West Virginia	2	26,000	71
Wisconsin	1	14,392	133
Wyoming	1	31,800	94

*Amendments are not subject to voter approval.

Source: Council of State Governments 2005, 37:10–11.

Efforts to Gain Political Advantage

One explanation for the many topics covered in state constitutions is straight-forward—simple politics. If a group gets its position on an issue included in a state's constitution, its opponents will have more difficulty trying to repeal or change the policy. This is really a matter of exercising power through the rules of the game. The Georgia Constitution is riddled with such provisions.

Earmarking. Like many state constitutions, Georgia's "earmarks" certain funds—that is, identifies revenue sources that must be spent for designated purposes. The most significant are motor fuel taxes, which Article 3, Section 9, Paragraph 6b of the state constitution requires be spent "for all activities incident to providing and maintaining an adequate system of public roads and bridges" and for grants to counties. Moreover, this money goes for these purposes "regardless of whether the General Assembly enacts a general provisions Act." Thus, the Constitution provides those groups interested in highway construction with guaranteed sources of funds. The 1992 amendment creating the lottery (Article 1, Section 2, Paragraph 8c) requires that net proceeds (after expenses and prizes) go to "educational programs and purposes," with the governor's annual budget including recommendations for the use of these funds. A 1998 amendment further restricts these funds.

In other cases, the Georgia Constitution merely permits the earmarking of funds. For example, Article 3, Section 9, Paragraph 6e permits the General Assembly to use taxes on alcoholic beverages for programs related to alcohol and drug abuse. Other provisions in the same section allow the legislature to create a variety of trust funds for programs ranging from the prevention of child abuse to promotion of certain crops.

Tax Breaks. The Georgia Constitution provides special tax treatment to various groups and activities over and above what the General Assembly enacts through tax laws. Examples in Article 7 include timber, one of Georgia's largest industries. As amended by voters in 1990, Section 2, Paragraph 3e requires that timber be taxed at fair market value only at the time of its harvest or sale, whereas timber previously was taxed annually at market value. This change produced a major drop in property tax revenues for some counties and school districts. A tax break for blueberry farmers that was offered as an amendment in 1994 was not ratified, however. Section 1, Paragraph 3c requires that certain agricultural land be assessed at 75 percent of its value, while Section 2, Paragraph 5 exempts part of the value of disabled veterans' homes from property taxes. Other sections of Article 7 authorize rather than require the General Assembly to provide certain types of tax preferences, as with taxes for homes listed in a historic register and heavy motor vehicles owned by nonresidents (Section 1, Paragraph 3d).[3]

Morality Issues. Various groups often attempt to use state constitutions to establish positions on controversial practices. For example, in 1919, opponents of the sale of alcoholic beverages orchestrated the passage of the Eighteenth Amendment to the U.S. Constitution. In 1933, however, Prohibition was repealed by the Twenty-first Amendment. Similar provisions exist in the Georgia Constitution. The 1983 Constitution retained a prohibition against whipping as a punishment for a crime. While some of those drafting the new document saw this provision as outdated, it was retained out of fear that the General Assembly might pass bills permitting whipping in schools or prisons.[4]

Like all of its predecessors since 1868, Georgia's 1983 Constitution prohibited lotteries—in this case, the prohibition appeared in Article 1, which covers the "Origin and Structure of Government" and the Bill of Rights. After being elected governor in 1990, Zell Miller convinced the General Assembly to submit an amendment to voters to create state-run lotteries whose proceeds must be spent on education. The amendment was ratified by a narrow margin in November 1992 following a strong campaign for passage by its supporters.

The most recent amendment proposed on a morality issue is the ban on same-sex marriage, which was ratified in 2004. By adding language to the state's constitution, proponents of this amendment have eliminated the possibility of a statute allowing same-sex marriage. This change also prohibits local governments from recognizing same-sex marriages within the state of Georgia, as with a couple moving to Georgia from a state with a different definition of marriage.

Limits on Policy Making. Constitutions affect politics by deciding who makes decisions, limiting the discretion of government agencies, and giving certain interests representation in the policy process. For example, Article 4 creates six state boards and commissions, and Article 8 creates two more for education. As noted earlier, the Constitution establishes important political ties between the State Transportation Board and the General Assembly, thereby reducing the executive branch's power over highways. An example of constitutional limits on the discretion of government agencies is Article 4, Section 3, Paragraph 2's requirement that military veterans receive preference in state civil service employment. Perhaps the most visible way the Georgia Constitution represents certain interests is through residency rules, as with requirements in Articles 4 and 8 that members from each congressional district serve on certain boards and commissions and that at least one member of the Board of Natural Resources come from one of the coastal counties.

State Court Decisions

A second reason for including policies in a constitution is to respond to state court decisions. For example, the Georgia Supreme Court might hold that a state law or an action by a local government violates the Georgia

Constitution, and almost the only way to undo the court's action is to amend the state constitution. A 1994 constitutional amendment (Article 3, Section 6, Paragraph 7) permits local governments to prohibit alcohol sales at clubs with nude dancing and was passed to circumvent a Georgia Supreme Court ruling that nude dancing was expressive conduct protected by the Georgia and U.S. Constitutions. Alcohol sales are not constitutionally protected, so regulating them is a way to try to drive nude dancing clubs out of business. The courts subsequently ruled that this approach was permissible under the Georgia Constitution.[5]

Several decisions by the Georgia Supreme Court during the 1980s created confusion about sovereign immunity (the ability of citizens to sue the state or its local governments). As a result, voters passed a 1990 amendment that attempted to clarify the matter.[6] Similarly, the 1983 Constitution added language to Article 9 to clarify a somewhat confusing series of cases regarding state, city, and county planning and zoning authority.[7]

The Federal Government and State Constitutions

A third way in which politics affects state constitutions is to satisfy some requirement of the national government. For example, the Georgia Constitution was amended in 1988 and 1992 to create a trust fund to provide medical services for the poor through the federal Medicaid program. Without the trust fund, money unspent at the end of the budgetary year would have to go to the state's general fund and could be used for any purpose, as specified elsewhere in the 1983 Constitution.[8] With the trust fund, the unspent money can be carried over to the next year to pay for medical care. Another example can be found in Article 3, which was written to satisfy federal court decisions about how legislative districts must be drawn.

Previous Georgia Constitutions

Each of Georgia's constitutions should be seen as a political response to some conflict, problem, or crisis (see table 3.2). In addition to substantive differences, the documents also vary in the methods used to draft and approve them. Seven of Georgia's constitutions were written by conventions composed of elected delegates. Two were prepared by bodies whose members were either appointed or included because they held specific offices. The

Table 3.2. Georgia's Ten Constitutions

Year Implemented	Revision Method (group responsible for proposing new document)	Major Characteristics
1777	Convention	Separation of powers, with most in the hands of the unicameral legislature.
1789	Convention	Bicameral legislature, which chose the governor; no bill of rights.
1798	Convention	Popular election of governor; creation of Supreme Court; greater detail than predecessors.
1861	Convention	Long bill of rights; first constitution submitted to voters for ratification.
1865	Convention	Governor limited to two terms; slavery abolished; Ordinance of Secession repealed; war debt repudiated; some judges made elective.
1868	Convention	Authorization of free schools; increased appointment power for governor; debtors' relief.
1877	Convention	More restrictions on legislative power; two-year terms for legislators and governor; governors cannot succeed themselves; most judicial appointments by legislature.
1945	Commission	Establishment of lieutenant governorship, new constitutional officers, new boards, state merit system; home rule granted to counties and cities.
1976	Office of Legislative Counsel (state employees, attorneys)	Reorganization of much-amended 1945 Constitution.
1983	Select committee (almost exclusively leaders from the three branches of state government)	Streamlining of previous document, with elimination of authorization for local amendments.

Source: Hill 1994, 3–20.

Constitution of 1976 resulted from a request by Governor George Busbee to have the Office of Legislative Counsel prepare an article-by-article revision of the Constitution of 1945 for the General Assembly. The 1861 constitution was the first to be ratified by voters.[9]

Eighteenth-Century Constitutions

Prior to its ten constitutions, Georgia had a temporary governing document in 1776. Three constitutions followed between 1777 and the end of the eighteenth century. The third had the longest life, lasting from 1798 to 1861.

The Rules and Regulations of 1776. Even before the American Revolution, Georgians were exerting their independence from England. Colonial Georgia, dependent on imports for most manufactured items, was hard hit by the various import taxes that had led to colonial protests. Public opinion in Georgia favored independence, and citizens mobilized to break with England. Georgia's first self-government was defined by the Rules and Regulations of 1776, which were adopted before the signing of the Declaration of Independence. Because the document was hurriedly written, it was short and simple. All current laws were maintained except those that conflicted with actions taken by the Continental Congress. The Rules and Regulations declared that governmental authority resided within the state, not with the monarchy, and that power originated from the governed. While this document was not officially a state constitution, many observers have noted that it served as one. The more formal separation from England represented by the Declaration prompted Georgians to adopt a more permanent state government and to write a new state constitution.

The Constitution of 1777. Georgia's first constitution included such now-familiar ideas as separation of powers among the legislative, executive, and judicial branches of government; proportional representation on the basis of population; and provisions for local self-government. This constitution, like the Rules and Regulations of 1776, included few expressed protections of individual liberties. Despite this omission, Georgia's political culture at the time was more liberal than that of other states, and the Constitution was written to empower the "common man," although only white males aged twenty-one or older who had paid property taxes in the previous year were permitted to vote. The Anglican Church was disestablished, and the document's wording was easily understood even by people unfamiliar with law. Citizens of the state who remained loyal to the British were encouraged or forced to move elsewhere—usually to Florida, which was controlled by Spain. Local control of the judiciary was ensured by the fact that no courts were established above the county level.

Few citizens noted the transition from the Rules and Regulations of 1776 to the 1777 Constitution. This document governed the state until the downfall of the Articles of Confederation in 1788. Georgia ratified the U.S. Constitution in January 1788—the fourth state to do so—and redrafted the state constitution in 1788 to reflect this monumental change in national government.

The Constitution of 1789. This document provided for a bicameral legislature. Although some accommodations were made for representation on the basis of population in the House of Representatives, all legislative districts were drawn within counties, which had between two and five representatives and one senator. Each slave was counted as three-fifths of a person, in accordance with the U.S. Constitution and to meet the demands of landowners seeking to enhance representation for areas with large plantations. The state capital was moved to Louisville; public education was mandated at the county level; and new counties were created and given representation in the legislature. In addition, the Constitution authorized the legislature to elect the governor and most other state officials except the legislature itself. Restrictions on voting included race, gender, age, residence, and the payment of taxes in the previous year.

The short-lived tenure of this constitution can be attributed to a public scandal that took place in 1789. The state legislature, attempting to overcome wartime debt, sold 15.5 million acres of land to speculators who had formed a number of companies named after the Yazoo River in South Carolina. The Virginia, South Carolina, Georgia, and Tennessee Yazoo Companies, among others, attempted to produce huge profits through land negotiations with several state legislatures. In Georgia, somewhere between 35 and 50 million acres of land were sold for about five hundred thousand dollars. Great public outcry resulted when citizens learned that these lands had been sold at a much lower price than expected and that many legislators held stock in the land companies. Georgians also were angered by allegations that bribery within the legislature had preceded debate on the sale of these lands. In 1798 a convention was called to draft a new constitution that would include provisions to void the sale as well as specifically to regulate the sale of lands by the state legislature.

The Constitution of 1798. This charter was written by a convention and retained much of the language of the previous document. However, it was much longer because it included increased detail about the legislature's authority. As time passed, this constitution was amended, among other reasons, to permit more democratic requirements for voting, to establish executive offices to handle some of the duties of the legislature, to outlaw the foreign slave trade, and to establish local governments. This constitution proved to be more enduring than its predecessors and remained in effect until the formation of the Confederacy forced the document's dissolution in 1861.

The 1860s and 1870s: Four Constitutions in Short Order

The Constitution of 1861. Secessionist fever at the start of the Confederacy could hardly allow the state constitution to go untouched. T. R. R. Cobb, the main author of the Confederate Constitution, also wrote the Georgia Constitution under the Confederacy. The size of the state legislature was reduced by permitting senators to represent more than one county. Judicial review was institutionalized in this document, and state judgeships were established as elective offices. The population was too concerned with preparation for war to pay much attention to the document or to the convention that produced it, and it was ratified with little fanfare. However, the Constitution of 1861 was the first submitted to the voters for approval in a referendum as well as the first Georgia constitution with an extensive list of personal liberties, including freedom of thought and opinion, speech, and the press. However, citizens were warned that they would be responsible for "abuses of the liberties" given to them. Naturally, the Georgia Constitution under the Confederacy included ideals of states' rights, and the governor was greatly empowered.

The Constitution of 1865. Reluctant Georgians drafted this document to accommodate the U.S. Congress's mandates for readmission to the Union. Only those men who expressed moderate political beliefs before and after the war were permitted to work on the document, which included provisions for the abolition of slavery, repudiation of Civil War debt, and repeal of the acts of secession. The North did not welcome this repeal, having insisted that the ordinance of secession instead be declared void. The 1865 Constitution also did not provide for the enfranchisement of the state's black population, although this omission was less likely to stir northern animosity since at the time blacks could vote in only six northern states. As a consequence of these perceived shortcomings, northerners pressured Georgians to rewrite their constitution just three years later to meet the requirements for reentry into the Union. Moreover, public opinion held that the Constitution of 1865 was the work of northern carpetbaggers trying to make quick fortunes in the postwar South or—worse yet in many Georgians' eyes—scalawags, southerners willing to cooperate with Yankees.

The Constitution of 1868. When the constitutional convention was called in 1867, most of Georgia's popular leaders boycotted the meeting. Many of the delegates, some of whom were black, could not find accommodations in the state capital, at that time in Milledgeville. Therefore, the convention was held in Atlanta, and the new constitution, perhaps in retaliation for Milledgeville's inhospitable treatment, specified Atlanta as the capital. The Constitution of 1868 met Congress's requirements for Georgia's readmission to the Union and, to the delight of most citizens, eliminated all debts incurred prior to 1865. The document also provided for public education funded by poll and liquor taxes, although this policy was not immediately implemented. Black citizens were ensured equal rights, at least on paper, and property rights for women were upheld. Moreover, some attempts were made to enhance the business climate, which was badly in need of a stronger tax base.

As a consequence of the high representation of poor and black citizens at this convention, the Constitution of 1868 was a liberal document for the times, particularly after blacks were seated in the General Assembly in 1870. Overall, the new constitution was widely unpopular because of its compliance with northern demands, which were symbolized by the presence of northern troops in the state until 1876. The document remained a symbol of southern defeat until a new constitution was ratified in 1877.

The Constitution of 1877. The new constitution signified a return to more conservative ideals. It reduced state officials' authority and shifted power to counties, most of which were rural. Most noteworthy was its not-so-subtle disenfranchisement of blacks and poor whites through the mandate that only those who had paid all back taxes would be eligible to vote. As the Constitution of 1877 was being drafted, factionalism erupted within the ranks of the Democratic Party. Many citizens who sympathized with the old southern culture were reluctant to compromise with those who called for economic development and progressive policies. An agreement was reached to comply with northern requirements for Reconstruction as well as demands from more industrialized northern states that the South continue to supply raw materials. This compromise stirred up a faction of the Democratic Party known as the Bourbons who were dedicated to pre–Civil War agrarian economic and social norms, white supremacy, and local and state self-determination. The Republicans found that the compromise left them with little power, and many years would pass before the Republican Party reasserted itself in Georgia.

The 1877 Constitution also codified the system of representation under which the six counties with the largest populations were represented in the lower house of the legislature by three members each, the next twenty-six most-populous counties by two each, and the remaining counties by one member. This three/two/one ratio became the basis for the Democratic Party's use of the county-unit system to elect statewide candidates, a custom that became state law in 1917 with passage of the Neill Primary Act.

The Constitution of 1877 was not well suited to changing conditions. For example, it forbade public borrowing, thereby eliminating the possibility of large-scale improvements in transportation or education financed by the state. In a state badly in need of postwar construction, this provision was ill-advised at best. The Constitution eventually included 301 amendments, many of which were temporary or dealt with local rather than statewide issues. Other amendments made Supreme Court justices elected officials, established juvenile courts and a court of appeals, empowered the elected Public Service Commission to regulate utilities, and modified the boards overseeing education.

The Constitutions of 1945 and 1976

The Constitution of 1945. With its many amendments, the Constitution of 1877 endured until 1945. At that point, dissatisfaction with the 1877 Constitution,

a careful study of the document in the 1930s, and prodding by Governor
Ellis Arnall led to the creation of a twenty-three-member commission to
draft a new constitution. The use of a commission rather than an elected
convention reflects the governor's wish to depoliticize the Constitution and
bring it up to date as well as the General Assembly's previous failure to muster the two-thirds vote needed to call a convention.[10]

The new constitution included few substantive changes; its main effect
was to condense its heavily amended predecessor. Perhaps the most notable
changes were the creation of the office of lieutenant governor and new boards
for corrections, state personnel, and veterans' services. One contested issue
was the ban against governors succeeding themselves, which the General
Assembly retained in the draft submitted to voters. Other controversies surrounded home rule for local governments and the poll tax. With a turnout
of less than 20 percent of those registered, voters approved the document by
slightly more than a three-to-two margin following an active campaign on its
behalf. Within three years, though, the new constitution had added its first
amendments. In fact, 1,098 amendments were proposed between 1946 and
1974. Voters ratified 826, of which 679 (82 percent) were local in nature.[11]

The Constitution of 1976. An effort to revise the 1945 constitution occurred
during the early 1960s, but a federal court ruling prevented voters from considering it during the 1964 general election. Another attempt died in 1970
when the House but not the Senate approved a document for submission to
the electorate.

After assuming office in 1975, Governor Busbee asked the Office of Legislative Counsel to draft a reorganization of the 1945 Constitution in time
for the 1976 election. After some revision by the General Assembly, voters approved the document in November of that year. With no substantive
changes in the new constitution, the General Assembly almost immediately
set out to consider a more thorough revision, creating the Select Committee
on Constitutional Revision during its 1977 session.[12]

The Constitution of 1983

Like its predecessors, Georgia's current constitution reflects the changing politics of the state yet maintains many characteristics considered
traditional: conservative fiscal policy, small government, and deference

to localities. However, the Constitution of 1983 was neither easily written nor quickly adopted. In fact, it is a good example of how factionalism can play a role in state politics.

Adoption

Between 1946 and 1980, Georgians were asked to vote on 1,452 proposed amendments (1,177 of them purely local in nature) and ratified more than 1,100. This process created an unwieldy document understood by only the most diligent of constitutional students. Because it so restricted the behavior of local governments, localities often had to amend the Constitution before they could make changes in taxation or municipal codes. For example, voters in Muscogee County voted on three amendments in 1966 and one in 1968 that applied only to their local governments and paved the way for the merger of the city of Columbus and Muscogee County governments in 1970.[13] Georgia voters became so annoyed with the large number of proposals that they began to vote them down. In 1978, the statewide ballot included more than 120 proposed changes in the state's constitution, one-third of which failed to pass.[14]

By the late 1970s, many citizens were pleased when Busbee sought to have the Constitution rewritten, although he may not have realized the difficulty of such a task. After beginning work in 1977, the Select Committee on Constitutional Revision, whose members included the governor, lieutenant governor, speaker of the House, attorney general, and eight other elected officials, debated the proposed constitution for three years. The committee appointed groups with broader citizen membership to revise individual articles of the Constitution for consideration by the General Assembly and the electorate. In November 1978 two articles were submitted to voters, who rejected them.[15]

Subsequent efforts by the committee and the 1980 session of the legislature failed to produce a new constitution. During its 1981 session, however, the General Assembly created the Legislative Overview Committee on Constitutional Revision, with thirty-one members from each house, to work with the Select Committee. These efforts produced a document that was approved in a 1981 legislative special session and modified at the 1982 session before being submitted to the electorate.

Like constitutional revisions generally, this one was quite political. Lobbyists and others representing specific interests were quick to get involved in the process, which former governor Ellis Arnall likened to "dancing with a grizzly bear."[16] Moreover, the process was a costly one, with some estimates of the tab for the 1981 special session at thirty thousand dollars per day.[17] A confrontation occurred between the speaker of the House of Representatives, Tom Murphy, and the governor over the powers to be granted to the legislature under the new constitution. This debate was fueled by the fact that previous constitutions had empowered the governor to name the presiding officers of the House and Senate as well as most legislative committee and subcommittee chairs. The governor had retained this intimidating power over the legislature until the 1960s, when it was changed by constitutional amendment.[18] Murphy wanted the legislature to retain various powers, while Busbee favored the delegation of some powers to bureaucratic offices and state boards. The governor and the General Assembly also disagreed regarding tax breaks and gubernatorial term limits. Some members of the legislature seemed more interested in having control over writing the new document than in its eventual passage. At one point, Busbee asked legislators to forget the proposal and spend the remaining days of the session on other topics.[19]

Voters reacted angrily to this potential loss of opportunity, and the members of the General Assembly returned after a weekend break determined to come to consensus. They eventually reached an agreement, and the resulting document was indeed much shorter than its predecessor. It also was written in gender-neutral and simpler language, making it easier for the average citizen to understand. Although many voters did not favor all of the new document's provisions, they approved it in November 1982 by a nearly three-to-one margin, and it took effect the following July. The new constitution was the product of long debate and of more than thirty-one hundred hours of work by more than two hundred people. Thousands of Georgians appeared at public hearings to argue for or against various provisions. Although some observers have argued that the new constitution represented an evolution rather than a revolution, the document made many noteworthy changes.[20] Its major provisions include

eliminating the requirement that local governments place changes in taxation, municipal codes, and employee compensation on the state ballot;

establishing a unified court system, consolidating the duties of justices of the peace and small claims courts into magistrate courts, and strengthening the state Supreme Court;

requiring nonpartisan election of state court judges;

enhancing the General Assembly's power to enact laws and appropriate taxes;

giving the Board of Pardons and Paroles power to stay death sentences;

incorporating an equal protection clause;

reducing the total amount of debt that the state may assume;

providing more open-to-the-public committee and legislative meetings; and

incorporating more formal separation of powers between the legislative and executive branches.

Even this more streamlined document has not closed the door on the amendment process. Between 1984 and 2004, eighty-three amendments were proposed, and sixty-three were approved (see table 3.3). Because the Georgia Constitution is so specific, amendments may be offered that affect only narrow interests, and voters often skip unfamiliar constitutional amendments.

The November 2000 election included seven proposed amendments. The only proposal defeated by voters (52 percent opposed) would have allowed changes in the way marine vessels are taxed. Three amendments were approved to allow benefits for law enforcement officials, firefighters, public school employees, and state highway employees killed or disabled in the line of duty. One allowed members of the General Assembly to be removed from office after conviction for a felony rather than after exhausting all of their appeals. Another amendment raised from five to seven years the amount of time that state court judges must have been able to practice law before they can begin their judicial service. Finally, voters approved a measure related to property tax relief.

The 2002 election included six proposed amendments. Voters rejected two of the six. The first defeated proposal (54 percent opposed) would have established separate valuation standards and property tax rates for low-income residential developments. The other (57 percent opposed) would have affected tax rates for commercial docksides used in the landing and processing of seafood. Of the four amendments approved by voters, two provided tax incentives for the redevelopment and cleanup of deteriorated or contaminated properties. Another established a program of dog and cat sterilization funded by special license plates. Finally, voters approved a measure to

Table 3.3. Proposed Amendments to the 1983
Georgia Constitution

Year	Number of Amendments Submitted to Voters	Number Approved
1984	11	10
1986	9	8
1988	15	6
1990	9	8
1992	8	7
1994	6	5
1996	5	4
1998	5	3
2000	7	6
2002	6	4
2004	2	2
2006	3	3
TOTAL	86	66 (78%)

Sources: Hill 1994 20–23; *Georgia Laws 1995 Session*,
3:CCCXVII–CCCXIX; Georgia Secretary of State,
Elections Division, *Georgia Election Results* (www.sos
.state.ga.us/elections/election_results/default.htm).

prohibit individuals from holding state office if they had defaulted on their federal, state, or local taxes. The November 2004 ballot included only two proposed amendments. One was an obscure question regarding the jurisdiction of the state Supreme Court. The other, a contentious measure banning same-sex marriage, attracted thirteen thousand more votes than the court measure.[21] In 2006, three measures were proposed and passed, including one restricting local government use of eminent domain.

Constitutional Distribution of Authority

Perhaps the most important aspect of the Georgia Constitution is what Melvin B. Hill Jr. calls its status as "a power-limiting document rather than a power-granting document."[22] Thus, many provisions specify things that the state of Georgia and its local governments may not do. Like most states, Georgia includes the ideal of separation of powers adopted by the Framers of the U.S. Constitution, although important differences from the national government exist.

Legislative Branch. On the surface, few differences between Congress and the Georgia General Assembly are apparent. Both are bicameral legislatures, with the presiding officer of the lower house chosen by its members and the leader of the Senate elected independently of its members. Unlike Congress, where only one-third of the Senate and the entire House are elected every two years, the whole General Assembly is up for election every two years. The General Assembly also meets for a limited time annually and lacks the salary and staff support found in Congress. However, the practices that have developed outside the respective constitutions most distinguish Congress from the General Assembly—in particular, the presiding officers at the state level have greater power (see chapter 7).

Executive Branch. Perhaps the most striking difference between the U.S. and Georgia Constitutions is the number of elected officials in the executive branch. The most visible elected executives are the governor and the lieutenant governor, although the latter's primary duties are legislative, as presiding officer of the Senate. While they may be compared to the U.S. president and vice president, the governor and lieutenant governor are not elected together and may represent different views and political parties. Georgia voters also elect to four-year terms their attorney general, secretary of state, superintendent of schools, and the heads of the Departments of Labor, Insurance, and Agriculture. The large number of elected officials limits the governor's power and authority because independently elected officials have little reason to respond to the governor's political needs. This arrangement differs substantially from the national government, where the heads of most agencies are nominated and may be fired at will by the president, with the only limitation being Senate approval of nominees.

Article 4 of the Georgia Constitution also provides for six multimember boards and commissions with legislative, administrative, and judicial responsibilities. Perhaps the most important is the Public Service Commission, whose five members are elected statewide for staggered six-year terms. The commission is responsible for regulating telephone services, utilities such as gas and electricity, communication networks, and transportation such as trucking and rail systems. Because the Public Service Commission

holds public hearings and considers rates charged to consumers, it functions in part as a judicial agency. It also handles enforcement and employs
inspectors and engineers, making the commission appear to be an executive
agency. Article 8 gives constitutional status to two other boards appointed
by the governor, one for elementary and secondary education and another
with jurisdiction over the state university system (see chapter 8).

Judicial Branch. The 1983 Constitution also maintained an independent judiciary. Unlike the federal legal system, the Georgia Constitution requires that
state judges be elected. Georgia's district attorneys (local officials responsible
for criminal prosecutions) are also elected. Thus, Georgia does not employ
the same checks and balances as at the national level, where, subject to Senate confirmation, local prosecutors are presidential appointees under the authority of the U.S. Department of Justice and judges are appointed for life.
Georgia's executive and judicial branches have some links, however, because
Article 6, Section 7 permits the governor to appoint people to vacant or
newly created judgeships. Another practice not found at the national level is
the attorney general's ability to issue advisory opinions, which have the force
of law in Georgia unless overturned in court (see chapter 9).

Local Government. Articles 8 and 9 of the Georgia Constitution establish a
framework for the operation of local government. These provisions are especially important because the U.S. Constitution says nothing about the matter
(see chapter 10).

Procedures

Constitutional Amendments. Georgia's constitution outlines several important
procedures, some of which differ significantly from those that appear in the
U.S. Constitution but resemble methods commonly used in other states (see
table 3.4). The most fundamental difference may be the method for carrying
out constitutional changes. In Georgia, the legislature can ask voters to create a convention to amend or replace the Constitution. The General Assembly can also propose amendments if they are approved by a two-thirds vote
in the House and Senate, a procedure that resembles the one at the national
level. While the U.S. Constitution requires ratification by three-fourths of

Table 3.4. Amending State Constitutions through Their Legislatures

Procedure	Approval Required	Number of States
Vote in Legislature	Majority	18
	Two-thirds	19*
	Three-fifths	9
	Other	4[†]
Number of Legislative Sessions	One	38*
	Two	12
Voter Approval	Majority on Amendment	44[‡]*
	Majority in Election	3
	Other	3[§]

* Method in Georgia.

[†]Includes three states that require larger majorities if passed in one session but only a majority if passed in two legislative sessions.

[‡]Includes five states with different majorities for certain types of constitutional changes.

[§]Delaware's constitution is amended by a two-thirds vote in two sessions of the legislature and does not require voter approval in a referendum.

Note: Eighteen states also allow their citizens to use the initiative process to place amendments on the ballot.

Source: Council of State Governments 2005, 37:12–14.

the states, Article 10 of the Georgia Constitution requires approval by a majority of voters casting ballots on the amendment. This provision is easier to comply with than the provisions in some state constitutions, which require a majority of those voting in the election, a threshold that can pose a problem when people vote for highly visible offices and skip complicated amendments further down the ballot.[23]

Lawmaking. The other major procedures outlined in the Georgia Constitution cover the legislative process and other legislative powers such as impeachment. Unlike the U.S. Constitution, Georgia's differentiates between local bills and those of statewide applicability (Article 3, Section 5), grants the governor a line-item veto for appropriations bills (Article 3, Section 7), and requires the state to adopt a balanced budget (Article 3, Section 9).

The Georgia Constitution in Practice: Rights and Liberties

Constitutions do more than establish governmental institutions and specify procedures. They also guarantee individuals' rights and regulate the government's ability to interfere with people's liberties. Amending a constitution is normally a very difficult process. Therefore, including rights and liberties in a constitution is designed to protect them better than if such guarantees could be reduced or eliminated simply by passing a law.

Article 1, Section 2, Paragraph 5 of the Georgia Constitution allows state courts to determine whether laws or actions comply with the state or U.S. constitution. This process of judicial review resembles that at the national level. Any law or administrative rule in Georgia, whether adopted by the state or by local governments, may be challenged in court. In addition, some private practices may be challenged, such as activities of businesses or individuals. Unlike the U.S. Constitution, in which most rights were added as amendments, Georgia's constitutions since 1861 have included a Bill of Rights as an integral part of the document. Article 1 of the 1983 Constitution includes twenty-eight paragraphs covering "Rights of Persons."

State constitutions may not infringe on liberties or rights protected by the U.S. Constitution. Because of dual state and federal citizenship and the Fourteenth Amendment to the U.S. Constitution, these federal guarantees are minimum standards, and states may grant their citizens broader rights. Some of the major provisions in Georgia's Bill of Rights have resulted in significant state court cases as well as federal court cases that have brought about substantial changes in Georgia and in the nation as a whole.

Right to Life, Liberty, and Property

Georgia Courts. Life, liberty, and property are the first rights listed in the Georgia Constitution—in Article 1, Section 1, Paragraph 1. Like guarantees in the U.S. Constitution, they cannot be abridged "except by due process of law."[24] State courts have found this guarantee to be broader than under the U.S. Constitution.[25] Georgia courts traditionally have found that the state has the power to regulate businesses as long as the regulation applies equally to all who engage in the same types of businesses and has some "rational relationship" to a valid purpose. Only when litigants show that their due process has been violated can they convince the courts that government regulation is "arbitrary" or "unreasonable." Thus, laws regulating the licensing and training of professionals have largely been upheld. The Georgia Supreme Court has held that a mandatory life sentence for a second drug conviction does not violate due process or equal protection despite statistical evidence that a disproportionate number of blacks serve life sentences under the law.[26]

The Georgia Supreme Court has taken a broad view of government compensation owed to the owners of private property taken for public use. All states and the federal government have some power of eminent domain (the taking of private property for public use such as expanding a highway, constructing facilities, and laying water or sewer lines). In 2006, the Georgia Constitution was amended to restrict the use of eminent domain. Local governments cannot take private property for purposes of private economic development, although taking of property for the public good remains constitutional. While most Georgia court decisions have permitted government to determine the size and use of land taken, restrictions have been imposed on compensation. The courts also have applied the notion of taking to regulation of private property: government regulation may be so restrictive that it has the same effect as seizing someone's land. In this regard, the Georgia Supreme Court has reviewed many cases dealing with land-use regulation and has tended to favor property owners over cities and counties, including forcing governments to pay for moving expenses and damages in addition to the land taken.[27] There are no landmark federal cases from Georgia dealing directly with this issue, although major concerns have been raised since the U.S. Supreme Court granted wide latitude in the use of eminent domain in a 2005 Connecticut case.[28]

Equal Protection

Georgia Courts. The second paragraph in Georgia's Bill of Rights (Article 1, Section 1, Paragraph 2) guarantees that "no person shall be denied the equal protection of the laws." This language mirrors the Fourteenth Amendment to the U.S. Constitution.[29] While the Georgia Supreme Court has held that the federal and state equal protection guarantees "coexist," the justices have acknowledged that the state may interpret the Georgia Constitution to offer broader rights than are available under the U.S. Constitution.[30]

A great deal of the controversy over equal protection involves government's classification of groups, with the courts being most vigilant regarding sex and race. In 1984, the Georgia Supreme Court found unconstitutional a law that provided benefits to children whose mothers were wrongfully killed but did not afford the same protection to children whose fathers were wrongfully killed.[31] The Court also struck down Atlanta's program to set aside a share of contracts for minority- and female-owned businesses because the city failed to demonstrate the need for a race-conscious program.[32] Local governments have continued to adopt set-aside programs, however, after studies to determine the effects of prior discrimination. Such policies remain highly contentious and must operate within guidelines laid out by the U.S. Supreme Court, which has become increasingly skeptical of such initiatives.

Perhaps more controversial have been several Atlanta ordinances dealing with gay rights. In 1995, the Georgia Supreme Court held that Atlanta could create a registry of unmarried couples (both heterosexual and homosexual) and forbid discrimination based on sexual orientation. However, the Court concluded that the city exceeded its authority by extending insurance benefits to the domestic partners of city employees.[33] The city has extended various protections based on sexual orientation,[34] although the Georgia legislature has limited their applicability to private clubs.[35]

Federal Courts and Discrimination. On the surface, the Fourteenth Amendment would seem to prohibit discrimination based on race. Yet Georgia, like other southern states, used a number of strategies to disenfranchise black citizens from the 1870s to the 1960s, including the poll tax, the white primary, and other restrictions eventually eliminated by federal legislation and court decisions (see table 3.5).[36]

The poll tax required citizens to pay an annual levy to be eligible to vote, thereby making it harder for the poor to vote. Georgia had used a poll tax earlier in its history, but the tactic became particularly restrictive when the 1877 Constitution made it cumulative, which meant that anyone who fell behind in the annual tax had to make back payments. The poll tax was not repealed until 1945, when Governor Arnall made it a major issue during the legislative session. In other southern states, the poll tax lasted until the Twenty-fourth Amendment to the U.S. Constitution banned it in 1964.

Table 3.5. Major Federal Cases on Discrimination Originating in Georgia

King v. Chapman 154 F.2d 450 (1946)	Building on a 1944 U.S. Supreme Court case covering Texas, the Court of Appeals found that the rules of Georgia's Democratic Party, which restricted voting in primary elections to whites only, violated the equal protection guarantee of the Fourteenth Amendment.
Heart of Atlanta Motel v. United States 379 U.S. 241 (1964)	Upheld the constitutionality of Title II of the Civil Rights Act of 1964, which prohibits racial discrimination in public accommodations.
Olmstead v. L.C. 527 U.S. 581 (1999)	Held that Georgia's practice of involuntarily institutionalizing disabled individuals judged capable of living in less restrictive settings violated the Americans with Disabilities Act of 1990.

Perhaps the most blatant attempt to disenfranchise blacks was the white primary, which restricted voting in party primaries to whites only. Blacks could participate in the general election, but their votes were inconsequential because Republican candidates seldom appeared on the ballot. Some Georgia counties adopted white primaries by the 1890s, and beginning in 1900, only whites could vote in the Democratic Party's primary elections. In a 1927 Texas case,[37] the U.S. Supreme Court held that it was unconstitutional for state law to restrict primary voting on the basis of race. At the time, the Democrats controlled virtually the entire South, and party leaders thereafter used party rules to enforce the white primary. Unlike general elections, which are processes of government, primaries could be regarded as activities of political parties, which are "private" organizations.

Not until 1944 did the U.S. Supreme Court hold that party rules enforcing a white primary also abridged the right to vote based on race.[38] A federal appeals court overturned Georgia's white primary the following year in *King v. Chapman*.[39] Perhaps the most immediate effect of this decision was in Atlanta, where business and political leaders began developing a coalition with the city's large black middle class.[40]

The Disenfranchisement Act of 1908, which voters approved as an amendment to the Georgia Constitution by a two-to-one margin, included three other provisions for voting: (1) a literacy test that required voters to read and explain any paragraph of the U.S. or Georgia Constitutions; (2) a property qualification that required voters to own forty acres of land or property valued at five hundred dollars; and (3) a grandfather clause that allowed U.S. or Confederate military veterans or their descendants to register to vote prior to 1914.[41] Implementation of the literacy test rested in the hands of local election officials, who exercised great discretion, especially their power to purge voter registration rolls of those judged to be unqualified.

As desegregation gained momentum during the 1950s and 1960s, the Georgia General Assembly produced an array of legislation to forestall the process.[42] Local school districts also tried to prevent or minimize desegregation, including the Chatham County school board's unsuccessful effort to claim that integration would heighten black children's feelings of inferiority.[43]

More recent controversies have centered on the use of affirmative action in admissions decisions at Georgia's public colleges and universities, including several years of litigation over policies at the University of Georgia. In 2003, however, the U.S. Supreme Court gave support to the limited use of affirmative action in college admissions in two cases involving the University of Michigan.[44]

The Civil Rights Act of 1964 was designed to end discrimination in public accommodations (hotels, restaurants, transportation, and so forth). In *Heart of Atlanta Motel v. United States*,[45] the U.S. Supreme Court took a broad view of the U.S. Constitution's commerce clause and upheld the Civil Rights Act as a valid exercise of Congress's authority. The Court rejected the motel's claim that it was a local business, ruling that because the motel served interstate travelers, its practice of refusing lodging to blacks obstructed commerce.

Not all discrimination falls under the Fourteenth Amendment. Congress has also passed laws dealing with characteristics such as religion, age, and disability. One of the leading cases regarding the disabled was based on the ways in which the Georgia Department of Human Resources had institutionalized people involuntarily after it was determined that such people could be placed in a community setting. In *Olmstead v. L.C.*,[46] the U.S. Supreme Court held that such action violated the protection of the 1990 Americans with Disabilities Act.

Federal Courts and Equal Representation. Since the early 1960s, federal courts have become increasingly active in the process of drawing districts for

Table 3.6. Major Federal Cases on Representation Originating in Georgia

Gray v. Sanders 372 U.S. 368 (1963)	Held that Georgia's county-unit system violated the Fourteenth Amendment's equal protection guarantee because it malapportioned votes among the state's counties.
Fortson v. Toombs 379 U.S. 621 (1965)	Upheld a lower court's 1962 decision that the Fourteenth Amendment required seats in the General Assembly to be apportioned with districts of roughly equal population rather than being based on county or other political boundaries.
Miller v. Johnson 515 U.S. 900 (1995)	Invalidated Georgia's congressional redistricting following the 1990 census as a violation of the Fourteenth Amendment's equal protection clause because race was the predominant factor in drawing district boundaries. The General Assembly had created three black-majority districts, with the Eleventh District having a very irregular shape.
Georgia v. Ashcroft 539 U.S. 461 (2003)	Held that courts reviewing redistricting under the Voting Rights Act must consider all relevant factors affecting minority voters, not just the chance of electing minority candidates.

legislative bodies. The courts have interpreted the equal protection guarantee of the Fourteenth Amendment to mean that one person's vote should have the same weight in an election as another person's; districts thus must have roughly equal populations (see table 3.6). After four earlier challenges had failed, in *Gray v. Sanders*,[47] the U.S. Supreme Court struck down the county-unit system as a violation of the Fourteenth Amendment's equal protection guarantee because the system malapportioned votes by underrepresenting urban residents. Other litigation also forced the General Assembly to redraw congressional districts in the state.[48] In *Fortson v. Toombs*,[49] the Court ruled that reapportionment for the General Assembly must be made on the basis of the population of the state rather than by county or other political boundaries. Each district must have roughly the same number of inhabitants.

Questions of representation have become increasingly linked to race since Congress passed the Voting Rights Act in 1965. This measure suspended use of literacy tests, allowed for federal election examiners and observers, and required affected state and local governments to receive approval from the national government before making changes in their electoral systems. The U.S. Department of Justice is especially wary of offering this "preclearance" when changes might dilute minorities' voting strength.

The U.S. Department of Justice objected to congressional redistricting by the Georgia General Assembly following the 1990 census. After two unsuccessful attempts to redraw districts, state lawmakers finally satisfied federal guidelines to protect minority voting strength in the 1992 elections.[50] Ironically, in 1995 those districts were ruled unconstitutional in *Miller v. Johnson* because race was a "predominant factor" used in drawing the district lines.[51] Similar litigation occurred following redistricting based on the 2000 census: in *Georgia v. Ashcroft*,[52] the U.S. Supreme Court again required Georgia to consider factors other than race in drawing legislative districts.

Rights Related to Expression and Association

Georgia's Bill of Rights includes a number of provisions designed to allow people to hold and express opinions, to associate with others, and to participate in the political process. The Georgia Constitution includes two paragraphs on religion as well as one on the press, another on the right to assemble and petition, and one on libel, which is not mentioned in the U.S. Constitution.

Georgia Courts and Freedom of Conscience and Religion. Religious freedom was the earliest liberty to be addressed by the drafters of the Georgia Constitution. Even the Rules and Regulations of 1776 included a provision for freedom of religion.[53] Article 1, Section 1, Paragraphs 3 and 4 of the Georgia Constitution include somewhat different language from the First Amendment to the U.S. Constitution. Perhaps the most striking difference is Georgia's limitation on religious practices: "But the right of freedom of religion shall not be so construed as to excuse acts of licentiousness or justify practices inconsistent with the peace and safety of the state." Thus, courts in Georgia have at times limited freedom of religion, including a decision that freedom of religion did not include the distribution of literature in public.[54] Nor has the Georgia Supreme Court extended freedom of religion to the use of controlled substances.[55] The state has also been drawn into controversies over links between religion and public school science courses, usually in relation to "creationism" and "intelligent design."[56]

Georgia Courts and Freedom of Speech and the Press. Georgia courts have adopted a broad interpretation of freedom of speech.[57] For example, while the U.S. Constitution held that screening of movies did not in and of itself violate free speech, the Georgia Supreme Court found that an ordinance requiring approval of a censor before screening movies was unconstitutional in the state.[58] The Court also held that banning people between the ages of eighteen and twenty-one from premises with sexually explicit performances constituted a violation of free speech.[59]

Free speech, as interpreted by the Georgia courts, includes limits. Indeed, Article 1, Section 1, Paragraph 5 of the Georgia Constitution says that people "shall be responsible for the abuse of that liberty," as in cases involving incorrect publication of delinquent debt, inaccurate information regarding criminal activity, or use of photographs for advertising without the subjects' permission. The Georgia Supreme Court has upheld an injunction against antiabortion protesters on the grounds that the protest was limited by reasonable restrictions regarding time, place, and manner.[60] The Court has held, however, that picketing was not protected free speech when the protest included an illegal strike.[61] The Court also upheld the state's "Anti-Mask Act," which targets groups such as the Ku Klux Klan by prohibiting intimidating or threatening mask-wearing behavior, despite a claim that the law violates a person's freedom of speech.[62]

The press does not have a constitutional right to withhold a confidential news source.[63] However, the media have received limited protection through a state law that allows reporters to be forced to turn over information from confidential sources only when the evidence is material and relevant, is necessary for one of the parties to prepare a case, and cannot reasonably be gathered by other means.[64] In terms of other publications, the Georgia Supreme Court has held that a city cannot prohibit the distribution of printed materials to homes.[65]

Controversies have swirled around language or behavior that many people judge offensive. For example, the Georgia Supreme Court struck down as too vague and a violation of free speech a state law attempting to outlaw bumper stickers considered profane.[66] Even greater debates have involved sexually oriented communication, particularly after the Georgia Supreme Court ruled that nude dancing was protected expression and overturned local regulations banning such entertainment as too broad or outside the authority granted to local governments.[67] As discussed earlier in the chapter, Georgia voters approved a 1994 constitutional amendment that increased local governments' control over nude dancing through their power to regulate alcoholic beverages, and the Georgia Supreme Court has held that such alcohol regulations do not violate free speech rights.[68]

Federal Courts and Freedom of Speech and the Press. During the past forty years the U.S. Supreme Court has considered many cases dealing with the First Amendment's guarantees regarding religion, speech, the press, and association (see table 3.7). Two major cases on obscenity originated in Georgia. In a 1969 decision, *Stanley v. Georgia,* the Court found that "the mere private possession of obscene matter cannot constitutionally be made a crime," which Georgia law had done. Police had a warrant to search a man's home for materials related to illegal gambling but found allegedly obscene material. The state claimed that certain types of materials should not be possessed or read and that obscene materials could lead to sexual violence or other acts. The Court rejected these claims, holding that although the state asserted the "right to control the moral content of a person's thoughts," such claims were "wholly inconsistent with the philosophy of the First Amendment." [69]

In a 1973 case, *Paris Adult Theatre I v. Slaton,*[70] the Supreme Court was asked to determine whether the state could ban a commercial theater's showing of films considered obscene. Here the Court reached an opposite result from *Stanley,* holding that the state had an interest in "stemming the tide of commercialized obscenity." The Court held that it did not make a difference that the films in question were shown only to consenting adults and that the business posted warnings of films' content and prohibited minors from entering. Instead, the Court held that the state had a valid interest in the "quality of life and the total community environment, the tone of commerce in the great city centers, and, possibly, the public safety itself."

The U.S. Supreme Court also used a Georgia case involving white supremacists to limit restrictions on protest. Forsyth County was the scene of several marches by civil rights supporters and countermarches by the Ku Klux Klan during the 1980s. To manage these events, the county commis-

Table 3.7. Major Federal Cases on Freedom of Speech and the Press Originating in Georgia

Stanley v. Georgia 394 U.S. 557 (1969)	Overturned a state law making private possession of obscene material a crime. The Georgia law was held to violate the First and Fourteenth Amendments to the U.S. Constitution.
Paris Adult Theatre I v. Slaton 413 U.S. 49 (1973)	Held that banning the showing of allegedly obscene films to consenting adults in a commercial theater did not violate the First Amendment or the right to privacy.
Cox Broadcasting Corp. v. Colin 420 U.S. 469 (1975)	Overturned a Georgia law prohibiting publication of the name of a rape victim obtained from public records.
Forsyth County, Georgia v. Nationalist Movement 505 U.S. 123 (1992)	Invalidated a local ordinance requiring participants to pay law enforcement costs for demonstrations and empowering the county administrator to determine how much to charge a group seeking a permit for a demonstration. The court found fault with the ordinance because it granted excessively broad discretion to the administrator, who was required to examine the content of a group's message in determining the fee to be charged for law enforcement protection.

sion adopted an ordinance requiring those seeking a demonstration permit to pay a fee for law enforcement protection. The county administrator had discretion over the size of the fee, which could not exceed one thousand dollars. One group refused to pay a hundred-dollar fee and sued the county. In *Forsyth County, Georgia v. Nationalist Movement*,[71] the U.S. Supreme Court found that the county ordinance contained no standards for the administrator to follow and was thus unconstitutional because it "contains more than the possibility of censorship through uncontrolled discretion [and] the ordinance often requires that the fee be based on the content of the speech" of the group seeking the permit.

Cox Broadcasting Corp. v. Colin[72] dealt with Georgia's law prohibiting publication of a rape victim's name. Pitted against each other were the desire to protect the victim's privacy and the freedom of the press. The Court held that it would violate press freedom to prohibit the publication of crime victims' names obtained from public records.

Rights of Those Accused and Convicted of Crimes

Article 1, Section 1 of the Georgia Constitution includes several provisions to protect people in dealing with the state's legal system, including conditions regarding searches, seizures, and warrants by law enforcement officials; access to the courts and the use of juries; the right to an attorney and to cross-examine witnesses in criminal cases; the right against self-incrimination; protection against excessive bail and "cruel and unusual" punishment; and a prohibition against double jeopardy.[73] Most of these guarantees parallel those in the U.S. Constitution's Bill of Rights, although Georgia has added other guarantees (see table 3.8). For example, Article 1, Section 1 of the state Bill of Rights explicitly prohibits whipping and banishment from the state as punishment for crimes, imprisonment for debt, and being "abused in being arrested, while under arrest, or in prison."

Georgia Courts. One of the most notable distinctions between the Georgia and U.S. Constitutions is that the state offers more protection to defendants against unreasonable searches and seizures by law enforcement authorities. In addition, Georgia has long recognized the right of indigents to have a lawyer appointed, although this right does not extend to civil cases.[74] A major problem with providing attorneys to poor criminal defendants has been in appropriating sufficient funds to make the guarantee work well.

Observers often argue that certain punishments are "cruel and unusual." Georgia courts have held that punishment exceeding the crime is, in some cases, constitutional. For example, fines larger than amounts taken by theft have been permitted. In some instances, defendants have been banished from certain counties, but the Georgia Supreme Court has not upheld banishment from the state as a whole. In 1972, the U.S. Supreme Court found Georgia's use of the death penalty to be unconstitutional because the state lacked standards to protect against unequal application of capital punishment.

Table 3.8. Major Federal Cases Affecting Those Accused or Convicted of
Crimes Originating in Georgia

Furman v. Georgia 408 U.S. 238 (1972)	Held that Georgia's methods of administering the death penalty violated the Eighth Amendment's guarantee against cruel and unusual punishment. The decision effectively ended executions in the United States for more than a decade.
Gregg v. Georgia 428 U.S. 153 (1976)	Upheld Georgia's revised law on capital punishment, which limited the crimes for which the death penalty could be imposed and specified the factors to be considered and procedures to be used in deciding when to impose capital punishment.
Coker v. Georgia U.S. 584 (1977)	Found that Georgia's imposition of the death penalty for the 433 crime of rape was grossly disproportionate and thus a violation of the Eighth Amendment's ban on cruel and unusual punishment.
Ballew v. Georgia 435 U.S. 223 (1978)	Held that a criminal trial using a jury of fewer than six members violated the Sixth and Fourteenth Amendment guarantees to a fair trial.
McCleskey v. Kemp 481 U.S. 279 (1987)	Rejected the claim that racial differences in the imposition of the death penalty violated the equal protection guarantee of the Fourteenth Amendment and amounted to cruel and unusual punishment in violation of the Eighth Amendment.
Chandler v. Miller 520 U.S. 305 (1997)	Held that Georgia's requirement that candidates for state office pass drug tests violated the Fourth and Fourteenth Amendment protections against suspicionless searches.
Georgia v. Randolph No. 04-1067 (2006)	Held that police cannot conduct a search without a warrant when one occupant of a dwelling gives them permission but the other occupant is also present and objects to the search.

Currently, Georgia law lists the conditions under which the death penalty may be sought and is in line with later U.S. Supreme Court rulings permitting executions. The Georgia Supreme Court has ruled that sentencing someone to life in prison for a second conviction for selling cocaine does not constitute cruel and unusual punishment.[75] Georgia's justices reached the opposite conclusion in 1989, however, in the case of executing someone who is mentally retarded.[76] Thirteen years later, a U.S. Supreme Court decision banned the practice nationally as cruel and unusual punishment.[77] Georgia courts have also grappled with concerns that prosecutors may discriminate in exercising discretion in requesting sentences for a crime.[78]

Federal Courts and Search and Seizure. Georgia has produced few major federal cases related to the search and seizure rights of criminal defendants found in the U.S. Constitution's Fourth Amendment. In 1997, however, the U.S. Supreme Court overturned a 1980s Georgia law requiring candidates for state office to pass a drug test. In *Chandler v. Miller,*[79] the Court held that the drug tests did not fall within the category of constitutionally permissible suspicionless searches. Indeed, the Court found that the test was essentially "symbolic" rather than being directed at some identifiable problem that might demand such a search. In 2006, the Supreme Court decided an important search and seizure case from Georgia. Police can search a home without a warrant if the inhabitant gives permission, including one spouse's permission when the other is not present. In *Georgia v. Randolph,*[80] however, both Randolph and his estranged wife were present. Although she gave the police permission to search, Randolph refused. The police searched the house anyway and seized evidence used to convict him of a felony. The Court held that conducting a search over Randolph's objection violated the Fourth Amendment protection against unreasonable searches and seizures, which means that the police would need to convince a judge that they had probable cause to obtain a search warrant when one of the occupants objects.

Federal Courts and the Rights of Criminal Defendants. The U.S. Constitution's Sixth Amendment includes the right to a fair trial, which is not spelled out in detail. Therefore, the courts have had to define what that right means in practice. Some of these cases have dealt with the size of trial juries and whether they must reach a unanimous decision. In a 1973 Florida case, the U.S. Supreme Court had permitted six-member juries in civil cases. In *Ballew v. Georgia*,[81] however, the Court ruled in 1978 that Georgia's use of five-person juries in misdemeanor cases violated the right to a fair trial, in part because of the reduced deliberation and bias in favor of the prosecution regarding hung juries. Article 1, Section 1, Paragraph 1b of Georgia's current constitution allows the General Assembly to permit six-member juries in misdemeanor cases or in courts of limited jurisdiction.

Federal Courts and the Death Penalty. Two appeals to the U.S. Supreme Court from Georgia during the 1970s became the landmark cases regarding the use of capital punishment in the United States. A 1972 case, *Furman v. Georgia*,[82] effectively ended executions throughout the country. Four years later, *Gregg v. Georgia*[83] allowed the state's rewritten capital punishment law to stand, thereby opening the door for states to resume executions.

How did these two cases differ? The members of the U.S. Supreme Court had a range of views regarding capital punishment, but the major concern was how the death penalty was applied. In *Furman*, the Court was concerned about both the lack of guidelines for deciding when to impose a death sentence and the wide variation in the use of the death penalty for similar crimes. The states then began revising their laws, and the Court decided several cases in 1976 based on the new statutes. In *Gregg*, the Court upheld Georgia's new capital punishment law, in part because it required specific findings by the jury regarding the facts of the crime and the character of the defendant; it also had a process for appellate courts to review death penalty cases.

Two other cases tested the constitutionality of the conditions under which Georgia imposed the death penalty. In *Coker v. Georgia*,[84] the U.S. Supreme Court held that the death sentence for the crime of rape was grossly disproportionate to the offense and thus violated the Eighth Amendment ban on cruel and unusual punishment. In *McCleskey v. Kemp*,[85] the Court confronted the issue of bias in imposing the death penalty. McCleskey presented a study showing that the use of the death sentence in Georgia was statistically related to the race of the murder victim and, to a lesser extent, to the race of the defendant. This pattern, he argued, violated the Eighth and Fourteenth Amendments. The Supreme Court rejected these claims, citing appellate courts' review of cases with facts similar to McCleskey's case.

The Right to Privacy

Georgia Courts. Like the U.S. Constitution, Georgia's does not mention a right to privacy. In 1904, however, Georgia became the first state to recognize a privacy right when the state's Supreme Court found this right in natural law and the guarantees of liberty found in the U.S. and Georgia Constitutions.[86] Privacy has been extended to the right of a prisoner to refuse to eat, even to the point of starvation,[87] and to a person's right to refuse medical treatment even if doing so was certain to lead to death.[88]

Federal Courts, Dual Citizenship, and the Right to Privacy. The U.S. Supreme Court first recognized a right to privacy in a 1965 Connecticut case dealing with government regulation of contraception. Since then, the courts have been forced to define the limits of privacy rights. These debates include two Georgia cases (see table 3.9). *Doe v. Bolton* remains almost unnoticed today, but this challenge to Georgia's abortion law was decided along with *Roe v. Wade* (1973), the more widely known Texas case in which the Supreme Court held that the right to privacy included a woman's right to abortion.[89]

The second Georgia case was *Bowers v. Hardwick* (1986),[90] which challenged Georgia's sodomy law as a violation of the right to privacy insofar as it applied to consensual sexual conduct and that contended that homosexuals faced constant threats of arrest and prosecution. The U.S. Supreme Court rejected the claim and upheld Georgia's sodomy law, which prohibited certain acts but did not specify the gender or sexual orientation of the participants.

Georgia's sodomy law provides a good example of the way in which dual citizenship can produce different rights under the state and U.S. Constitutions. The Georgia Supreme Court reinforced the *Hardwick* decision in

Table 3.9. Major Federal Cases on the Right to Privacy Originating in Georgia

Doe v. Bolton 410 U.S. 179 (1973)	Decided along with *Roe v. Wade*, this case overturned Georgia's ban on abortions as a violation of a woman's right to privacy.
Bowers v. Hardwick 478 U.S. 186 (1986)	Held that the right to privacy did not protect consensual homosexual sex from prosecution under Georgia's sodomy law.

1996, ruling in *Christensen v. State* that the state's sodomy law did not violate Georgia's right to privacy.[91] In 1998, however, the Georgia Supreme Court ruled in *Powell v. State,* a case involving a heterosexual couple, that "insofar as it criminalizes the performance of private, non-commercial acts of sexual intimacy between persons legally able to consent, [the sodomy law] 'manifestly infringes upon a constitutional provision' . . . which guarantees to the citizens of Georgia the right to privacy."[92] Shortly thereafter, however, the Court rejected the claim that Georgia's right to privacy also protected commercial sexual activity.[93]

Thus, while any state's law criminalizing sodomy would not violate the federal right to privacy as applied in *Bowers v. Hardwick,* state courts around the country could consider such a law in violation of broader rights guaranteed in their state constitutions. That possibility changed rather dramatically in 2003, however, when the U.S. Supreme Court's *Lawrence v. Texas* decision overturned sodomy laws in those states that still had them.[94]

The most recent frontier in battles over privacy rights involves medical treatment. A 1997 U.S. Supreme Court decision left the door open for states to either ban or allow doctor-assisted suicide. This produced a conflict when former U.S. Attorney General John Ashcroft attempted to keep Oregon from implementing its law allowing the practice, and in January 2006, the Court sided with Oregon.[95] Although major federal cases on this subject have not originated in Georgia, such disputes will undoubtedly continue in the face of breakthroughs in medical treatment and research.

The Continuing Significance of Georgia's Constitution

A constitution does not provide a sacred or unchanging blueprint for government. Constitutions are essentially political documents, and individuals, businesses, political parties, and interest groups often fight vigorously about interpreting and amending constitutions. Lawsuits have contended that Georgia's methods of selecting judges and juries are racially biased.[96] By approving an amendment to create a state-sponsored lottery in 1992, voters gave the governor, legislature, and bureaucracy millions of dollars to distribute to programs and individuals but also paved the way for firms to profit from the production, sale, and marketing of lottery tickets. Another amendment granted a property tax break for growing timber. The 1992 amendment (Article 8, Section 5, Paragraphs 2 and 3) requiring that local school board members be elected and superintendents be hired allows boards to recruit superintendents from anywhere. Under the old system of electing school superintendents in some counties, only local residents could run for the office.

As these examples demonstrate, constitutions help distribute political and economic power. Constitutions also adopt policies that under other circumstances might be put into practice simply by passing a law. Given the extensive detail in the Georgia Constitution, voters undoubtedly will face proposed amendments every even-numbered year as various interests try to modify the document to achieve their ends. Indeed, the popularity of the HOPE scholarship program seems to have given birth to a regular series of proposed amendments supposedly designed to protect the program—and enhance the image of the Republicans and Democrats who support those amendments.[97]

If voters ratify a large number of amendments, the Constitution might become unwieldy and difficult to interpret. A second possibility is that Georgians will become so annoyed with proposals on the ballot that they rebel by voting against amendments. Finally, interest groups, political parties, and members of the General Assembly might regularly use constitutional change as just another way to achieve their political ends. If so, Georgians might treat amendment battles as just an ordinary part of the election process, although the phenomenon would not approach the scale on which western states use ballot initiatives. None of these scenarios bodes well, however, for the durability of the 1983 Georgia Constitution.

CHAPTER 4

Public Opinion

Public opinion is the foundation for participation and helps set the limits of acceptable action by government officials and others. Candidates, the media, parties, interest groups, and others also expend great effort to understand or influence public opinion. People often hold diverse opinions, a situation that can make it difficult for policy makers to decide what to do regarding a particular issue. On some occasions, the public may line up overwhelmingly on one side of a question; at other times, large numbers of people are undecided or have no opinion about an issue. Still, a variety of organizations use polls to determine what the public thinks.[1] Scholars are especially interested in the ways that ideology and political culture relate to people's attitudes.

Ideology and Political Culture

Ideology

Ideology refers to "a set of fundamental beliefs or principles about politics and government: what the scope of government should be; how decisions should be made; what values should be pursued."[2] Researchers and the public alike usually discuss ideology in terms of "liberal" and "conservative." "Although these words are used in a variety of ways, generally liberalism endorses the idea of social change and advocates the involvement of government in effecting such change, whereas conservatism seeks to defend the status quo and prescribes a more limited role for governmental activity."[3] Studies generally classify people's ideology in two ways: (1) whether they call themselves liberal, moderate, or conservative and (2) the degree to which they identify with liberal or conservative positions on specific issues.

A 2004 national poll of the voting electorate found that 23 percent of Americans self-identified as liberal or somewhat liberal, while 32 percent called themselves conservative or somewhat conservative. Another 26 percent chose to label themselves as middle-of-the-road, and a surprising 20 percent claimed not to have thought about the matter. These findings reflect limited change from 1992, when the same poll found that 31 percent of respondents self-identified as conservative, 20 percent as liberal, and 23 percent were middle-of-the-road. These data reinforce the image of Americans as not tending toward extreme beliefs. Differences in ideology exist along educational, religious, racial, and regional lines, however.[4]

Georgians have long been known for traditional values, conservative politics, and a general distrust of government. Evidence suggests that this traditional conservatism persists. In a 1992 poll conducted by the Survey Research Center at the University of Georgia, 9.5 percent of all respondents indicated that they were liberal, 29.3 percent identified themselves as conservative, and 54.1 percent said they were moderate.[5] A poll taken in 2004 shows those figures to be fairly stable, with 10 percent of respondents self-identifying as liberal, 34 percent as moderate, and 30 percent as conservative.[6] Naturally, political opinion among Georgia's residents varies by economic status, educational levels, age, gender, race, and geography.

A few studies have compared states. Robert S. Erikson, Gerald C. Wright, and John P. McIver used CBS News/*New York Times* surveys to rate the prevailing ideological patterns of residents in the lower forty-eight states. With 18.8 percent liberal and 36.6 percent conservative, Georgia's rounded score placed it behind sixteen other states considered more conservative. The most conservative states were in the South and Great Plains (see figure 4.1), a pattern

Figure 4.1. Ideological Patterns among the States

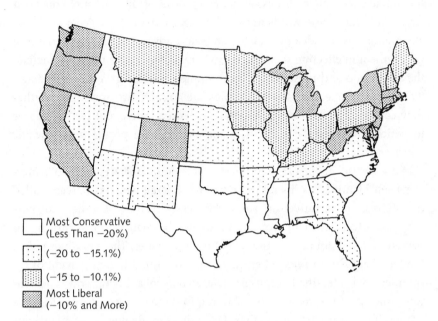

Most Conservative
(Less Than −20%)

(−20 to −15.1%)

(−15 to −10.1%)

Most Liberal
(−10% and More)

Note: Public's self-identification of its ideology is averaged for 1976–1988; state scores are equal to the percentage liberal minus the percentage conservative.

Source: Erikson, Wright, and McIver 1993, 18.

consistent with popular images of many states. The ideological patterns of the individual states remained quite stable during the thirteen years examined by Erikson and his colleagues.[7] A later study by Paul Brace, Kevin Arceneaux, Martin Johnson, and Stacy G. Ulbig found that ideological changes do occur in some states over long periods of time, but this phenomenon did not occur in Georgia.[8]

Virginia Gray created an index of policy liberalism and used it to rank all of the states on several policy dimensions: she found that Georgia's scores tend toward conservatism (see table 4.1). Scores range from one (most liberal) to forty-eight (most conservative). Georgia ranks forty-fifth on policy liberalism, forty-second on gun laws, and thirty-sixth on abortion policies. The state achieved its most conservative ranking—forty-eighth among the states—on policies related to temporary assistance to needy families (TANF).

Table 4.1. Gray's Index of Policy Liberalism among the States

State*	Policy Liberalism†	Gun Law Index	Abortion Index	TANF‡ Index	Tax Progressivity
Alabama	38	36	27	33	40
Arizona	32	31	17	31	32
Arkansas	42	41	32	44	26
California	1	2	5	7	5
Colorado	19	19	20	25	27
Connecticut	5	3	4	26	28
Delaware	10	22	26	12	1
Florida	47	18	23	45	46
Georgia	**45**	**42**	**36**	**48**	**21**
Idaho	37	35	28	46	7
Illinois	18	6	25	27	38
Indiana	28	30	35	41	35
Iowa	23	9	21	24	22
Kansas	30	32	30	23	20
Kentucky	33	46	46	37	15
Louisiana	44	47	48	10	41
Maine	15	48	13	21	9
Maryland	12	4	7	42	19
Massachusetts	4	1	19	22	16
Michigan	22	14	42	16	36
Minnesota	6	12	16	3	8
Mississippi	40	33	41	32	33
Missouri	21	13	44	15	25
Montana	8	44	12	6	2
Nebraska	26	16	40	13	14
Nevada	36	28	15	18	48
New Hampshire	16	27	8	9	39
New Jersey	14	5	10	40	29
New Mexico	11	25	11	2	34
New York	2	7	6	5	13
North Carolina	29	10	22	47	10
North Dakota	46	43	47	30	31
Ohio	24	20	38	36	12
Oklahoma	34	38	18	39	23

(*continued*)

Table 4.1. Continued

State*	Policy Liberalism[†]	Gun Law Index	Abortion Index	TANF[‡] Index	Tax Progressivity
Oregon	7	24	2	20	6
Pennsylvania	25	23	45	8	37
Rhode Island	9	8	33	4	11
South Carolina	20	11	29	19	3
South Dakota	48	37	39	35	45
Tennessee	41	26	31	28	44
Texas	31	45	14	11	42
Utah	39	29	43	29	30
Vermont	3	40	3	1	4
Virginia	35	17	34	38	17
Washington	17	15	1	17	47
West Virginia	13	34	9	14	18
Wisconsin	27	21	37	43	24
Wyoming	43	39	24	34	43

*Alaska and Hawaii are not included.

[†] 1 = most liberal; 48 = most conservative.

[‡] TANF = temporary assistance to needy families.

Source: Gray 2003, 4.

Georgia achieved its most liberal ranking on Gray's indexes in the area of tax progressivity, ranking twenty-first among the states.[9]

The notions of how democracies work—and ought to work—anticipate that elected officials and the policies they enact will to some extent reflect the public's beliefs. Erikson, Wright, and McIver compared state ideology from 1976 to 1988 with a range of state policies around 1980 on education, social welfare, consumer protection, gambling, criminal justice, support for the federal Equal Rights Amendment, and tax progressivity.[10] For most states, the dominant ideology of their residents and the ideological drift of public policy matched well. In the case of Georgia, policy tended to be somewhat more conservative than the ideological leanings of the state's residents.

Several factors could account for this pattern. For one, those surveyed could differ from those who vote in state elections. Also, the legislative process may be geared toward more conservative views than those held by Georgians as a whole. Indeed, Erikson and his collaborators found legislators slightly more conservative than predicted based on the ideology of Georgia residents. Nationally, legislators and congressional candidates appear more moderate than local party chairs and national convention delegates; such Democratic activists tend to be more liberal and their Republican counterparts more conservative than the public.[11]

Political Culture

Both scholarly research and everyday conversation frequently compare states in terms of their political cultures. Political culture develops from each state's historical, economic, social, and political values. The public's prevailing attitudes about government contribute to a state's political culture. State political cultures generally have been classified as individualistic, traditionalistic, moralistic, or some mix of the three. An individualistic political culture is characterized by active participation based on private motivations. In contrast, a moralistic political culture includes broad support for the role of politics in promoting a just society and the expectation that citizens will participate actively. In traditionalistic cultures, politics is geared to preserving existing relations, and participation is concentrated among elites.[12]

Like most of the southern states, Georgia is considered to have a traditionalistic political culture. Moralistic culture is most common among states in the Upper Midwest and West, while individualistic culture is prevalent in the Ohio Valley and East. These notions are consistent with the view of Massachusetts as very liberal and Idaho as very conservative. Regions are far from homogeneous, however. As figure 4.1 indicates, most of the South is more conservative than Georgia, but so are the Dakotas.

Although much of the research on political culture is historical, recent public opinion data identify ideological and partisan variations among the states that cannot be explained by demographic factors such as gender, race, and age. Scholars attribute these differences to variation in states' political culture, which is associated with policy differences.[13] Variation also exists among types of communities, with cities tending to be more liberal and small towns more conservative.[14] Moreover, some research suggests that states may have multiple political cultures, with important differences among regions within states.[15]

Efforts to analyze variation in ideology and political culture include complaints about how oversimplified the "red state/blue state" view is for identifying Republican/conservative and Democratic/liberal areas, respectively.[16] Indeed, Georgia's image as a red stronghold ignores some areas that are strongly Democratic (blue) or quite mixed (purple). Thus, even though Americans are highly mobile and are touched by the national media, prevailing attitudes can diverge significantly from place to place.

Efficacy

Another underlying characteristic associated with attitudes about public policies is political efficacy, which is the degree to which citizens believe that they impact political systems. As noted earlier, in a democratic society, public views are expected to translate into political action, at least to some degree. Political efficacy is often measured to test the level of cynicism in society. People who believe that their views or actions influence change have high levels of efficacy. Citizens who consistently feel that their views are ignored or that political leaders do not know or care about citizens' views have low levels of political efficacy. High levels of political efficacy are linked to higher levels of voting turnout and other forms of participation in political life. Low levels of efficacy are linked to political alienation. Efficacy levels can be assessed by asking poll respondents about the degree to which politicians listen to constituencies or whether respondents are optimistic or pessimistic that they can have a personal impact on the political process.

In 2004, researchers conducted a poll to assess the level of political efficacy among Georgia residents. The poll found that Georgians were more optimistic about their ability to impact government than were most Americans. Previous reports indicated that approximately 47 percent of Americans believed that they had little say in what government does, but only 35 percent of Georgians expressed this level of pessimism. In addition, although 66 percent of Georgians felt that politicians elected to Congress quickly lost touch with their constituencies, this figure fell below the 75 percent of nationwide respondents who responded in that manner.[17]

Georgians are also more likely to feel efficacious about their ability to impact local rather than national government. A majority of respondents (53 percent) in the same 2004 poll indicated that they expected their local government to pay some (42 percent) or a lot (11 percent) of attention to their complaints. Only 45 percent of respondents indicated that they expected some or a lot of attention from national government. A similar question asked respondents how much influence they felt they had over government decisions. Georgians were more likely to express opinions of efficacy over government decisions at the local level than at the national level (see figure 4.2). Georgians expressed optimism in other ways as well. When asked about whether they viewed government as a necessary evil or a place where people come together for positive change, a majority (64 percent) se-

Figure 4.2. Georgians' Opinions on Influence over Government Decisions

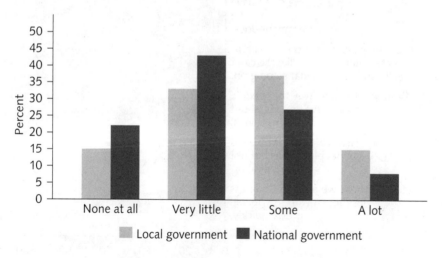

Note: Reponses to the question, "How much influence do you think someone like you can have over [local/national] government decisions?"

Source: Vinson Institute of Government 2004.

lected the more optimistic, positive change response, while only 28 percent of respondents described government as a necessary evil; 8 percent selected neither option.

Not all of the news in the poll was positive. Many respondents expressed views indicating low levels of political efficacy (see figure 4.3). A majority of respondents indicated that they thought congressional representatives quickly lost touch with people, that political parties were interested only in getting votes, and that public officials cared little about public opinion. A substantial minority of respondents also indicated that government was so complicated that they had difficulty understanding what was going on and that they had no say about what the government does.

Political efficacy is an important concept: many studies have shown that it is linked to political behavior, including voting, and civic engagement on many levels. Georgians overall express more optimistic views than citizens of the nation as a whole, but many residents of the state clearly feel low levels of

Figure 4.3. Measures of Political Efficacy among Georgians

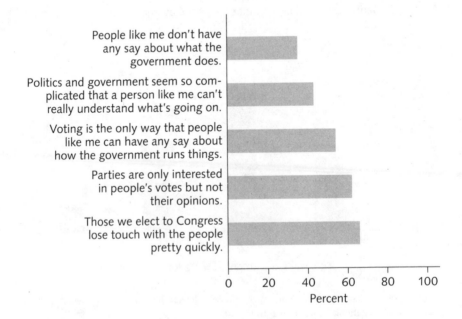

Source: Vinson Institute of Government 2004.

political efficacy, especially when asked about national government officials and policy.

Georgians' Positions on Contemporary Issues

Georgia has changed significantly in some ways during the past generation, so it is unclear to what extent public opinion in the state still reflects a traditionalistic political culture. Probably the best way to address the question is with up-to-date polls on current issues.

Georgians' Assessment of Key Issues

While political culture is characterized by stability, the public's sentiments about important issues can change quite readily. Following September 2001, respondents were more likely to indicate that they feared terrorist attacks. They also expressed high levels of satisfaction with President George W. Bush's performance. However, these rankings began returning to issues more closely associated with state politics only one year after the 9/11 events.[18] Georgians identified education and economic concerns as the most salient issues in 2002 and 2005 (see table 4.2). From 2001 to 2005, poll respondents expressed growing concern with the economy, which resulted in changes in the percentage of Georgians who gave Bush a strong approval rating as president. In addition, concerns regarding terrorism varied from 2001 to 2002, and by 2005, the survey did not include the issue as a separate question.

Education and the economy consistently remain high-priority issues for Georgians. Social issues receive modest priority. In 2005, as the state and national economies rebounded, fewer than 2 percent of respondents indicated that health/medical insurance was the most important problem, and only 1 percent indicated that poverty was the most important issue. Consistent from year to year is the approximately 10–12 percent of respondents who indicate that they have no opinion regarding what is the most important issue facing the state.[19] In a separate 2005 poll, 44 percent of Georgia residents felt that the economy was improving, while 36 percent felt that economic condi-

Table 4.2. Georgians' Views of the Most Important Problem Facing the State, 1991–2005

	1991	1996	2001	2002	2005
Education	20.7%	19.5%	22.0%	30.3%	24.5%
Unemployment	8.4%	4.7%	10.8%	9.7%	7.6%
Economy	8.8%	3.7%	6.3%	8.0%	7.1%
Crime	7.5%	23.7%	3.7%	6.5%	6.9%
Drugs	18.6%	7.9%	4.0%	3.7%	6.2%
Fear terrorist attack*			64.6%	33.1%	
"Strongly approve" of President George W. Bush			54.0%	36.0%	7.7%

* The polling questions to ascertain fear of terrorism differed in 2001 and 2002. These percentages indicate those who said they were "very" and "somewhat" fearful in 2001 and respondents who indicated that they were "fearful" in 2002. In 2005, the survey recoded fear of terrorism as one of the most important issues facing the state but did not list it as a separate question.

Sources: Georgia State University Applied Research Center; University of Georgia Survey Research Center.

tions were getting worse. Georgians' outlook on the economy during 2004 and 2005 was consistently more optimistic than opinions on the economy held by residents of other states.

Not all opinions are ideological or partisan. Georgians often are concerned with more narrow and timely issues, such as current bills facing the General Assembly or the governor's popularity ratings. Many of these issues are salient only for a brief period but nevertheless provide important indicators of Georgians' underlying views.

The Controversy over the State Flag

One issue that has persisted for several decades is the Georgia flag. In 1993, Governor Zell Miller sought to change the state flag adopted in 1956. Although Miller withdrew this proposal, it divided the populace along

fairly predictable lines. The Georgia General Assembly passed many resolutions in the mid-1950s designed to show defiance of U.S. Supreme Court
rulings on desegregation in schools and other public places. Georgia's reactions to these rulings included a temporary revocation of teaching cer-
tificates for teachers who belonged to the National Association for the Advancement of Colored People, a resolution that declared the actions of the
Supreme Court "null, void and of no effect," and a publication written by
Governor Herman Talmadge, *Segregation and You*. In this charged environment, Georgia's flag was changed in February 1956 to include the Confederate battle emblem.[20] Whether the flag was intended as a symbol of defiance or as a remembrance of Confederate war heroes is a question of some
debate.

Polls taken in 1992 indicated that the majority of Georgians did not want
to change the flag to eliminate the Confederate emblem, but opinions varied
along racial lines, with 52 percent of blacks and only 18 percent of whites
supporting change. Moreover, younger Georgians were more likely to support modifying the flag, with 38 percent of those aged between eighteen and
twenty-nine indicating support, 34 percent of respondents aged thirty to
forty-four backing a change, and 17 percent of those aged forty-five to sixty-
four favoring a change. The poll also uncovered differences between metropolitan Atlanta and other areas: 38 percent of metropolitan Atlanta residents
favored change, versus 20 percent of residents in the rest of the state. Support
for change was also stronger among Georgians with higher levels of education. A spring 1993 poll conducted by Georgia State University found that
35 percent of Georgians supported a change in the flag, while 55 percent opposed the move. Moreover, Governor Miller's approval rating varied sharply
between supporters and opponents of the 1956 flag.[21]

Although Miller withdrew his attempt to change the flag, the issue resur-
faced in 2000 when his successor as governor, Roy Barnes, determined that
the flag should be changed. During his first term, Barnes met with state officials and citizens and presented the legislature with a new flag design, which,
after much debate and public controversy, was adopted and began to fly over
the State Capitol in January 2001. Many opponents of the flag change worked
hard to unseat Governor Barnes. Confederate heritage groups felt that a public referendum should have been held to determine a new flag. When Barnes
was defeated in his bid for reelection, those groups anticipated that the new

governor, Sonny Perdue, would offer a referendum that included the 1956 flag. However, the state legislature approved a compromise flag, and Governor Perdue signed his approval on May 8, 2003, giving Georgia its third state flag in slightly over two years.[22]

A subsequent public vote to approve the new flag was held, but it limited voters' choices to the most recent flags and did not include the 1956 flag. Voters approved the 2003 flag, effectively ending the flag debate. In 2004, supporters of the 1956 flag sought legislative support for yet another referendum but failed to attract sponsors for the measure.[23]

The flag debate illustrates the sustainability of public opinion on an issue over time, although even long-held beliefs may vary within groups. A decade of polling data shows clear differences in opinion on support for the 1956 flag (see figure 4.4). Although each of the groups presented exhibited some variation, differences between groups were more evident. Black respondents consistently were more likely to indicate that they wanted to change the 1956 flag. White survey respondents were much less likely to express support for change. In addition, differences between urban and rural respondents are clear: rural respondents were less likely to indicate that they wanted the 1956 flag to be changed.

The flag controversy also illustrates how public debate can prompt change in opinion. The debate surrounding the changes in 2000 and 2001 tended to raise support for changing the flag among all of the respondents polled. For example, from 1992 to 2000, rural residents' support for changing the flag remained close to 22 percent. However, during the height of the debate, support for changing the flag rose to more than 30 percent of all respondents. In a poll taken after the flag change, more than 40 percent of rural respondents indicated that they favored the change. White respondents' support for the flag change also grew during that period. In the winter of 2001, more than 30 percent of white respondents indicated that they favored change, an increase from less than 27 percent for the previous eight years.[24] By the spring of 2004, polling data indicated that most Georgians were no longer concerned about the flag. The Georgia State Poll indicated that almost half (45 percent) of respondents neither liked nor disliked the new flag; only 21 percent expressed dislike for the latest of Georgia's official flags, and 76 percent indicated that they believed the flag issue was a distraction from more important issues facing the state.[25]

Figure 4.4. Percentage Supporting Change of the 1956 Confederate Emblem Flag, by Race and Residence

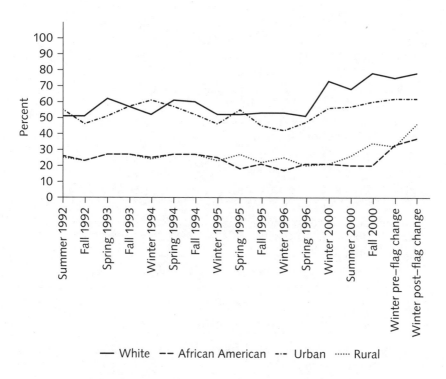

Source: Compiled by authors from Georgia State University Applied Research Center, Georgia State Poll, 1992–2000.

Other Recent Issues

Taxes. Georgia's conservative ideology suggests that most residents favor reduced taxes and services. In 2004, as the state faced budgetary hard times, more than half of the respondents to a Georgia State University poll indicated that the state should reduce expenditures to balance the budget, compared to only 5 percent who thought the budget shortfall should be addressed by higher taxes.[26] However, the same poll indicated that Georgians would approve of tax increases if they came with assurances that the revenues would be spent in specific ways (see figure 4.5). For example, more than

Figure 4.5. Georgians' Support for Increased Taxation

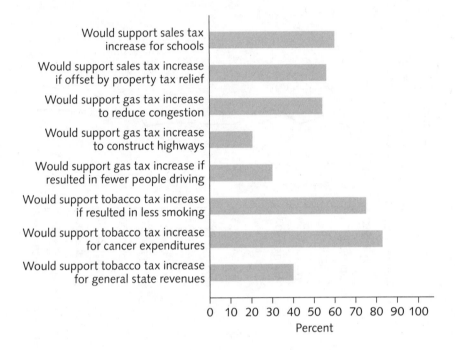

Source: Compiled by authors from Georgia State University Applied Research Center, Georgia State Poll, Winter 2005.

60 percent of the respondents said that they would support state income tax increases if the revenues generated by the tax increase went to local schools, and 56 percent indicated that they would support such a tax if it were offset by property tax rollbacks. When asked about gasoline taxes, 54 percent of the respondents indicated that they would support higher gas taxes if the increase were directed at solutions to reduce congestion. More than 34 percent of those polled indicated that they would support gas tax increases if the monies were used specifically for highway construction, and 30 percent said that they would support the increase if it resulted in people driving less. Tobacco taxes were the most popular among the respondents, with more than 75 percent saying that they would support such increases if it caused

people to smoke less and 83 percent saying they would support increased taxes if the funds were used for cancer prevention efforts. In contrast, only 40 percent of respondents said that they would support the tobacco tax increase if the money were used to support government expenditures generally.[27]

Racial Issues. Georgia has a long political history of racial conflict. Recent data shed some light on contemporary attitudes. A January 1995 survey by Georgia State University found that one-third of Georgians thought race relations were improving, a jump from just 25 percent in 1994.[28] Racial differences persist, however. An April 1995 poll found that roughly equal proportions of blacks and whites agreed that affirmative action plans do more harm than good. Yet only 25 percent of whites disagreed with that view, as opposed to 33 percent of blacks.[29] Twenty-two percent of whites agreed that affirmative action programs help compensate for past injustice, while 40 percent disagreed. A reverse pattern existed for blacks: 42 percent agreed and 24 percent disagreed with the statement.[30] By 2002, the Georgia Poll indicated that 37 percent of the Georgia population felt that affirmative action was still necessary. A 2004 poll asked respondents whether the average African American's income was better, worse, or just about the same as that of white residents. Forty-nine percent of respondents said that income was about the same, while 31 percent believed that white incomes remained higher and just 7 percent felt that African Americans were better off than whites.[31]

Immigration. As noted in chapter 2, Georgia's population is rapidly growing, in part because of increased numbers of immigrants. For many Georgians, the increased population, as well as the concurrent culture change, is a salient issue. Opinions on immigration vary (see table 4.3).[32] Respondents in the Atlanta metropolitan area were more likely than other state residents to view immigration as beneficial to the state. Respondents with higher levels of education were also more likely to view immigration as a benefit. Surprisingly, political ideology did not seem to have much of an effect on Georgians' opinions regarding immigration. As the data indicate, Georgians are fairly evenly split on the issue of immigration, with

Table 4.3. Respondents' Views on Increased Population as a Result of Immigration, Summer 2005

	Total of All Respondents	Region of the State		Level of Respondent Education				Respondent Self-Identified Ideology		
		Atlanta Region	Rest of the State	High School Diploma or Less	Some College	College Degree	Post-graduate Work	Conservative	Moderate	Liberal
More Benefit Than Harm	44%	48%	40%	38%	35%	51%	58%	46%	45%	40%
More Harm Than Benefit	34%	34%	35%	41%	37%	30%	27%	33%	35%	36%
Little Effect	16%	14%	17%	12%	23%	13%	12%	15%	15%	15%
Not Sure/Did Not Answer	6%	5%	9%	9%	6%	5%	3%	6%	5%	9%

Note: Percentages are rounded and may not total 100.

Source: Vinson Institute of Government 2005a.

44 percent of respondents saying that it was more beneficial than harmful and 34 percent indicating that they thought it was more harmful than beneficial.

Public Officials' Performance

Surveys in many states have begun to track public assessments of how well public officials do their jobs. The spring 2004 Georgia State Poll included a number of such questions. At that time, 53 percent of the respondents indicated that they approved of how President George W. Bush was handling his job. Support for Bush remained high in Georgia throughout his first term and midway through his second term, but by 2005, polls reflected a downward turn in his popularity nationwide, with his approval ratings dipping into the 35–39 percent range.[33] When compared to respondents in other states, voters in Georgia are more likely to support Bush's agenda, which coincides with the state's traditional conservative culture (see figure 4.6).[34]

All polling data are subject to variability. Question wording, sampling, and the timing of polls can affect outcome.[35] The spring 2004 approval rating for President Bush recorded by the poll at Georgia State University (53 percent) varies from that collected by the University of Georgia (61.5 percent). Such

Figure 4.6. Georgians' Approval Ratings for President George W. Bush, 2001–2005

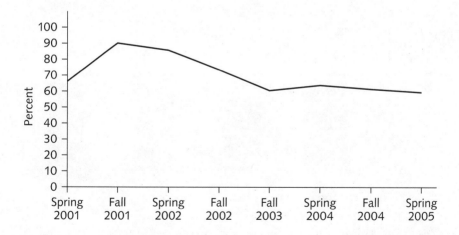

Source: Compiled by authors from Georgia State University Applied Research Center, Georgia State Poll, 2001–2005.

approval ratings are best understood when the same question is asked across a long time span. However one analyzes the various surveys of presidential popularity in Georgia, two conclusions are clear: Bush's overall popularity in the nation and the state is down from a very high point during the fall of 2001, and residents of Georgia are more likely to approve of the president than are residents of the rest of the nation as a whole.

The University of Georgia's Survey Research Center also periodically measures gubernatorial approval ratings. These polls have found relatively stable approval ratings for Governor Perdue (see figure 4.7). From the fall of 2003 to the spring of 2005, approval ratings for the governor varied by only 2 percentage points, remaining close to 64 percent, a strong contrast from the drop in President Bush's approval ratings from 90.1 in the fall of 2001 to 60.6 in the fall of 2003. Such change may also be a function of the timing of the survey. For example, Bush's ratings also leveled out during the 2003–2005 period after their previous strong fluctuations.

Signs indicate, however, that Georgians' views of the state and the nation differed in 2003. The Georgia State Poll included two questions on the direction of the nation and the state, and Georgians took a more pessimistic view of the country as a whole than of their state (see figure 4.8).[36] Many

Figure 4.7. Georgians' Approval Ratings for Governor Sonny Perdue

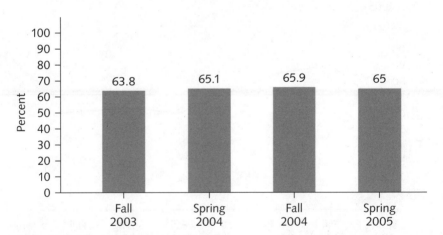

Source: Compiled by authors from Georgia State University Applied Research Center, Georgia State Poll, 2003–2005; data available at www.src.uga.edu/surveys/GA-Poll.

Figure 4.8. Respondents' Views on the Direction of the Nation and of Georgia

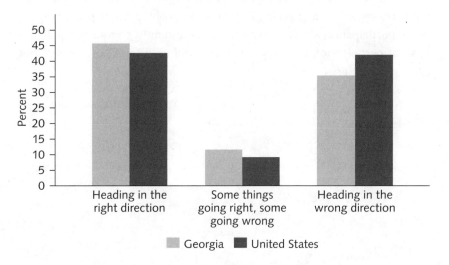

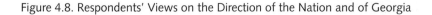

Source: Georgia State University Applied Research Center, Georgia State Poll, Winter 2003; data available at http://aysys.gsu.edu/srp/georgiastatepoll/gastatepoll_winter03.pdf.

Georgians said that the state was heading in the right direction but the nation was heading in the wrong direction. When asked about the state legislature, 10 percent of respondents said that they felt well represented by the legislature, 53 percent felt that their views were somewhat represented, and 14 percent indicated that they were not well represented. Five percent of respondents said that they were not sure whether the Georgia General Assembly represented their views. The remaining respondents did not respond to this poll question.

A series of polls conducted between 2001 and 2005 included a similar question regarding trust in the Georgia General Assembly.[37] Public confidence in the General Assembly (as measured by the percentage of respondents who indicated that they had "quite a lot" or a "great deal" of confidence in the legislature) remained between 15 and 25 percent during those four years. This level of confidence was lower than the ranking given to the courts, public schools, the police, and other public institutions.

People do more than hold attitudes. They often act on their views in a variety of ways—discussing politics, contacting government officials, signing petitions, or even engaging in protest or violence. Some people choose not to participate at all. The most common—and most commonly studied—form of participation is voting. Chapter 5 will examine Georgia's elections and voting patterns.

CHAPTER 5

Voting and Elections

Electoral participation in Georgia has long been a source of scholarly curiosity and public debate. Historically, this interest focused on factionalism under one-party Democratic rule, use of the county-unit system and runoff elections, low voter turnout, and the power of interest groups. Since the 1970s, however, a variety of changes have reshaped Georgia politics, especially in the areas of political parties, black political gains, and the growing power of suburban voters.

This chapter and the next focus on political participation. This chapter examines different types of elections, electoral procedures, voter turnout, and voting trends, while chapter 6 contrasts voting to interest groups and political parties, the two most common forms of participation in which individuals cooperate or join organizations to influence politics.

Elections

Public opinion makes its mark throughout the political system but perhaps nowhere more than in the electoral process. Indeed, elections reflect the way that politics operates within a state and provide indicators of the electorate's political culture. Georgia elections have produced some interesting results over the years, but one constant has remained—Georgia has one of the nation's lowest participation rates on Election Day.

Statewide Contests

General Elections. Types of elections vary by state, but all states have general elections in which voters choose from among a number of candidates to fill an office. In most states, including Georgia, voters select party nominees from a group of potential candidates in a primary election. Some states also use party conventions to nominate candidates for certain offices.[1]

Primaries. States hold several different types of primaries. The two most common are labeled "closed" and "open." Twenty-eight states hold closed primaries. Under this system, voters must register as a member of a particular party or as an independent, and only registered members of a given party may vote in its primaries. Independents are not permitted to vote in any party's primary.

Twenty states, including Georgia, hold open primaries, in which those eligible to vote in the general election may vote in any party's primary. In Georgia and ten other states, voters must tell workers at the polling place which party's ballot they wish to use. The other nine states with open primaries permit voters to choose one party's ballot in secret. Such open primaries permit people to vote strategically. For example, members of one party with few contested offices could vote for the weakest candidates in the other party's primary.[2]

Georgia holds two primaries in presidential election years, a March presidential preference primary and a July primary to determine candidates for state and local offices. In the presidential primary, voters must select one party's ballot and choose one of its candidates. Until 1992, Georgia's presidential primary was held on "Super Tuesday"—a date used by almost all southern states to increase the region's influence, especially within the Democratic Party.

Georgia's 2004 presidential primary occurred on March 2, approximately midway through the primary season. On the Republican ballot, George W. Bush ran unopposed. Nine candidates appeared on the Democratic ballot. John Kerry, the eventual nominee, led the field with 46.8 percent of the vote, and Georgians placed John Edwards, who later became Kerry's running mate, second with 41.4 percent of the vote. Each of the remaining candidates tallied less than 7 percent. Because the presidential preference primary does not include other offices on the ballot, voters tend to select the party ballot where there is opposition.[3] Other than to show popular support, Republican voters had little reason to cast ballots for Bush, who was running unopposed. A total of 161,374 Republicans did cast ballots in support of the president. However, 626,738 voters chose the Democratic ballot, which featured a full slate of candidates. In 1996, with President Bill Clinton unopposed on the Democratic ballot and Bob Dole facing intraparty competition among the Republicans, more Georgians voted in the Republican contest than in the Democratic primary, the first time that phenomenon had ever occurred.[4]

Each political party's primary results in the selection of delegates for its national convention, where its presidential nominee is formally chosen. Georgia law allows each party's state executive committee to determine the method for selecting delegates, who are required to vote at the convention for the candidate whom they are pledged to support until the candidate is nominated, gets less than 35 percent of the delegate votes, or releases delegates from their obligation. In any case, delegates are not legally bound beyond the second ballot for president in the unlikely event that a convention proves that competitive.[5] For example, in the 2004 presidential race, of the 102 Democratic delegates sent to the convention, 86 were pledged to candidates, but 16 of the state's Democratic delegates were unpledged at the time of the convention as a result of either party rules or the withdrawal of candidates from the presidential race. The process of awarding delegates to the conventions begins well before the primary. The national party approves each state's methods for selecting delegates, although they generally are assigned in proportion to each candidate's share of the vote in the primary.

Runoffs. In most states, the individual who receives the most votes in an election is declared the winner, but others require that the winner of a primary or general election receive more than a certain percentage of the votes cast. Ten states, including Georgia, hold runoffs if no single candidate captures 50 percent of the vote. North Carolina also employs runoffs but reduced the threshold from 50 percent to 40 percent in 1989. Georgia's runoff was originally adopted in 1917 but was changed in 1964 when the county-unit system of election was abandoned. The logic behind the runoff system is based in part on the assumption that elections should reflect the will of the majority of the electorate. In states that have a tradition of one-party politics, candidates have faced their strongest opposition in the primaries. If only a plurality were required in such states, it would be possible to achieve elected office by finishing first in a primary with many candidates and receiving well under 50 percent of the vote. The runoff was intended to prevent such occurrences. Not surprisingly, most of the states currently using runoffs are southern states with a history of one-party domination.[6]

Observers have frequently debated whether the runoff is necessary or discriminates against female and minority candidates. Several legal challenges have arisen over the continued use of the runoff in southern states. Many opponents argue that the 1964 Georgia version of the runoff was intended to dilute black voting strength and to prevent black candidates who led in the primary from making it to the general election.[7] In primary runoffs for state and federal offices in the South between 1970 and 1986, virtually no difference in the success rate of the primary leader occurred when the two candidates were of the same race. When the candidates were of different races, however, black front-runners in primaries won runoffs only 50 percent of the time when facing white opponents. In contrast, white leaders defeated black runners-up 90 percent of the time. Similar results exist in runoffs for county offices in Georgia from 1970 to 1984, where black front-runners defeated white opponents in runoffs 50 percent of the time but white primary leaders beat black runners-up 84 percent of the time.[8]

Some critics of the runoff argue that the "Solid South" no longer exists and that primaries no longer determine who will hold office. Thus, other arguments against the runoff deal with the cost and confusion surrounding so many elections as well as the related concern that divisive primary and runoff campaigns may weaken a party's ultimate nominee in the general election.[9] Despite the criticism of primary runoffs, the U.S. Supreme Court permitted their continued use in 1999 when it refused to hear an appeal of a Georgia case.[10]

One study found that in the 215 runoffs held in Georgia between 1970 and 1986 for Congress, the legislature, and statewide offices, the leader in the primary won 69 percent of the time in the runoff. This success rate contradicts a popular impression that a weakened front-runner generally loses to a coalition of voters who backed other candidates in the primary. The track record was worse, however, for the 83 incumbents in those 215 runoffs: just 48 percent of the incumbents who led in the primaries went on to win their runoffs; of those incumbents who finished second, only 20 percent were runoff victors. The same study reported that at the county level from 1970 to 1984, the primary leader won the runoff 71 percent of the time.[11] In a 2005 poll of Georgia's county commissioners, 37 percent indicated that county races were usually decided in the primary, with little or no opposition in the general election. Another 14 percent indicated that county races were most often decided in runoffs. Forty-one percent of the respondents indicated that county races were most often decided in the general election, and 6 percent of the commissioners responded that election outcomes in their counties varied significantly from one cycle to the next.[12]

Georgia has traditionally held runoffs after primaries, but a runoff was held in 1992 after a general election between candidates for the U.S. Senate. In that instance, a third candidate prevented front-runner Wyche Fowler, the Democratic incumbent, from earning more than 50 percent of the vote. His Republican opponent, Paul Coverdell, won the runoff. Following the Fowler-Coverdell runoff, the General Assembly passed a law reducing the winning percentage in general elections from 50 percent plus one vote to 45 percent. Without this change, Democrat Max Cleland would not have defeated Republican Guy Milner in the 1996 Senate race. Cleland's victory was also noteworthy in that it was one of the only two victories for Democratic Senate candidates in the South during 1996. In 1998, the General Assembly extended the law to statewide constitutional offices, including secretary of state, attorney general, and the commissioners of insurance, labor, and agriculture.[13] Prior to these changes, Georgia was the only state to require a 50 percent margin of victory in general elections.

Referendum, Initiative, and Recall. States also conduct elections that do not involve candidates for office. The most common of these elections are referenda, in which legislative bodies place issues on the ballot to elicit public approval. Critics often complain that asking people simply to vote yes or no on a question is not a good way to decide complex issues. Georgia voters are accustomed to referenda on whether to amend the state constitution. They are also often asked to decide whether local governments should levy sales taxes or be permitted to go into debt to pay for public improvements such as roads and buildings.

In some states, citizens may place issues on the ballot through a petition process, usually without the approval of elected officials. Such citizens' initiatives began in 1898 and are now permitted in twenty-four states as a method of amending constitutions or adopting laws. Between 1976 and 1996, 597 statewide initiatives took place, 98 of them in California and 86 in Oregon. From 1996 to 2002, another 300 initiatives were placed on state ballots, increasing the average from 45 to 50 per year. Of the total number of initiatives proposed, approximately 40 percent are adopted. Controversial initiatives in recent years have focused on taxation, term limits for elected officials, and environmental concerns. Recent initiatives have focused on minority issues, including gay rights and affirmative action repeal. Such campaigns are becoming increasingly specialized and expensive. Reported spending on California's 1998 measures reached more than $196 million.[14] The Georgia Constitution does not permit initiatives, although the General Assembly studied the matter in 1995.[15]

Recalls are special types of elections that remove public officials from office before their terms have expired. Recall of state officials is allowed in Georgia and eighteen other states; recall of local officeholders is more widely permitted.[16] Some states exempt certain officeholders, usually judges, from the recall process. In Georgia, all persons who occupy elected state or local offices, even those appointed to fill unfinished terms, are subject to removal. Recalls are placed on the ballot through a petition process. For statewide office, petitions must include valid signatures totaling 15 percent of the number registered to vote at the last election that included the office in question; at least one-fifteenth of these signatures must be obtained in each congressional district. Those wishing to circulate such petitions must first meet requirements to begin the process; they then have a limited time to complete the petitions once they are issued by election officials—ninety days for statewide office and thirty to forty-five days for lesser officials, depending on the number of signatures required. When enough signatures of eligible voters have been obtained, recalls are placed on a ballot, with voters simply voting yes or no on the question of whether to remove the official. If an office becomes vacant through recall, a special election is held.[17]

Election Procedures

Official decisions about procedures such as voter eligibility standards, redistricting, timing, and election administration can have a substantial impact on elections. Much of U.S. political history is a story of removing barriers to voting. The same can be said of Georgia.

The Right to Vote. Changes in registration requirements may alter turnout or promote certain election outcomes. As discussed in more detail in chapter 3, the poll tax, literacy tests, the white primary, and other restrictions on black votes persisted until the 1960s.

In 1965, Congress passed the Voting Rights Act, which removed the last legal hurdles to enfranchising blacks. The act has subsequently been renewed several times. The law suspended use of literacy tests, allowed for federal election examiners and observers, and required affected state and local governments to receive approval from the federal government before making changes in their electoral systems. The U.S. Department of Justice is especially wary of issuing this "preclearance" for any changes that could dilute minorities' voting strength.

The Voting Rights Act did not have immediate effects. A 1966 Supreme Court decision turned back a challenge to the law's basic provisions by the state of South Carolina. Litigation over application of the law has been frequent, however. In Georgia, the estimated percentage of blacks registering to vote rose from 27 percent in March 1965, before passage of the act, to 53 percent in September 1967. During the same period, however, white registration rose from 63 to 80 percent. One study of electoral turnout in presidential and off-year elections indicates that black voters remain less likely to visit the polls than do white voters. Comparing electoral returns in 1996 and 1998, George H. Cox and Raymond A. Rosenfeld found that black voters were overall less likely to turn out and that black males in particular had significantly lower turnout rates than did other race and gender groups (see table 5.1). Many observers credit the act with aiding the election of black officials. The number of blacks elected to state and local offices in Georgia rose from 21 in 1968 to 266 in 1981, with the vast majority serving as members of city councils and school boards.[18]

In other extensions of the franchise, Georgia became the first state to reject the Nineteenth Amendment to the U.S. Constitution in 1919. When enough other states ratified the amendment, however, women received the right to vote, and Georgia's white women went to the polls for the first time in 1920. In 1943, voters ratified a state constitutional amendment that made Georgia the first state to grant the franchise to eighteen-year-olds.[19]

Redistricting. Prohibiting certain groups from voting is an obvious way to influence elections, but more subtle means also exist. Probably the oldest and

Table 5.1. Georgia Election Turnout by Race and Gender, 1996 and 1998

Race/Gender Group	1996 Presidential Year Turnout*	1998 Off-Year Turnout*
Black Females	58.4%	45.5%
Black Males	49.1%	38.7%
White Females	64.2%	47.2%
White Males	64.4%	49.3%
All Other Voters	50.9%	28.4%

* Calculated as a percentage of registered voters.

Source: Cox and Rosenfeld 2001.

most practiced is redistricting. States redraw district boundaries for their legislatures and the U.S. House of Representatives following each U.S. Census. Gerrymandering, or the practice of drawing districts to achieve political outcomes, is one method by which incumbents may protect their political careers, minority political parties may be prevented from gaining legislative seats, rural or urban districts may dominate, and the voting strength of minority groups may be diluted. Since the 1960s, several factors have influenced redistricting in Georgia, especially actions by the federal courts, implementation of the Voting Rights Act, and the rise of the Republican Party.

Although it did not originate in Georgia, the U.S. Supreme Court's 1962 decision in *Baker v. Carr* affected the state.[20] This landmark ruling and its progeny forced states to draw legislative districts on the basis of population rather than political boundaries such as county lines. The "one person, one vote" standard requires districts of equal population, although slight variation is tolerated. In Georgia, a string of federal court decisions eliminated the county-unit system, the rotation of state Senate seats among the counties in a district, and rural overrepresentation in the General Assembly.[21] In addition to pressures regarding black representation, redistricting in Georgia has been complicated by a shift in party control of the legislature. When the Democratic-controlled General Assembly drew legislative and congressional districts, Republicans offered strong criticism of what they believed to be gerrymandering to ensure Democratic electoral victories. Since the Republicans have taken control of the General Assembly, district lines have been redrawn several times to undo the advantages to Democratic candidates and to appease the U.S. Department of Justice.

Redistricting is a difficult and politically entangling process. Interest groups such as the American Civil Liberties Union and the National Association for the Advancement of Colored People often play an active role, and politicians concerned for their careers are not easily pleased by the results. Party competition and local elites complicate the process. Legislatures today are assisted in the redistricting process by computers and map-writing software. While these technical advancements may make some aspects of the job easier, they certainly do not make it less controversial.

The General Assembly faced the difficult task of redistricting after the 2000 census. Blacks and Republicans felt they had much to gain in the redistricting process for the U.S. House as well as the General Assembly's 180 House and 56 Senate seats. As a consequence of population growth, Georgia's number of U.S. representatives grew from 11 to 13, and its electoral vote thus went from 13 to 15. Some of the districts drawn were oddly shaped, while others generally followed boundaries of counties or other jurisdictions. Republicans, who obtained the majority in the General Assembly after the first round of redistricting, wanted to change the boundaries again. The controversy grew complicated, and district lines for congressional and state legislative seats changed in every election from 2002 to 2006. The controversy spilled over to include a challenge of authority between the Democratic state attorney general Thurbert Baker, and Republican Governor Sonny Perdue. The attorney general argued that he had state constitutional authority to challenge district lines in federal court, while the governor argued that he should decide when the state would address issues to the federal courts. Baker eventually won the argument, but the courts also ruled that the lines drawn by the Republican-dominated General Assembly could stand.[22]

Georgia has also had an unusual history with the use of multimember districts (which elect more than one representative). Because campaigns generally cost more in multimember districts than in single-member districts, multimember districts tend to favor candidates who are incumbents or who have strong financial backing. Observers saw the elimination of multimember districts as a benefit to minority candidates. Between 1971 and 1981, the number of seats in the Georgia House held by blacks grew from thirteen to twenty-one through the elimination of some multimember districts.[23] The shift in the state's electorate prompted Democrats to reintroduce multimember districts, drawing many suburban districts so that they were represented by multiple representatives, who ran for specific, numbered seats within each district. This approach would have required candidates to campaign across a wider area than candidates running in single-member districts, thereby increasing costs. The multimember districts were short-lived, however, and by 2004, the General Assembly no longer included multimember district representatives.[24]

Following both the 1990 and 2000 censuses, Georgia's district maps were reviewed by the U.S. Justice Department and contested in federal courts before being approved. In 2004, after partisan control of the General Assembly shifted and the governor and attorney general entered the fray, a panel of federal judges drew the districts that the state legislators could not. As the 2006 General Assembly elections approached, district lines for the General Assembly seemed likely to change—midway through the decade—in part for political gains. Indeed, one bill was introduced in January 2006 to redraw Georgia Senate districts around Athens for the primary elections six months later.[25] Multiple changes in district lines after a census are likely to confuse voters, but the state must adjust to shifting standards of compliance with the Justice Department and federal courts as well as deal with influences of political parties, interest groups, and incumbents seeking political advantage.[26]

Timing. Length of terms and the related scheduling of elections can also have important consequences, as can be seen by comparing turnout in congressional races. Since 1968, turnout in presidential elections nationwide has hovered around 50–55 percent of the voting-age population.[27] In contrast, turnout in off-year congressional elections remained under 40 percent since 1974 and fell below 35 percent in 1998 and 2002.[28]

The Georgia Constitution requires that members of the General Assembly be elected for two-year terms in even-numbered years. The governor and other statewide officeholders have four-year terms and are elected in even-numbered years between presidential elections. Although Georgia's governor has been elected for a four-year term ending in the off year since 1942, this practice has become the norm nationally since the 1960s as state political parties have tried—apparently with success—to protect gubernatorial nominees from association with unpopular presidential candidates.[29]

Georgia's municipal elections do not take place at the same time as major state and national races; with a handful of exceptions, these municipal contests are nonpartisan. With no party identification of candidates on the ballot, voters must rely on other cues, such as name recognition. Many people argue that nonpartisan elections 'discourage participation, especially when not held with elections for higher offices, and favor candidates who are more organized or spend more campaign monies on advertising.[30]

Election Administration. The U.S. Constitution leaves administration of elections in the hands of the states. This has produced some interesting differences in voter registration, voter information and outreach efforts, and rules for polling places and absentee ballots.[31]

The requirements for registering can limit participation in elections. At one time, states required voters to register months ahead of scheduled elections. The earliest deadline now is thirty days before a general election—the requirement in Georgia and thirteen other states. Maine, Minnesota, New Hampshire, Wisconsin, and Wyoming permit voters to register on Election Day, while North Dakota does not require registration.[32] Prior to 1993, when Congress outlawed the practice, some states removed voters from registration lists if they had not voted for a specified number of years. Even though later deadlines may facilitate registration, the locations and times for registering may deter would-be voters. Information campaigns using the media, direct mail, and toll-free phone numbers also may increase voter registration and turnout. The same is true of registration drives targeted at specific groups such as students and outreach efforts such as multiple registration sites, candidate forums, and distribution of sample ballots.[33]

Debates regarding voter registration intensified during 2005–2006 when the General Assembly changed the procedures regarding the types of identification that would be accepted at polling places. Arguments focus on whether the law targets certain groups and the impact the procedures might have on voter fraud. The federal courts overturned Georgia's first law on the matter, leading to passage of a replacement bill in early 2006.[34] Just before the 2006 general election, the new law was found to be too restrictive. The original law allowing seventeen forms of identification, including those without photo, remained in effect, but voters arrived at the polls uncertain which of the three laws applied.

Rules governing polling places and absentee ballots can affect election results and can stir up controversy. Whenever ballots are improperly marked, such as when a voter selects more than one candidate or votes both a straight party ticket and for a candidate of the opposing party for a specific office, ballots are declared void. Georgia became the first state to adopt electronic ballots statewide, eliminating many of these voting errors. In the 2000 presidential election, only some of the counties had adopted electronic voting procedures, but by 2004 all counties had. Comparing voting accuracy in the two elections reveals that voting errors due to "undervoting" (failing to vote in the presidential race) or "overvoting" (voting for more than one candidate in a single race) were drastically reduced. Undervoting rates went from 3.5 percent in 2000 to 0.39 percent in 2004.[35] However, new voting technologies have not convinced some election observers that the machines are foolproof, and some citizens express concern about the lack of paper ballots to back up electronic voting data. Despite such concerns, most Georgians have been pleased with the new voting technologies.[36]

Changes in Georgia's absentee balloting have also generated controversy. With anyone allowed to vote by absentee ballot without having to state a reason, critics argue that current law has led to voting fraud, particularly with elderly voters and votes cast by deceased citizens whose names remain on voting rolls. Early or advance voting constitutes a relatively recent change in Georgia's voting process. Early voting is strictly for convenience of voters, and no reason is required for advance voting in the state. Polls remain open at centralized county locations for one week prior to the general election. In the November 2004 election, many polling places reported long lines of advance voters, and some 367,000 voters cast ballots before Election Day.[37]

Changes at the federal level may affect voting in Georgia. In 1994, an estimated 55 percent of Georgians age eighteen or older were registered to vote, compared to 62 percent nationwide. The so-called motor-voter law of 1993 requires states to permit eligible voters to register at various government agencies, such as driver's license offices. Georgia added more than eight hundred thousand new registrants, the majority in metropolitan Atlanta. These new voters tended to be younger and less partisan than other registered voters: 47 percent were under age thirty, compared to 16 percent of those previously registered; 42 percent considered themselves independent, versus 29 percent of previously registered voters. On Election Day, many poll workers had to make last-minute verifications to permit voting by registered citizens who had not made the list. Some motor-voter registrants waited hours for verification, while others simply gave up.[38] Data from 1999–2000 indicate that half of all new voting registrations in Georgia took place in motor vehicle offices.[39] Higher levels of registration and other procedural changes may work with other factors to improve Georgia's record of having one of the lowest turnout levels in the nation.

Turnout in Georgia Elections

For most of the past century, Georgia's voter turnout was extremely low. Between 1920 and 1946, less than 20 percent of voting-age adults (less than 30 percent of voting-age whites) voted in Georgia's Democratic primaries for governor and U.S. senator. Turnout was not much different in presidential elections, not surprising given the Democratic lock on the South's electoral votes during the period. Several factors account for this pattern. Poll taxes and literacy tests posed barriers to voting by blacks and poor whites. Few candidates ran as Republicans, given the party's association with the North and Reconstruction. The real political contests took place during the Democratic primaries, in which only whites were permitted to vote until the mid-1940s. Within this context, incumbents held office for long periods of time, and voters were apathetic.[40]

General Elections

Voting changed with the rise of partisan competition and the civil rights movement. Turnout in presidential elections in the South through 1948 hovered between 20 and 25 percent of the voting-age population, roughly the same rate as in Democratic primaries for governor and five to ten points above turnout in gubernatorial general elections. Turnout in presidential elections rose sharply beginning in 1952 and surpassed that for other races. By the mid-1960s, gubernatorial contests also changed in the South, with general election turnout exceeding that for Democratic primaries. In Georgia, 62 percent of those registered voted in the 1962 gubernatorial primary, but only 23 percent of registered voters cast ballots in the general election. The pattern reversed in 1966, when 45 percent of those registered voted in the primary and 54 percent voted in the general election.[41]

Turnout obviously is affected by the prestige of the offices on the ballot. Even among southern states, Georgia has traditionally had some of the lowest turnout rates (see table 5.2). Between 1960 and 2004, Georgia ranked

Table 5.2. Turnout in Georgia, 1988–2004

Year	Type of Election	Georgia Turnout of Registered Voters	Georgia Turnout of Eligible Voters	U.S. Turnout of Registered Voters*	U.S. Turnout of Eligible Voters*	Registered Voters (Georgia)
1988	Presidential Primary	38%	22%			2,574,296
	General Election	62%	39%	56%	50%	2,934,816
1990	General Election	52%	31%			2,772,816
1992	U.S. Senate Runoff	39%	25%			3,177,061
	General Election	73%	47%	78%	55%	3,177,061
1994	General Election	51%	30%			3,003,527
1996	Presidential Primary	19%	12%			3,433,747
	Primary	27%	17%			3,602,231
	General Election	60%	42%	66%	49%	3,811,284
1998	Primary	24%	16%			3,817,393
	General Election	46%	32%			3,910,740
2000	Presidential Primary	44%	25%			4,383,314
	Primary	36%	21%			4,474,686
	General Election	56%	43%	68%	51%	4,648,210
2002	Primary	12%	9%			4,667,555
	General Election	43%	32%			4,726,083
2004	Presidential Primary	24%	15%			4,585,422
	Primary	35%	21%			4,698,007
	General Election	67%	51%	86%	57%	4,951,955

* Presidential years only.

Sources: Compiled by authors from the following Web sites: Georgia Secretary of State (www.sos.state.ga.us), U.S. Census Bureau (http://factfinder.census.gov), Federal Elections Commission (www.fec.gov), U.S. Election Assistance Commission (www.eac.gov), U.S. Office of the Federal Register (www.archives.gov/federal-register/index.html).

among the bottom four states in turnout of eligible voters in every presiden-tial election. Even Georgian Jimmy Carter's presence on the ballot in 1976 and in 1980 did not raise the voters' interest enough to break this cycle, and Geor-gia placed forty-ninth in turnout in both those elections. By 1992, turnout in Georgia rose to 47 percent, still far below the nationwide rate of 55 percent. In 1996, about the same number of Georgians voted as in 1992, but because the state's population had grown during that period, overall turnout declined to 42 percent of those eligible to vote and about 60 percent of those registered. In 2004, a record 3.3 million Georgians turned out to vote—more than two-thirds of those registered but only about 57 percent of those eligible. Only three states ranked lower in turnout of voting-age adults, and only seven had smaller percentages of registered voters turning out.[42] Georgia's turnout in off-year elections is also anemic—generally around 30 percent and again among the lowest of the states. In 2006, there were 2,122,185 votes cast for governor, a turnout of approximately 48 percent of those registered. Competition up and down the ballot may constitute one factor that affects turnout: between 1982 and 1986, only two states had less-competitive races for their legisla-tures. Studies over the past thirty years have indicated that in state elections, Georgia is more competitive than ever before, but in terms of presidential voting, Georgia's electoral votes go consistently to the Republican nominee.[43]

Primary Elections

In the six primaries listed in table 5.2, turnout of eligible voters remained below 30 percent. The July 9, 1996, primary was unusual, with few contested races beyond the six-man field vying for the Republican nomination for the U.S. Senate seat being vacated by the retirement of Democrat Sam Nunn. Turnout for the primary, which occurred less than two weeks before the start of the Olympic Games in Atlanta, was less than 20 percent. Campaign-ing for runoffs, including the GOP contest for the U.S. Senate nomination, was more difficult than normal because of the media attention devoted to the Olympics, which ended two days before the election.

One notable change has been rising turnout and competitiveness in Re-publican primaries. Fewer than 15 percent of those voting in the contested 1970 and 1974 gubernatorial primaries chose the Republican ballot. By 1992, however, roughly the same number of Georgians chose to vote in the Re-publican and Democratic presidential primaries. By 2004, voters selecting a

Republican ballot in the state primary outnumbered those selecting Democratic ballots by 51 to 49 percent. However, turnout remained low overall, with only about one-third of registered voters casting ballots. One problem with low turnout in primaries is that such elections may be dominated by activists and relatively extreme elements in each party rather than more moderate voters. When activists control the primary results, candidates must appeal to more extreme views during the primary season, then moderate their positions during the general election campaign to win.[44]

Runoff Elections

Turnout in statewide runoffs has occasionally surpassed 25 percent of the voting-age population; however, in 46 percent of Georgia's primary runoffs between 1970 and 1986, more votes were cast than in the primary. This drop-off is smaller than that in all but one of the states using runoff elections.[45] The November 1992 elections were the first in which runoffs followed a general election rather than a primary, and turnout was instrumental in the Republican wins for the U.S. Senate and Georgia Public Service Commission. In the Senate race, the number of votes on November 24 was 1,300,000—1,000,000 fewer than for the general election. Democratic Senator Wyche Fowler led Republican challenger Paul Coverdell 1,108,416 to 1,073,282 on November 8, but three weeks later, Coverdell won 635,114 to 618,877. Eighteen counties switched parties in the runoff, and all of them went to Coverdell.[46] Turnout was especially low in the August 1996 runoff for the Republican nomination for U.S. Senate: about 1,200,000 people had voted in the July 9 primary, but fewer than 500,000 voted in the runoff between Guy Milner and Johnny Isakson, which occurred just two days after the Olympic closing ceremonies. In the 2002 statewide runoff, fewer than one-tenth of registered voters cast ballots.[47]

Political Campaigns in Georgia

Before modern television campaigns, Georgia elections were legendary for corruption, fiery speeches, and mass rallies. Among the most noteworthy on the stump were Tom Watson in the 1890s and Eugene Talmadge from the 1920s through the mid-1940s. Both men became famous for their racial appeals to rural whites. Courthouse gatherings were prominent under the county-unit system, where statewide candidates who won a county got all of its unit votes. With rural counties overrepresented in this system and their leaders often capable of delivering votes for a price, no county was too small to ignore.[48]

Some aspects of Georgia elections have changed little in generations, while several new wrinkles have developed. The constants include candidates' efforts to cultivate favorable images and to mobilize support. Perhaps the greatest changes involve the technology and cost of campaigning, the Republican Party's increased vitality in the state, and Georgia's growing importance on the national political stage.

Campaign Costs

Running a statewide campaign is expensive. One analysis estimated the cost of the average gubernatorial campaign between the 1970s and early 1990s at $8.6 million per state, or $3.87 per registered voter (adjusted for inflation to 1993 dollars). Georgia ranked nineteenth during that period, with an average cost per campaign of $7.7 million, or $2.42 per registered voter—less than the figure for thirty-three other states. Cost for gubernatorial elections spiked sharply beginning in 1999, and overall costs have jumped 119 percent since 1977.[49] In his unsuccessful 2002 bid for reelection as Georgia's governor, Roy Barnes raised a record $20 million. His opponent, Sonny Perdue, raised and spent less than $5 million. Given that just over 2 million votes were cast in that election, the estimated cost per vote had risen to $12.28.[50] Even in 2004, without a governor's race at the top of the ticket, candidates for statewide executive, legislative, and judicial races raised an average of $11.46 per vote cast.[51] In that year, candidates who planned to run for governor in 2006 collected more than $5 million, and Governor Perdue raised another $10.4 million during 2005 for his reelection.[52] Perdue eventually raised and spent $13.5 million, and his opponent, Mark Taylor, raised just under $10 million. The 2006 election was not as close as previous gubernatorial races, and costs per vote were down. Excluding amounts spent directly by parties, Perdue spent $6.36 per vote and Taylor spent $4.71.[53]

Campaign costs fluctuate based on the office for which candidates are running. In 2002, Mark Taylor's successful bid for lieutenant governor cost close to $6 million, while financing for Cathy Cox's successful race for secretary of state reached only $1.5 million. In a race for a U.S. Senate seat, winning candidate Johnny Isakson raised and spent more than $8 million, while his opponent, Democrat Denise Majette, lost with a campaign budget that

Table 5.3. Average Amount of Money Raised by Candidates in Georgia, 2004

| Type of Office | By Outcome | | By Incumbency | | | |
	Winners	Losers	Incumbents	Challengers	Open Seats	Total Candidates
Judicial Statewide	$553,666	$264,535	$553,666	$264,535	N/A	2
Other Statewide	$236,193	$33,207	$236,193	$38,132	N/A	6
State House	$61,285	$25,419	$61,590	$24,265	$28,922	353
State Senate	$161,398	$52,263	$157,461	$37,480	$37,840	154

N/A = Not applicable.

Source: Institute on Money in State Politics 2006.

exceeded $2 million. In the 2006 midterm elections, statewide judicial candidates spent $90,753 on average, and other statewide candidates (Secretary of State; Attorney General; Labor, Insurance, Public Service, and Agriculture Commissioners) spent an average of $259,000. Totals for the Georgia House races reached $8.5 million, and Senate candidates spent $6.2 million.[54]

This level of spending may also indicate the extent to which the two political parties are prepared to contest statewide races.[55] As these examples illustrate, more money does not automatically translate into electoral victory; however, in 2004, winners raised more than twice as much money as losers overall, and incumbents had more fund-raising success than did challengers (see table 5.3).

In most cases, funds come from large corporate and individual contributors or from large corporations through political parties. Corporations often create political action committees (PACs) to contribute to candidates. Candidates may also create PACs to raise and spend money on their behalf. PACs are especially important in campaigns for federal offices because corporations and unions cannot give directly to candidates. Instead, a PAC solicits donations from an organization's members. Georgia law, in contrast, permits corporations and unions to donate funds directly to candidates for state and local offices. Prior to 1992, Georgia had even fewer restrictions on campaign contributions; in that year, however, the General Assembly tightened the rules for donations, prohibiting legislators from directly receiving contributions while the legislature is in session and prohibiting commissioners from accepting money from the utilities and organizations that they regulate (see chapter 6).

Georgia sets its limits for campaign contributions for statewide office at $5,000 for each primary and general election and at $3,000 for runoffs following primaries and/or general elections. Thus, a candidate whose name appears on primary, runoff, and general election ballots can receive $13,000 from a single donor. Each donor to a candidate for the Georgia General Assembly or any other office that lacks a statewide constituency is limited to $2,000 for primary and general elections and $1,000 for runoffs.[56] Each contributor is also restricted to $2,500 per statewide referendum (such as a constitutional amendment).

These regulations do not inhibit lobbyists and legislators. For example, although lobbyists may not provide money for campaigns during the legislative session, they may entertain legislators during that period. Some PACs consistently contribute to Georgia's electoral campaigns. From 2000 through 2004, the Civil Justice PAC, representing the interests of trial lawyers, contributed more than $1.5 million to Georgia candidates. Other top spenders during that period included real estate agents ($1.1 million), the Medical Association of Georgia ($823,000), and AFLAC insurance ($700,000). Contributions from medical, dental, hospital, and nursing PACs combined to top $3.5 million.[57] It is not surprising that trial lawyers and medical PACs would contribute so much during the sessions in which the state legislature considered—and passed—medical tort reform legislation.

Other loopholes in the contribution limits exist. Children and spouses of donors may also contribute. Friends and family members can coordinate their contributions. In many instances, several checks for the maximum contribution arrive in one envelope, a process that is often referred to as "bundling" and that some political analysts believe has the effect of a single contribution.[58] Moreover, Georgia imposes no limits on contributions to political parties.[59] Candidates may also use their personal funds to finance their campaigns. In his unsuccessful bid for the governor's office in 2006, Mark Taylor spent just over $1 million of his own money. In that year, Georgia candidates (including Taylor) contributed over $4 million in personal finances to their campaigns.

Candidates may accrue campaign donations for future elections, and many collect large sums even when running unopposed. A large political war chest may discourage future opponents or prepare an incumbent for future campaigns for higher office. In 2001–2002, twenty-two incumbent Georgia

Table 5.4. Campaign Contributions for State Legislature
by Party, 1996–2004

Year	Democratic Candidates	Republican Candidates
1996	$5.77 million	$5.37 million
1998	$9.00 million	$7.42 million
2000	$9.59 million	$7.28 million
2002	$14.20 million	$10.00 million
2004	$12.12 million	$17.28 million

Sources: James Salzer, "Georgia GOP Finds There's Money in
Winning," Atlanta Journal-Constitution, May 9, 2005, A1;
Institute on Money in State Politics 2006.

legislators running unopposed raised a combined $2.3 million for campaigns.
Many of these candidates then contributed funds to other candidates of their
party. In one case, Democrat Terry Coleman contributed $134,100 to the
campaigns of fellow Democrats whose votes he needed in his successful bid
to become speaker of the House. Some observers criticize such practices, but
candidate-to-candidate giving is legal and has a long history in the state.[60]

Campaign contributions often flow to those most in power. For many
years, Republican candidates faced an uphill battle to raise campaign funds.
In 2004, with Republicans in the governor's office and in control of the legislature, the party's candidates for the General Assembly for the first time
outpaced their Democratic opponents (see table 5.4).

Projecting an Image and Mobilizing Support

Some of the biggest changes in state campaigns have occurred in uses of media. Radio and television ads designed to reach thousands of potential voters
at once have replaced meetings with small groups of constituents across the
state. In Georgia, estimates on campaign spending for governor indicate that
seventy-five cents of every dollar go to advertising. A thirty-second commercial on an Atlanta area station in 1990 cost between one thousand and
three thousand dollars during the day (for programs such as soap operas or
game shows) but soared to as much as seven thousand dollars during popular prime time series.[61] In 1996, a thirty-second political ad cost between

eight thousand and fifteen thousand dollars, depending on the viewer ratings for programs running at the time when ads are aired. Public-access-channel advertising could be much cheaper in 1996—as little as eight hundred dollars for thirty seconds—but reached fewer people. Radio spots in markets similar to Atlanta ran between six thousand and forty-five thousand dollars. The average cost for one cable network spot ranged between three thousand and five thousand dollars, while premium network spots averaged closer to ten thousand dollars.[62] Many candidates now use Web-based media, but one concern with this approach is the degree to which voters must seek out information rather than having it presented to them. The use of Internet campaign advertising and fund-raising is likely to rise. Howard Dean's 2004 presidential campaign relied heavily on Internet resources and provided a model for low-overhead fund-raising. Virtually all candidates for office in Georgia have Web sites, and the General Assembly maintains lists of e-mail addresses so that constituents can contact their representatives. Candidates also use the Web to send out campaign literature, conduct unofficial polls, and seek contributions. In 2002, in support of gubernatorial challenger Sonny Perdue, the Republican Party created a controversy by posting on a Web site a film depicting incumbent Roy Barnes as a large rat. Newspapers then picked up the story, generating additional attention for the ad.

Candidates must take care when launching negative media attacks on their opponents, as such attacks have created backlashes against some candidates. Political consultants advise candidates on how best to present themselves to the public, and polls determine how and why the electorate reacts to the candidates with favorable or unfavorable opinions. In Georgia's 2002 Senate race, Saxby Chambliss and Max Cleland exchanged bitter rhetoric, resulting in some criticism from voters and the press.[63] However, candidates trailing in the polls or who see clear political advantage face strong temptations to go negative.[64] Negative campaigns may become more common in the wake of decisions by the U.S. Supreme Court and Georgia's attorney general that have made it easier for committees not affiliated with candidates to campaign without disclosing their activities.[65]

In addition to paid advertising, candidates try to secure free media coverage that boosts their campaigns. This frequently is done by staging events that journalists and camera crews will cover. Candidates also try to secure statements of support from interest groups and prominent individuals. A similar and long-standing practice is for newspapers to endorse candidates.

The 2000 and 2004 Presidential Elections

In the controversial 2000 election, which pitted Republican George W. Bush against Democrat Al Gore, Georgians voted in large numbers. More than 190,000 Georgians registered in the days just before the election, and more than 2,500,000 voters turned out.[66] Although polls had predicted that Bush would carry the state, national outcomes were not as clear, and the perception of a tight race may have fueled the high turnout numbers.

Gore was most successful in central Georgia, which has the state's highest percentages of African American residents. Gore also had the most success among women and among lower-income voters (see table 5.5). Those who described the most important attribute of the new president as "honesty" were overwhelmingly more likely to vote for Bush, while those who selected "experience" as the most important factor were more likely to chose Gore. Approximately 9 percent of Georgia's voters cast ballots for the first time, and about 65 percent were married. More than two-thirds worked full time at the time of the election, and 39 percent had children at home.[67]

The 2000 presidential race may have been marked by electoral controversy, but it was also affected by the scandals of the second Clinton administration, from which Gore attempted to distance himself. Exit polls showed that Georgia voters in 2000 held some negative opinions of Clinton. Two-thirds of the voters said that the Clinton presidency would most be remembered for scandal, and an equal number blamed Clinton for a recent downturn in the economy. Forty-one percent of the respondents in the exit poll identified themselves as Democrats, while 38 percent called themselves Republicans and 21 percent identified themselves as independents.[68]

Despite the Bush victory, congressional Republicans did not post strong showings in 2000. In Georgia, Bush's coattails did not bring the election of Mack Mattingly, who lost to Democrat Zell Miller for a U.S. Senate seat, or smooth the way for Republican challengers for U.S. House seats: every Democratic incumbent was reelected.[69]

In 2004, Georgia's voters remained mindful of the war in Iraq and the economy.[70] As in 2000, perceptions of a tight race may have helped boost turnout in the state to a record 3.2 million votes. However, pollsters had predicted the outcome in Georgia long before the polls opened. Even though nationwide polling data indicated that Kerry's challenge to President Bush was very close, Georgia voters clearly fell into the Bush camp. Bush coat-

Table 5.5. Patterns of Support among Georgia Voters in 2000 Presidential Race

Demographic Group	Voted for Bush	Voted for Gore
Gender		
Men	53%	43%
Women	42%	54%
Race		
Black	7%	91%
White	69%	26%
Family Income		
Under $15,000	37%	54%
Over $100,000	57%	43%
Most Important Factor		
Honesty	80%	N/A
Experience	N/A	82%
Age		
18–29	49%	45%
30–44	54%	40%
45–59	53%	45%
60+	50%	49%

Note: Percentages may not equal 100 because of votes for other party candidates; percentages for some categories were not reported.

Source: "@Issue," Atlanta Journal-Constitution, November 12, 2000, C4.

tails were more in evidence than had been the case four years earlier, and Republicans took control of both chambers in the Georgia General Assembly.

Turnout among young Georgians was slightly lower than expected, with the turnout for those aged between eighteen and twenty-nine declining by three percentage points from 2000—bad news for Kerry, since young Georgians voted overwhelmingly for the Democratic nominee. Churchgoing voters and those who favored the war in Iraq supported Bush. Voters who indicated in exit polls that the "war on terrorism" was more important than the war in Iraq were more likely to vote for Kerry. Among those Georgians who said that they were better off economically than they had been in 2000, 83 percent voted for Bush.[71]

Central, rural Georgia, which had supported Gore in 2000, shifted to produce Republican victories for Bush and for candidates for state offices. More than 80 percent of voters in Forsyth, Cherokee, Cobb, Gwinnett, and Hall Counties selected Bush. Richmond County (which includes the city of Augusta) and Bibb County (Macon) overwhelmingly favored Kerry (79 and 77 percent, respectively). Gwinnett County, which has many new immigrant voters, contained areas of Democratic support, even though the county over-all favored Bush.[72]

Bush may also have benefited from the placement on the ballot of a pro-posed amendment to the Georgia Constitution to ban gay marriage. Interest groups working in support of the ballot measure increased attention to and turnout in the race, and those who favored the ban voted overwhelmingly for Bush. Voters for Bush also tended to make up their minds earlier in the campaign. Kerry captured the votes of 55 percent of Georgians who decided on a candidate on Election Day and 56 percent who decided within thirty days prior to the election. Voters who reported feeling "positive" about their vote choice as opposed to voting "against" the other candidate were more likely to vote for Bush.[73]

Recent Gubernatorial Campaigns

The reelection of Sonny Perdue in 2006 was a clear indication that Georgia is one of the safest states for Republican incumbents. Although Democrats nationwide held on to all governors' seats previously occupied by Democrats and took an additional six states, the outcome of the race in Georgia was es-tablished long before the election. Moreover, although President George W. Bush's low approval ratings and the concern over the war in Iraq connected Republican candidates to Bush's policies in other states, Georgia voters did not remove their support from Perdue and other Republican incumbents. As discussed in chapter 4, this was due in part to the fact that Bush's popularity was higher in Georgia than in the United States as a whole.[74]

Across the southern states, Republicans recently have done well. In the 2004 Presidential election, Kerry did not connect well with southern voters, and Bush's conservative orientation convinced many to vote for him and for his party. In the 2006 races for state offices in Georgia, Republican incumbents held on to the offices of Insurance Commissioner and School Superintendent, but Democratic incumbents retained their positions as Labor Commissioner, Agriculture Commissioner, and Attorney General. Republican candidates were succcessful in attaining the offices of Secretary of State and Lieutenant Governor, both open seats formerly held by Democrats. The governor's wide margin of victory was also a measure of Republican success in Georgia in 2006. Perdue's reelection, however, did not have a strong coattail effect for candidates in the Georgia General Assembly. Republicans held on to their majority in both chambers, but added no new seats in the Senate and only two in the House.[75] Overall, Georgia Republicans fared better than those in most other states, and in 2006 Georgia was one of the most loyal of the "red" states. This is a far cry from the era of Democratic Party dominance described by V. O. Key Jr. in 1949, but it is emblematic of Georgia's conservative heritage.

Political Parties and Interest Groups

Americans may take political parties and interest groups for granted, but both have received extensive criticism. The earliest and most vocal critics included the drafters of the U.S. Constitution, who designed the American political system to control what James Madison labeled in *The Federalist* no. 10 the "mischiefs of faction." Madison complained about the many factors that "divided mankind into parties, inflamed them with mutual animosity, and rendered them much more disposed to vex and oppress each other than to cooperate for their common good." Nonetheless, political parties developed during George Washington's tenure as the nation's first president, and interest groups have existed for virtually as long.

Political parties and interest groups are formal organizations that connect citizens with public officials. Thus, they are often labeled "linkage" institutions. The characteristics and influence of such organizations vary among the states. Parties and interest groups also have changed over time. This chapter traces these patterns generally and in Georgia.

Political Parties in the United States

The Many Meanings of "Political Party"

Political parties can generally be thought of as coalitions that seek to win elections and control government. The goal of winning elections has led parties to perform a wide range of functions: recruiting and supporting candidates, distributing propaganda, mobilizing voters, providing citizen access to government officials and processes, and forging coalitions on issues. Parties may also exercise power after elections by pressuring officials to maintain the party position on issues, influencing executives and legislatures to place loyal party members in positions of power, and threatening to withhold future support.

Political parties operate at three levels: as formal organizations, in government, and among the electorate.[1] In the United States, these three components operate relatively independently of one another. As formal organizations, the national and state parties exist as both permanent and temporary entities. The permanent apparatus includes party officials, committees, and workers. The two major national parties as well as most of their counterparts at the state level have headquarters, budgets, and paid staff that function on a permanent basis, not just during campaigns. The temporary features include caucuses, primaries, and conventions used during election years to choose candidates and party leaders, develop platforms, and establish rules for party governance.

The party in government consists of candidates and officeholders using a given party label. The United States, unlike many democracies, has almost no ways to force such leaders to adhere to party positions on issues. This occurs because candidates pick the party label they use, although there was a time in U.S. history when party leaders chose candidates. Moreover, individual candidates now cultivate loyal followers, build campaign organizations, and raise funds for election contests. Nevertheless, party affiliation remains quite important when elected executives appoint officials to important government jobs and legislatures choose presiding officers and committees.

The party in the electorate is a somewhat elusive concept since there are few requirements for calling oneself a member of a political party in the United States. Although some states require citizens to identify their party or call themselves "independent" when registering to vote, what is known about the composition of U.S. parties is based on public opinion surveys that ask people to name the party (if any) with which they identify. Most surveys also try to determine the strength or weakness of a person's ties to a given party. The details and history of such surveys have allowed scholars to examine how Americans' identification with the two major parties relates to other conditions, including a president's popularity and the economy's performance. The bottom line remains, however, that party identification in the United States is simply a person's feeling of loyalty.

Dynamics of the American Party System

Americans may take for granted or criticize the options offered them by the current two-party system, yet U.S. political parties have displayed historical and geographical variation.[2] A number of political parties arose and disappeared by 1860, but the major issues that divided them remained fairly constant and quite volatile: the power of the national government versus that of the states, economic interests, and slavery. Even though the Democrats and Republicans emerged from the Civil War as the nation's dominant parties, they have experienced challenges from a variety of minor parties that formed because of ideology, issues, or support for individual leaders. These include the Populists in the 1890s, Theodore Roosevelt's "Bull Moose" candidacy in 1912, and segregationist challenges to Democratic presidential candidates in the South in 1948 and 1968. Minor parties appear on the ballot in most states today. In Georgia, the Libertarian Party places candidates for statewide offices on most ballots. Although their share of the vote seldom exceeds 5 percent, they can drain off enough support from Democratic or Republican candidates to affect election outcomes.[3]

In addition to external challenges, the Democrats and Republicans have endured shifts in their core groups of supporters.[4] For example, blacks have moved overwhelmingly to the Democratic Party, which has also developed strong support from women and Jews. Republicans, conversely, have gained support over the past thirty years among white southerners and white ethnics in northern urban areas, two groups that previously had been key members of the Democratic coalition that began with Franklin Roosevelt's New Deal of the 1930s. The Democratic Party's membership has now become more associated with liberal ideology, while conservatives have become an increasingly large majority of the Republican Party. Many of these shifts have been associated with controversial issues such as the Vietnam War, civil rights, government taxing and spending, and abortion.

Perhaps the most enduring characteristic of American parties has been their lack of centralized control, a situation that differs substantially from what occurs among European parties. This lack of central authority has grown since the 1830s, when the selection of presidential candidates by party members in Congress was replaced by candidate selection by conventions of delegates chosen at the state and local levels. A generation ago, V. O. Key Jr. emphasized the decentralized nature of American political parties, particularly their lack of tight organization at the national level and the great differences among them from state to state.[5] Today, while national parties may be thought of as collections of state parties, they are also important players in financing campaigns, recruiting congressional candidates, conducting polls and other research, and training political operatives.

The states of the former Confederacy have occupied an important position within the decentralized party system. The region's unusual features include a long domination by the Democratic Party and the resultant differences with the remainder of the nation, southern support for Republican presidential candidates after World War II, growing competition between the two major parties at the state and local levels, and the shifting composition of the Democratic and Republican coalitions. Georgia has not been immune to these developments, which have profoundly affected the state's politics.

Partisan Change

Georgia has a long history as a Democratic stronghold, but elections since the 1980s indicate that the state is no longer bound by this tradition. Trends include changes in the composition of the parties, stronger support for Republican presidential candidates, and Republican gains in local and state elections.

The "Solid South" and Democratic Factionalism

The idiosyncrasies of southern politics have long been the subject of research and popular discussion. Key's 1949 classic, *Southern Politics in State and Nation,* argued that the region's politics were hampered by the electorate's non-involvement, the problems of a largely agrarian society within the world's major industrial nation, and the nagging burdens of racial strife and political corruption. It is ironic that the Democratic Party has come to represent support for civil rights, since maintaining segregation traditionally provided the foundation for Democratic rule in the South.

Prior to the Civil War, the Whig Party represented the views of states' rights advocates and the Republican Party was more closely allied with a strong Unionist ideology. After the Civil War, the Republican Party forced its will on the people of the vanquished Confederacy. To Georgians and other white southerners, Republicans were synonymous with the carpetbagging Yankees who profited from southern misfortunes during Reconstruction. Newly enfranchised blacks were likely to ally themselves with the Republican Party in the post–Civil War South, while antiblack rhetoric strongly tied white voters to the Democratic Party. White supremacy and black disenfranchisement were essential to Democratic dominance. Those who attempted to tie the races together based on shared issues, as the Populists tried with farming interests, found that fear of black empowerment superseded any other bond that might sway whites.[6]

Key noted that the lack of party competition within the South produced politics that were essentially party-free. Since all candidates were Democrats, the real contests developed in the Democratic primary, not the general election. This is not to say that differences did not exist among candidates, but factions formed within the Democratic Party, and personal loyalties came to hold paramount importance. This arrangement produced some rather flamboyant political personalities, notably the Longs of Louisiana, George Wallace in Alabama, and the Talmadges of Georgia.

Georgia's historical lack of party competition was associated with strong factions within the Democratic Party. Following Reconstruction, a faction known as Bourbons held power within the party, advocating white supremacy, local self-governance, and resistance to national policies. Stability was more the goal than was sound government. Thus, the Bourbons provided little in the way of policy but held office under leaders such as Governor Alfred Colquitt. Other Bourbons fared well with political rhetoric emphasizing that they had fought in the war, represented the South, and strongly supported white supremacy. Members of this group included Joseph Brown, who served as U.S. senator and governor; John Gordon, who became a U.S. senator; and Henry Grady, best known as editor of the *Atlanta Constitution*.

Unlike most other Bourbons, Grady did advance some new ideas, among them manufacturing's value to the Georgia economy.[7] However, Grady and his peers never strayed far from what they considered traditional southern values. In fact, it would have been politically unwise not to support such widely held views.

At times, true ideological differences divided the party, as with the Arnall-Talmadge struggle for power during the 1940s. The Talmadge dynasty (Eugene and his son, Herman) was particularly important because it clearly divided Democrats into Talmadge and anti-Talmadge forces. Eugene Talmadge was perpetually a candidate in Georgia's Democratic primaries, appearing on every ballot from 1926 to 1946.[8] The Talmadges were particularly strong in rural areas, where class and race appeals were well received. Ellis Arnall's 1942 election as Georgia's governor represented a break from traditional politics in the state, and his administration included establishment of the Board of Regents to insulate the university system from political control, repeal of the poll tax, and establishment of a state merit system of employment. Arnall served only a single four-year term. Herman Talmadge was elected governor in 1948 and remained a powerful figure until, amid scandal, he lost his final bid for reelection to the U.S. Senate in 1980.

Democratic presidential candidates seeking the South's solid bloc of electoral college votes carefully attended to the region's racial concerns. One way to maintain control of the party's nominating process was to restrict those who could participate. Among states in the Southeast, only Florida held presidential primaries. Delegates to the national conventions from other southern states were chosen by party caucuses or by the state Democratic Party committee (as was the case in Georgia), not by the general population. National party platforms carefully avoided civil rights, which might alienate southern whites. Moreover, New Deal policies in the 1930s and 1940s benefited the southern economy, furthering ties to the Democratic Party.[9]

The social programs of the 1930s may well constitute part of the reason why black voters began to join the Democratic Party in the South, and the party came under increasing pressure nationally to adopt civil rights as a core of its platform in later years. As early as 1948, with Harry Truman as its candidate, the Democratic Party began to voice mild support for broadening civil rights. While this strategy prompted some rural white voters to abandon the party as well as the loss of some electoral votes to the States' Rights

Party, the Democrats cultivated stronger support for civil rights. With the elimination of barriers to black enfranchisement, the Democrats tapped into a loyal bloc of black voters in southern states. Together, these developments sowed the seeds of change in the two major parties, change that became more evident in the 1980s and 1990s.

Party Coalitions

In 1968, blacks accounted for 10 percent of all southern delegates to the Democratic National Convention. By 1988, African Americans comprised one-third of the region's delegates, higher than the overall proportion of blacks in the South. Blacks made up 44 percent of Georgia's delegation.[10] Today, black voters are far more likely to identify with the Democratic Party than with the Republican Party, especially in the South. On the flip side, the Democratic Party in the South has seen a wholesale loss of white voters.[11] Analysis of black turnout in Georgia primaries illustrates how Democratic candidates rely on African American votes. In 1996, 33 percent of all Democratic primary ballots were cast by black voters; by 2004, that figure had risen to 47 percent, making black voters virtually essential to winning many contested Democratic primaries.[12]

Racial differences are also seen in electoral outcomes. Almost all of Georgia's black General Assembly members are Democrats, as were the blacks elected as attorney general and labor commissioner from the 1990s through 2006. Georgia's Republican leaders have made efforts to attract black voters, however. The state's first Republican governor in more than century, Sonny Perdue, appointed a black jurist to the Georgia Supreme Court, and Republican legislative leaders proclaimed historic the election of the first two black Republicans to the state legislature. However, both of these representatives were elected in districts that are majority white, and few people doubt that the Democratic Party retains the loyalty of a large majority of Georgia's black voters.[13]

Following the 2004 elections for the Georgia General Assembly, Republicans held the majority in both the Georgia House and Senate for the first time in 130 years. The Republican majority resulted in part from several members of the General Assembly switching from the Democratic Party to the Republican Party, including some who changed right after the election. The Republican Party systematically courted newly elected members to ensure a majority. Party switching by elected officials in Georgia, while relatively new, has constituted a pattern since the 1990s. Even Perdue began his political career as a Democrat.

Change is also occurring within the electorate. Nationwide surveys indicated that during the 1990s, more southern voters identified themselves as Republicans than had been the case in previous decades. Between 1987 and 1994, Democratic partisan identification fell by 16 percent among southerners.[14] Along with blacks, women and elderly voters are still more likely to be Democrats than Republicans in the South, but many working-class males are more comfortable within the Republican Party. However, the electorate's shifting partisan loyalties may now be leveling off.

In surveys conducted in 2001 and 2005, the University of Georgia asked questions regarding party affiliation and ideology (see figure 6.1). These surveys are of all Georgia residents, not just voters, but reflect relatively stable

Figure 6.1. Party Identification and Ideology among Georgia Residents

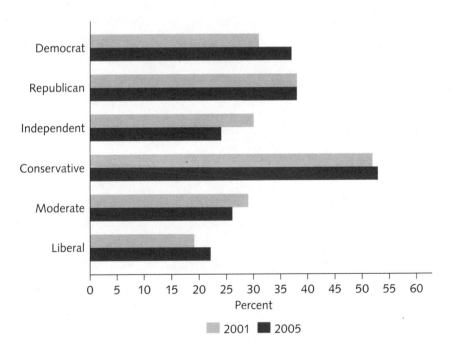

Sources: Vinson Institute of Government, University of Georgia, Peach State Poll, 2001, 2005 (www.cviog.uga.edu/peachpoll).

party identification over that four-year period. Because these two polls have a margin of error of ±3 percent, differences in party identification and political ideology remained virtually unchanged over this period. The percentages of respondents who identified themselves as Democrats and Republicans, respectively, were very close. However, the much larger percentage of respondents who thought of themselves as conservative rather than liberal gave the Republican Party an advantage in the state. Many observers believe that conservative Democratic voters are likely to find the more conservative Republican candidates appealing. Party crossover voting—that is, voting for the candidate of the opposing party—is more common among Georgia's Democratic voters than among the state's Republicans.[15] When asked which party was doing a better job in Washington, D.C., more than 44 percent of respondents chose the Republican Party, while only about 37 percent selected the Democratic Party (see table 6.1).

Support for Republican Presidential Candidates

Republican presidential candidates have enjoyed support from the South since 1964. Georgia has been less likely to cast electoral votes for Republican candidates than its southern neighbors, largely as a consequence of the presence of a Georgian, Jimmy Carter, as the Democratic nominee in 1976

Table 6.1. Georgians' Impressions of Washington Partisans, 2005

Question: Who Is Doing a Better Job in Washington?		
Response	Number	Percentage
Democrats	154	36.6
Republicans	188	44.7
Neither Democrats nor Republicans	54	12.8
Other	25	5.9
TOTAL	421	100.0

Source: Vinson Institute of Government, University of Georgia, Peach State Poll, 2005 (www.cviog.uga.edu/peachpoll).

Table 6.2. Georgia Presidential Vote Distribution, 1944–2004

Year	Republican Candidate	%	Democratic Candidate	%
1944	Dewey	17.3	Roosevelt	82.4
1948*	Dewey	18.3	Truman	60.8
1952	Eisenhower	30.3	Stevenson	69.7
1956	Eisenhower	33.3	Stevenson	66.4
1960	Nixon	37.4	Kennedy	62.5
1964	Goldwater	54.1	Johnson	45.9
1968[†]	Nixon	30.4	Humphrey	26.7
1972	Nixon	75.0	McGovern	24.6
1976	Ford	33.0	Carter	66.7
1980	Reagan	41.0	Carter	55.8
1984	Reagan	60.2	Mondale	39.8
1988	Bush, G. H. W.	59.8	Dukakis	39.5
1992[‡]	Bush, G. H. W.	42.0	Clinton	44.3
1996	Dole	47.5	Clinton	46.1
2000	Bush, G. W.	55.0	Gore	43.2
2004	Bush, G. W.	58.0	Kerry	41.9

* Strom Thurmond, States' Rights Party candidate, received 20.3% of the popular vote for president in Georgia in 1948.

[†] George Wallace, American Party candidate, received 42.8% of the popular vote for president in Georgia in 1968.

[‡] Ross Perot, an independent candidate, received 13.6% of the popular vote for president in Georgia in 1992.

Sources: Georgia Department of Archives and History 2004; Scammon and McGillivray 1993, 1996; "Voting and Registration," U.S. Census Bureau (http://www.census.gov/population/www/socdemo/voting.html).

and 1980 (see table 6.2). Democratic presidential candidates' difficulty in attracting southern votes results in part from the region's conservative bent and the particular candidates nominated in recent presidential races. During the 1980s, Democratic candidates such as Walter Mondale and Michael Dukakis often took more liberal stands on issues than the southern electorate or even southern Democrats. Georgia cast its electoral votes for Bill Clinton in 1992 but did so by only a slim margin. Moreover, the 1992 election included a strong showing by independent presidential candidate Ross Perot, whose Georgia supporters accumulated 137,182 signatures on a petition to assure that his name would appear on the ballot.[16] Prior to the Clinton victory, only two Democratic presidential candidates in thirty-two years had carried Georgia—Carter in 1980 and John F. Kennedy in 1960—and Georgia returned to the Republican fold in 1996, giving Bob Dole a narrow victory over President Clinton. In 2000 and 2004, George W. Bush posted two clear victories in Georgia, with margins comparable to that achieved by President George H. W. Bush in 1988 (see table 6.2).

Increases in Republican Officeholders

The 1994 elections ushered in dramatic changes throughout the United States, as Republicans, who had slim majorities in the U.S. Senate several times during the 1980s, won control of both houses of the U.S. Congress for the first time since 1953. Yet Georgia's legislature remained heavily Democratic, and Georgia did not elect its first post-Reconstruction Republican governor until 2002, the last of the former Confederate states to do so. Nevertheless, Republicans have gained at all levels of Georgia's government, an especially impressive showing in light of the party's virtual extinction in the state a generation ago.

Statewide Offices. Republicans offered no opposition to the Democratic nominee for governor before the mid-1960s. However, Barry Goldwater carried Georgia while being defeated soundly for the presidency in 1964 and seemed to give a shot in the arm to the state's Republicans. In 1966, the Republican Party nominated Congressman Howard "Bo" Callaway for governor. Although he received the most votes in the general election, he did not receive more than 50 percent of the vote. The law required that the General Assembly select a governor if no candidate received a majority, and legislators chose Democratic candidate Lester Maddox. Despite this setback, five of Georgia's constitutional officers switched to the Republican Party in 1968. None ever won elective office again.[17]

Republican fortunes remained pallid until 1990, when Johnny Isakson won 45.7 percent of the votes for governor in his loss to Democrat Zell Miller. The two parties also ran tight races in 1994 and 1998, as Guy Milner, a well-financed Republican candidate, sought the office in two election cycles (see table 6.3). In 2002, in defiance of polling numbers that indicated that he

Table 6.3. Georgia Gubernatorial Vote Distribution, 1966–2006

Year	Republican Candidate	%	Democratic Candidate	%
1966*	Callaway	46.7	Maddox	46.2
1970	Suite	40.7	Carter	59.3
1974	Thompson	30.9	Busbee	69.1
1978	Cook	19.3	Busbee	80.7
1982	Bell	37.2	Harris	62.5
1986	Davis	29.5	Harris	70.5
1990	Isakson	45.7	Miller	54.3
1994	Milner	47.1	Miller	52.9
1998	Milner	44.1	Barnes	52.5
2002	Perdue	51.4	Barnes	46.3
2006	Perdue	57.9	Taylor	38.2

* Ellis Arnall received 5.4% of the vote as a write-in candidate. In the absence of a majority, the Georgia General Assembly elected Lester Maddox governor.

Sources: Scammon and McGillivray 1993; Georgia Secretary of State (http://www.sos.state .ga.us/elections/election_results/default.htm).

would go down to defeat, Republican challenger Sonny Perdue unseated the incumbent Democratic governor, Roy Barnes. In 2006, two strong Democratic candidates emerged: Cathy Cox, the incumbent Secretary of State, and Mark Taylor, the Lieutenant Governor. Following a bitter primary battle dominated by negative campaign ads, Taylor won without a runoff, achieving 52 percent of the vote.[18] Although some polls indicated that Cox might have fared better against Perdue in the general election, Taylor's appeal, especially in southern Georgia, and his campaign organization won the primary.[19] Although Cox lost the election, some political observers in the state see her as a viable candidate for future races, and it is likely that voters will see her again.[20]

Other races also indicate that the Republican Party now has a loyal voting base in Georgia. Republicans have held a majority of the seats on the Public Service Commission since the 1990s. By 2004, in addition to holding the governor's office and majorities in both chambers of the General Assembly, Republicans served as superintendent of schools and insurance commissioner. Democratic candidates in 2004 held on to the offices of lieutenant governor, secretary of state, agriculture commissioner, attorney general, and labor commissioner. In 2006, when Democrats Cathy Cox and Mark Taylor both decided to run for governor, their decision left the offices of secretary of state and lieutenant governor open. Republican candidates took both. In the Republican primary for lieutenant governor, early front-runner Ralph Reed lost to State Senator Casey Cagle. Reed's well-financed campaign lost momentum after his association with disgraced Washington lobbyists became public.[21] In the general election Cagle faced Jim Martin, a former state legislator and commissioner of the state's Department of Human Resources. Cagle won with 54 percent of the vote and became the state's first Republican lieutenant governor. In the race for secretary of state, Fulton County Commissioner Karen Handel defeated her Democratic opponent, state legislator Gail Buckner, by the same margin.[22] No Democrat has been elected to an open statewide seat in Georgia since 2002.[23]

The General Assembly. Elections for the state legislature have also become more likely than ever to produce Republican victories. As late as 1950, Republicans in the Georgia General Assembly numbered under 2 percent of the total. By 1971, only 12 percent of the House and 15 percent of the Senate were Republican, and in 1984 the numbers remained relatively unchanged.[24] In actual numbers, Georgia Republicans built a strong beachhead in 1992. The GOP won 15 of the 56 Senate seats (27 percent), gaining 4 new members; the number of Republicans in the House jumped from 34 to 52 of the 180 members (29 percent). These gains may have resulted in part from redistricting, but they were extended in the summer of 1993, when Republicans won special elections for two vacant Senate seats.

The GOP further chipped away at the Democratic majority in the General Assembly in the 1994 elections. The House of Representatives changed to 114 Democrats and 66 Republicans, while the Senate had 21 Republicans and 35 Democrats. Democrats retained 63 percent of the seats in the General Assembly, a number higher than the party's overall 52 percent share of seats in the forty-nine state legislatures using partisan elections. By 2004, however, Republicans took over the majority in the Georgia General Assembly by taking 99 of the 180 House seats and 34 of the 56 Senate seats. In 2006, Georgia Democrats were able to hold on to their 22 seats in the Senate. Republicans made small inroads in the House, increasing their majority to 106. It should be noted that although only 99 of the victors in 2004 had been Republicans, party changing had increased the Republican lead to 103 in the two-year interim.[25] These gains are small but show a consistent improvement in Republican numbers in both chambers over the past decade.

Changes in Georgia reflected changes in the South as a whole. Between 1990 and 1994, the GOP gained almost two hundred seats in southern legislatures.[26] In 2004, Republicans achieved majorities in at least one chamber of the state legislatures of Virginia, South Carolina, North Carolina, and Florida.[27] In the same year, Republican candidates captured five U.S. Senate seats formerly held by southern Democrats.

In Georgia, the members of each party in the General Assembly form a caucus to plan strategy, select party members to serve on legislative committees, and determine who will serve as legislative leaders. Recent changes in partisanship have enhanced the power of the Georgia Republican Caucus. Republicans now chair all committees, and Democrats find themselves in the unfamiliar position of minority party. Members of the minority party often attempt to offer unified opposition to the majority party, but doing so requires Georgia Democrats to overcome differences based on urban and rural representation. For example, many rural Democrats voted with the Republicans to ban homosexual marriage.[28] However, Democrats are not the only ones to make adjustments; lobbyists, too, must take note of Republican dominance.

Congress. Republican candidates for the U.S. Senate and House of Representatives had limited success in Georgia until the 1990s. Mack Mattingly, the first Republican elected statewide since Reconstruction, lost his Senate seat in 1986 after only one term. Many observers argued that Mattingly's lone victory had resulted in large part from anti–Herman Talmadge sentiment, yet Mattingly did well in many areas of the state, notably suburban Atlanta.[29] One pollster estimated that Mattingly attracted only 9 percent of the black vote and was soundly defeated in the black-majority counties of southwestern Georgia. Mattingly also had little appeal and party organization in rural areas.[30]

Even though Mattingly lost to Democrat Wyche Fowler in 1986, Paul Coverdell recaptured the seat for the GOP in 1992. Despite early polls indicating that Fowler's lead was substantial, Coverdell closed the gap in the final weeks of the campaign. Fowler received only 49 percent of the vote to Coverdell's 48 percent; a Libertarian candidate garnered 3 percent. Under Georgia law requiring that a successful candidate receive at least 50 percent of the vote, a runoff election was held: Republican voters turned out in greater numbers than did Fowler supporters, thereby winning the seat for Coverdell.

Before the 1992 election, only a few Republicans from Georgia had been elected to the U.S. House of Representatives. Bo Callaway rode Barry Goldwater's coattails to a victory in 1964. Pat Swindall was elected to the House from the Fourth District during the 1980s but lost his seat amid public scandal over money laundering. Newt Gingrich held a seat in the 1980s but defeated his Democratic opponent by only one thousand votes in 1990 and faced strong opposition within the Republican Party in 1992. His tight margins of victory were particularly noteworthy given his national prestige: he served first as House minority whip and later as speaker of the House. Seven of Georgia's eleven congressional districts elected Republicans in 1994, while the Democratic winner in another district switched parties in 1995.

In 1996, these eight Republicans and three Democrats won reelection even though some of them faced voters in vastly reconfigured districts after the federal courts redrew district lines. In fact, voters in the new Eleventh District elected Republican John Linder even though he did not live there at the time of the November election. Following the 2000 census, Georgia gained two seats, and in 2004, Democrats won six of the state's thirteen seats, with seven going to the Republicans. In 2006, Democrats held on to their six seats in the House, with only one incumbent, Cynthia McKinney, not returning to office. McKinney's tenure in the House was noted for its controversy, especially after her confrontation with security personnel in the U.S. Capitol. She was defeated in the Democratic primary by challenger Hank Johnson, who later won the seat in the general election. All other incumbents, Democrat and Republican, returned to office. Two Democrats, John Barrow of the 12th district and Jim Marshall of the 8th district, won by very narrow margins.[31] These changes in partisan representation support the notion that Georgia is now a competitive two-party state.

Local Offices. Republicans are becoming more numerous at the local level in Georgia as well. The party's strength remains somewhat unclear, however, because almost all cities elect their officials on a nonpartisan basis. Among counties, though, one-tenth of the commissioners and 7 percent of all officials were Republican by 1992. In addition, the percentage of school board members who identify with the Republican Party increased from 4.4 percent in 1981 to 8.2 percent in 1991. The Republican share of other elected offices—sheriffs, probate judges, tax commissioners, school superintendents, and the like—has also increased.[32] In some counties, loyal voting bases virtually ensure Republican majorities. Cobb County, for example, has become a stronghold of the Republican Party, and in 2005 only one of the county's five commissioners was a Democrat.

Other Atlanta suburbs that have become Republican strongholds in Georgia are Gwinnett and Fayette Counties. These areas have high numbers of new residents—many from more traditionally Republican parts of the country—and high personal incomes, providing a seedbed for Republican candidates. However, the growing number of black and Latino registered voters in suburban Atlanta counties could shift the balance. All congressional districts in metropolitan Atlanta experienced a rise in the number of black voters from 2000 to 2005.[33] Party activists keep a close watch on demographic change and will move quickly to push for advantageous districts and policy positions that ensure partisan electoral success.

Maintaining a Two-Party System

If Georgia is to sustain two competitive political parties, both the Republicans and the Democrats must do more than attract voters and win some elections. They must have strong state organizations, strategic links to the national parties, and firm foundations at the local level. All of these phenomena require leadership and other resources.

Party Organization

Party structure and activity traditionally have been conspicuously weak in Georgia. In fact, the absence of a Republican presence in Georgia until the 1990s may in part explain the lack of a strong Democratic party organization. With virtually no opposition, Democrats had little need for a strong organization.[34] A mid-1980s poll of state and local party activists throughout the United States found that Democrats were more likely than Republicans to rely on large fund-raising events (93 to 72 percent, respectively). In contrast, 90 percent of the Republicans identified direct mail and telephone contacts as the most important for fund-raising, compared to 67 percent of the Democrats. Another review indicated that state parties strengthened in the 1990s, especially in southern states.[35] Georgia is a good example of such state party growth.

Beginning in the mid-1980s, Georgia's Republican Party made a concerted effort to build political strength. In 1992, all 159 counties for the first time had

Republican Party offices. At the county level, party activists distribute campaign literature and lawn signs, conduct voter registration drives, transport
voters to the polls, and organize campaign events. Such activists may be instrumental in recruiting candidates for office, campaigning on behalf of candidates, and raising campaign funds. State party building also benefits from
support by the national organizations. State party chairs in the mid-1980s
ranked the Republicans higher on all forms of assistance (campaign funds,
data processing, mail costs, voter registration efforts, and the like) provided
by the national party. Assistance to state Republican parties was greatest in
southern states, where Republicans had the greatest disadvantage.[36]

Grassroots Activism

In addition to being organized, political parties require leadership and resources, particularly at the local (grassroots) level. One 1990s study examined county chairs and precinct committee members of both political parties
in Georgia. These activists were predominantly white and male, had high
incomes, and were well educated. Some differences existed, with Democratic
precinct activists more likely to be black and the GOP including a higher
share with college degrees and incomes of fifty thousand dollars or more.
The county chairs in both parties were more commonly male than were the
precinct activists.[37]

Brad Lockerbie and John A. Clark reported several differences in the political careers of the party activists they studied.[38] Republicans were more
likely than Democrats to have held some previous position in their party.
The Republicans had less service, though, with more than 40 percent of the
county chairs having fewer than ten years' experience, compared to 13 percent for the Democrats. A quarter of the Democrats came to their party positions after holding public office; fewer than 10 percent of Republicans traveled this route. In many ways, these patterns illustrate the development of the
two parties in Georgia, with the Democrats drawing more from established
public officials and the Republicans developing a local base among people
with limited political experience who move quickly through the party ranks.

As one might expect, local activists in the two parties differed in their
positions on issues, with the Democrats more liberal and Republicans more
conservative on economic, racial, health care, and foreign policy matters.
Fewer policy differences existed between the parties' rank and file, although
men and women were more likely to disagree within the Democratic Party

than within the Republican Party. The GOP had internal divisions over abortion and between those calling themselves "fundamentalists" and others. Surprisingly, Democratic activists thought it important to support party candidates even if they disagreed with them (55 percent) to a greater degree than did Republican county chairs and precinct workers (33 percent). Both groups of activists, though, believed that candidates should not compromise to win election and should place more importance on discussion of divisive issues than on party organization and unity.[39]

Research suggests that local party activists differ somewhat from those who gave campaign contributions to candidates for the General Assembly in 1992. John Clark and John Bruce call the latter "checkbook" activists. Both groups are overwhelmingly white, male, and well educated. Georgia's median annual household income amounted to roughly twenty-nine thousand dollars in 1992, but that figure rose to more than fifty thousand dollars among party activists and soared to more than one hundred thousand dollars for contributors. In addition, the checkbook activists offered more support for political compromising than did party activists. With the exception of abortion, grassroots Democratic activists tended to be more liberal on issues and grassroots Republicans more conservative than their respective parties' contributors. In cases such as beliefs regarding the national government's proper role in promoting economic security, however, all four groups were predominantly conservative in Georgia.[40] The differences between local party activists and campaign contributors suggest that candidates in Georgia may occasionally face a difficult balancing act in raising money for their campaigns and motivating party loyalists to work on their behalf.

The Future of Party Politics in Georgia

When Key examined politics in the South during the 1940s, he concluded that one-party politics hindered the region's development. Nearly two generations after Key's assessment, Georgia Republicans are competing effectively with the long-dominant Democratic Party, and the Libertarian Party won enough votes in 1992 to force two statewide runoff elections. These changes may encourage broader political debate, increase voter turnout, produce a more varied pool of candidates, and change the General Assembly.

Despite the growth of the Republican Party, in 2004 Georgia Democrats held six of thirteen congressional seats and five of eight constitutional offices. In 2006, Democrats lost two open seats to Republicans, one for secretary of state and one for lieutenant governor. Two Democratic incumbents almost lost their U.S. House seats to strong Republican opposition.[41] Despite nationwide Democratic gains for congressional and gubernatorial candidates, Georgia Republicans maintained their seats in Congress and in the governor's office. Still, change can be noted within the parties as well as between the parties. Shifts in the composition of the major parties may produce difficult adjustments for each, such as the conflict within the Republican Party between traditional members and religious conservatives and the effort of Democratic officeholders to distance themselves from national party leaders.[42] The growing racial polarization between the parties also could make Georgia politics even more partisan and strident. Still, the growing number and power of interest groups in Georgia politics threatens the influence of both major parties.

Interest Groups

Interest groups provide an avenue for influence in addition to those available from elections and other forms of participation. Unlike political parties, interest groups do not necessarily seek to win elections and control government. Nor are they composed of the diverse membership typical of political parties. Rather, they comprise like-minded individuals who pursue public policies on which they all agree. Those who join groups in the United States tend to have higher incomes and more education than the general population, a situation that should not be surprising given the amounts of time and money and the skills that can be required for membership. Unlike voting, where each person's vote has the same weight, interest groups allow people to act on the strength of their concern about an issue by investing varying amounts of time and money.[43]

Most interest groups are organized to further economic goals. Examples include labor unions, groups representing professions such as doctors and real estate agents, and industries such as oil producers and cotton growers. Other types of groups have proliferated since the 1970s, including social welfare, educational, ethnic, religious, and public affairs organizations. Also increasingly common are single-issue groups such as those dealing with abortion or the environment as well as law firms, consultants, and others who offer services as lobbyists for hire. Not everything interest groups do is strictly political, however; they also provide members with training and information.[44]

Strategies

Lobbying. Perhaps the most widely recognized—and criticized—activity of interest groups is lobbying, which is the process of communicating information to officials to influence policy. Those engaged in such endeavors include contract lobbyists hired by clients, in-house lobbyists who work for an organization or business, those representing government agencies, citizen volunteers who promote causes on an unpaid basis, and private individuals acting on their own behalf. While lobbying activity is often discussed in terms of legislatures, interest groups can also lobby the executive branch. Beyond the testimony, office visits, and research or reports provided by traditional lobbyists, lobbying also can include mobilizing grassroots members of an organization and using the media to promote goals.[45]

Donations. Another frequent strategy of interest groups is the distribution of money and other benefits (trips and so forth) to public officials. Although public attention occasionally focuses on scandal related to monetary benefits for public officials such as the 2006 case of Washington lobbyist Jack Abramoff, little evidence shows that officials exchange their action for such benefits. In fact, groups often reward candidates both for their past support and to make sure that such "friends" have sufficient campaign funds to win reelection. Some groups even give donations to multiple candidates competing for the same office, especially when no incumbent is running. Such donations seek to influence policy by trying to place supportive people in key positions. Corporations and unions cannot give money directly to candidates for federal offices, so they form political action committees (PACs), which solicit contributions from individuals and donate pooled money to candidates' campaign committees. Practices and regulations regarding nonfederal offices differ substantially among the states.[46]

The Courts. Many groups also use the legal system to promote their interests. This approach includes efforts to influence the selection of judges and prosecutors. Most state and local judges and district attorneys are chosen by public election, thereby prompting groups to recruit, endorse, and fund such candidates. Just because federal legal officials are appointed does not mean that politics is not involved in their selection.

Interest groups can also file lawsuits and submit legal briefs even when they are not one of the parties to a case, as a means of shaping the way that courts apply the law. Evidence indicates that since the mid-1960s, these amicus curiae ("friend of the court") briefs have become increasingly common and involve a wide array of interests, although the findings vary among the states.[47]

Other Strategies. Beyond these conventional methods of influencing policy, interest groups also engage in protests, which can be either legal or illegal. The illegal lobbying category also includes strategies such as violence and bribery. Protest and violence often are designed to get public attention and support for a group that has not achieved its goals using other means.

Interest Groups in the States

Although scholars, the media, and the public have devoted great attention to the proliferation and activities of interest groups in national politics, such organizations are important at the state and local levels as well. Observers have traditionally cited business, labor, education, agricultural, and local government groups as the most active in the states. Since the 1970s, a larger and more diverse set of interest groups has developed, including those involved in social issues as well as individual companies and local governments lobbying on their own despite belonging to general membership organizations. One study during the 1990s found that associations representing schoolteachers were the most influential groups in forty-three states, followed by general business organizations (for example, chambers of commerce), bank associations, manufacturers, labor unions, and utilities.[48]

Discussions of general patterns can cloud important differences among the states. Ronald J. Hrebenar and Clive S. Thomas have studied state interest group activities for many years, producing a method of state comparison (see table 6.4). The Hrebenar-Thomas classification divides state interest group activities into five categories: (1) dominant, where interest groups retain an overwhelming influence over state policy making; (2) dominant-complementary, where interest groups have a strong policy influence; (3) complementary, where interest groups share influence with other political forces; (4) subordinate-complementary, in which interest groups supplement other, more dominant, political forces; and (5) subordinate, in which interest

Table 6.4. Classification of the Fifty States According to the Overall Impact of Interest Groups in 2002, with Comparison to Classification of 1985

Dominant	Dominant-Complementary	Complementary	Subordinate-Complementary	Subordinate
5 states	26 states	16 states	3 states	none
Alabama	Alaska (−)	Colorado	Michigan (−)	
Florida	Arizona	Connecticut (+)	Minnesota	
Montana (+)	Arkansas	Delaware (+)	South Dakota (−)	
Nevada (+)	California	Hawaii (−)		
West Virginia	**Georgia**	Indiana		
	Idaho	Maine		
	Illinois (+)	Massachusetts		
	Iowa (+)	New Hampshire		
	Kansas (+)	New Jersey		
	Kentucky	New York		
	Louisiana (−)	North Carolina		
	Maryland (+)	North Dakota		
	Mississippi (−)	Pennsylvania		
	Missouri (+)	Rhode Island (+)		
	Nebraska	Vermont (+)		
	New Mexico (−)	Wisconsin		
	Ohio			
	Oklahoma			
	Oregon			
	South Carolina (−)			
	Tennessee (−)			
	Texas			
	Utah			
	Virginia			
	Washington			
	Wyoming			

Note: + or − indicates changes noted from 1985 to 2002 by Thomas and Hrebenar.

Source: Thomas and Hrebenar 2003.

groups have a minor role in policy making. Neither Hrebenar and Thomas's 2002 analysis nor their earlier studies have categorized any of the fifty states in the subordinate category. Georgia is categorized with twenty-five other states in the dominant-complementary group. Moreover, Hrebenar and Thomas have not noted changes in the degree to which interest groups dominate the policy process in Georgia since their analysis was first published in 1985.[49]

Differences among states may be especially great in the South, where the historical lack of competition among political parties helped to nurture a network of influential interest groups. The region's interest groups have changed during the past three decades with the decline of rural political control, the rise of the Republican Party, racial change, and economic and population growth. More diversity among interest groups has replaced a system dominated by agriculture, local governments, and churches. State capitals now have more groups; public employees and state agencies have become important political participants; groups have developed more elaborate tactics, including more extensive and sophisticated lobbying; most states have seen a rise in the use of contract lobbyists; and interest groups have received more attention, both from the media and in the form of increased regulation. As one might expect, Georgia has not been immune to these changes.[50]

Interest Groups in Georgia

Interest groups are nothing new to Georgia politics. During the 1940s, Key concluded that organized interests were few and represented Georgia's major corporations, including utilities such as Georgia Power, other companies regulated by the state, firms opposed to Franklin Roosevelt's New Deal, and Atlanta's commercial leaders.[51] For much of the 1950s and 1960s, political disputes centered on racial and urban-rural issues. Although racial change was not easy, Georgia's business leaders, especially those often described as Atlanta's business elite, promoted moderation as a means of achieving economic growth. They also promoted the state as an active player in development. From this base, the number and types of groups have expanded as state government has grown and economic issues have taken center stage.[52]

It is somewhat difficult to get a firm grip on Georgia's system of interest groups because legal requirements for reporting their activities were extremely lax until the 1990s. In the early 1970s, roughly 300 people registered to lobby the General Assembly. During the 1990 legislative session, however, one tally found 1,059 registered lobbyists, with 27 percent working for businesses or business associations. The next-most-common registered lobbyists were professional associations and unions (20 percent), those grouped in the ambiguous category of "registered agents" (18 percent), and groups advocating social issues (17 percent). No other type of interest constituted more than 4 percent of those registered to lobby.[53] A similar count for the 1991 legislative session identified 947 lobbyists, 48 percent of whom represented individual companies or business associations. Notable growth occurred in the number of health and education lobbyists: whereas 25 such groups had registered in 1975 (11 percent of the total), 143 registered in 1991 (14 percent). Similarly, advocacy, social cause, and "public interest" groups multiplied from 32 in 1975 to 136 in 1991 (14 percent).[54] Moreover, the total number of registered lobbyists continues to grow, topping 3,000 by 2006.[55]

A census of lobbyists does not distinguish between those who are highly influential and those whose efforts have little impact. Generally identified among the most influential groups in Georgia are banks, business associations (especially the statewide chamber of commerce), the Medical Association of Georgia, the Georgia Association of Educators, the state Department of Transportation, Home Depot, Coca-Cola, and Delta Air Lines. Other observers would include on such a list the Georgia Power Company, the Georgia Poultry Association, AFLAC insurance, the organizations representing Georgia's cities and counties, the Board of Regents of the University System of Georgia, and firms recently relocated to Georgia, such as United Parcel Service. The debate on tort reform dominated much of the 2005 legislative session; the preceding year, the Georgia Trial Lawyers' lobbyists made more campaign contributions than any other group.[56]

Interest group systems differ dramatically among the states. Perhaps more importantly, groups' activities also can vary within a state over time, as has been in the case in Georgia, where interest groups until recently escaped both state regulation and media attention.

Regulation of Interest Groups

It may be a gross understatement to say that Georgia has seldom been a leader in regulating interest groups.[57] Until 1992, Georgia was one of the only two states that did not require lobbyists to report their activities, although lobbyists did have to register and wear an identification badge while in the Capitol. Certain actions, such as getting paid based on the outcome of specific bills and discussing pending matters on the floor of the House and Senate during the session, were illegal, however.

During 1991 and 1992, Secretary of State Max Cleland and some of the media, particularly the Atlanta daily newspapers, campaigned for ethics reform—laws governing the behavior of interest groups and public officials.[58] The issue was quite controversial, but the General Assembly amended the state's "ethics in government" law in 1992. The new procedures transferred lobbyist registration from the secretary of state to the State Ethics Commission, set an annual registration fee (except for governmental and nonprofit organizations), and required those registering to wear an emblem labeled "Lobbyist" while in the Capitol. The law also mandated that lobbyists disclose their expenses, the public officials on whom money is spent, and the specific bills for which they are lobbying; they are not required to disclose their compensation. Reports are filed monthly when the General Assembly is in session as well as at two other times during the year.[59] However, the law set no limits on how much legislators could accept in the way of meals, gifts, trips, or similar benefits.

Passing lobbyist regulation is not the same as enforcing it, and critics complained that the General Assembly gave the State Ethics Commission insufficient staff and budget to monitor lobbying. The most frequent criticism was that lobbyists did not list specific legislators or bills when filing reports. One tally found that only 138 of the 3,800 reports covering the 1993 legislative session listed a bill or general subject discussed at events paid for by registered lobbyists. Only 7.5 percent of the expenditures were reported to be directed at specific legislators.[60] Other observers have complained that organizations do not report activities not funded by their lobbyists—for example, trips financed by a company.

As with lobbying, Georgia placed few limitations on contributions to candidates' campaigns until the 1990s. Unlike laws governing federal elections, Georgia law permits companies and unions to donate directly to candidates' campaigns. Disclosure of donations has been required since the 1970s, but there were no limits on such amounts until 1990 (see table 6.5). Of course, many companies and individuals contribute to more than one candidate, and candidates can spend unlimited amounts of their personal money on their campaigns.

Table 6.5. Georgia Campaign Donation Limits, 2006

Type of Election	Type of Office	Donation Limit
Primary	Statewide	$5,000
Primary Runoff	Statewide	$3,000
General Election	Statewide	$5,000
General Election Runoff	Statewide	$3,000
Primary	All Other	$2,000
Primary Runoff	All Other	$1,000
General Election	All Other	$2,000
General Election Runoff	All Other	$1,000

Source: Georgia State Ethics Commission (http://ethics.georgia.gov).

Some sectors can be identified as heavy contributors (see table 6.6). Lawyers as a group contributed more than one-tenth of the $51,557,621 raised for all 2004 statewide, state legislative, and state judicial races; the largest chunk ($456,638) came from the Georgia Trial Lawyers Association.[61] Although 2006 campaign contribution data are incomplete, over $60 million in contributions had been recorded by December 2006. Many organizations contribute to more than one candidate in the same race. For example, the Humane Society contributed a relatively small $500 in the 2004 elections, dividing that amount equally between Democrats and Republicans.

Lobbying

Lobbyists, especially the more professional and experienced ones, remain active between legislative sessions, although the pace quickens when the General Assembly is meeting.[62] Interest groups engage in a variety of activities to press their points of view: testifying at hearings, dispensing information, providing favors, and sponsoring events. Some of these actions are aimed at securing the passage of legislation. Others are defensive—that is, designed to defeat bills a group opposes. Some generally seek to create goodwill for the organization. All attempt to build winning coalitions of interests, not always an easy task.

Information. Testifying and otherwise providing information can be very useful to interest groups and public officials alike in a state such as Georgia,

Table 6.6. Fifteen Largest Sector Donors in Georgia, 2004 Elections

Type of Contributor	Number of Contributions	Total Amount of Contributions for 2004 Elections	Percentage of All Contributions
Lawyers	8,003	$5,216,721	10.12%
Finance, Insurance, and Real Estate	8,539	$5,071,984	9.84%
Health	7,453	$3,994,966	7.75%
Candidate Contributions (Including Self-Contributions)	1,272	$3,724,686	7.22%
General Business	3,958	$2,338,943	4.54%
Construction	3,123	$2,215,701	4.30%
Political Parties	2,371	$1,735,305	3.37%
Other/Retiree/Civil Servants	2,764	$977,223	1.90%
Transportation	1,406	$678,403	1.32%
Agriculture	1,218	$657,505	1.28%
Energy and Natural Resources	1,436	$646,562	1.25%
Labor	933	$572,580	1.11%
Communications and Electronics	603	$352,034	0.68%
Ideology/Single Issue	275	$246,216	0.48%
Defense	7	$13,150	0.03%

Source: Institute on Money in State Politics 2004.

where legislators are part-time officials who receive low pay and limited staff support. Providing facts about pending legislation and mobilizing members of a group are not always sufficient for success, however. Officials' willingness to listen and defer to the judgment, expertise, or power of a group and its lobbyists is also important. There are even customs about where certain lobbyists position themselves in the halls of the Capitol to talk to representatives and senators during the legislative session.[63]

Favors. Interest groups also use events and favors, such as receptions, dinners, seminars, trips, tickets, and other gifts. Lobbyists spent $1.1 million entertaining Georgia lawmakers during 2005.[64] Critics claim that such tactics buy access and influence in legislative and executive branch decisions. Some of these items are generally available to members of the General Assembly during the legislative session, such as soft drinks provided by Coca-Cola, newspapers supplied by Delta Air Lines, hotel hospitality suites furnished with food and beverages, the annual Wild Hog Supper sponsored by various agricultural interests, and a doctor on call provided by the Medical Association of Georgia. Similar benefits throughout the year include tickets to professional and college sporting events, with buffets for legislators before University of Georgia football games. Beyond favors that seem more general in nature, others appear targeted at those with substantial influence. For example, prior to 1991, Georgia Power offered state officials inexpensive leases on its lakefront property.[65]

Lobbying is not limited to business interests. During 2006, the Georgia Municipal Association registered eight lobbyists, Emory University had seven, and the Association County Commissioners and the state Department of Transportation had thirteen registered lobbyists each.[66] Although the Board of Regents of the University System of Georgia had only one registered lobbyist in 2004, the University of Georgia and Georgia Tech have provided executive and legislative leaders with tickets to football games. Other groups use the political system to promote policies consistent with certain ideologies, values, or ways of life. These include groups both supporting and opposing firearms regulation as well as religious groups.[67]

Relationships. Interest groups' success depends in part on building strategic relationships, and critics complain about the extent to which legislators serve on committees related to their occupations. For example, the ten members of the Senate Banking and Financial Institutions Committee in 1993 included the chair of a bank board of directors and a man who represented a lending company as part of his law practice. On the one hand, these senators could be regarded as having special expertise regarding banking; on the other hand, they faced some accusations of favoritism.[68]

Government officials also try to build useful alliances. One study of state agencies found that they benefit from their insider status in the General Assembly, which requires them to expend less energy than private lobbyists do on courting legislators. Government representatives also occupy a favorable position for keeping legislators informed. Agency influence varies, however. The most effective agencies are those with substantial discretion and resources that make them capable of providing benefits to legislators' districts and constituents—not surprisingly, other lobbyists identified the Department of Transportation as the most influential with the legislature.[69]

While building alliances is important, the proliferation of groups can pit some interests against others. For example, lawyers, doctors, and insurance companies were very active in the 2005 legislative debate on medical malpractice tort reform. Nine of the top ten contributors in 2004 had strong interests in the outcome of that legislation (see table 6.7). Disagreements among particular industry entities may be especially troublesome for organizations representing a diverse membership, as with the Georgia Chamber of Commerce's position as the leading group promoting general business concerns. The same can be said of the Georgia Municipal Association, which includes scores of cities that often have competing interests and can find itself in conflict with the groups representing county governments and school boards.

In many ways, newspaper headlines often give the appearance that interest groups seduce public officials; however, the relationship is a two-way street. Groups do not necessarily direct their spending toward passive officials; lobbyists' largesse and politicians' power mean that some interests may fear *not* providing favors. Indeed, one former lobbyist wrote to a newspaper arguing that "for far too many years" a culture had existed in which legislators "openly demanded" favors from lobbyists.[70]

Campaigns

In addition to lobbying, many interest groups also donate money to election campaigns, both for candidates and for referendum questions. The 1986 election was the last campaign in which unlimited donations were permitted for state offices, and PACs donated more than $3.5 million to candidates. Of course, the introduction of regulation has not resulted in a decrease in overall campaign spending by individual PACs (see table 6.7). However, not all interest group donations come from PACs. Georgia law permits individuals, companies, and associations to give money to campaigns for state and local offices.

As Georgia's electorate expands, the scope of state government grows, and the two major parties remain competitive, the cost of campaigns undoubtedly will rise. Thirty million dollars may soon become low end for combined

Table 6.7. Highest PAC Contributors in Statewide, State Legislative, and State Judicial Campaigns, 2004

Contributor	Amount
Georgia Trial Lawyers Association Civil Justice PAC	$456,638
Georgia Dental Association	$261,300
Georgia Association of Realtors	$226,950
Georgia Association of Educators	$224,250
Medical Association of Georgia	$213,000
MAG Mutual Insurance	$186,300
Georgia Hospital Association (HOS PAC)	$161,400
Independent Insurance Agents of Georgia (IIAG)	$157,900
Georgia Highway Contractors Association	$156,093
Georgia Alliance of Community Hospitals	$147,550

Source: Institute on Money in State Politics 2004.

spending by the major parties' gubernatorial candidates. As a result, some observers expect that successful gubernatorial candidates will have to raise large sums of money early in their campaigns, primarily in metropolitan Atlanta. This development in turn could strengthen ties between politicians and interest groups. Observers have long expressed concerns about whether campaign contributors buy political access or favors with donations to candidates, a fear that gained credence in 1996 when the press obtained a memo from state school superintendent Linda Schrenko directing her chief of staff to give priority to campaign contributors when scheduling appointments.[71]

Concerns have been raised about campaign funding loopholes such as the fact that companies cannot give to the campaigns of elected officials whose agencies regulate the companies but employees may do so as individuals. Critics have chided recent insurance commissioners, for example, for accepting—and soliciting—campaign contributions from people whose businesses the insurance commission regulates. Observers have also questioned candidates' use of leftover campaign money for personal purposes. Finally, donations to political parties essentially remain unregulated. In 2004, party committees received upward of $13 million, more than one-fourth of all political contributions at the state level for that year. Donors may route large sums of money to campaigns over and above the amounts given to candidates, which state law limits.[72] Similarly unregulated are donations to committees tied to officials, as with a fund connected to Speaker of the House Glenn Richardson, a Republican. During 2005, the fund collected more than $175,000, much of it from interest groups and their lobbyists, with funds used for polling, personnel, technology, and similar support. Richardson's fund resembled one maintained by his Democratic predecessor.[73]

Interest groups are also involved in elections that have no candidates—that is, referendum campaigns. Georgia has no initiative process permitting citizens to circulate petitions placing policy questions on the ballot. Thus, the referenda most familiar to Georgians are proposed amendments to the state constitution, local votes to adopt sales taxes or to use debt financing for public projects, and questions tied to local bills passed by the General Assembly (for example, consolidating the Athens and Clarke County governments).

Interest groups can be very active in referendum campaigns when the groups have substantial financial stakes in the outcome. For example, the state's voters approved a 1990 constitutional amendment that substantially reduced the local property tax burden for timber and agricultural land. The amendment was promoted as environmentally responsible because lower taxes could encourage forest preservation and planting. Major timber companies were significant backers of the amendment, including a reported contribution of thirty-two thousand dollars by Georgia Pacific. The amendment produced tax savings for these companies, but other taxpayers had to pay more to make up for the lost revenue.[74]

Grassroots Pressure

Traditional lobbying and the use of campaign money are not the only strategies employed by interest groups. Some also mobilize their members to write or call public officials. Groups such as the National Rifle Association and the AARP (originally known as the American Association of Retired Persons) have a reputation for being very effective with such efforts. Groups also use media campaigns to promote their goals and images. They also "go public" by rating legislators according to roll call votes. In such cases, a group identifies bills it considers important and then rates legislators according to the percentage of bills on which they voted "correctly."

A similar tactic during campaign years is to rate candidates according to their answers on questionnaires about issues important to a group. Opponents are often saddled with derogatory labels, as when an environmental group calls the twelve lowest-rated legislators the "Dirty Dozen." With ratings goes the sometimes subtle threat of a group's members voting en masse against candidates who do not measure up to a group's standards. Georgia's Christian Coalition regularly uses this approach, labeling those with acceptable ratings "profamily" and distributing thousands of scorecards to would-be voters. Prior to the 2004 elections, candidates received an eighty-two-question survey from the Christian Coalition, which printed the results and distributed them to five hundred thousand Georgia church members just before Election Day. Some questions have arisen over judicial candidates answering such surveys, which include responses indicating agreement or disagreement with Supreme Court decisions. Some candidates who refused to answer the questionnaire also expressed concern about how results might be presented to the public.[75] In addition, the Christian Coalition reached out to Georgians by paying for television spots highlighting traditional families during the debate on the 2004 constitutional ban on gay marriage. The Christian Coalition has tax-exempt status, which means that it cannot directly endorse candidates, but it can and does use financial means to promote values and spotlight candidate views that can easily translate into political agenda.

The Christian Coalition and many other grassroots organizations also attempt to influence policy by registering voters. The same-sex marriage controversy prompted not just supporters of the ban but also its opponents, including Georgia Equality, to reach out to voters through registration drives. One representative of that group estimated that political mobilization against the ban on gay marriage would cost $1 million.[76] Despite their efforts, the constitutional amendment to ban gay marriage received more than 76 percent of the vote.

Litigation and Protest

Interest groups outside the political mainstream often have few resources to achieve their policy goals through normal legislative and executive channels. In fact, they often have to defend themselves against laws or bureaucratic decisions. Under such conditions, groups use other avenues to achieve their policy. One important strategy is to turn to federal and state courts. Civil rights organizations used the federal courts, for example, to eliminate state actions that restricted blacks' right to vote.[77] Groups such as the American

Civil Liberties Union exist primarily to take on court cases. Some of these cases can be quite controversial, however, as when the American Civil Liberties Union successfully represented a student seeking to eliminate prayers before high school football games as a violation of the U.S. Constitution's prohibition against the establishment of religion. A similar lawsuit by a public employee organization challenged a state law requiring mandatory drug tests for all state and local government job applicants. The law was declared unconstitutional in the federal courts in 1990 as a violation of both the guarantee against unreasonable search and seizure and the right to privacy.[78]

Groups also use protests to dramatize their position or create political pressure. This was the case during much of the 1960s, when civil rights groups used peaceful protest to turn U.S. public opinion against racial segregation. Both sides in the abortion debate use a variety of protest strategies such as picketing. Worker organizations such as unions have limited influence in Georgia, so they have held rallies at the Capitol to dramatize what they argue are inadequate payment levels from the fund set up to compensate workers injured on the job.[79]

Supporters and opponents of Georgia's 2004 constitutional amendment banning gay marriage have used court action and protest to further their agenda. Opponents of the ban first attempted to block its placement on the ballot through the courts and then worked after its passage to have the amendment declared unconstitutional in federal court. They also organized protests against the ban at the State Capitol. Supporters of the amendment also worked with lawyers to make sure that the language of the amendment would not prevent its placement on the ballot. Their "Family Day" at the Capitol in part constituted a demonstration of support for passage.

Political Participation and the Future of Georgia Politics

Some observers might argue that little has changed since V. O. Key Jr. described Georgia politics in the 1940s. Although the Democratic dominance that lasted through the 1990s gave way to a Republican governor and GOP majorities in the General Assembly, business interests still retain substantial influence over the policy process. Yet linkage institutions have become more complex during the past fifty years. Georgia has a competitive two-party system, although voters' party loyalty is declining.[80] Moreover, the composition of the two major parties has changed, possibly with serious consequences for ideological and racial conflict. Georgia has many more interest groups than was the case a generation ago, and their ability to use resources—primarily money—may be more important than ever in the electoral and policy processes. Thus, with levels of participation already low, the changing nature of parties and interest groups may offer few avenues in which most Georgians can influence government. In fact, the cost of elections and lobbying may breed further distrust of politics.

CHAPTER 7

The Legislature

The Framers of the U.S. Constitution expected legislatures to be the branch of government closest to the people. In Thomas Jefferson's view, legislators were to be citizen-lawmakers who applied the values of the community to government without placing themselves above average citizens.

The U.S. Congress and many states have left behind the idea of the citizen-legislator in favor of the professional politician. The Georgia General Assembly, however, may be characterized as a citizen legislature in that members must maintain other sources of income, districts are relatively small, and most members have no ambitions for higher office. Yet the General Assembly, like other legislatures, does not perfectly reflect the people it purports to represent.

The Fifty State Legislatures

State legislatures have much in common.[1] For example, legislators are charged with the duties of representing the people of their districts, reapportioning districts following the census, enacting laws, adopting taxing and spending measures, overseeing enforcement of current laws, and interceding on behalf of constituents. Every state except Nebraska has a bicameral legislature, elects its legislature on a partisan basis, and has an upper chamber called the

Table 7.1. State Legislatures

Characteristic	Minimum	Maximum	Georgia
Length of Term (Years)			
Lower House	2 (44 states)	4 (5 states)	2
Senate	2 (12 states)	4 (38 states)*	2
Total Members	49 (NE)	424 (NH)	236
Lower House	40 (AK)	400 (NH)	180
Senate	20 (AK)	67 (MN)	56
Annual Salary, 2004	$200 (NH)[†]	$99,000 (CA)	$16,200
Number of Committees, 2005[‡]			
Lower House	9 (AK, MD)	45 (MS, WI)	34
Senate	8 (MD)	39 (MS)	25
Republican % of Seats, 2005			
Lower House	13.1% (MA)	81.4% (ID)	55.0%
Senate	13.2% (RI)	80.0% (ID)	60.7%

* Nebraska's unicameral legislature is the Senate, whose members serve four-year terms. Senators in Illinois and New Jersey are included in this total, although some serve for two years.

† Another nine states only reimburse legislators at a daily rate during the legislative session.

‡ Excludes states relying primarily on joint committees for most substantive work.

Source: Council of State Governments 2004, 37:130–132, 142–143, 176– 177.

Senate. Forty-one states call their lower chamber the House of Representatives, and forty-four states hold annual legislative sessions.

Differences do exist among legislatures, especially in terms of provisions in state constitutions and statutes (see table 7.1). Among the formal distinctions, size varies from a low of 49 in Nebraska's unicameral legislature to a high of 424 in the small state of New Hampshire. Georgia, with 236 members, has the third-largest legislature. Qualifications such as minimum age, terms of office, length of residence, and term limits also vary. Georgia is one of twelve states using only two-year terms; thirty-two states elect members of their upper chambers to four-year terms and members of their lower chambers for two years. Regular legislative sessions range from off-year limits of thirty calendar days in New Mexico and Virginia and twenty legislative days in Wyoming to unlimited length for annual sessions in fourteen states. Leadership, procedures, and compensation also differ widely.

In addition to the characteristics imposed by state constitutions and laws, legislatures also differ in their informal traits, one of which observers have labeled "legislative professionalism."[2] One often-used distinction is among professional, hybrid, and citizen legislatures. Professional legislatures are composed largely of career politicians who devote large portions of their time to legislative work and who often do not hold other jobs. For many of these persons, election to the legislature is a means of achieving other goals as well as an accomplishment in its own right. Professional legislatures have high compensation levels, long legislative sessions, and large numbers of staff members to assist legislators. One classification includes nine states in this category.[3]

At the other extreme are citizen legislatures, which have short sessions, low levels of pay, and very limited staff support. Members generally have outside careers, often in business or law, although they can use legislative service as a springboard to run for higher office. Georgia is among the sixteen states with a citizen legislature. The remaining twenty-five states are classified as hybrid because their combination of compensation, session length, and staff fall between the two extreme categories. One study found that in thirty-one of the forty-one legislatures for which 1998 data were available, at least 60 percent of members had outside careers, with a high of 93 percent in Indiana and a low of 27 percent in California. Georgia's 62 percent ranked the state thirtieth in the percentage of members with outside careers.[4]

Legislators tend to be fairly similar. Most are males, have lived in their state or district long term, hold professional occupations, and are of higher socioeconomic status than the state population as a whole. They also tend to be well educated and are generally highly involved in local and community organizations. Diversity has increased, although wide variation exists among the states. By 2006, more than 22 percent of legislators in the fifty states were women, as opposed to 4 percent in 1969. Similarly, 8 percent of legislators in 2003 were black, a substantial jump from the 1970 level of 2 percent.[5]

The Georgia General Assembly: Constitutional Provisions

Georgia's legislature is officially named the Georgia General Assembly, and its two chambers are called the House of Representatives and the Senate. All Georgia legislators are elected to two-year terms in November of even-numbered years. Should a seat become vacant during the legislative session, a special election is held to fill the position.

Legislative Districts

Since Georgia's earliest legislatures were based on county representation, the General Assembly initially had at least one representative for each county. As the number of counties grew to 159, the legislature became relatively large. Moreover, as local population grew at differential rates, county-based representation proved problematic when small, sparsely populated counties had the same number of votes as larger counties. In addition, each Senate district included three counties, with the seat rotating among the counties. Thus, the real power in the legislative branch was concentrated in the House, where members could hold unlimited tenure.[6]

Redrawing legislative districts occurs following the U.S. census held every ten years. In the 1960s, federal courts ruled that all representation within state legislatures must be based on population rather than county. Since then, Georgia has eliminated the rotation system for state senators, all 56 of whom are now elected from single-member districts. With the adoption of the Constitution of 1983, the Senate has been restricted to no more than 56 members, while the House has been required to have at least 180 members. Thus, the legislature could enlarge the number of representatives in the House or decrease the size of the Senate as long as the courts uphold the constitutional mandates on size.

The House of Representatives has employed a combination of single-member and multimember districts over the years. Multimember House districts provide for election of candidates to a "post," or position, within the district. If District A elected three members to the House, it would have three times the population of a single-member district. Candidates would file to run for one of the three posts within the district. Thus, someone running for the House in District A, Post 3, does not compete with candidates for District A, Post 1, although the electorate consists of the same voters. Georgia eliminated multimember House districts following the 1990 census, but the General Assembly reinstated them after the 2000 census. Those multimember districts were eliminated following a series of lawsuits, however, and all 180 members of the House now represent single-member districts. Based on Georgia's population of almost 8.2 million in the 2000 census, each member of the House has roughly 45,500 constituents, and each Senate district has approximately 146,000 residents.

The General Assembly used a special session to draw new districts following the 2000 census. The session was expected to be quite interesting because it included not only the General Assembly's districts but also Georgia's seats in the U.S. House of Representatives, which increased from eleven to thirteen as a result of population growth. As in most instances of redistricting, the majority party—in this case, the Democrats—drew maps designed to ensure the election of its candidates. Two federal lawsuits were filed that impacted Georgia's new districts. In the first, two dozen Republicans argued that the new plan violated one person, one vote principles. In an unrelated case, the U.S. Supreme Court established new standards for redistricting that required a review of the 2001 districts for the Georgia Senate.[7] The confusion surrounding the maps resulted in districts shifting before and after the 2002 elections, with final maps drawn not by the General Assembly but by a federal court just three months prior to the 2004 state primaries. Candidates who had represented districts for many years found that they no longer lived in their home districts and could not move in time to meet the twelve-month residency requirements for the 2004 elections.[8]

Redistricting controversies also affected the balance of power between the governor and Georgia's attorney general. Governor Sonny Perdue, a Republican, asked that a court case filed by the state regarding state Senate districts be withdrawn. Attorney General Thurbert Baker, a Democrat, refused to withdraw the suit, stating that the attorney general, not the governor, had the authority to make legal decisions for the state. The dispute ended up in court, and the Georgia Supreme Court decided in Baker's favor in September 2003.[9]

Qualifications of Members

Article 2, Section 2 of the Georgia Constitution requires that persons seeking office in the General Assembly be registered voters, U.S. citizens, and Georgia citizens for at least two years. It also mandates that representatives live within their districts for at least one year, a requirement that may force incumbents to run against each other after districts are redrawn. Those elected to the Senate must be at least twenty-five years old, whereas members of the House must be twenty-one or older. Persons may not simultaneously run for more than one office or in the primaries of two political parties. Also ineligible are persons on active military duty, those who hold other elected or civil offices within the state (unless they resign), and convicted felons. Therefore, members of the Georgia General Assembly may not hold other state or county offices or be employees of the state or faculty at state colleges or universities. However, people may serve on local school boards and run for the General

Assembly. A 1990 state law required candidates to pass a drug test, but the U.S. Supreme Court ruled this measure unconstitutional in 1997.[10]

Legislative Sessions

According to Article 5, Section 2 of the Georgia Constitution, the state legislature meets annually in regular session for forty legislative (not calendar) days beginning on the second Monday in January. The General Assembly may be called into special session by the governor, who sets the agenda, or by agreement of three-fifths of the members of each chamber. Special sessions may be called to deal with unexpected crises, such as natural disasters, budgetary shortfalls, or other state emergencies. Special sessions may not last longer than forty legislative days and generally cannot be used for matters unrelated to the official agenda.

Compensation

Article 2, Section 4 of the Georgia Constitution allows members of the General Assembly to set their salaries by law, although any raise cannot take effect until the term of office after the raise is approved. Setting salaries by law is the procedure in most states, although some set salaries in their constitutions, and twenty states use compensation commissions, at least in part, to set salaries or other compensation for legislators.[11]

According to the National Conference of State Legislatures, in 2005, members of the Georgia General Assembly received $16,524 per year plus mileage and expense allowances. Twenty-four states had annual legislative salaries higher than Georgia's, led by $110,800 per year in California, $79,650 in Michigan, and $79,500 in New York. Another four states paid legislators at least $50,000 annually, and an additional ten states had annual salaries of at least $30,000. On the other end of the spectrum were states that provided legislators only token payments, as in New Hampshire, where legislators received only $200 for their two-year term. Eight states paid a fixed amount for each day or week that the legislature was in session rather than an annual salary, including ten dollars per day (plus expense allowances) in Alabama.[12] Georgia legislators' salaries are tied to raises for state workers, with the lawmakers receiving half the percentage increase given to state employees. Thus, legislators set their own salaries indirectly for coming years when they include employee pay raises in the state budget.

Like all but six states, Georgia pays a per diem to legislators for expenses. In 2004, members of the General Assembly received $128 per day during the legislative session and for committee service when the legislature was not in session. In 2006, legislators increased their per diem to $178 to match federal rates. Long-distance telephone expenses are free, clerical help is provided, and each legislator receives an additional amount for general expenses.

The Georgia General Assembly: Characteristics of Members

The United States has nearly 7,400 state legislators (1,971 senators and 5,411 members of lower houses).[13] Among the significant characteristics of legislatures are turnover in membership, demographic characteristics, and partisan makeup. All of these have changed to some degree during the past generation, especially in Georgia.

Membership Turnover

State legislatures are relatively stable institutions, although turnover is higher in elections following redistricting. Vacancies can occur for several reasons, including death, resignation, retirement (for a host of reasons), defeat in a primary, and loss of a general election. One study discovered that lower-house turnover averaged 21 percent between 1984 and 1990. That research also found that 54.4 percent of new members in lower houses in 1979–1980 remained in office in 1983–1984, but only 27.1 percent remained as long as 1989–1990. In senates, 62.2 percent remained through 1983–1984 and 33.6 percent served through 1989–1990.[14]

In 1994, most turnover nationally occurred because legislators did not seek reelection. In only five bodies did less than 80 percent of incumbents running for reelection win: Missouri Senate (69 percent), Nevada Senate (75 percent), North Carolina House (74 percent), Washington House (74 percent), and Wyoming Senate (78 percent). Similarly, 20 percent of the seats in state legislatures changed hands between 1994 and 1996, although turnover was 30 percent or higher in Arizona, California, Idaho, Louisiana, Maine, New Hampshire, New Mexico, Oregon, and South Dakota. Redistricting occurred after the 2000 census, and of all seats up for election in 2002, turnover reached 33 percent in state senates and 27 percent in state houses.[15]

One of the major factors affecting turnover since the 1990s has been term limits. Beginning in 1990, when voters approved initiatives in California,

Colorado, and Oklahoma, a total of twenty-one states eventually limited the number of terms that people could serve in their legislatures. However, courts overturned term limits in four states, and they were repealed in Idaho and Utah. Thus, by 2005, just fifteen states had term limits. Still, term limits have shaken up the political landscape. They were first applied in 1996, when 26 of 151 House members and 4 of 35 senators in Maine could not seek reelection; in California, 22 of the 80 members of the Assembly (the lower house) had to relinquish their seats. In 1998, term limits forced the retirement of 50 of the 100 members in the Arkansas House and 63 of 110 members in the Michigan House. In 2000, half of the lower houses in Michigan and Florida were ineligible for reelection. For the 2002 election, 322 legislators in eleven states had to give up their seats; in 2004, the total was 262, including significant numbers of legislative leaders and committee chairs.[16]

Longevity has been somewhat higher in the Georgia General Assembly than in other state legislatures. Georgia has never adopted term limits for its 236 legislators. Sixty-six percent of the twenty-nine men and women newly elected to the House in 1979 remained in office during 1983–1984, as did 55.2 percent in 1989–1990. In the Senate, five of the six first-time senators in 1979 were still there in 1983–1984, but only one remained by 1989–1990.[17]

In Georgia, turnover has been associated with both partisan change and redistricting. Democrats maintained control of the General Assembly in the elections of 1998 (34–22 in the Senate, 102–78 House) and 2000 (32–24 Senate, 104–74 House), but the new century has accelerated change, especially with the redistricting that has occurred. In 2002, 10 of Georgia's 56 state senators did not appear on the November ballot, and another 6 lost in the general election. Those 16 new members represented a 29 percent turnover. Aided by the party switching of 4 senators, Republicans took control of the Senate (30–26) for the first time since Reconstruction. In the Georgia House, 40 of the 180 representatives did not make it to the general election in 2002, either because they gave up their seats or because they lost a primary. The remaining 140 incumbents all won reelection, however, producing a turnover rate of 22 percent, a surprisingly low figure for a redistricting year.

One factor in turnover in Georgia is the constant redistricting process. In 2000, 2002, and 2004, incumbents faced districts different from the ones that had elected them in the previous election cycle. For some incumbents, redistricting meant that they no longer even lived within district boundaries, and in last-minute changes in 2002, candidates were caught off guard by the requirements on length of residency. It was too late for the incumbents to move into the new boundaries of the districts they had represented in the past. Other incumbents realized that they would have to face off in elections with colleagues of their own party. Faced with changing their residence or rebuilding a base in a new district, many incumbents chose to retire. In 2004 alone, fifty seats were left open by retiring incumbents.[18]

Demographic and Occupational Characteristics

In addition to more first-time legislators, the 2004 elections brought other changes to the General Assembly (see figure 7.1). In the House, the 180 members included 34 women in 1993 and 36 in 1995. A decade later, that number had increased only to 37 (21 percent). The Georgia Senate included 7 women after the 2004 election, the same as after the 1994 election. Thus, 18.6 percent of the General Assembly was female in 2005, slightly below the national figure of 22.5 percent. In this measure, Georgia trailed Florida, North Carolina, and Texas but finished ahead of the other seven former Confederate states, including the national low of 10 percent in Alabama. Georgia is well below the high of 34 percent in Maryland and the other legislatures that were at least 30 percent female in March 2005: Arizona, California, Colorado, Delaware, Kansas, Nevada, New Hampshire, New Mexico, Vermont, and Washington.[19]

The number of blacks remained unchanged at 9 following the 1992 redistricting and elections for the Georgia Senate but increased to 31 in the House. After the 1994 elections, blacks added 1 seat in each chamber, for a total of 10 senators (18 percent) and 32 representatives (18 percent). Following the 2006 election, blacks again held 10 seats in the Senate (18 percent) but their number increased to 39 in the House (21.6 percent).[20] A generation earlier, of course, the institution included only whites.

At least one constant remains in the composition of Georgia's legislature—the presence of lawyers. In 1985, 46 of the General Assembly's 236 members were attorneys (19 percent); the next-largest occupations were farmers (27 members) and real estate professionals (26 members). The 1995 General Assembly included 45 lawyers (33 percent); 25 retirees; 13 members associated with real estate sales, development, construction, and contracting; and 16 working in insurance. In 2005, the General Assembly included at least 32 lawyers (14 percent), a figure exceeded by the 60 (25 percent) who

Figure 7.1. Composition of the Georgia General Assembly, by Race and Gender, 1990–2006

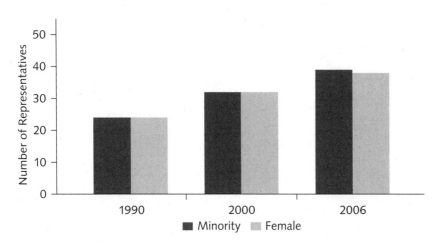

Source: Calculated by the authors from publications of Senate Public Information Office and House Public Information Office, Georgia General Assembly.

identified themselves as business owners, chief executive officers, or self-employed. The presence of business executives is probably much larger, but the reporting system treats separately professions such as consulting, while some members reported their field of work (for example, insurance) without indicating their ownership status. These patterns differ somewhat from those in the U.S. Congress, where 217 of the 535 representatives and senators in 2005 (41 percent) listed law as a previous occupation.[21]

Partisan Composition: The Rise of Georgia Republicans

Perhaps more startling than demographic shifts in the General Assembly have been partisan changes (see figure 7.2). Democrats dominated Georgia politics from the late 1800s into the 1980s. Republicans established a presence following Georgia's support for Republican presidential candidate Barry Goldwater in 1964, and slow but steady gains followed. Republicans held fewer than 20 percent of the seats in the General Assembly into the 1990s.

Following the 1992 election, the number of Republicans grew from 34 to 52 in the House (29 percent) and from 11 to 15 in the Senate (27 percent).

Figure 7.2. Partisan Affiliation, Georgia General Assembly, 1976–2006

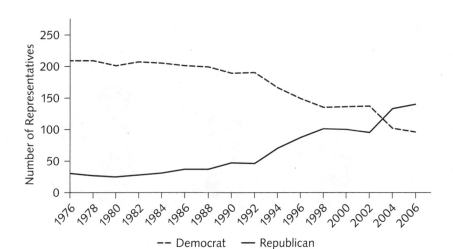

Source: Compiled by the authors from publications of Senate Public Information Office and House Public Information Office, Georgia General Assembly.

The GOP's share of seats increased slightly in 1994, 1996, 1998, and 2000. The real breakthroughs occurred in 2002 and 2004. Republicans, aided by 4 party switchers, gained control of the Senate in 2002, the same year that Sonny Perdue became Georgia's first Republican governor in more than a century. In 2004, Republicans expanded their control of the Senate from 30 to 34 seats (61 percent).

Going into the 2002 election, Democrats controlled the House 105–74 and saw almost no erosion in their share of seats. However, perhaps a harbinger of things to come was the general election defeat of Tom Murphy, a Democrat who had served as speaker of the House since 1973. In the 2004 election, the Republicans recorded huge gains to take control of the House, winning 96 seats and adding 2 party switchers, thereby gaining control of both houses of the legislature to complement a Republican in the governor's mansion.[22]

In 2006, Republicans made small inroads, maintaining their steady progress. What makes this a particularly noteworthy accomplishment for the Republicans is that it is counter to the trend seen in other states in 2006, when Democrats gained control of a majority of state legislatures. In fact, many observers note that Georgia may be one of the strongest Republican states in the union.[23]

Legislative Leadership

Article 3, Section 3 of the Georgia Constitution provides for the selection of presiding officers in each chamber. In the Senate, the lieutenant governor serves as president, just as the vice president of the United States is formally the presiding officer of the U.S. Senate. Thus, the presiding officer of the Senate is chosen by Georgia's voters in a statewide election, although the winner is elected independently of the governor. The Georgia Senate also elects one of its members as president pro tempore should the presiding officer require replacement. In the House, the representatives elect a speaker from among their members along with a speaker pro tempore.

Legislative leadership in Georgia resembles that in most states. Forty-two states have a lieutenant governor, with twenty-four elected on a ticket with the governor and eighteen elected independently. All lieutenant governors are first in line to succeed to the governorship in their states, but their power in the legislative branch varies. Twenty-nine states in addition to Georgia (including Nebraska's unicameral legislature) make the lieutenant governor the presiding officer of the Senate. In the remaining twenty-four states, the Senate chooses its own presiding officer.[24] Like Georgia, the lower house in the other forty-eight bicameral legislatures elects one of its members as speaker. Twenty-five of these forty-eight states also elect a speaker pro tempore; the other twenty-three legislatures either have no such position or have their speaker appoint someone.

Informal norms sometimes guide leadership selection. One study that examined legislative leadership in the states over almost fifty years found that twenty-eight lower houses and thirty-three senates had a norm of one or two terms for leaders from 1947 until 1968. From 1968 through 1980, three or four terms became more common in both chambers. From 1981 to 1992, twelve lower houses had a norm of presiding officers serving five or more terms; the same was true of eighteen senates. Georgia is one of a handful of states where long service as a presiding officer was a norm from 1947 to 1992.[25]

Party Caucuses

In reality, party members generally make decisions on leadership positions before the session begins. A meeting of Republican legislators in each chamber—the House Republican Caucus and the Senate Republican Caucus—elects its party's leaders. Democratic caucuses do likewise for their House and Senate leaders. For example, Republican senators chose their leadership for the 1995 session the week of the November 1994 elections, while House members picked their leaders the week after the election—roughly two months before the General Assembly convened. In 2002, when Republicans won control of the Senate, the longtime Democratic speaker of the House, Tom Murphy, was defeated for reelection. Although behind-the-scenes campaigning occurred among caucus members, House Democrats chose their leaders less than two weeks after the November 5 election, with Representative Terry Coleman officially elected speaker after the House began its new session the following January. In the Senate, Republicans also moved quickly to choose their leaders for the session that would start two months later.[26]

Members of each caucus are expected to remain loyal to their party nominee when floor votes are taken for presiding officers. Thus, a nomination by the majority party caucus is tantamount to election on the floor. Party caucuses also meet to discuss official positions on major issues and to set priorities. Leaders of the caucuses influence the legislature's agenda by devising strategies, promoting party positions on bills, and using the media to promote their goals.

Leadership in the House of Representatives

The Speaker. The speaker of the House has broad powers going beyond those officially granted to the office, including the ability to change the order of bills appearing on the calendar and to control floor debate through recognition of members, suspension of debate, and decisions about the appropriateness of amendments. The speaker may also maintain order on the floor, require attendance by members to obtain a quorum, and control activity in the visitors' galleries. In addition, the speaker is second in line to succeed the governor, after the lieutenant governor.

Perhaps the speaker's greatest power is the ability to appoint the members of the committees that will review and draft legislation. The speaker also determines the committees to which bills are sent for review. These powers provide House members with strong incentives to cooperate with the speaker. The speaker may attend any and all committee meetings as an ex-officio member and is a voting member of the powerful Rules Committee. In general, the speaker does not vote on bills as do other members of the House. There are four instances in which a speaker may vote during the floor debate: (1) when the House is tied on any floor vote, (2) when a requirement for a two-thirds or three-fifths vote is short by one vote, (3) when the speaker's vote would cause a tie, or (4) when the House is holding an internal election.

Longevity can increase the speaker's unofficial power, as in the case of Murphy. The House changed dramatically during Murphy's tenure, and he withstood several attacks on his power and prerogatives, especially in the early 1990s. Opponents accused him of being both dictatorial and vengeful; supporters viewed him as someone who maintained order and stability in the 180-member House as the institution and the state changed over the years. These concerns were heightened at the end of the 1994 legislative session when the seventy-year-old speaker suffered a heart attack. He finally lost power when his constituents turned him out of office in 2002 by nine hundred votes out of almost twelve thousand cast.

In the speaker's absence, the speaker pro tempore, who is elected by the membership of the House, presides. The speaker may appoint other members to preside temporarily over the House as needed. Whenever presiding over the House, the speaker pro tempore or other representatives hold the same powers of debate regulation as the speaker.

Other Leadership Positions. Another powerful office is that of majority leader, who is chosen by the party caucus. The majority leader and caucus officers may also assist the speaker in determining the party's position on important issues. Party whips are elected to assist in this process and may be instrumental in convincing other party members to vote along party lines.

The minority leader, caucus officers, and minority party whip are chosen by the caucus and perform much the same duties as their majority party counterparts. Naturally, the minority party exerts less influence within the chamber than does the majority party.

Unlike the lack of formal links between the U.S. president and Congress, in Georgia one member in each chamber serves as liaison to the governor's office. The governor picks the administration floor leader in the House, who may introduce or sponsor measures from the governor's legislative agenda.

Leadership in the Senate

The Lieutenant Governor. The leadership in the Senate in many ways resembles that of the House, but important differences exist and can be attributed to the smaller size of the Senate and its constitutional mandates. Unlike the speaker of the House, the lieutenant governor is not elected from a district but by statewide vote, which makes the position fairly visible to the electorate. As presiding officer, the lieutenant governor is referred to as president of the Senate. Unlike the speaker, the president of the Senate may not vote under any circumstances.

The long dominance of the Democratic Party once guaranteed that the presiding officer and majority of members in the Senate came from the same political party. Duties included assigning senators to committees, referring bills to committee, and controlling debate and order on the Senate floor. The authority of lieutenant governors represents a combination of constitutional provisions, laws, and Senate rules. This became painfully obvious to Democratic Lieutenant Governor Mark Taylor following the November 2002 elections. The new Republican majority changed Senate rules to remove the lieutenant governor's control over committee assignments and diminish the office's authority in other ways. In 2005, after the Republicans also gained a majority in the House, the new speaker denied Taylor the traditional role of presiding over the joint session of the House and Senate that hears the governor's annual State of the State speech.[27] Following the 2006 election of Republican Casey Cagle as lieutenant governor, Republican leaders announced the restoration of these powers to the office.

Other Leadership Positions. The president pro tempore, who is elected from the majority party, can fill in as presiding officer. The Senate also has the positions of majority and minority leader as well as majority and minority whip. As in the House, these positions are selected by the party caucuses, which also select senators to chair the caucuses, develop their parties' positions on important issues, and try to persuade senators to vote the party line on bills. As in the House, the administration floor leader designated by the governor introduces the governor's legislative agenda in the Senate.

Legislative Staff

Staffing in state legislatures differs dramatically from congressional staffing. In 2004, twenty-six of the fifty states provided senators with year-round personal staff, primarily at the state Capitol. The other states provided year-round shared staff at the Capitol or gave senators shared or personal staff only during the legislative session. A similar pattern existed among the forty-nine lower houses: twenty-three states had year-round personal staff at the Capitol, in the district, or both. Far more common is the assignment of permanent staff to committees and chamber or party leaders. The fifty states had just over 28,000 permanent staff members in 2003, a slight increase from 1988 and 1996 but 66 percent higher than the almost 17,000 permanent staffers in 1979. The flip side of this growth is a decline in session-only staff in the states from slightly more than 10,000 in 1979 to 6,912 in 2003. Altogether, state legislatures utilized 34,979 staff members in 2003, ranging from a high of 3,428 in New York to lows of 75 in South Dakota and 82 in Vermont. Staff totals amounted to fewer than 200 in another eight states and to more than 1,000 in six more.[28]

The Georgia General Assembly furnishes its members with limited staff support. Both the House and the Senate are assisted by personnel who provide a wide variety of services—messengers, clerks, doorkeepers, and others. They generally are assisted by student interns during the legislative session. These housekeeping duties are not taken lightly. The clerk of the House and the secretary of the Senate are charged with filing all papers necessary for the proper functioning of the chambers. They compile the House and Senate journals after the close of the session and manage other necessary clerical functions.

The Georgia General Assembly also has professional staff positions designed to deal with the complex duties and diverse policy questions that come before the legislature. This expertise is concentrated in research and budget offices in each chamber. Staffing was also affected by the 2002 election results. The new speaker in the Democratic-controlled House added a press secretary, policy analyst, and administrator to his staff. After the Republicans won their first majority in the Senate in more than a century, they created a separate budget office rather than share one with the Democratic House. Republican Senate leaders added other staff positions as well. All of these changes reflect both new leaders and efforts by the two parties to bolster their ability to contend with each other. In the end, the National Conference of State Legislatures reported that in 2003, the General Assembly had 603 permanent staff as well as 220 session-only staff, ranking Georgia twelfth among the states in the total number of legislative staff. The 2003 total of 823 staff members shows steady growth from 742 in 1996, 679 in 1988, and 600 in 1979.[29]

The Committee System

Comparing the Fifty States. Committees have become key parts of the way modern legislatures organize to do their work, but substantial differences exist among the states. In 2005, the number of senate committees ranged from four to thirty-nine, while house committees varied between six and forty-five. Six states utilize standing committees made up of house and senate members. These joint committees are a major reason several legislatures have very few standing committees in each chamber. Committee systems also vary in how members and chairpersons are selected. Of the fifty senates in 2005, fifteen had presiding officers appoint committees, while the remainder used a range of other procedures. In thirty-eight of the forty-nine lower houses, the speaker appointed committee members. The remainder relied on one or more of the following: committees, shared responsibility between the speaker and minority leader, party caucuses, and seniority. Slightly less variation occurred in the methods for choosing which members would chair committees. Seventeen of the senates had presiding officers pick committee chairs, while forty-two of the forty-nine lower houses gave this responsibility to the speaker.[30] This system displays the unusual power of presiding officers in state legislatures, which may be based in part on the need to get work done during limited sessions and the parties' desire to promote an agenda when they are in the majority.

Georgia: Types of Committees. The Georgia Constitution permits each chamber of the General Assembly to set its own procedures. It would be difficult for each member to be highly prepared on every issue that comes before the legislature, and it would be impossible to conduct debate on issues with everyone included in all discussions, particularly given the General Assembly's large size and brief sessions.[31] Therefore, standing (permanent) committees have been established to deal with issues that require regular attention. In 2005, the House operated with thirty-five committees, and the Senate had twenty-four (see table 7.2). House committees are generally larger, with the Appropriations Committee having sixty-eight members in 2005; Senate committees have an established size of between four and twenty-eight members. Senators serve on four to six committees; representatives normally are assigned to three or four committees.

All members of the House or Senate may occasionally have an interest in an upcoming piece of legislation or other important matter. In such cases,

Table 7.2. Standing Committees of the Georgia General Assembly, 2006

Senate	House of Representatives
Agriculture and Consumer Affairs	Agriculture and Consumer Affairs
Appropriations	Appropriations
Banking and Financial Institutions	Banks and Banking
Economic Development	Children and Youth
Education and Youth	Defense and Veterans Affairs
Ethics	Economic Development and Tourism
Finance	Education
Health and Human Services	Ethics
Higher Education	Game, Fish, and Parks
Insurance and Labor	Governmental Affairs
Interstate Cooperation	Health and Human Services
Judiciary	Higher Education
Natural Resources and the Environment	Human Relations and Aging
Public Safety and Homeland Security	Industrial Relations
Reapportionment and Redistricting	Information and Audits
Regulated Industries and Utilities	Insurance
Retirement	Intergovernmental Coordination
Rules	Interstate Cooperation
Science and Technology	Judiciary
Special Judiciary	Judiciary, Non-Civil
State and Local Government Operations	Legislative and Congressional
State Institutions and Property	Reapportionment
Transportation	MARTOC (oversight of MARTA)
Veterans and Military Affairs	Motor Vehicles
	Natural Resources and the Environment
	Public Safety
	Public Utilities and Telecommunications
	Regulated Industries
	Retirement
	Rules
	Science and Technology
	Special Rules
	State Institutions and Property
	State Planning and Community Affairs
	Transportation
	Ways and Means

Sources: Georgia House of Representatives, "2005–2006 House Committees" (http://www.legis.state.ga.us/legis/2005_06/house/commroster.htm); Georgia Senate, "Senate Committees List" (http://www.legis.state.ga.us/legis/2005_06/senate/index.htm).

the entire chamber may relax parliamentary procedure and meet as one large committee. The Committee of the Whole permits less formal procedures and more open discussion. At the other extreme, a committee of one may be appointed to permit a single legislator to receive a per diem allowance while conducting research on a bill, writing a report, or performing other official business, even when the legislature is out of session. Committees of one are temporary assignments.

Some committees include members of both the House and the Senate. These are joint committees and may be standing or ad hoc. Georgia has fewer joint standing committees and relies on them less than do other states, but on occasion they can reduce confusion between the chambers and iron out differences between standing committees before legislation is drafted. Joint committees are especially useful in the budget process, where time is an important factor. Conference committees are temporary joint committees formed when bills passing the House and Senate differ in language or intent. In such cases, compromises must be made to ensure that both chambers will consider the same bill for passage.

Committee Membership and Leaders. Members of House and Senate committees generally retain their assignments until they request another assignment or vacate their seats. Leadership within the committees is not guaranteed, however, and is appointed in the House by the speaker. When Republicans gained control of the House in the 2004 election, they adopted several innovations to the committee system designed to enhance the power of their leadership. Perhaps the most visible and controversial was the speaker's authority to designate an unlimited number of "hawks." Like the speaker, speaker pro tempore, majority leader, and majority whip, hawks were considered ex officio members of all House committees and subcommittees. All of these party leaders had committee voting rights with the exception of the speaker, who was allowed to vote only in the Rules Committee. Thus, if legislation favored by party leaders encountered trouble in committee, they could mobilize the hawks. As one might expect, House Democrats reacted negatively to this flexible definition of committee membership.[32]

The lieutenant governor lost the authority to control committee appointments as president of the Senate in 2003, when Democrat Mark Taylor faced the new Republican majority. The Committee on Assignments, which includes the lieutenant governor, the president pro tempore, and the majority leader, now selects committee members and leaders. This arrangement has left the Republicans with a two-to-one majority on this crucial committee.[33] Committee leadership is exercised by a chair, vice chair, and secretary (the important exception here is the House Appropriations Committee, which operated with six vice chairs in 2005). Committee and subcommittee chairs are aware that their positions depend on continued good relations with the chamber leadership.

In addition to standing committees, other committees may be formed to deal with issues on an ad hoc basis. These temporary committees may be formed to watch over the implementation of a new bill or to deal with a one-time-only project such as the 1996 Olympics. Interim committees are established between sessions to investigate issues or to write reports that will be presented to the entire chamber when it is again in session. These committees disband when their tasks are complete, and members are not guaranteed continued assignment on future committees.

Committees and Legislators' Goals. Committees do more than allow legislatures to work more efficiently. They also provide a way for legislators to pursue re-election, issues that are important for their districts, policies they consider important, and a variety of other goals. Although committee assignments allow members to develop expertise, specialization has been criticized on occasion as a conflict of interest when members sit on committees related to their occupations or businesses. Committee work also can help legislators obtain campaign funds from interest groups. Committees also permit legislators to use "pork barrel" politics—legislation that can provide benefits for specific constituencies. Traditional examples include public works projects such as highways.

The House Higher Education Committee, for example, has jurisdiction over the thirty-five colleges and universities in the University System of Georgia, the more than sixty campuses under the Department of Technical and Adult Education, and the HOPE Scholarship Program. In 2005–2006, the committee had seventeen members (nine Republicans and eight Democrats). Perhaps more interesting than the committee's partisan makeup was its geography. The Democrats came from districts that included Georgia Tech, the University of Georgia, Valdosta State University, Georgia Southwestern State University, Columbus State University, and Augusta State University. The Augusta representative's district was next to one that included the Medical

College of Georgia. In addition, the Democrat from Jonesboro had a district next to one that included Clayton State University, and another member's district included a private institution, Emory University.

The nine Republicans represented districts without large institutions. The committee chair came from Douglasville, home to one of the four campuses of West Central Technical College. One member's district included North Georgia College and State University, another represented the district with Waycross College, and the vice chair's district was home to South Georgia College. The remaining Republicans included one from Cobb County, one from Rockdale County, and two from Gwinnett County. These four members may not have had readily apparent interests within their districts, but their areas had important technical colleges. In addition, the General Assembly approved legislation in 2005 to create a state college at a site in Gwinnett County where several state institutions were offering programs and degrees. Moreover, students from Cobb and Gwinnett Counties were the two largest beneficiaries of HOPE Scholarship dollars, with upward of $470 million awarded to more than 105,000 students from September 1993 through May 2005. Fulton County students ranked third in the state, receiving almost $211 million during this period but with a smaller share of students using their awards to attend University System institutions. The ninth Republican was from Griffin, where the University of Georgia's College of Agricultural and Environmental Sciences has operated a campus for many years and where degrees were offered starting in 2005.[34]

Types of Legislation

Like other legislatures, the Georgia General Assembly spends significant time considering bills introduced by its members in hopes that they will be passed and become part of state law. Bills before the General Assembly can be classified as resolutions, general legislation, and local legislation.[35] All currently enforceable statutes are published in the *Official Code of Georgia Annotated,* which is updated periodically to include both new laws and legal opinions on implementation of current law.[36]

Resolutions. Much of what the General Assembly considers is not intended to be implemented as statute. Some of the items brought up for consideration are statements of legislative opinion and may be enforceable only on the membership of the legislature itself. For example, the legislature may wish to honor an individual or a sports team, in which case the General Assembly might pass a resolution describing the honoree's achievements. Resolutions also might be used to create special committees, determine compensation for citizens who have been injured or suffered damages by state actions, or set requirements for legislative staff. The resolution has little impact on other citizens of the state but does express the approval of the state government.

Resolutions might be passed to require the General Assembly itself to behave in a specific manner, as with rules of conduct, scheduling, or agreements on budgetary matters. In some cases, one chamber passes resolutions to establish rules only for its members, but joint resolutions require passage by both chambers, as in the case of budgetary resolutions. Resolutions generally do not require the governor's signature since they do not involve implementation outside the legislature, although they might be passed in much the same way as other legislation. However, joint resolutions that are enforceable as law require the governor's signature and may be vetoed.

Proposed amendments to the Georgia Constitution are special cases of joint resolutions that must receive favorable votes from two-thirds of each chamber. The proposed amendments are then placed on the ballot for public approval by a majority of the voters. The governor has no formal role in this process but may exercise influence in proposing amendments and mobilizing public opinion before the referendum.

General Legislation. General legislation has application statewide—for example, laws regarding election procedures or speed limits on state highways. Local governments may not pass ordinances that contradict general law. Most general legislation intended to change existing law will specify exactly which statutes will be changed, but any new legislation supersedes past legislation. For this reason, the passage date may be important. Only the most recently passed legislation remains applicable.

Local Legislation. Local legislation refers to those laws passed by the Georgia General Assembly that apply only to specific cities, counties, or special districts within the state. The General Assembly retains the power to govern localities through the passage of local legislation, which Article 3, Section 5 of the Georgia Constitution specifies may not contradict general legislation and may not be used to change the tenure of particular local officials. Local legislation can, however, create or change political boundaries.

The passage of local legislation differs in some ways from the passage of general law. Local bills must be preceded by a period of advertisement in which citizens of the jurisdiction concerned are notified of the potential law—usually in local newspapers. Legislators from the district(s) involved generally speak on the floor of the legislature, and other lawmakers normally defer to them because the bill typically affects only the districts of members sponsoring the local bill. This pattern of local courtesy is reciprocal. For this reason, most local legislation passes without dissent. Unlike the required three readings of general bills, local legislation requires only one reading, and sometimes only the title is read. Because so little debate takes place, the General Assembly at times votes on several local matters at once.

The Georgia General Assembly is notable for its involvement in local matters and limited grant of authority to local governments (see chapter 9). As a result, local legislation comprises a large share of the statutes adopted by the legislature (see table 7.3). Georgia ranks in the middle of the states in legislative workload: twenty-eight legislatures considered more bills than the 1,437 that came before the Georgia General Assembly in 2003, including more than 14,000 in New York, more than 11,000 in New Jersey, and more than 5,500 each in Illinois, Massachusetts, and Texas.[37]

How a Bill Becomes a Law

This section describes the path that a bill follows from introduction in the House of Representatives to enactment as law, in accordance with Article 3, Section 5 of the Georgia Constitution. Not all legislation will follow all of these steps outlined; in fact, most legislation stalls early in the process, but all contingencies are covered here to provide a complete description.

Introduction and Referral

All legislation starts out as an idea conceived by legislators or brought to them by lobbyists, other politicians, private citizens, corporations, or interest groups. Only members of the General Assembly may introduce legislation. Bills generally are written by several persons and may be sponsored

Table 7.3. Bills Introduced and Passed in Regular Sessions of the Georgia General Assembly, 1980–2004

Year	Total # Bills Introduced	# Bills Passed			Local Acts as % of Total Bills Passed
		General	Local	Total	
1980	1,817	419	347	766	45.3
1981	1,598	353	486	839	57.9
1982	1,891	358	395	753	52.4
1983	1,199	310	273	583	46.8
1984	1,658	385	398	783	50.8
1985	1,429	344	430	774	55.5
1986	1,893	381	532	913	58.2
1987	1,574	352	456	808	56.4
1988	1,781	427	266	693	38.3
1989	1,542	404	310	714	43.4
1990	1,316	437	332	769	43.2
1991	1,556	374	234	608	38.5
1992	1,497	507	363	870	41.7
1993	1,559	327	305	632	48.3
1994	1,239	354	300	654	45.9
1995	1,575	298	222	520	42.7
1996	1,121	338	225	563	40.0
1997	1,515	298	213	511	41.7
1998	2,117	306	218	524	41.6
1999	1,386	219	242	461	52.5
2000	1,836	333	170	503	33.8
2001	1,290	205	191	396	48.2
2002	2,014	256	365	621	58.8
2003	1,437	199	215	414	51.9
2004	2,038	208	186	394	47.2
TOTAL	39,878	8,392	7,674	16,066	47.8

Source: Georgia General Assembly, Legislative Services Committee and Office of Legislative Counsel, Summary of General Statutes Enacted, 1980–2004.

by multiple legislators. The legislative staff or the Legislative Research Office may assist in the drafting of a bill. In some instances, Georgians may use legislation passed by other states as a model. Bills may be introduced in either chamber of the General Assembly or at the same time in both chambers. One exception to this is proposed legislation dealing with public revenues or appropriation of public money, which is constitutionally mandated to begin in the House of Representatives.

Bills to be introduced are filed with the clerk of the House of Representatives. Bills must adhere to a specific format dictated by the constitution and observed procedures. Each bill begins "BE IT ENACTED BY THE GENERAL ASSEMBLY OF GEORGIA" and has a summary title that describes the bill's intent. The title of the bill must directly relate to the content of the proposed legislation, and bills are constitutionally restricted to no more than one purpose. The Georgia Constitution mandates that all bills be read three times from the floor on three separate days. Because the title is required to be a summary of intent, reading the title only substitutes for reading the entire bill. A second reading of the bill two days after introduction will also be of the title only. The Constitution forbids the introduction of bills that deal with specific individuals or that might limit the General Assembly's constitutional authority. Article 3, Section 6 also forbids population bills (those that apply to jurisdictions of a certain population) and bills that would have the effect of limiting business competition or creating monopolies within the state.

After a bill is introduced in the House, the speaker determines which committee will review the proposal. Because committee jurisdictions overlap to some degree, the speaker's choice of a committee has some influence on a bill's outcome. The speaker may choose to give a bill to a committee that is likely to receive it favorably, amend it in certain ways, or even kill it.

Committee Action

Once assigned to a committee, the bill may be referred to a subcommittee, where a smaller number of legislators might have more time to devote to its content. Not all bills are referred to subcommittees, however. Whether a committee or subcommittee works on the legislation, a number of courses may be followed at this stage. Public hearings may be held on the proposed legislation. Lobbyists or other interested parties may testify regarding the bill's potential impact or the need for more legislation in a particular area. The media may follow the bill at this stage, and Article 3, Section 4, Paragraph 11 of the state constitution requires that the public be permitted to attend committee meetings. Such "sunshine laws" are designed to allow public scrutiny at this stage of lawmaking, which generally occurs outside of the public's view. The committee or subcommittee may determine that further study is necessary, or members may decide that the legislation is unnecessary or undesirable, in which case it will not be acted on further. They may also recommend that a bill be passed or amended. In some instances, the bill will go forward from the committee with a recommendation that it not be passed by the full chamber. A bill reported unfavorably indicates some disagreement within the committee and that at least one legislator is confronting the majority. Such action would not be taken lightly, as it might have negative political consequences.

On occasion, legislators who do not serve on the committee considering a bill might have an interest in its passage. In such instances, a motion may be made on the floor of the House to bring the bill to a floor vote, even over the committee's objections. These motions represent a clear challenge to the committee leaders' decisions and must be supported by at least two-thirds of the members present.[38] Forcing a bill out of committee does not ensure its passage, and bills sent to the floor may simply be referred to other committees, in which case the process begins again. The Senate does not permit such floor challenges, and committees may choose not to act on any bills in their jurisdiction.

Scheduling Floor Debate

After a bill has made its way out of committee, it must be placed on the calendar to receive attention on the floor. In the first half of the legislative session, placement of a bill on the calendar is achieved through the General Calendar of the clerk of the House, but as the session progresses, time on the floor becomes more strictly guarded. During the final twenty days of the session, the House Rules Committee meets daily to set the Rules Calendar, a list of which bills will be discussed on the floor that day. The Rules Committee may select for daily consideration any bill that has been reported favorably by a standing committee. Thus, the Rules Committee may decide that the House never acts on a particular piece of legislation, even if a standing committee favors it. Members of the Rules Committee therefore hold substantial power over legislation, especially because most committees do not finish work on many bills early enough in the session to place them on the General Calendar. The chairs of the Rules Committees in both chambers are strong political forces in the General Assembly: little legislation that does not meet their approval is likely to pass. Moreover, in the House, the speaker is a voting member on the Rules Committee: the speaker's attendance at Rules Committee meetings clearly indicates that the speaker wants certain bills to appear on the calendar.

Floor Action

After being placed on the calendar and called up for discussion, bills are read on the floor for the third time. At this point, members are free to propose amendments and debate various issues relative to the bill's content. Debate is controlled by the presiding officer of each chamber. Restrictions on debate time are set by House and Senate rules, and there is no provision for filibuster. Those legislators who wish to speak on the merits or disadvantages of a bill must obtain permission from the presiding officer, who may allow questions from the floor. The chair of the committee that reported the bill receives a special allocation of time to discuss the bill, and dissenting opinions also have floor time prior to the vote.

Bills are passed by a simple majority of the entire membership of each chamber, although several exceptions to this rule exist. Tax legislation, proposed amendments to the Constitution, veto overrides, punitive action against a member of the General Assembly, and motions to change the order of business require two-thirds majorities. Procedural changes may require only a majority of those members present. In most instances, votes are taken using electronic voting boxes located on legislators' desks. At other times, votes are taken by voice or a show of hands. Voice votes generally are used for less controversial issues, as are votes by hand counts. In some cases, a roll call vote may be taken in which legislators are individually called on to respond "Yea" or "Nay." For important voting procedures, such as a veto override, both electronic and roll call voting may be used. After a bill has achieved a majority vote in one chamber, it must be passed in identical form by a majority vote in the other chamber to continue on the path to becoming a law.

Bills are transmitted from one chamber to another after careful proofreading. Transmittal is a formal procedure governed by strict rules and normally takes several days. During the more frantic days of the session, transmittal of bills may be expedited. In one famous 1964 effort to beat the deadline for the end of the session, a legislator hung from the balcony to stop the hands of the clock just before midnight. Although he did not fall, his precarious position caused him to knock the clock off the wall and break it, thus allowing debate to continue. In later interviews, one of his colleagues admitted, "We'd been imbibing."[39] To prevent a logjam of legislation in the final days, the Senate will not accept House bills after the thirty-third day of the session. The House has no such constraint, but its rules recognize the need to deal with the Senate's limitation. This date is known as "Crossover Day" because it is the last time a bill can cross over between the two chambers for a first reading to be considered during the session.[40]

In most cases, bills passed by the Senate and those passed by the House are similar but not identical. The presiding officers of the House and Senate then bring together a conference committee to work out the differences between the two versions of the bill. This committee may comprise members of the standing committees that previously had jurisdiction over the bill, but it must include only legislators who voted in favor of the bill's passage. Conference committees may recommend substantial changes in the bill but may not deviate from the bill's original intent. They also must act quickly and may not report a bill back to either floor of the General Assembly with an unfavorable recommendation.

When a conference committee has worked out the final language of a bill, it must again receive a majority in each chamber. This final passage must produce an identical bill passed by a majority of the House and a majority of the Senate. The final version is then certified by the clerk of the House and the secretary of the Senate prior to being sent to the governor. Failure by either chamber to pass the conference committee's version of a bill generally spells its death. In some cases, the conference committee may again be asked to rework the bill for further consideration.

The Governor

Article 3, Section 5 of the Georgia Constitution gives the governor authority to act on legislation passed by the General Assembly that would have the effect of law, except for changes in the Constitution. If the governor signs the bill, it becomes law on a specified date—usually July 1, the start of the fiscal year. If the governor fails to act on a bill, it will become law following a six-day waiting period (for bills passed during the first thirty-four days of the session) or following a forty-day waiting period (for bills passed during the final six days of the legislative session). Thus, bills may sit on the governor's desk after adjournment of the legislature and become law even if the governor does not sign them. In some cases, the governor will veto legislation. If the governor vetoes a bill after the adjournment of the General Assembly, the next legislative session may take up action on the veto.

Like forty-two other states, Georgia provides for two types of vetoes, full and item (often called line-item veto), although Georgia's item veto applies only to appropriations bills.[41] A full veto is a rejection of an entire bill. The governor will transmit a vetoed bill back to the legislature with an explanation of the objections. The General Assembly is then free to either modify the bill to meet the governor's expectations or to try to override the governor's veto with a two-thirds majority in each chamber. Veto overrides are not easily accomplished, and the General Assembly has not overridden the full veto of any governor since 1974.

Item vetoes are rejections of specific passages in appropriations bills. Reconsideration of bills in which specific funding has been vetoed is not necessary, and the governor's actions officially reduce the appropriation. Thus, the item veto can be a tool to enhance a governor's power vis-à-vis the legislature. For example, Governor Zell Miller vetoed a 1992 line item for $479,479 that was listed under the Education Department's budget for "special projects." Miller indicated that the vague entry left him unable to determine how the money was to be used. Subsequent investigation of this expenditure revealed that over the preceding six years, the speaker of the House and other key legislators had maintained control of approximately $2.5 million in public money, spending much of it in their home districts without the governor's approval. While the media attention surrounding this disclosure labeled it a "slush fund," the attorney general's office took no legal action.[42]

As is true in the legislature, the end of the session is a busy time for the governor, with many pieces of legislation reaching the governor's desk at the same time. At the end of the 1992 session, Governor Miller signed more than one hundred pieces of legislation in a single day, almost half of the total for that session.[43] After a bill has been signed into law, it takes precedence over previous legislation. Exceptions to the July effective date for laws are bills that specify another date, local bills, constitutional amendments, or resolutions that deal with the operation of state government agencies or budgets.

Factors Influencing the Legislative Process

The legislative process involves more than constitutional or legal requirements. Of the many actions that can affect the legislative process, two of the important ones are the pressures brought to bear by lobbying and the norms that affect legislators' behavior.

Lobbying

Interest groups have an important role in the political process (see chapter 5). All interest groups have the same goal—creating and maintaining policy in accord with their objectives—and work in all three branches of government to do so. An organization's ability to influence public policy depends on the number of people or other resources it possesses, its organization, its cohesion, and other factors.

Lobbying got its name from the fact that many policy advocates would wait outside the floor of legislature chambers—in the lobbies—to speak to legislators before they cast votes. Although lobbyists are not permitted on the floor of the Georgia House or Senate, representatives from organized groups still wait to speak to legislators in the Capitol's corridors. The lobbying process has had rather negative connotations and was declared unconstitutional in Georgia prior to the implementation of the 1983 Constitution. The definition of what should be considered lobbying was left to the legislature, and the practice existed despite its supposed unconstitutionality.

Lobbyists in the Georgia Legislature. In Georgia, lobbyists were divided for many years into two camps: urban and agricultural interests. By the 1990s, a coalition interested in economic development blurred some of the boundaries between these two groups, and an economic growth lobby became a driving force in Georgia politics. Economic development is so widely accepted as a governmental function that it may be impossible to separate the interests of government from economic growth. Business groups commonly have ties to the legislative committees that regulate them.[44] Recent actions suggest that this business coalition remains quite successful in the legislative process.

Some observers argue that the growth of the economic development lobby is beneficial because it has diminished urban-rural and racial divisions. Those representing other interests might not evaluate the political scene as optimistically. For example, social welfare lobbyists are less likely to succeed in Georgia's political climate for a number of reasons. First, Georgians are often wary of social welfare spending by government. Second, the Georgia Constitution requires a balanced budget, and programs that operate on public funds must fight vigorously for budgetary allocations. Finally, social welfare groups have traditionally had less success in building coalitions with legislators than have economic development lobbyists. Environmental groups have faced similar obstacles to success.

Government agencies also have a vested interest in public policy. For example, the Department of Corrections has a strong interest in decisions regarding the staffing, funding, and operation of prisons. Agencies lobby for policy through their interaction with lawmakers, their influence on the information available to the legislature, and their prestige as experts and government officials. Some evidence indicates that agencies are more influential when they can provide services or projects for legislators' districts or help with constituent concerns.[45]

Success for lobbyists depends in part on effective use of time, money, and information. In general terms, that phenomenon has translated into campaign contributions and other benefits to legislators. Such established relationships permit long-term lobbyists a head start on their competition. One analysis found that interest groups spent more than $900,000 lobbying the legislature in 2004, including more than $780,000 for entertainment and nearly $30,000 for tickets to sporting events. Efforts included individual meals and huge social events, plus free food and beverages at the Capitol provided by the Georgia Association of Convenience Stores. During 2004, the Georgia Chamber of Commerce, Georgia Soft Drink Association, and Coca-Cola each spent more than $20,000 on lobbying; Georgia Power spent almost $44,000; and the Savannah Chamber of Commerce emerged as the big spender at $50,024. Entertainment spending has been complemented in recent years by more grassroots mobilization, including efforts by educators, environmentalists, and Christian conservatives. With limited staff resources, legislators often rely on lobbyists and interest group members for information.[46]

Lobbying Regulation. Lobbyists attempting to influence public policy in Georgia must register for each legislative session and pay a filing fee to the five-member State Ethics Commission, which was created by the 1986 Ethics in Government Act. While in the Capitol building, lobbyists must wear identification badges that identify them as "Lobbyist" and disclose their organization. Statements must be filed to delineate an organization's purposes and expenses.

Critics have expressed concern over practices such as providing meals, entertainment, and travel for legislators. Others have complained about the "revolving door" through which former officials turn to lobbying when they leave government service. However, prior to the 1992 session, Georgia's lobbying laws were among the least restrictive in the fifty states. Media reports linked a bill passed in the legislature to international money laundering and a Georgia-based bank. This coverage and efforts by Georgia Secretary of State Max Cleland helped lead to increased control of lobbying. These initiatives received strong support from "good government" groups and some members of the media. Lawmakers were greatly divided, however, but despite objections by House Speaker Tom Murphy, an ethics bill passed. The measure limited lobbyists' campaign contributions, clarified the state's bribery laws, and for the first time required lobbyists to disclose what they spent to influence legislation.[47]

Even with the changes adopted in 1992, Georgia remained among the least restrictive states in terms of lobbying regulation. One study covering 1990–2003 compared states in terms of lobbying definitions, prohibited activities, and disclosure requirements. On a scale of regulation that ran from zero to eighteen, Georgia moved from a score of one in 1990–1991 to eight in the mid-1990s, where it remained through 2003. Eighteen states posted scores between twelve and seventeen, while another thirteen states scored eleven or twelve.[48] More recently, Governor Sonny Perdue promoted more stringent ethics legislation after his election in 2002 but met with limited success, even after his fellow Republicans took control of the General Assembly.[49]

Legislative Norms

Some observers argue that norms of behavior are necessary to achieve stability and efficiency within legislatures, whether at the state or federal level. Norms may be quite simple (a consistently friendly manner toward those in positions of power) or very complex (practices adopted toward committee chairs or deference to colleagues on local legislation).

Several norms appear to further the interests of individual legislators as they pursue policy goals or influence within the General Assembly. Since some traditions of behavior have no written guidelines, norms are often noted subjectively by observers or adhered to by participants. In other cases, norms of behavior may be based in part on written legislative bylaws. Major norms in the Georgia General Assembly include behavior toward colleagues on and off the floor, patterns of reciprocal voting, and the use of loyalty and limited seniority in committee assignment and leadership positions.

Collegiality. Rules of the House and Senate prohibit disruption of activity on the floor. While total silence is not maintained and side conversations are more the rule than the exception, members do not applaud or hiss at comments made from the floor. Nevertheless, members often move freely around each chamber during debate. In the Senate, members are forbidden to pass between the speaker and the presiding officer. While on the floor, members speak to each other only through the presiding officer. Thus, someone wishing to ask a question would first ask the presiding officer whether the speaker would yield the floor for a question. Direct address is not permitted, and legislators refer to each other in formal language such as the "gentleman from the Seventy-second District" or by the courtesy titles Mr., Mrs., and Ms.[50]

Rules also prohibit legislators from making disparaging remarks about the General Assembly or other members. This institutional loyalty officially governs only remarks made on the floor or in the House and Senate journals but is generally practiced outside the chambers as well.

Work and Reciprocity. Members are expected to do their share of the work. Because all members of the Georgia General Assembly are required to vote on all legislation unless excused before the vote is called, they are expected to be informed on most issues coming up for votes. Although all legislators cannot be fully informed on all matters, the committee system provides a means for members to rely on each other for information and support. In the General Assembly, as in most other legislatures, members are expected to defer to the work of a committee when its bills come to the floor for votes. In turn, members of other committees expect the same deference when their bills come to votes. Thus, the norm of reciprocity is apparent in the behavior of members of the House and Senate. While procedures are available to bring a bill to the floor without the approval of the relevant committee, legislators risk alienation from their peers with such a violation of reciprocity.

After bills receive committee recommendations and are presented for floor votes, most of the debate is assumed to have already taken place. Bills that would divide the members are not likely to progress that far in the law-making process. Therefore, unanimous or nearly unanimous floor votes are not uncommon. This is not to say that there is no debate on the floor or that close votes do not sometimes occur, but members generally avoid the public display of divisiveness that such debate would produce. Compromises are reached in more private settings, such as committees or even behind the scenes. The members' cohesiveness may be explained in a number of ways. It may indicate that members are concerned about the public appearance of such debate and believe it violates the stability of the institution. Moreover, a publicly voiced debate would certainly have a loser as well as a winner, and no member looks forward to the possibility of losing in public. Finally, the short length of the session and limited time permitted for debate also force members and leaders to build consensus if they hope to pass any legislation regarding a particular matter.

Seniority and Loyalty. Those members who have attained positions of power within the chamber generally retain those positions until they are no longer in office or the presiding officer removes them. Positions such as committee chair, vice chair, and secretary are generally awarded based on some combination of loyalty and the number of years served on a committee (seniority). However, seniority does not in and of itself guarantee that someone will become a committee's chair. For example, Bobby Lawson and Ken Poston lost committee positions in 1993 after backing an unsuccessful bid to unseat Tom Murphy as speaker of the House.[51] Some legislators have built successful public careers despite violating traditional norms and being considered outsiders. Many observers considered Cynthia McKinney a political outsider during her tenure in the Georgia General Assembly, but she nevertheless won election to the U.S. House of Representatives in Georgia's newly created Eleventh District in 1992, the first black female to represent Georgia in Congress.

The New Face of the General Assembly

As noted throughout this chapter, the Georgia General Assembly is in a period of transition. Reapportionment following the 1990 and 2000 censuses has changed the balance of power to allow the election of more suburban, black, and Republican members. Norms of behavior also remain in a state of flux, especially given the restrictions of new ethics legislation and recent calls for still tighter regulation of lobbying. In addition, the state's electorate is growing and changing, in part as a result of recent migrants from other states. More Georgians now ally themselves with the Republican Party, new interest groups have appeared on the scene, and partisan change will affect the way lobbyists and candidates conduct political activity. Sponsorship of legislation, floor debates, and roll call votes may become increasingly conflictual as the two parties attempt to stake out agendas that differentiate them more clearly from each other in voters' eyes. Such conflicts may be especially pronounced whenever the state enters a period of divided government (as in 2003–2005), with the governorship and either chamber of the General Assembly controlled by different parties. The new face of politics in Georgia may also have a profound effect on priorities and public policy.

CHAPTER 8

The Executive Branch

Two important features characterize Georgia's complex executive branch: the workings of the plural executive and dramatic changes in recent decades. Unlike the national government or a private business, where a chief executive chooses and fires key subordinates, most states use a plural executive in which authority is divided among a state's governor and a series of elected department heads. Voters around the country choose just over three hundred executive officials in statewide elections—a very slight decline since the early 1970s. Ten states also elect members to multimember boards.[1] A few exceptions to this system of dissipated authority exist. The only state official elected by voters in Maine, New Hampshire, New Jersey, and Tennessee is a governor. Alaska and Hawaii voters choose only a governor and lieutenant governor, while Virginia elects these two officers and an attorney general (see table 8.1).[2]

State constitutions require the election of many members of these plural executives; laws provide for other positions. The tasks of these officeholders vary significantly, and advocates of this system see it as promoting accountability to voters and furthering checks on the power of other officials. Financial monitoring, for example, is assigned to elected auditors, comptrollers, and treasurers as well as appointed officials. Spreading around this control over money made eminent sense to constitution drafters in the 1800s as a way to prevent corruption. The same might be said of attorneys general,

Table 8.1. Executive Branch Officials Elected in the States

Office	Number of States Electing	Method of Selection in Georgia
Governor	50	Elected Statewide
Lieutenant Governor	42	Elected Statewide
Secretary of State	36	Elected Statewide
Attorney General	43	Elected Statewide
Agriculture Commissioner	13	Elected Statewide
Insurance Commissioner	11	Elected Statewide
Labor Commissioner	5	Elected Statewide
Education Superintendent	14*	Elected Statewide
Utilities Commissioners	7	Elected Statewide[†]
Treasurer	36	Appointed by Governor[‡]
Auditor	23	Chosen by Legislature

* Another eight states elect their boards of education.

[†] Georgia's Public Service Commission consists of five members elected to six-year terms.

[‡] Tasks performed by director of finance, who is appointed by the governor.

Source: Council of State Governments 2005, 37:233–238, 350–351.

whose independence in investigating and prosecuting could provide a check on other state officials. Nevertheless, the 1900s saw increased centralization in the states, both in terms of the states increasing their power relative to their local governments and governors gaining authority relative to legislatures.[3]

The Governor

Even under the plural executive, governors are generally the most powerful political figures in their states. Their clout arises from the formal authority granted in a state's constitution as well as several other sources of power, including laws, the media, public opinion, ties to political parties and interest groups, and personal characteristics.

Formal Authority

Several studies have attempted to compare the power of governors. Thad Beyle of the University of North Carolina has developed a scoring system that ranks governors based on institutional and personal power.[4] Beyle uses a scale ranging from one to five for a variety of items that comprise each type of power and then averages these numbers to determine overall assessments of institutional and personal power. The two averages can then be added to produce a measure of total power ranging between one and ten.

Institutional power includes the governor's tenure potential, veto power, budgetary control, and appointment power; the number of separately elected executive officials; and the degree to which the governor's party controls the state legislature. The last item, of course, is not fixed but can vary among different governors and for the same governor over time. Formal power can also differ significantly from a politician's willingness and ability to use it, which means that power can vary significantly from one governor to another.

Based on 2002 data, the average for institutional power in the fifty states was 3.5. However, this measure of the fifty governors' institutional power has increased somewhat since 1960.[5] Only six states scored 4.0 or higher in 2002; another thirty-eight states scored between 3.0 and 3.9. Along with three other states, Georgia scored 2.8 in institutional power, just ahead of the low score of 2.7 registered by Alabama. The main reason for Georgia's ranking was the large number of separately elected officials and the governor's very weak appointment power. This was balanced somewhat by strong budgetary and veto authority. These differences are discussed in more detail later in the chapter.

Tenure. One source of power in Beyle's scoring of gubernatorial authority is the four-year term, which has become the norm among the states over the past three decades. One extreme in tenure potential exists in fourteen states where governors face no limit on the number of consecutive terms. At the opposite pole is Virginia, which does not allow governors to succeed themselves.[6]

Georgia's 1877 Constitution limited the governor to two consecutive two-year terms. A 1941 constitutional amendment provided for a four-year term but prohibited governors from succeeding themselves. That limitation was changed in 1976 to permit successive terms, but the lifetime limit for any governor remained at two terms. The 1983 Constitution permitted two consecutive four-year terms with no lifetime restriction on the time of a governor's service (earning a score of four out of a possible five from Beyle). Article 5, Section 1 of the Georgia Constitution places no limits on the number of consecutive terms that other statewide elected officials may serve.[7]

Veto Power. The governor's veto power in Georgia is considered very strong (five out of five points) because it includes the standard veto of bills, the item veto of specific lines in appropriations bills, and substantial legislative majorities to override the veto. Nineteen states allow the item veto for a broader range of bills than just appropriations. At the low end, seven states received a score of two for requiring a special majority to override a veto but failing to grant their governors an item veto. This group includes North Carolina, whose governor lacked any veto power until voters approved a constitutional amendment in 1996.[8]

In Georgia, the governor's veto power is included in the legislative article of the Constitution, which describes the process for enacting laws. Under the provisions of Article 3, Section 5, the governor has six days to act on a bill while the General Assembly is in session. If the General Assembly has adjourned for the session or for more than forty days (like a recess), the governor has forty days after adjournment to act. When vetoing a bill, the governor is required to return it to the chamber where it originated within three days during the session or sixty days after adjournment. After the General Assembly has received a veto message, the originating chamber immediately may consider the vetoed bill. A bill becomes law if the governor does nothing—neither approves nor vetoes it.

In Georgia, overriding the governor's veto so that a bill can become law requires the approval of two-thirds of the members of each chamber, not just of those present. If an override fails in either house of the Georgia General Assembly, a bill is dead, but those bills vetoed during adjournment can be overridden during the next legislative session. Finally, the authority to veto specific items within a bill is limited to appropriations bills, which gives the governor the power to kill spending for specific projects without having to veto an entire budget. Twenty-five states have more lax requirements for overriding a gubernatorial veto: six require only a majority of those elected; six mandate three-fifths of those elected; and thirteen specify three-fifths or two-thirds of those present for the override vote.

The Budget. Beyle rates Georgia's governorship a three in terms of budget-making authority, primarily because of the legislature's virtually unlimited power to change the budget submitted by the governor. The Constitution directs the governor to prepare the state's annual budget and submit it to the General Assembly during the first five days of the regular session. Agencies submit their requests to the Office of Planning and Budget, which reports to the governor. The Office of Planning and Budget, in turn, develops the draft appropriations bill, which is the starting point for budget debates in the legislature. Georgia's governors have not always had so much authority. The legislature dominated the budgetary process until 1931, and the executive's position was strengthened in 1962 when what was then called the Budget Bureau was placed under the governor's authority with a budget director and staff support.[9]

Elected and Appointed Officials. Beyle assigns Georgia the lowest score possible for two indicators related to a governor's ability to control or manage the bureaucracy: the number of competing elected officials and the power to appoint officials in six key areas—health, education, highways, corrections, public utilities regulation, and public welfare. In each of these six major policy areas, Georgia's top officials are chosen by voters or by boards (discussed later in the chapter). In the case of the Board of Transportation, the governor does not even appoint the members; they are chosen by the General Assembly.[10] Like the majority of states, Georgia elects a lieutenant governor, attorney general, and secretary of state. Georgia is among the few states, however, that allow voters to pick the school superintendent and the agriculture, insurance, and labor commissioners as well as the five members of the Public Service Commission, which regulates utilities.

This does not mean that Georgia governors have few positions to hand out. Governors' influence is indirect, primarily through their power to appoint boards and propose the budget. Gubernatorial control over boards and commissions is weakened because terms are long and staggered, which means some time may need to pass before a governor's appointees constitute a majority. For example, members of the University System Board of Regents, which adopts policies and selects administrators for Georgia's public colleges and universities, serve staggered seven-year terms, posing a challenge to any governor who seeks to alter the board's composition and policies. During his first year in office (2003), Governor Sonny Perdue appointed only four of the eighteen members of the Board of Regents. However, he also appointed members to a wide range of state boards and authorities, ranging from the regulatory boards for the construction industry, athletic agents, opticians, and nursing home administrators to agencies with significant budgets and policy-making authority, such as the Board of Education and the Georgia Lottery Corporation.[11]

Perhaps the most important appointment power of Georgia governors is their constitutional authority to fill vacancies in the executive and judicial branches without Senate confirmation. Obviously, a governor's impact is greatest when appointing the first members to a new board or commission, as Governor Perdue did with the Georgia Land Conservation Council in 2005.[12] In the case of elected positions, the appointment power allows the governor to pick someone who immediately becomes the incumbent in the next campaign. This can be especially important in appointing judges, who tend to be reelected quite handily. Governor Perdue appointed ten judges to trial courts during his first year in office. He had the ultimate opportunity in 2005, when he appointed his top legal adviser to a vacancy on the Georgia Supreme Court.[13]

Gubernatorial Party Control. The last type of institutional power Beyle examines is party control of the legislature. Georgia's governors once appeared quite powerful by this measure because of the Democratic Party's long hold on the governorship and history of overwhelming legislative control. While Georgia governors encountered little partisan opposition, disagreements occurred over policy, ideology, and personality. Moreover, for much of the twentieth century, Georgians divided into factions loyal to different Democratic candidates for governor.[14] All of that changed in 2002, however, with Perdue's election as Georgia's first Republican governor since Reconstruction.

During his first two years, Perdue governed with a Republican Senate but faced a Democratic House. Divided government—that is, no single party in control of the governorship and both houses of the legislature—became increasingly common in the states during the 1900s. In 1984, only sixteen of the forty-nine states with partisan elections had governors whose parties did not control their state legislatures; in 1994, that number reached thirty states. After the 2004 elections, twenty-nine states had divided government, twelve had unified Republican control, and eight were controlled by Democrats.[15] In Georgia, unified party control came full circle with the election of 2004, when Republicans won a majority in the House to give them control of the legislature and governorship for the first time in more than a century.

Gubernatorial Leadership

Formal authority constitutes only part—some observers would suggest a very small part—of a governor's political power. Also important are governors' personal power, which Beyle defines to include the size of their electoral mandate, the degree to which they have moved up a state's political ladder, the potential time they may remain in office, and their ratings in public opinion polls. Obviously, these factors vary both among governors and over the course of an individual governor's time in office.

In 2004, Beyle's measure of personal power rated Georgia at 4.0, somewhat above the fifty-state average of 3.7. The major reason that Georgia did not post a higher score was Governor Sonny Perdue's narrow victory margin in 2002 and the degree to which he did not move to the governorship following a climb from other major offices.[16]

Still, Beyle's analysis ignores other factors that affect a governor's performance in office. Scholars often call these factors "enabling resources," and they include staff assistance and access to information, which permit governors to reach decisions independently of the state legislature, interest groups, and other organizations. One study has found that the nation's governors have increased these resources between the late 1970s and early 1990s.[17] Another study found that the Georgia governor's office had a staff of seventy-seven in 2004, which ranked it tenth in size among the states— essentially the same as its rank in total population.[18] Personal power, enabling resources, and a variety of individual characteristics are important in governors' leadership ability, which is often discussed in terms of the way they perform certain roles or functions.[19] Some of the major gubernatorial roles include policy maker, chief legislator, manager of the executive branch, and symbolic leader.

Policy Maker. This role involves governors' ability to set the public agenda.[20] Of course, governors cannot always choose the issues they emphasize. Some issues are perennial—that is, they arise during every legislative session. Probably the most apparent is the budget, which must be adopted each fiscal year or, in a few states, every two years. Georgia governors can use the budget to emphasize certain programs, agencies, or policies. Given its brief annual session and limited staff, the Georgia General Assembly historically has produced a budget within 1 or 2 percent of the governor's recommendation, although modifications occur in the relative shares going to various programs.[21]

Other perennial concerns are the services that consume the major share of state budgets: education, highways, corrections, health care, and social welfare. Because of the prominence of these functions, governors mention them often in State of the State addresses and propose policies to improve service quality or access.

States also face cyclical issues, which grow in public concern and then decline. Examples include the burst and then rapid leveling off of interest in the environment during the 1970s. The same was true of energy after the Arab oil embargo in 1973, economic development in the mid-1980s, education reform in the late 1980s and again after 2000, and state budget problems during the recessions of the early 1990s and following the 2001 terrorist attacks.[22]

Governors also must confront transitory issues, which appear suddenly and then vanish after they are dealt with. Examples include ethics reform following a scandal, changing the drinking age in response to federal law, or the response to a natural disaster. Concern over an issue can vary widely among the states at the same point in time, and issues may shift among the transitory, cyclical, and perennial categories over time. In particular, economic development gained great significance during the recession of the 1980s, and most states adopted a wide range of financial incentives, training programs, and similar tactics by the end of the decade. These programs were maintained and expanded even as unprecedented growth occurred during the 1990s. With the growing globalization of the economy and the recession following September 11, 2001, jobs and investment—as well as security— became perennial issues for governors and other state officials.[23]

Georgia's governors have used several strategies to set the public agenda. Perhaps the most common is the news conference—which, of course, a variety of officials, interest groups, and individuals use to promote their views. Speeches to groups and staged events also allow governors to promote their policies. Perhaps the most visible is the State of the State address to the General Assembly at the beginning of each legislative session. Official prestige usually assures the governor of coverage by the state's television stations and daily newspapers.[24]

Another common practice is the use of commissions to study issues and report their findings and recommendations to the governor, who can then use these results to propose major policy changes. Such commissions can include officials and private citizens and thus can yield several advantages in agenda setting. First, these commissions tap the talents of individuals and organizations outside government. Second, service by prominent and well-connected citizens can increase the visibility and acceptance of the commission's conclusions, thereby helping to upstage other proposals in the same policy area, lending an air of objectivity to proposals, and including representatives of affected groups in the commission's work. Third, depending on its composition and links with various other leaders, a commission can help formulate compromises or other proposals that have a high likelihood of passing the General Assembly. Indeed, a commission may be useful in pressuring legislators to adopt the governor's proposals. Finally, a commission's report can alert officials, interest groups, and the general public to a problem and mobilize these people to support a specific remedy.

Georgia's governors have used study commissions to consider policy changes that have the potential to generate significant opposition from legislators, agencies, local officials, and interest groups. One was the Growth Strategies Commission created in 1987 to deal with land-use planning, building codes, and permit systems. To minimize opposition by local leaders, the thirty-five-member commission appointed by Governor Joe Frank Harris worked with business leaders and representatives of Georgia's cities and counties to establish a system of long-term planning that starts at the local level and works its way through regional and state approval. In addition, the process was phased in slowly after the enactment of planning legislation in 1989.[25]

One of Governor Zell Miller's earliest actions was the appointment of a 1991 commission to consider a perennial issue, the performance of the state bureaucracy. Miller touted the commission in statements about his achievements and agenda. Less than four years later, however, Miller set up the Governor's Commission on Privatization to identify services to be turned over to the private sector as means of saving the state money.[26] Shortly after taking office in 2003, Sonny Perdue launched a similar effort to improve efficiency in state government, appointing leaders in business and other fields to his Commission for a New Georgia.[27]

Not all gubernatorial commissions lead the state to adopt policy innovations. At times, a governor may decide to ignore a commission's recommendations for political or other reasons. In May 1991, for example, Miller created the Local Governance Commission, which recommended some major changes in local government. The commission proposed greater local control over the structure of city and county government, modifications in revenue systems, and new standards for providing local services. These proposals would have eliminated several small governments and elected positions, including sheriffs. In the face of some vigorous opposition, the governor did little to promote the commission's ideas during the 1993 legislative session, although some of the report's recommendations became law.[28]

Chief Legislator. In examining the legislative role of the nation's governors, Alan Rosenthal identifies several powers: initiation, rejection, provision, experience, unity, publicity, popularity, and persuasion.[29] In addition to the budget and the policy-making strategies discussed earlier, Georgia governors have several other methods of initiation. One is submission of bills to the General Assembly, where the governor selects one member in each chamber to serve as the administration's floor leader. Another is support for ideas proposed by legislators, agencies, or interest groups. A third is calling a special session of the legislature to address some issue or problem the governor deems important, at least symbolically. One study of the early 1990s, when the Democrats controlled both the governorship and the General Assembly, found that votes on the floor of the legislature in favor of Governor Miller's agenda varied among identifiable groups of Democrats. During election years, however, members of Miller's party increased their support for the governor's bills, while Republican support declined.[30]

The governor's power of rejection is substantial, in part because of the full and item-veto authority. The governor can also benefit from the fact that the legislature does not pass most major bills until the end of the legislative session, providing more time for review before (and politicking after) deciding to veto a bill. Georgia governors have exercised their veto power only sparingly (see table 8.2). In 2004, when Governor Perdue faced a Senate controlled by his fellow Republicans and a House controlled by Democrats, he vetoed 19 of the 1,944 bills and resolutions enacted by the General Assembly (1 percent). In the other forty-one states that held regular legislative sessions that year, the number of vetoes ranged from 0 in five states to 78 in New York and 154 in Maryland. The majority of states, however, had fewer than 10 vetoes.[31]

Georgia has seen limited use of the item veto. Other states have made it more difficult for governors to use the item veto because their legislatures have combined larger appropriations into fewer lines. Thus, a governor vetoing a large lump sum would have to kill a whole range of programs in addition to the one targeted with the veto.[32]

In assessing a governor's prior experience, Rosenthal concludes that "the years spent in the house or senate, the time served in gubernatorial office, and future tenure prospects do make a difference" in a governor's legisla-

Table 8.2. Gubernatorial Vetoes of Bills, 1981–2005

Legislative Session	Governor	Full Vetoes	Item Vetoes Number	Item Vetoes Amount
1981	Busbee	12	3	$0
1982	Busbee	12	2	0
1983	Harris	12	2	0
1984	Harris	16	4	0
1985	Harris	4	4	8,000,000
1986	Harris	6	4	0
1987	Harris	9	5	0
1988	Harris	9	6	0
1989	Harris	10	4	0
1990	Harris	18	7	70,000
1991	Miller	13	10	5,000
1992	Miller	27	16	38,595,089
1993	Miller	16	10	0
1994	Miller	4	11	9,864,199
1995	Miller	14	14	9,042,422
1996	Miller	18	7	342,500
1997	Miller	15	11	9,417,245
1998	Miller	13	8	3,950,520
1999	Barnes	6	4	0
2000	Barnes	11	4	1,500,000
2001	Barnes	7	5	76,000
2002	Barnes	10	7	55,000
2003	Perdue	19	6	403,000
2004	Perdue	19	9	288,135
2005	Perdue	15	15	9,243,226

Note: Data cover only bills and regular legislative sessions. One resolution was vetoed in 1984; two resolutions were vetoed in 1991; and five item vetoes occurred during the 1991 special session.

Sources: Georgia General Assembly, Legislative Services Committee and Office of Legislative Counsel, *Summary of General Statutes Enacted, 1981–2005; Acts and Resolutions of the General Assembly of the State of Georgia, 1997–2005.*

tive success.[33] Experience does not automatically provide power, but it can furnish governors with connections, favors, and knowledge that further their influence in state legislatures. Beyle examined the career paths of the 225 individuals who served as elected governors between 1970 and 1994. Only 8 percent held no prior political office, and the state legislature was the most important starting point: 38 percent of all governors were members of their state legislatures when elected to the governorship.[34]

Georgia's governors have seldom lacked political experience. Of the twelve men who took office between 1947 and 2003, only Lester Maddox might be considered a political outsider. He did not have that status for lack of trying, however: Maddox was defeated for mayor of Atlanta in 1957 and 1961 and for lieutenant governor in 1962 before becoming governor in 1967. All of Georgia's other governors served in the General Assembly or in some statewide elected position, while Herman Talmadge was heir to a family political legacy.[35]

The power of unity refers to a governor's ability as an individual rather than as part of a collective body to take action and gain the attention of the public and the media. This gubernatorial power can be limited by competition with other elected officials. With no limit on reelection, Georgia's lieutenant governor can build power and visibility to compete with the governor, as can other members of the plural executive, who can undercut a governor's legislative program.[36]

The final three gubernatorial powers identified by Rosenthal—provision, publicity, and popularity—seem quite closely linked. Provision refers to governors' ability to fulfill legislators' needs.[37] Governors can directly bestow some benefits on legislators: appointing or hiring people, attending events, and writing or phoning on legislators' behalf. Somewhat more indirectly, providing benefits for a district can aid both the legislator and the governor—for example, by including specific items in the state budget and through the long-standing practice of making allocations from the governor's emergency fund.[38]

Publicity surrounding major policy initiatives, especially in election years, may enhance a governor's popularity, although the popularity of the nation's governors is most often driven by state and national economic factors.[39] After launching his reelection campaign, Miller announced proposals to distribute unanticipated revenues from the state lottery, adopt a modest income tax cut, and shift his emphasis on two hot issues, the state flag and welfare reform.[40]

In summarizing governors' many powers in the legislative process, Rosenthal concludes, "Each of these powers alone is not sufficient to make a governor 'chief legislator.' But taken in combination, they are impressive. Together they allow the governor to persuade legislators—directly and personally, and indirectly through the media—that what he or she wants by way of policy, expenditures, and operations is what they ought to grant, in their own interests. . . . Given their advantages, it is a wonder that governors ever lose. But the fact is that legislatures have significant power of their own and the will to use that power."[41] Moreover, that success is affected by other participants in the political process, particularly interest groups, and can vary with the formal power of legislatures as well as their professionalism—that is, whether being a legislator is a part-time job or offers full-time, well-paying employment.

Manager of the Executive Branch. The governor is at least formally the state's chief administrator. It is difficult, though, to speak of governors "managing" the bureaucracy in the same way that executives in the private sector issue orders, change policies, or hire and fire subordinates, in part because of the plural executive, civil service protection for state employees, and political constraints. Thus, governors often retain only indirect influence such as appointments and the budget.[42]

Some states have chosen to increase a governor's ability to manage the bureaucracy through the power of reorganization in their constitutions or statutes. Twenty-seven states, including Georgia, permit their governors to reorganize the bureaucracy by issuing executive orders. The remaining states require their legislatures to enact measures to reorganize the executive branch. The last such effort in Georgia occurred in the early 1970s, when the General Assembly did so in response to a request from Governor Jimmy Carter.[43]

The nation's governors also vary in their salaries and staffs. When the Council of State Governments compared governors in December 2004, only eighteen states paid their chief executives less than $100,000 per year. Georgia's governor received $127,303. Seven states had gubernatorial salaries of at least $150,000, including a high of $179,000 in New York. The Georgia Governor's Office had a staff of eighty-seven people in 2004. Governors in thirteen states had office staffs of fewer than twenty-five people, while those in Florida, Illinois, Louisiana, New Jersey, New York, and Texas employed more than one hundred people each.[44]

Governors also use pressure against agencies. In 1996, for example, Georgia's appointed state school board had been feuding for some time with

Linda Schrenko, the Republican elected state school superintendent in 1994. To end the conflict, Governor Miller, a Democrat, called on the entire board to resign. Similarly, Perdue pressured members of the school board to resign before he was sworn in as governor. Perdue also obtained resignations from the head of the Department of Human Resources and the chair of the powerful transportation board, both of whom were already in office when he was sworn in as governor.[45]

Symbolic Leader. The last gubernatorial role is the symbolic one of defining a state's image. Governors may face pressure to emphasize certain policies and to portray them in particular ways. During desegregation conflicts in the 1950s, for example, Georgia Governor Marvin Griffin played to white voters at home in opposing desegregation, but his approach gave people outside the South a negative opinion of him. His actions also contrasted with those of local officials in Atlanta and elsewhere who adopted more moderate positions on race in hopes of promoting their communities to outsiders, especially investors.[46]

As Georgia grew after the desegregation battles, governors played a major role in promoting the state as both a place to invest and a source of products and services. Carter made several promotional trips within the United States, including a session to persuade movie industry leaders to film in Georgia. He also visited Latin America, Europe, and Israel. His successors did likewise, extending gubernatorial visits to Japan, Korea, and Canada in addition to the traditional ventures in Europe. Miller scheduled a trip to Russia during his first year in office, and Perdue has made several trips outside the United States, including one to Canada.[47]

Constitutional Officers

As table 8.1 indicated, the Georgia Constitution requires the statewide election of six officials in addition to the governor and lieutenant governor: secretary of state, attorney general, school superintendent, commissioner of insurance, commissioner of labor, and commissioner of agriculture. According to Article 5, Section 3 of the Constitution, these elected department heads must have reached the age of twenty-five, been U.S. citizens for at least ten years, and been Georgia residents for at least four years before assuming office. The attorney general is also required to have had seven years as an active-status member of the State Bar of Georgia, which supervises the legal profession in the state. The Constitution leaves it to the General Assembly to spell out the power and duties of these officers, to determine their salaries, and to fund their agencies. Article 5, Section 4 includes a procedure under which four of the eight constitutional officers can petition the Georgia Supreme Court to hold a hearing to determine if a constitutional officer is permanently disabled and should be replaced.

Constitutional officers possess power independent of the governor because of the prerogatives of their offices and their ties to the constituencies they serve. The attorney general, for example, exercises great discretion regarding the handling of litigation to which the state is a party. In addition, the attorney general's office issues opinions on the legality or constitutionality of actions taken by the state.[48] Similarly, the insurance and agriculture commissioners have substantial power to regulate certain types of businesses. However, they are sometimes seen as advocates of the industries they oversee, as when the agriculture commissioner participates in programs sponsored by food producers or processors.[49]

The narrow focus of their positions also means that constitutional officers' natural constituencies—for votes and campaign money—are the interests affected most directly by their decisions.[50] In 2002, for example, incumbent insurance commissioner John Oxendine raised more than $3 million for his reelection. Between April and June, just before he ran unopposed in the Republican primary, Oxendine reported receiving more than $169,000 in contributions, including six donations of $5,000 and another ninety between $1,000 and $2,500. Of these ninety-six contributions of $1,000 or more, twenty-eight came from people listed as in the insurance business, another ten were in health care, eight were in law, another eight were in banking or finance, and thirty-eight were in other lines of business. Oxendine reported another $110,000 in contributions after he won reelection on November 5, 2002, with 64 percent of the vote, including fifty-two contributions of $1,000 or more plus $5,000 from the president of a major Atlanta hospital and another $5,000 from his wife.[51] Similar contribution patterns can be found for other candidates for constitutional offices.

In addition to having conflicts with the governor, constitutional officers may do political battle with one another. In 1995, for example, Oxendine refused to collect a premium tax on church-owned insurance companies providing coverage to churches, which he argued was unconstitutional. A fellow

Republican, Attorney General Michael Bowers, filed suit against Oxendine to force him to collect the tax unless the legislature passed a law exempting such companies. Oxendine relented.[52]

Boards and Commissions

States commonly assign decision making in certain policy areas to multi-member boards rather than departments headed by individuals. Georgia is no exception, and its boards and commissions vary in their origin, authority, organization, operations, and political power. A few have their authority spelled out in the Georgia Constitution; many others have been created by law or executive order.

Constitutional Boards and Commissions

The Constitution provides for eight boards and commissions (see table 8.3). These are among the most powerful agencies in Georgia, in part because any changes in their basic authority and membership require a constitutional amendment rather than passage of a law by the General Assembly. Their power is also reflected in the resources they control. In 2005, for example, the University System Board of Regents had a budget of roughly $3.5 billion, slightly less than half of which was state funds. Some funds are earmarked in the Constitution: Article 3 requires that state motor fuel taxes, which were expected to total more than $634 million in fiscal 2005, must be spent for "an adequate system of public roads and bridges." That provision gives substantial power to the Department of Transportation, which had a total budget of more than $1.6 billion in fiscal 2005.[53]

The Constitution insulates these boards from political pressure to some degree by providing members with relatively long and staggered terms. In the case of the State Board of Education and the University System Board of Regents, the Constitution specifically prohibits the governor from serving on the board. This restriction was put in place in reaction to events in the 1940s, when Governor Eugene Talmadge, whose office entitled him to a seat on the board, conducted a purge of administrators accused of promoting racial integration, leading to a loss of accreditation for Georgia's public colleges and universities.[54] Originally created by an 1879 statute and intended to regulate railroads, the Public Service Commission subsequently

Table 8.3. Constitutional Boards and Commissions

Board/Commission	# Members	Membership Selection
Education	13*	One member per congressional district; appointed by the governor to seven-year terms subject to Senate confirmation.
Natural Resources	18*	One member per congressional district plus five at-large members (at least one of whom is from a coastal county); appointed by the governor to seven-year terms, subject to Senate confirmation.
Pardons and Paroles	5	Appointed by the governor to seven-year terms, subject to Senate confirmation.
Personnel	5	Appointed by the governor to five-year terms, subject to Senate confirmation.
Public Service	5	Elected statewide on a partisan ballot for six-year terms.
Regents	18*	One member per congressional district, plus five at-large members; appointed by the governor to seven-year terms, subject to Senate confirmation.
Transportation	13*	One member per congressional district; elected by majority vote of General Assembly members whose districts overlap any of the congressional district.
Veterans Services	7	Appointed by the governor to seven-year terms, subject to Senate confirmation.

* Membership varies along with Georgia's number of seats in the U.S. House of Representatives, which increased to thirteen following the 2000 census and reapportionment.

Source: Constitution of the State of Georgia, art. 8, sec.2; art. 8, sec. 4; art. 4, secs. 1–6.

had its reach extended to other utilities and its membership enlarged and made subject to election. The commission received constitutional status in 1943 after voters approved an amendment.[55] In contrast to such arm's-length relationships, the State Transportation Board may seem like the essence of pork-barrel politics. One member is chosen for each congressional district by the state legislators whose districts overlap it—and benefit from highway construction.

Most constitutional boards and commissions use some geographical representation. Assigning one seat per congressional district has the effect of assuring South Georgia seats on boards that otherwise might be dominated by people from the Atlanta area. It also means the size of a board can change as Georgia receives additional seats in the U.S. House of Representatives.

Statutory and Executive Boards

Beyond the small number of constitutional boards and commissions are many more created by law or executive order, including more than three dozen examining boards for professionals in such fields as accounting, libraries, and wastewater treatment. Statutes have established well over one hundred other boards and commissions to oversee, study, or make recommendations for various agencies and programs. Examples include the Council on Aging, State Forestry Commission, Lake Lanier Islands Development Authority, Teachers Retirement System, and World Congress Center Authority. Finally, governors can create commissions, boards, and task forces that provide advice on various issues and usually go out of existence after their missions.

Critics have long attacked the operation of Georgia's boards and commissions, including licensing boards' infrequent disciplining of professionals they oversee. Observers also have faulted the quality and background of gubernatorial appointees, the decisions and expenses of board members, and the use of outside consultants.[56]

The Bureaucracy

Public bureaucracies face a variety of competing goals and pressures. Citizens want government to be efficient yet expect it to be open and fair, responsive to their demands, and accountable for its actions. Unlike the relationship between private firms and their customers, how public bureaucracies operate is often decided through the political process. These tensions affect agencies and public employees, who must interact with clients, the governor, the legislature, courts, interest groups, and the media.

State Employees

Most states have long struggled to set up personnel systems that promote efficient and effective government while protecting government workers from partisan politics. Georgia has used various approaches and now operates with several personnel systems. Georgia emulated other states and in 1943 established a "civil service" system in which permanent employees are hired and rewarded on the basis of qualifications and performance, not party or personal loyalties. Such workers are hired under the state merit system—what the public normally thinks of as "bureaucrats." That system changed, however, when the legislature followed Governor Miller's recommendation and closed the merit system to employees hired after July 1, 1996. Those new employees lack the protections of the merit system, and agency managers have more flexibility in rewarding, disciplining, and terminating state workers. Other employees remain under separate systems, including many upper-level management jobs or positions in the governor's office, the Georgia Lottery, the attorney general's office, the legislature, most authorities, and the University System of Georgia.[57]

The U.S. Census Bureau conducts its Census of Governments every five years. The 2002 census revealed that Georgia had the equivalent of 123,000 full-time state employees, an increase of 7.8 percent from the 114,000 counted ten years earlier. In contrast, state employment grew 10 percent nationwide during that time. Georgia had 143 state workers for each 10,000 residents in 2002, slightly below the national average of 147 and down from 168 ten years earlier (a reduction of almost 15 percent). Such comparisons can be hazardous because states differ significantly in the distribution of responsibilities among state and local governments, the private sector, and nonprofit organizations. The relative size of Georgia's public payrolls seems larger when factoring in local government employment (cities, counties, school districts, authorities), which reached 352,000 in 2002, 22 percent higher than the 1992 figure. Georgia has 411 employees per 10,000 population, ranking it tenth among the states. Georgia's 2002 total of 554 state and local workers per 10,000 residents is quite close to the national average of 542. Critics have blasted this level of public employment as excessive, although some see it as a result of the state's large number of counties.[58] Debates have also focused on the composition of the state workforce, especially regarding gender and race.[59]

State Agencies

In 1991, the Governor's Commission on Effectiveness and Economy in Government identified 258 agencies: 8 interstate agencies, 35 major executive departments, 40 examining and licensing boards, 42 authorities and public corporations, 57 nondepartment agencies with executive functions, and 76 advisory boards.[60] There is little reason to believe that this wide range of agencies has changed substantially since that time. A majority of state workers were located outside metropolitan Atlanta, with many at public colleges, universities, and technical schools.

Size and Budget. As one might expect, agencies differ in the resources they control. During the 2006 fiscal year, when the state budget totaled more than $18.6 billion, eight agencies received more than $500 million (see table 8.4). No relationship necessarily exists between an agency's appropriations and the size of its workforce, however; the Department of Education has only a modest number of staff members, but its large budget is the result of its mission to distribute substantial sums to Georgia's local school districts for a wide variety of purposes. Other departments receive substantial amounts from the federal government and other sources.[61]

Organizational Change. State bureaucracies are not as immutable as many critics contend. Over the years, most states have created, abolished, or altered agencies. Some of these changes occurred because of political conflicts between different branches of government, governors' efforts to gain greater control over the bureaucracy, increased public concern over certain issues, or interest group pressure.

Like most states, Georgia has modified its executive branch on a somewhat regular basis. Two major reorganizations stand out: during the single term of Governor Richard Russell, when the General Assembly increased the governor's power in 1931, and the 1972 reorganization under Governor Jimmy Carter that reduced the number of departments to twenty-two. These two changes increased the governor's ability to manage the bureaucracy through budgeting, better coordination and planning, and appointments.[62]

Table 8.4. State Funds Appropriated for Major Agencies,
Fiscal Year 2006

Agency	Appropriation (in $ million)	Percentage of Total State Appropriation
State Board of Education	6,439.7	34.5
Department of Community Health	2,259.9	12.1
University System of Georgia	1,812.8	9.7
Department of Human Resources	1,372.3	7.4
Department of Corrections	927.2	5.2
Department of Transportation	619.1	3.3
Student Finance Commission	559.5	2.9
Department of Revenue	538.7	2.8

Note: Total state appropriations for fiscal 2006 equaled $18.654 billion.

Source: Georgia Governor's Office of Planning and Budget 2006, 23–25.

Many states have created agencies in response to actions by the federal government or growing public concern over certain issues. In Georgia, the Council for the Arts was established in 1964 as federal funding in this area expanded. The Office of Consumer Affairs was created in 1969 when such issues became more prominent in the United States. Three-quarters of the states lacked such agencies prior to the 1970s. Georgia's 1972 reorganization followed a pattern established in most states of creating comprehensive departments to manage major policy areas: human resources (a range of agencies serving the poor), transportation (to take a broader view than in the prior Highway Department), and natural resources (replacing a series of departments that had dealt separately with conservation issues since the 1940s). Most states also created separate departments to deal with local governments—Georgia's Department of Community Affairs was spun off from existing agencies in 1977.

In the 1980s, Georgia mirrored many other states by establishing agencies to manage public radio and television resources (1981), improve coordination among the numerous organizations in the criminal justice system (1981), and cope with a range of environmental problems (1986). During the following decade, changes in the state bureaucracy were tied to both pressing issues and changes in federal policy, including the creation of PeachCare, Georgia's part of a program established by the U.S. Congress in 1997 to help states provide low-cost health insurance for the children of the working poor. PeachCare originally formed part of the Department of Medical Assistance. With the rising costs of health care to the state—including PeachCare, Medicaid, and medical care for state employees—in 1999, the legislature adopted a proposal by Governor Roy Barnes to reorganize Georgia's many health programs into the new Department of Community Health.[63] In 2005, the Department of Driver Services was created, encompassing most of the duties of the former Division of Motor Vehicles (DMV). Other DMV services were transferred to the Departments of Public Safety, Revenue, and Transportation and the Public Service Commission. Governor Perdue made these changes to respond to critics of the DMV's services.

Managing Public Agencies. Public management can be difficult for a variety of reasons. Unlike the simple goal of profit in the private sector, agency objectives can be vague or even in conflict with one another. Assessing achievement is also complicated. How does one decide, for example, if schools produce an acceptable "product" for the state? Many agencies do furnish processes—renewing licenses, checking tax forms, registering voters—where workers' accuracy and efficiency can be monitored. Yet selecting indicators to use for evaluation remains a problem, as does interpreting "success."[64] Many of these matters are open to competing political interpretations.

In addition to multiple goals and performance measures, public sector managers typically must respond to multiple "bosses." Department heads must work closely with the governor, legislature, and interest groups. Gubernatorial influence will be highest with managers whose selection requires the governor's approval. In contrast, department heads elected by voters or appointed by boards without the governor's consent normally will be more concerned with influencing the legislature, whose members frequently call to get information about programs, discuss regulations, complain about service delivery, request a project or service for their district, and seek jobs or contracts for constituents.[65] The General Assembly also earmarks some agency funds for local projects in members' districts—what critics often call pork-barrel spending—such as classroom buildings, museums, sewer improvements, senior centers, and similar items.[66]

Given this complex administrative environment, government leaders often look for new and better ways to provide services. During the 1990s, this effort was associated with a "reinventing government" movement that aimed to reshape public management to be more results-oriented, entrepreneurial, and customer-driven.[67] By the end of the decade, a major effort to evaluate management by state governments was funded by a grant from the Pew Charitable Trusts. Research teams at Syracuse University's Maxwell School of Citizenship and Public Affairs and at *Governing* magazine analyzed the states in five areas: financial management, capital management, human resources, managing for results, and information technology.

The Government Performance Project issued grades in 1999 and 2001. In 2001, Georgia received a B− in the first four categories and a C− in information technology, leaving the state with an overall grade of B−. The 2001 grades represented a slight improvement over 1999 in every category except human resources; the state's overall grade was a C−. Few states received grades of A− or A: just ten in financial management, five in capital management, three in human resources, five in managing for results, and six in information technology. Only three states received an average grade of A− or A over all five categories: Michigan, Utah, and Washington.[68] A second study characterized these five categories as "top-down" change and focused more on "bottom-up" changes in state management: this study ranked Georgia third among the states in 1998.[69]

As in other states, Georgia's citizens and officials undoubtedly will continue to look for ways to make government more efficient and responsive. Doing so will not be easy, as James Q. Wilson points out: "Many, if not most, of the difficulties we experience in dealing with government agencies arise from the agencies being part of a fragmented and open political system. . . . The greatest mistake citizens can make when they complain of 'the bureaucracy' is to suppose that their frustrations arise simply out of management problems; they do not—they arise out of governance problems."[70]

Limits on Executive Power

Although granted extensive authority, Georgia's executive branch faces a variety of legal and political constraints on its power. Legal constraints include Georgia's constitution, laws, and courts. The nature of U.S. federalism means that the executive branch is also constrained by the U.S. Constitution and federal law. The executive branch also confronts political limits. This may be especially true of governors' efforts to push proposals through the General Assembly. As chapter 6 indicates, interest groups can influence the executive branch's ability to propose and implement policies. Agencies also face constraints imposed by public opinion, especially when it is coupled with citizen action.

Even though Georgia's executive branch has grown in size and power over the past generation, it still faces significant external challenges to its authority. It also must deal with internal tensions among the governor, elected department heads, the permanent bureaucracy, and established agency procedures and norms. Such political checks may escalate with competition between the two major political parties.

CHAPTER 9

The Legal System

The U.S. legal system includes a complex set of institutions and participants—courts, judges, prosecutors, lawyers, and a wide range of others, among them agencies such as corrections systems and law enforcement (see chapter 11). Complexity also occurs because of U.S. federalism. Because Americans are citizens of both the United States as a whole and a particular state, they fall under the jurisdiction of two constitutions and two sets of laws. In effect, the national government operates one legal system, while the fifty states operate a parallel set of legal systems.[1]

Complexity also exists because of the many types of law.[2] One distinction is the hierarchy among laws created by different institutions. At the highest level is constitutional law, which is more difficult to change than other types of law. Next in the hierarchy is statutory law, which consists of rules established by legislatures and must conform to the U.S. and respective state constitutions. Third is administrative law, which must conform to the statutory law authorizing it and is usually quite detailed.

Courts also make law. Common law evolved from British law and includes rulings not based on constitutional or statutory law. Instead, common law makes interpretations based on custom and previous decisions. Cases in equity evolved in Britain when common law provided no remedy or seemed unfair. Actions at equity generally involve an order to a named party, as when

a court issues an injunction ordering someone to fulfill a contract. This compares to actions at law, where a party would have to sue for compensation
after being injured by another.

An important procedural difference in the legal system exists between
civil and criminal law. In criminal cases, the government brings action
against an alleged offender, who must be convicted if there is proof beyond
a reasonable doubt. Penalties normally consist of imprisonment, probation,
fines, or community service. Civil cases can be brought by government or
private parties who have disputes. The standard for a verdict is the prepon-
derance of the evidence, which is lower than in criminal cases. The typical
penalty is some form of financial compensation.

The U.S. legal system has received extensive criticism. Complaints have
focused on crime rates, bias in law enforcement, overcrowded jails and prisons, recidivism, the jury system, the high costs of using the courts, clogged
court dockets and the attendant delay in deciding cases, damage awards in
tort cases, ineffective or poorly organized agencies, and the quality of personnel. As these topics suggest, the legal system is linked closely to politics
and policy making.

State and Local Governments in the Legal System

State and local governments are major players in the U.S. legal system, despite rhetoric from politicians and interest groups calling on the national
government to do more, especially regarding crime and private lawsuits. In
2001, state and local governments spent more than $111 billion on criminal
justice—everything from police protection to judges to corrections. State
and local governments employed the full-time equivalent of more than
1.5 million police and corrections workers in 2002, and 90 percent of the
more than 1.3 million prisoners in 2002 were housed in state rather than federal prisons.[3]

Like most states, Georgia provides substantial resources to its legal system.
In fiscal year 2005, the General Assembly appropriated roughly $1.5 billion
to the major agencies in Georgia's legal system (see table 9.1). This amount
included more than $150 million for the judicial branch and $1.3 billion for
the major executive agencies, with the largest single allocation going to the
Department of Corrections. City and county governments also have major
roles, primarily in law enforcement.

Table 9.1. Appropriations for Georgia's Legal System, Fiscal Year 2006

Judicial Branch	
Supreme Court	$7,969,323
Court of Appeals	$12,968,792
Superior Courts	$51,252,671
District Attorneys	$48,181,467
Juvenile Courts	$1,632,983
Public Defender Standards Office	$11,167,007
Executive Branch	
Department of Corrections	$997,005,543
Board of Pardons and Paroles	$49,847,069
Department of Juvenile Justice	$296,512,793
Georgia Bureau of Investigation	$65,891,012
Department of Public Safety	$102,255,376
Department of Law (Attorney General)	$146,705,539

Source: Georgia Governor's Office of Planning and Budget 2006, 23–25, 39–41.

Georgia's Courts

Organization and Jurisdiction

Like the federal government and most other states, Georgia has an elaborate system of trial and appellate courts (see figure 9.1).[4] Trial courts apply laws to the facts in specific cases, as when they render a verdict of guilt or innocence in a criminal case. Appellate courts review the actions of trial courts to determine questions of law—whether statutes or constitutional questions were interpreted or applied correctly. Unlike the U.S. Constitution, which grants Congress broad authority regarding the legal system, the Georgia Constitution includes substantial detail about the operation of trial and appellate courts, the selection and conduct of judges, the election and performance of district attorneys, and a range of procedures.

Trial Courts. At the lowest levels are approximately four hundred local courts—primarily municipal courts dealing with traffic matters, local ordinances, and other misdemeanors. These courts also process warrants

Figure 9.1. Structure of Georgia's Court System

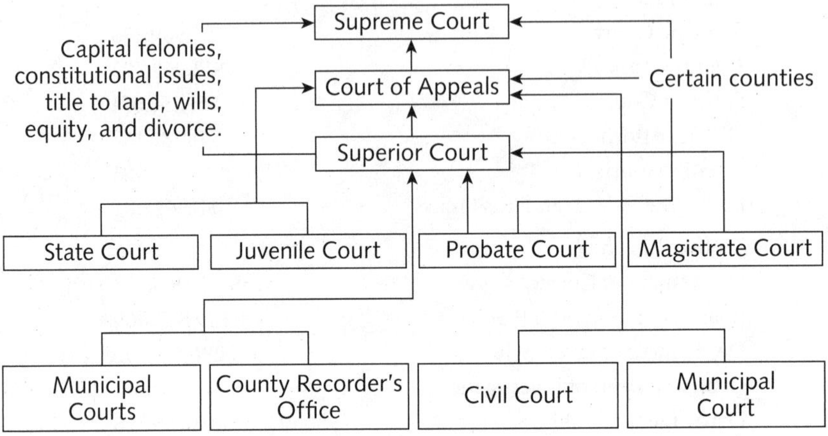

Source: Judicial Council of Georgia and Administrative Office of the Courts 2004, 6.

and may conduct preliminary hearings to determine probable cause in criminal cases. Local acts passed by the General Assembly determine the qualifications and selection method for municipal court judges.

Other courts deal with specific areas of the law. The Georgia Constitution requires a probate court in each county. These courts are headed by an elected judge and deal with wills, estates, marriage licenses, appointments of guardians, and involuntary hospitalizations of individuals. Probate courts may also issue warrants in some cases.

Each of Georgia's 159 counties also has a juvenile court, with a judge chosen by superior court judges in each circuit. In smaller counties, juvenile court judges may serve part time or superior court judges may serve in juvenile court. There are no jury trials in juvenile courts, and records are generally sealed to protect minors. Minors occasionally are tried in state or superior courts if a jury trial is warranted. In July 2004, 120 judges and associate judges served Georgia's juvenile courts.

Magistrate courts in each county deal with bail, misdemeanors, small civil complaints, and search and arrest warrants as well as with civil suits with claims of fifteen thousand dollars or less. As in juvenile courts, magistrate courts do not hold jury trials. In 2004, there were also seventy state courts, which hear some civil cases and may hear traffic violations or other misdemeanors. Jury trials are permitted in state courts. Overlap may be a problem in counties that have state courts because superior courts hold concurrent jurisdiction.

The Georgia Constitution designates superior courts as Georgia's trial courts of general jurisdiction. The state is divided into circuits (forty-nine in 2007) that vary in population and size. Each county has its own superior court, but judges may handle cases in more than one county within a circuit. They hear divorces, most cases involving civil disputes, land title cases, felonies, and equity cases. Jury trials are held in most cases. In 2006, Georgia had 193 superior court judges.

Appellate Courts. Like most states, Georgia has two levels of courts to hear appeals. Members of both courts are elected to six-year terms on a nonpartisan ballot. Cases decided at lower levels may be appealed to the State Court of Appeals, except in cases where the Supreme Court has special jurisdiction. The Court of Appeals was created in 1907 to relieve some of the burden on the Supreme Court and does not hear cases involving constitutional questions, land title disputes, the construction of wills, murder, election contests, habeas corpus, extraordinary remedies, or divorce and alimony; the Court of Appeals also does not hear cases where original appellate jurisdiction lies with the superior courts. From 1961 to 1996, the Court of Appeals had nine judges, but in response to calls to increase the size of the court, the governor and legislature added a tenth judge in 1996 and two more in 1999.[5] All appeals to the court are heard by a panel of three judges, who must agree unanimously to dispose of a case; if one judge dissents, the case may be heard by a panel of seven Court of Appeals judges.[6]

The Supreme Court has seven justices who choose whether to hear appeals from lower courts through the process of certiorari, or request for information, from lower courts. The court also is charged with hearing all cases regarding the Georgia Constitution, the U.S. Constitution (as it applies within the state), the constitutionality of laws, and elections. It also may hear cases on appeal from the Court of Appeals or decide questions of law from other state or local courts. It has authority to review all cases in which a sentence of death may be given. The Supreme Court is also involved in administering the state court system and regulating the legal profession.

The Work of the Courts

Trial Court Dockets. In 2004, more than 366,000 cases were filed in Georgia's superior courts—an average of 1,897 per judge (see table 9.2). A decade earlier, Georgia had fewer judges as well as 40,000 fewer cases filed, and the per-judge average dropped over that span. Of the 2004 cases, 63 percent were civil matters and 37 percent were criminal. Almost two-thirds of the civil cases dealt with domestic relations (for example, child custody, divorce), while 58 percent of the criminal cases involved felony charges. More cases are filed each year than are disposed of, producing a buildup of open cases.

Lower-level courts have more cases filed than superior courts, but the time involved in the disposition of each case is often less because paying of fines and filing documents does not take up court time. Because state courts do

Table 9.2. Caseload of Georgia Courts, 2004

Court	Number of Courts Reporting	Cases Filed
Supreme Court	1 of 1	1,976
Court of Appeals	1 of 1	3,238
Superior Courts	49 of 49	366,132
State Courts	71 of 71	904,611
Juvenile Courts	159 of 159	157,265
Probate Courts		
Civil Cases	142 of 159	91,718*
Criminal Cases	71 of 91	168,293
Magistrate Courts		
Civil Cases	148 of 159	422,286[†]
Criminal Cases	146 of 159	884,720[‡]
Municipal Courts	45[§]	237,390

*Excluding 69,395 marriage licenses and 56,590 firearms licenses.

[†] Eleven counties did not report; twenty-eight counties failed to provide data for all four quarters.

[‡] Thirteen counties did not report; twenty-nine counties failed to provide data for all four quarters.

[§] Number of municipal courts that sent data to the state.

Source: Judicial Council of Georgia and Administrative Office of the Courts 2005.

not exist in all counties and reporting of caseloads is not mandatory, figures on their workloads are only estimates. In 2004, data for Georgia's seventy-one state courts indicate that more than 904,000 cases were filed, 58 percent of them involving traffic charges.[7]

In excess of 157,000 juvenile cases—45 percent dealing with delinquency—were filed statewide in 2004. Although gaps exist in the data, probate courts had 91,718 civil cases in 2004, plus 69,395 marriage licenses and 56,590 firearm licenses. The seventy-one probate courts reporting complete criminal offense data for 2004 had more than 168,000 cases filed, 97 percent of them traffic charges. The largest volume of cases occurs in magistrate courts. For the counties reporting in 2004, magistrates faced more than 420,000 civil filings, issued almost 346,000 warrants, and had nearly 1.3 million criminal and civil cases filed.

Appellate Court Workloads. Cases heard at the appellate level are time-consuming and receive much media attention. In 1993, Georgia's Court of Appeals had the highest average of opinions per judge for any state, but the addition of three judges to the court enabled the creation of more three-judge panels to handle the many appeals for which written opinions are issued. In 2004, the Court of Appeals disposed of 3,435 cases, more than 2,500 of them direct appeals.[8]

The Supreme Court disposed of 2,055 cases in 2004 but resolved only 347 with formal opinions. The court also denied 569 petitions for a writ of certiorari and 237 applications for a writ of habeas corpus. The court also considered 79 cases of attorney discipline.

In addition to the formal changes in jurisdiction and procedures that can occur because of constitutional amendments and laws, courts are affected by their rules and informal practices. The Georgia Supreme Court has discretion to decide whether to hear certain types of appeals through its authority to issue writs of certiorari. Between 1993 and 2001, the Supreme Court received more than 5,600 petitions for certiorari but agreed to review only 8 percent of these cases, a substantial decrease from the 15–20 percent of certiorari petitions granted from 1978 to 1988.[9]

Written dissents by justices who disagree with the majority of the court in a case increased dramatically from the 1840s to the early 1900s and again through the 1950s. Through the early 1980s, most dissents occurred in civil cases. By 2001, dissents were almost equally common in civil and criminal cases. Moreover, by 2001, only about one-third of the dissents in cases were by a single justice, compared to just over 50 percent from the early 1900s through the 1950s.[10] The Supreme Court has also altered its habits in issuing per curiam opinions, which do not identify their authors. From the 1840s through the early 1980s, most per curiam opinions merely affirmed decisions by the Court of Appeals in civil cases. By 1998–2001, though, 90 percent of per curiam opinions dealt with attorney discipline.[11]

One study compared the success of parties who appealed their cases to the Georgia, North Carolina, and South Carolina Supreme Courts. Individuals filing appeals in Georgia had less than a 30 percent chance of winning without groups filing supporting briefs; that number rose to 45 percent in South Carolina and to 47 percent in North Carolina. With interest group support, the chances of winning on appeal increased to 44 percent in Georgia and to more than 60 percent in the other two states. In general, this study confirmed the importance of repeat players compared to one-shot participants in producing favorable outcomes in appellate courts.[12]

Controversies. Despite images of the law as impartial, debates have swirled over the workings of the courts. One deals with authorities' use of their discretion—that is, with prosecutors making decisions about which charge or penalty to pursue based on the backgrounds of the victim and the accused.[13] More general concerns about racial bias have also been raised.[14] Observers long complained that the jury system was biased in favor of the accused because defendants could remove two potential jurors from the pool for every one that the prosecution struck. In 2005, however, following pressure by supporters of a deceased crime victim, the legislature passed a law giving the prosecution and defense in criminal cases the same number of strikes from the pool of potential jurors.[15]

Other criticisms have concerned civil cases. One statewide poll during the mid-1990s suggested that most Georgians believed that personal injury cases were clogging the courts, were growing rapidly in number, were too often decided by juries instead of settled out of court, and produced awards that were too large—the respondents estimated the average award at $200,000. However, research on four counties representing urban, suburban, and rural areas for 1990–1993 indicates that an image of runaway tort litigation does not fit Georgia's courts. More than 43,000 civil cases were filed in Bibb, Irwin, Gwinnett, and Oconee Counties during the four years studied, but fewer than 5 percent were tort claims, while 70 percent concerned domestic relations. More than two-thirds of the tort cases were vehicle-related, and less than 5 percent dealt with medical malpractice. More than 80 percent of the plaintiffs and defendants were individuals rather than businesses, government agencies, or other organizations. Moreover, just 5 percent had jury verdicts, while another 1 percent featured verdicts by judges. Most cases were disposed of without trials. Overall, the plaintiffs prevailed in 51 percent of the trials with an average award of $27,868, far below the estimated $200,000.[16]

Critics also focus on delays in criminal trials and executions of those sentenced to death in the belief that dragging out trials and putting off executions weakens the deterrent effects of punishment. Conversely, death penalty opponents cite cases where delay has allowed new evidence to exonerate someone sentenced to die. Opponents also fault prosecutors for the way they use their discretion, particularly when seeking the death penalty can aid a district attorney's reelection chances. These issues are especially salient in Georgia, which gave rise to the major death penalty cases decided by the U.S. Supreme Court during the 1970s. Georgia ranked sixth in number of executions (thirty-six) between 1977, when the death penalty was reintroduced, and 2004. On January 1, 2006, the state had 109 inmates on death row.[17]

Some evidence indicates that Georgia juries are less willing to sentence defendants to death since a 1993 law added a sentence of life without parole. (Previously, convicted criminals sentenced to life in prison could be eligible for parole.) In addition, some prosecutors negotiate plea bargains of life without parole to avoid the lengthy and costly appeals that accompany death penalty cases.[18]

Judicial Agencies

Georgia's legal system is administered by several organizations.[19] One of the major agencies is the Judicial Council, which was created in 1973 and is composed of twenty-four trial and appellate judges. The chief justice of the Georgia Supreme Court chairs the council, which evaluates the need for new courts, court circuits, and personnel. The council also may conduct studies of other aspects of the judicial system. Several other councils provide support and research for different types of courts. The Council of Superior Court Judges, for example, uses several committees to study various aspects of the workings of superior courts.

Another key agency is the Administrative Office of the Courts, which was created in 1973 and reports to the Judicial Council. The office provides the judicial branch with administrative support and research and serves as a public information office, disseminating information on caseloads, judges, and the like to interested officials and citizens. The Administrative Office of the Courts works with various organizations that provide training and education, such as those for court administrators, reporters, and interpreters.

The Judicial Qualifications Commission sets standards for judicial conduct and holds hearings to determine whether judges are guilty of misconduct. The Institute of Continuing Judicial Education holds seminars and conferences to train judges, clerks, judicial secretaries, and other court personnel.

Providing attorneys for the poor in criminal cases has remained controversial since a series of U.S. Supreme Court decisions during the 1960s.[20] Historically, complying with such decisions was a decentralized matter in Georgia, with the state's counties choosing several methods of providing counsel for indigent defendants. In 2001, about half of Georgia's counties used a system in which judges appointed attorneys, with compensation varying by county. In another fifty-nine counties (38 percent), indigent defense was put out for bid by firms, like many local government services. In the remaining twenty-one counties (13 percent), the county funded and staffed a public defender's office to represent poor defendants, much like any other county government agency. The state provided some financial support for indigent defense. However, debates over the different approaches to indigent defense led the Georgia Supreme Court to create a commission in 2000 to study the issue.[21]

The commission's work became more critical as the federal courts expanded the conditions under which indigents were entitled to an attorney, including a 2002 case from Alabama in which the U.S. Supreme Court ruled that someone who receives a probated or suspended sentence that could lead to imprisonment had the right to be represented by a lawyer. The Georgia General Assembly responded to these demands in 2004 and created a statewide system with a public defender's office in each judicial circuit. The system, which operates under the supervision of the Georgia Public Defender Standards Council, was expected to cost more than $40 million annually, with the money coming from increases in court fees, fines, and bail bonds. Counties can opt out of the system if they can demonstrate to the council that an adequate system is already in place.[22]

In addition to these agencies, the Attorney General's Office serves as prosecutor for capital felony cases at the state level as well as counsel for the state and its agencies. The attorney general is an elected official, but lawyers may be hired as assistant attorneys general to work in this office as in any other state agency.

Most criminal cases are handled at the local level by district attorneys, with one elected in each judicial circuit for a four-year term on a partisan ballot. Each serves as prosecutor for the state in superior court and must have been a member of the state bar for three years prior to election.

Judges, Juries, and Lawyers

In addition to establishing courts, the states oversee key participants in the legal system. The most important regulations include qualifications, selection, and procedures for judges, juries, and attorneys.

Judicial Qualifications and Selection

Judicial Selection in the States. Unlike the national level, where judges are nominated by the president and confirmed by the Senate, the states employ five methods of choosing judges.[23] Some elect judges in partisan elections; other states hold nonpartisan elections; others require that judges be appointed by the governor; three states have at least some judges elected by the legislature; and still others allow for the selection of judges under a merit system of screening by nominating commissions that submit candidates to a state's governor. Once in office, such judges stand periodically for election. Some states use several selection methods: one recent tally listed eight states with partisan election of judges, thirteen with nonpartisan elections, fifteen relying exclusively on merit appointment through a nominating commission, four employing gubernatorial appointments, and two (Virginia and South Carolina) with legislative election of judges. Another nine states combined merit selection with other methods of selecting appellate and general trial court judges.

Each selection method has its detractors and advocates, and Henry Glick has noted that "state selection systems do not make much difference in determining who becomes a judge."[24] Gubernatorial appointment has existed

since colonial times, but election became common by the 1820s. Some research suggests that appointment systems improve gender diversity in state
supreme courts.[25] Critics of elections complain about judges who may be too
political; opponents of appointment argue that judges are not accountable to
the public. Since the 1940s, states have increasingly adopted merit plans, although that approach does not take politics out of the equation. State nominating commissions tend to have more elite backgrounds than the general
public, generally include some members loyal to the governor, and often
reflect splits within the legal profession. Only a small percentage of judges
selected under merit plans get voted out of office. More generally, one study
found that only 20 percent of state supreme court races between 1980 and
1995 were close (defined as the winner getting less than 55 percent of the
vote). Elections were more likely to be close, however, in nonpartisan contests without an incumbent running and in partisan races, where more than
one-third were close, even with incumbents on the ballot.[26]

Underlying all these debates is the growing public recognition that courts
not only enforce laws but also make policy. At the trial level, research findings are mixed on whether judges' race, ethnicity, and gender are associated
with disparities in the sentences they hand down to various types of defendants.[27] However, one study has found that black trial judges are harsher
than their white counterparts when imposing sentences.[28] Some evidence
also shows that limits on judges' flexibility can reduce racial disparities
in sentencing.[29]

Appellate courts are important policy makers, in part because they define
the scope of rights under state constitutions, can create or expand important
legal doctrines, and use a variety of factors in deciding individual appeals.[30]
For example, state appeals courts have been drawn into debates over such
controversial issues as same-sex marriage. Judicial discretion is one reason
that governors try to use court appointments to change policies as well as a
reason that judicial elections have become more contentious in recent years,
especially as rules governing judicial campaigns have loosened. Judicial elections have become more partisan, increasingly aggressive, more like other
media-based campaigns, and more costly. In 2004, candidates spent more
than $39 million in forty-four judicial contests. Candidates for a state su-
preme court seat in West Virginia raised $2.8 million, while interest groups
spent another $4.5 million; two candidates in Illinois spent a combined
$9 million, to which interest groups and political parties added $4.4 million.[31] One study comparing the states found that spending in state supreme

court elections between 1990 and 2000 was highest for races in which there was no incumbent running, where the terms were longer, where the number of seats on the ballot was low, and where the volume of tort cases was high.[32]

Judicial Selection in Georgia. Georgia has a long-standing commitment to electing judges, although Article 6, Section 7 of the Georgia Constitution lists some requirements regarding age, residence in counties or circuits, and membership in the state bar.[33] The Constitution specifies that members of the Supreme Court and Court of Appeals be elected in statewide elections on a nonpartisan ballot for six-year terms and must have been authorized to practice law for seven years prior to election. The justices of the Supreme Court choose a chief justice from among themselves.

Superior court judges are also elected in nonpartisan elections but serve four-year terms and are elected by the voters within each circuit. State court judges are elected in nonpartisan countywide elections and serve four-year terms. Juvenile court judges are appointed by the superior court judges of the counties they serve.

Most probate judges are elected in partisan county elections, but seventeen counties hold nonpartisan elections. In counties with more than ninety-six thousand residents, probate judges are required to meet age and other qualifications. Georgia's magistrates are appointed or elected, depending on the county. In some cases, chief magistrates are elected in partisan county elections and appoint other magistrates to serve concurrent terms. Qualifications, selection, and terms of office for municipal court judges vary widely and are set by the cities in which the judges serve.

Judicial elections have usually been low-key affairs, with incumbents seldom facing challengers. Changes are becoming apparent, however. In 1996, a candidate for the Georgia Court of Appeals ran a thirty-second television commercial criticizing the incumbent for writing an opinion overturning a conviction in a child molestation case. Georgia's judicial conduct rules prohibit judicial candidates from announcing their views on disputed issues, and the Georgia Judicial Qualifications Commission criticized the ad but did not attempt to remove it from the air.[34]

In 2006, a bitter battle for a seat on the Georgia Supreme Court cost the incumbent $1.1 million in campaign expenditures. Despite a vigorous media campaign by her challenger, Justice Carol Hunstein won by over 63 percent of the vote. Recent heated races may be a harbinger of things to come in Georgia's nonpartisan judicial elections. The district attorney in Cobb County helped raise money for the opponent of an incumbent judge. Even more visible were the interest groups and large amounts of money involved in several judicial races. The Georgia Christian Coalition surveyed candidates for appellate courts on five controversial social issues: seven of the nine refused to fill out the questionnaire; the two who provided answers agreed with the organization's positions. One candidate had the backing of Governor Sonny Perdue in trying to defeat a Supreme Court incumbent endorsed by a major teachers organization, labor unions, and the state's gay rights lobby. A race for a seat on the Court of Appeals included another Perdue endorsement, one candidate who raised more than $2.7 million, and litigation that forced a runoff four months after the July election. Even a state court race in Gwinnett County saw the two candidates raise a total of almost $150,000 with two weeks remaining before their runoff election.[35]

Despite the requirement that judges be elected, appointment is important for filling vacancies and new judgeships, especially since most judges easily win reelection. Except in magistrate, probate, and juvenile courts, Article 6, Section 7 of the Georgia Constitution authorizes the governor to appoint someone to serve the remainder of a judge's term when a position becomes vacant for any reason. The governor thus has substantial power to shape the composition of the judiciary. The Judicial Nominating Commission assists the governor in making appointments, although the selection process includes input from political leaders and members of the legal profession.[36] One study calculated that between 1968 and mid-1994, 66 percent of superior court judgeships were filled by appointment.[37] Observers have expressed concern that political connections can play a large role. For example, going into his 2002 reelection campaign, Governor Roy Barnes had considered 173 finalists while filling 53 judgeships. Sixty of the 120 not chosen had contributed a total of $136,400 to Barnes's campaign, while 44 of the 53 chosen gave a total of $165,300, with additional contributions coming from some of their relatives and associates.[38] When a vacancy occurred on the Georgia Supreme Court in 2005, Perdue appointed his personal legal adviser.[39]

All judges, whether appointed or elected, are subject to the Georgia Recall Act of 1989. The seven-member Judicial Qualifications Commission may also remove judges from office, discipline them, or forcibly retire them if they are found guilty of willful misconduct while in office, are convicted of crimes, willfully and persistently fail to perform duties, are habitually intemperate, engage in prejudicial conduct that brings the judicial office into disrepute, or become disabled to the extent of seriously interfering with the performance of judicial duties. The commission's findings and recommendations are subject to review by the Georgia Supreme Court.

Juries

Citizens may be chosen to serve on either trial (also known as petit) juries or grand juries. While trial juries are the better known to the public because of media coverage of some criminal cases, grand juries are important in determining how and if a case will proceed against a defendant.

Each county has a board of jury commissioners that chooses members of both trial and grand juries. The commissioners are required to develop jury pools composed of "a fairly representative cross section of the intelligent and upright citizens of the county" and do so by relying on driver's licenses or similar state-issued identification, voter registration lists, or other lists of residents.[40] Once called, jurors must serve or face contempt of court. Employers must excuse jury-related absences. Observers have lodged complaints over the years about the fairness of the size and composition of the pools of potential jurors in various counties. Both the General Assembly and the courts have stepped in to deal with such problems, including a 2002 Georgia Supreme Court ruling that Hispanics were to be treated as a distinct group when considering the representativeness of a pool.[41]

Trial Juries. Trial juries in civil and criminal cases can vary in size according to the level of the court and the laws of the jurisdiction. A jury defendant can choose whether to have a judge render a verdict. Juries serve as the ultimate decision-making institution for court cases but must operate within the confines of the law and the evidence presented within the courtroom. Many factors may sway juries, including both formal influences such as a judge's instructions and informal issues such as the appearance of a defendant or witnesses.[42]

With rare exceptions, the U.S. Constitution requires that citizens tried for criminal offenses are entitled to trial by jury.[43] Anyone who faces a punishment of more than six months in prison must be tried by jury, but the size of the jury may vary between twelve (as it is in federal cases) and six, depending on the state. Some states require unanimous jury decision, as does the federal government, while other states require a specific majority on a twelve-person jury. The U.S. Supreme Court has required states to use unanimous decisions with six-person juries.[44]

In Georgia, jury size is determined by the level of the court; some court decisions do not require juries at all. Because appellate courts review the actions of lower courts and do not hold trials, juries are not used. Magistrate courts and juvenile courts never hold jury trials, and other lower courts seldom use juries. State courts have six-member juries, while superior court juries have twelve members. Juries in civil cases consist of six or twelve members, depending on the dollar amount of damages sought and whether either party in state court requests a jury of twelve rather than six members. In Georgia, unanimous decisions are required in criminal cases but not in other trials.[45]

The size of a jury pool for a case varies by county. The state has set a minimum pool size of thirty for felonies and forty-two for capital cases; other pools are generally twice the size of the trial jury. The members of the trial jury are selected from among the members of the pool. Judges may excuse potential jurors from service because of family emergencies, work schedule conflicts, or other unavoidable hindrances. Such excuses usually only postpone service rather than permanently excuse the juror. Both sides in a case then question potential jurors, a process known as voir dire. If an attorney can convince the judge that a potential juror cannot be impartial, the person is removed from the pool for cause. Georgia permits an unlimited number of such juror challenges. Those excused or struck for cause are replaced to maintain the required pool size.

Each side also receives a limited number of peremptory strikes, for which attorneys do not have to give a reason for removing potential jurors from the pool. Attorneys generally use peremptory strikes to try to shape a jury in their favor. The U.S. Supreme Court has limited litigants' ability to remove potential jurors on the basis of race or gender, although some observers remain concerned that this practice continues in more subtle forms.[46] The number of peremptory strikes depends on the required size of the jury. Since 2005, each side receives fifteen peremptory strikes in death penalty cases, nine in other felony cases, and three in misdemeanor trials.[47] In civil cases, the plaintiff and defendant also receive an equal number of strikes. When both sides have used all their strikes, the remaining pool members comprise the jury.

Grand Juries. More than half the states use grand juries to issue indictments in criminal cases. All other states make grand jury indictments optional, with the prosecutor filing an information to enter a formal charge against someone. New Jersey, South Carolina, Tennessee, and Virginia require grand juries for all indictments. Georgia is one of fifteen states that requires a grand jury for felony indictments. Six states require grand jury indictments for capital crimes, and Pennsylvania does not empower grand juries to indict.

Grand juries in most states consist of eighteen to twenty-three citizens selected in the same manner as trial juries. Grand juries may be used to determine whether enough evidence exists to bring a case to court. In this, they serve the same function as preliminary hearings in determining whether probable cause exists to support an indictment. The difference between a grand jury and preliminary hearing lies in the powers of the prosecuting attorney. Because the grand jury is charged with determining whether sufficient evidence exists, only the prosecution is heard, business is conducted in secret, and the defense has no right to cross-examine witnesses. In addition, grand jury decisions need not be unanimous. Many commentators have argued that these characteristics make grand juries unnecessary and merely a rubber stamp for the prosecutor.[48]

Grand juries in Georgia consist of between sixteen and twenty-three members and issue presentments (reports) in addition to indictments. Grand juries selected school boards in some counties until the state constitution was amended in 1992; evidence shows that this process was inaugurated in the 1870s to minimize the influence of black voters.[49] Grand juries also have broad powers to study county government records and activities, issue reports, and make certain decisions. In 1996, for example, a twenty-one-member commission appointed by a grand jury reviewed the performance of the recently merged governments of Athens and Clark County and issued a final report as a presentment to the superior court judge.[50]

Lawyers

The United States had more than 950,000 lawyers in 2004. Women comprised 29.4 percent of the total, blacks constituted 4.7 percent, and Hispanics made up 3.4 percent. The nation's law schools have conferred more than 35,000 degrees annually since the 1980s. In 1975 women received only

15 percent of the law degrees awarded, but by 2002 that figure had risen to 48 percent.[51]

Legal services generally are provided in exchange for a fee; people with low incomes may, therefore, lack access to lawyers. A series of court cases has guaranteed free legal representation to poor criminal defendants in cases that could result in jail sentences, although, as discussed earlier in this chapter, each state has set up a system for providing attorneys. The national government and the states also provide some legal assistance to the poor in civil matters.[52]

Legal Education. Lawyers generally receive training in two ways—formal education provided by law schools and ongoing education for practicing attorneys. Although some are for-profit entities, most law schools are housed within universities, including many public institutions that use tax money to train professionals in a variety of fields in addition to law. Law schools are accredited nationally by the American Bar Association. Georgia's accredited programs in 2005 included state-funded programs at the University of Georgia and Georgia State University as well as private programs at Emory and Mercer Universities.

Law schools generally offer three-year courses of study that prepare students to pass the state bar exam, which is a prerequisite for practicing law. In his widely adopted text on the legal system, Glick has summarized this training: "Law schools put heavy premiums on business law, with relatively little emphasis on other areas such as consumer law, civil rights, or environmental law. The major thrust is learning the basics of business problems and serving business clients."[53]

Lawyers' education does not end with law school and the bar exam, however. Continuing education also is available, usually through publications, formal courses, and seminars at professional conferences. Lawyers in Georgia are required to attend at least twelve hours of continuing legal education annually under the supervision of the Commission on Continuing Lawyer Competency. Sponsored by the State Bar of Georgia and the state's accredited law schools, the Institute of Continuing Legal Education also offers a wide range of continuing education courses.[54]

Regulation of the Legal Profession. Many people are surprised to learn that the training and regulation of lawyers are left largely to the states and the legal profession itself. Oversight of any profession or industry can often become controversial, especially at the state level, where few organized interests may represent consumers or others affected by the regulated industry. According to Glick, "One of the important characteristics of a state-regulated profession is that it has the authority to do work that is prohibited of others. . . . Despite internal differences that frequently occur among lawyers, protecting the profession is the one issue on which most lawyers close ranks."[55] Lawyers have more difficulty doing so than do doctors, Glick adds, because lawyers have lower status than medical professionals, have less control over their clients, and perform work that is often not easy to separate from routine procedures conducted by nonlawyers. For example, requiring attorneys for certain property transactions can bring lawyers into conflict with another powerful interest regulated by the states, real estate groups.[56] Critics have charged that state bar associations limit the size and activities of the legal profession, thereby increasing the cost of legal services. Competition has increased in recent years, however, as the U.S. Supreme Court has outlawed certain regulations and lawyers have begun advertising.

At the national level, the American Bar Association sets rules regarding ethical conduct in the legal profession. Enforcement is left to the states, usually through their supreme courts and bar associations. In Georgia, the state bar association functions as a self-governing administrative arm of the Supreme Court and processes complaints. From May 1, 2005, through April 30, 2006, Georgians filed 2,719 grievances with the state bar, all but 384 of which were dismissed based on the factual record. Following review by an investigatory panel, 252 cases were referred for prosecution, with confidential discipline imposed on 40 attorneys. The state bar referred the most serious incidents to the Georgia Supreme Court for a hearing and possible public discipline. Some cases are continued from one year to the next, but during 2005–2006, 28 attorneys were disbarred or voluntarily surrendered their ability to practice law, 27 more were suspended, and another 6 received some form of reprimand or admonition.[57]

The Future of Georgia's Legal System

Elected officials, police, prosecutors, the courts, and corrections agencies face pressure to solve a host of problems, many of which may not be soluble. Politically, this situation has translated into efforts to criminalize more behavior and stiffen penalties. Indeed, each candidate for public office seems to try to create a tougher image than his or her opponent. In 2005, 26 percent of Americans polled by the Gallup Organization reported "a great deal" or "quite of lot" of confidence in the criminal justice system, an 8-point drop from a year earlier but 6–11 points above the levels in the mid-1990s.[58]

State courts have been drawn into this maelstrom. They are being asked to improve their efficiency, in part through technological improvements and alternatives to traditional lawsuits. They also stand on the front lines of debates over biases in the law, the legal profession, and the judiciary. Changes over the past few decades and growing interest group involvement in judicial elections suggest that Georgia's legal system will no longer constitute a relatively invisible part of state government. In fact, the legal system may become even more visible as it grapples with controversial issues and becomes more politicized.

Local Government and Politics

Georgia had more than 1,400 local governments in 2002, and the 2007 U.S. Census Bureau count will undoubtedly show that the number has continued to increase. This chapter considers the state's crucial role in controlling local governments, describes the organization and functions of local governments, examines citizen participation and policy making in Georgia communities, and compares Georgia to other states. These are important topics because Georgians depend on local governments for a wide range of basic daily services, including police and fire protection, water, and schools. Georgians also expect local officials to be accessible and responsive to concerns. Yet the effectiveness of any local government is influenced by organization, state and national governments, and the actions of other communities.

The Foundations of Local Government

Georgia's local governments include counties, cities, and special districts. Unlike many states in the Midwest and New England, Georgia has no townships that provide services in rural areas; instead, counties assume such responsibilities. Counties and cities are considered general-purpose local governments because they provide a wide range of services and have received broad authority from the state. In Georgia, like most states, counties also serve as administrative arms of the state, performing tasks such as jailing and prosecuting people, providing public health services, processing vehicle license plates, and maintaining necessary records such as those for real estate and marriage. Special districts are limited to a single service or a narrow range of functions. Probably the most visible examples are school districts.

As in other states, local government in Georgia changed after World War II: the total number of local governments increased more than 48 percent between 1952 and 2002 (see table 10.1). This contrasts sharply with the nation as a whole, where the number of local governments dropped almost 25 percent over that period, primarily as a consequence of the elimination of more than fifty thousand school districts. Special districts almost tripled in the United States during the same fifty years, however. Even looking only at the thirty years between 1972 and 2002, when the total number of local governments in the United States grew 12.3 percent, the total in Georgia increased 16.5 percent.

In addition to an overall increase in local governments, Georgia has also witnessed a change in the mix of government types (see table 10.2). The number of counties in Georgia has remained constant at 159 since the 1930s. The number of cities grew slightly from 475 to 528, while the total for school

Table 10.1. Number of Local Governments in the United States and Georgia, 1952–2002

	United States		Georgia	
Year	Total	% Change	Total	% Change
1952	116,756		975	
1957	102,341	−12.3	1,120	14.9
1962	91,186	−10.9	1,218	8.8
1967	81,248	−10.9	1,203	−1.2
1972	78,218	−3.7	1,243	3.3
1977	79,862	2.1	1,263	1.6
1982	81,780	2.4	1,268	0.4
1987	83,186	1.7	1,286	1.4
1992	86,692	4.2	1,297	0.9
1997	87,453	0.9	1,344	3.6
2002	87,849	0.5	1,448	7.7

Sources: U.S. Census Bureau 2002a, 3–6; U.S. Census Bureau 2006c, table 416.

Table 10.2. Number and Type of Local Governments in Georgia, 1952–2002

Year	Counties*	Municipalities	School Districts	Special District
1952	159	475	187	154
1957	159	508	198	255
1962	159	561	197	301
1967	159	512	194	338
1972	159	529	189	366
1977	159	529	188	387
1982	159	531	187	390
1987	159	531	186	410
1992	159	534	183	421
1997	159	532	180	473
2002	159	528	180	581

* The Census Bureau counts Georgia's consolidated city-county governments as municipalities. This table treats them as counties, however, because they maintain the functions of counties and continue to elect county officials, particularly constitutional officers such as sheriffs.

Sources: U.S. Census Bureau, Census of Governments, various years.

districts held fairly steady. The major change occurred among special districts, which grew from 154 to 581 (an increase of 277 percent). These special districts perform functions such as housing and community development (201), hospitals (107), sewer and/or water service (60), soil and water conservation (38), health (27), and administration of airports (25).

Critics have often taken aim at Georgia's substantial number of small local governments. The General Assembly responded to this situation in 1993 by passing legislation that used grants and rules to encourage consolidation and elimination of smaller jurisdictions. As a result, 188 cities had their charters revoked on July 1, 1995, because they did not provide three of eleven listed services, hold regular meetings, or conduct elections.[1]

The U.S. Constitution and Local Governments

The U.S. Constitution says nothing about local governments. It does refer to states, however, and its provisions and federal laws extend to governments created by the states. The basic responsibility for establishing and regulating local governments, then, rests with the fifty states, each of which has created a distinct system of local government. The legal doctrine underlying state-local relations is known as Dillon's Rule, and it treats local governments as "creatures of the state" with only those powers explicitly granted, clearly implied from explicitly granted powers, or essential to meeting responsibilities.[2] This doctrine can restrict local officials' discretion but also means that local government authority is often open to interpretation, debate, and—not surprisingly—litigation.

State Methods for Limiting Local Governments

One means of restricting a local government is its charter, which is comparable to a constitution. States grant charters to local governments much in the same way that they establish procedures for private companies to incorporate or nonprofit organizations to form. The process by which a new municipal government is created and granted a charter is known as incorporation. Charters typically cover governmental organization, procedures for selecting officials and conducting public business, powers of taxing and spending, requirements for providing public services, and other basic features.

A second constraint is state control over local governments' territory. The boundaries of a new government are specified when it is incorporated. In addition, states also regulate annexation (a city's extension of its boundaries to include unincorporated territory) and consolidation (the merger of two or more local governments). States also limit local officials' discretion with mandates—that is, standards, functions, procedures, or other rules that impose obligations or prohibitions (discussed later in the chapter). States justify mandates in terms of minimum standards for local governments throughout the state, but local government officials complain that mandates substitute state priorities for local priorities and impose significant costs on local governments.

The Georgia Constitution and Local Governments

Georgia's Constitution is very detailed regarding local government. In fact, Article 9, which is devoted to counties and municipalities (cities), comprises more than 15 percent of the document. Parts of Article 8 ("Education") and several other sections also treat local government.

Local Government Organization and Authority

The Constitution is somewhat more specific regarding counties than it is regarding cities and special districts. Article 9 even restricts the number of counties to a maximum of 159, although no such limit applies to other governments. The article also requires all counties to have certain elected officials. These "constitutional officers" include a clerk of the superior court, judge of the probate court, sheriff, and tax commissioner (or tax collector and tax receiver), each of whom serves a four-year term. The Constitution permits state law to spell out the characteristics of local legislative bodies such as county commissions and city councils.

Article 6, which covers the judicial branch, prescribes the procedure for electing the various judges and the district attorney in each judicial circuit, which can include one or more counties. Every county, however, must have at least one superior, magistrate, and probate court.

The Georgia Constitution goes to some lengths to prohibit counties from taking actions that would affect local school systems or any court. The document also lists functions that cities and counties may perform if they choose, including offering public transportation, providing health services and facilities, operating libraries, and enforcing building codes. This provision is especially important to counties, which were first authorized to provide urban services by a constitutional amendment ratified in 1972. Article 9 also allows counties and cities to use planning and zoning, to take private property, to make agreements with one another, and to consolidate. Other sections cover intergovernmental relations, local taxation and debt, and various types of districts.[3]

Home Rule

The constitution also provides home rule. In most states, this means that a local government receives broad powers to write and amend its charter and to take any action not prohibited by the state. Home rule has proven more limited in Georgia than in many other states, however. Georgia has a long-standing reputation for granting relatively little authority to its cities and counties to determine their form of government. However, it has granted local governments flexibility in carrying out their functions. Unlike the majority of states, Georgia does not divide its cities into "classes" (usually based on population), with different levels of authority granted to each class.[4]

A major reason for this limited local power is the Constitution, which places many restrictions directly on counties and cities. It also permits the legislature to adopt local laws. While general laws are applied uniformly statewide, a local law applies to the city, county, or special district specified in the bill. Although local laws cannot conflict with general laws, the General Assembly uses such laws to modify the workings of cities, counties, and special districts. Local bills cover a wide range of topics. For example, the General Assembly had to establish procedures for citizens to vote on merging the governments in Athens–Clarke County in 1990 and in Augusta–Richmond County in 1995. Many other states prohibit the adoption of local laws.

A significant share of all legislation adopted by the General Assembly is local (see chapter 6). To be reported from committee, local bills must have the support of state legislators from the affected city or county. An unofficial norm of local courtesy then dictates that the rest of the House or Senate defer to the judgments of the delegation from the city or county named in the bill. The dilemma is that communities must depend on the General Assembly to determine their future. Moreover, state legislators have the power to act without formally involving local officials or residents.[5]

Financial Constraints

Article 9, Section 4 of the Georgia Constitution generally permits the General Assembly to address the question of how local governments can raise and spend money. In contrast, debt is covered in substantial detail. Georgia employs two major restrictions common among the states. One is that debt cannot exceed 10 percent of the assessed value of taxable property within the jurisdiction. The other requires that voters approve new debt by a simple majority in an election. However, these provisions apply only to general obligation debt—borrowing in which the local government pledges tax revenues to pay off bonds sold to raise money. The Constitution also places an annual limit on the amount that can be borrowed on a short-term basis.

The requirement for voter approval of debt has numerous loopholes. Revenue bonds are the major exception to the required voter approval and debt limitation. Revenue bonds are backed not by taxes but by revenues from projects financed by the bonds. Airport bonds, for example, are generally paid off with parking revenue, aircraft landing fees, rents from airlines and concessionaires, and the like. With all types of local government borrowing, though, the real limit is investors' willingness to buy bonds issued by a government.

Georgia Law and Local Governments

State control does not stop with the Constitution. The General Assembly has wide latitude to regulate local governments, including territory and mandates dealing with services, personnel, finances, and procedures.

Territory

The state's major focus regarding territory is procedural and is based on long-standing differences between counties and cities in the United States. At least until World War II, municipal governments served developed areas needing a wide range of services, while counties provided minimal services in rural locations. Thus, as areas became urbanized, they would form city governments or become part of existing municipalities. While this remains the pattern in many states, Georgia counties have provided urban services since the 1970s.

Creating New Local Governments. Georgia originally had only 2 counties, although that number had grown to 32 by 1832. Counties proliferated significantly during two periods: 37 were created between 1850 and 1860, bringing the total to 132, and another 24 were added in the early twentieth century, enhancing rural political power under the county-unit system. Fulton County's merger with two less-well-off counties during the 1930s reduced the total to its present level of 159. Only Texas has more.[6] Although the General Assembly can create new counties, the current number is the maximum allowed by the Constitution.

More common has been the creation of municipalities and special districts. Like other states, Georgia uses its general laws to specify guidelines for incorporating a municipal government, but granting a charter to a city requires a local law.[7] To incorporate, a new municipality must have at least two hundred residents and a minimum density of two hundred people per square mile, cannot be closer to an existing municipality than three miles, and must have at least 60 percent of its area subdivided into lots used for nonagricultural purposes.

The Georgia Constitution and general laws permit special districts. Perhaps the most important characteristic of special districts is their relative independence from county and city governments, especially in the case of Georgia's local school systems. In contrast, various authorities and districts maintain ties to general-purpose local governments. The legislature can either create such districts by local law or authorize cities and counties to establish them.[8]

Annexation and Consolidation. The state also sets ground rules for changing the boundaries of local governments. General law includes procedures to change a county's boundaries, but such events are virtually nonexistent. Annexation and consolidation efforts are much more frequent.

Georgia municipalities can annex through local acts of the General Assembly, passage of a resolution by a city with a subsequent referendum in the area proposed for annexation, or two petition processes. One type of petition permits cities to annex adjoining territory if requested in a petition signed by the owners of 100 percent of its acreage. The other method allows the petition to be signed by the owners of 60 percent of the property and 60 percent of the voters in the area under consideration. Under both processes, the city must hold a public hearing and pass an ordinance to complete the annexation. The state has also authorized cities to annex unincorporated areas—islands—of fifty or fewer acres surrounded by the cities.[9]

While annexation might seem to be an incremental change in boundaries, consolidation appears more radical because it can altogether eliminate some governments. General law for merging cities with counties in Georgia is quite brief, and the General Assembly considers each consolidation on a case-by-case basis using local laws. Consolidations require majorities in each of the governments being merged. This can be troubling to consolidation backers, as when Rockdale County voters approved a merger with Conyers (the county's only municipality) in 1989, but the consolidation failed in Conyers.[10]

Georgia has been among the most active states in considering city-county consolidations, with 30 proposals on local ballots between 1933 and 2003 (see table 10.3). Yet voters have approved only four mergers: Columbus and Muscogee County, Athens and Clarke County, Augusta and Richmond

Table 10.3. City-County Consolidation Referenda in Georgia

Location	Year
Macon–Bibb County	1933
Albany–Dougherty County	1954
Albany–Dougherty County	1956
Macon–Bibb County	1960
Columbus–Muscogee County	1962
Athens–Clarke County	1969
Brunswick–Glynn County	1969
Columbus–Muscogee County	1970*
Augusta–Richmond County	1971
Athens–Clarke County	1972
Macon–Bibb County	1972
Savannah–Chatham County	1973
Augusta–Richmond County	1974
Augusta–Richmond County	1976
Macon–Bibb County	1976
Athens–Clarke County	1982
Tifton–Tift County	1984
Lakeland–Lanier County	1986
Brunswick–Glynn County	1987
Augusta–Richmond County	1988*†
Conyers–Rockdale County	1989
Athens–Clarke County	1990*
Griffin–Spalding County	1991
Metter–Candler County	1994
Ellaville–Schley County	1994
Augusta–Richmond County	1995*
Griffin–Spalding County	1997
Hawkinsville–Pulaski County	1999
Waycross–Ware County	2000
Cusseta–Chattahoochee County	2003*

* Passed

† Voided under the federal Voting Rights Act.

Sources: U.S. Advisory Commission on Intergovernmental Relations 1982, 398–399; Georgia General Assembly 2005b, 3:300A–334A; *Columbus Ledger-Inquirer,* June 18, 2003, C1.

County, and Cusseta and Chattahoochee County. Despite setbacks, consolidation backers have been persistent: the 1995 Augusta referendum was the area's fifth; residents of Macon and Athens have voted four times on consolidation.[11]

Politics and Local Government Boundaries. Drawing the boundaries of local governments may seem like a pretty mundane matter, but such changes can lead to hot debates because of their effects. For example, adding territory can provide city officials with larger tax bases, additional federal or state funds, more utility customers, lower demand for services, and even supportive voters. Similarly, by incorporating a new city government, residents secure greater political influence than if they had only their larger county government, especially in matters such as land-use regulation. Developers and manufacturers can also use boundary changes to obtain better infrastructure or lower development costs and regulation. Annexation and consolidation also add population, which allows boosters to portray a community as larger and growing. Indeed, one of the first reactions to the 1995 Augusta–Richmond County consolidation vote was that its larger size would "put Augusta on the map." Race and class divisions also characterize many incorporation, annexation, and consolidation debates, particularly when affluent white suburbanites and black city residents anticipate changes in their political power or social and economic conditions. Such debates became more common in Georgia during the 1990s and continued into the new century with conflicts such as the incorporation of a new city of Sandy Springs just north of Atlanta, although that debate began during the 1950s.[12]

Services

The state plays a key role in trying to guarantee that Georgians, no matter where they live, receive local government services that meet certain minimum standards. For example, various local services affecting environmental quality come under the supervision of the Georgia Department of Natural Resources. Requirements include certification of supervisors of local water and sewer systems and reports to the state of results from periodic tests of water samples. Local governments must also meet standards regarding waste disposal.

Other state actions are designed to encourage public safety and health—for example, minimum standards for full-time and volunteer fire departments as well as the licensing and inspection of local emergency medical services. Georgia has statewide building codes, although localities can impose stricter requirements. The state also sets standards and provides funds for county boards of health and uses financial incentives to encourage local governments to provide certain types of services, as with the requirement that counties without emergency management organizations are not eligible for disaster assistance.

Personnel

Georgia sets standards for public servants in the Constitution, state law, and agency rules. These requirements cover those elected to office as well as those hired or appointed. Some standards cover minimum qualifications to hold an office, while others regulate behavior after taking office.

Elected Officials. Those elected at the local level in Georgia must satisfy very few state requirements.[13] To run for most city and county offices, candidates must file a notice with local election officials. They cannot have been convicted of certain offenses, including election law violations. The state has set thirty days as the minimum time candidates must reside within the area from which they would be elected. In partisan elections, candidates can compete for only one party's nomination. The state permits local governments to charge a filing fee within certain limits. Beyond such minimum standards for candidates, new city council and county commission members have been required since 1990 to attend a training and education course to prepare them for their "positions of public trust."[14] Additional standards apply to some officials, such as county coroners.[15]

Appointed Officials. Some appointed officials exercise substantial authority on their own; others are members of boards that make decisions collectively. Appointed executives such as city and county managers, city attorneys, and city clerks can be fired almost any time a majority of the local governing body chooses to do so. The state still sets standards for such jobs, however. Since the early 1990s, full-time city clerks must complete a training course at their employers' expense.[16] This mandate might seem trivial, but clerks maintain government records, keep minutes of various public meetings, publish and distribute a wide range of official notices, and perform similar tasks that must meet numerous legal requirements. Similarly, municipal court judges, who are not necessarily lawyers, have been required since 1991 to complete a training course and annual training thereafter.[17]

Local governments also appoint citizens to various boards, commissions, authorities, and advisory groups. Some appointed bodies have substantial power to shape public policy, and seats on them are highly desired. Builders, developers, and neighborhood activists, for example, frequently compete for appointments to planning commissions, which review land-use plans and rezoning requests.[18] Citizens also serve on boards that supervise airports, hospitals, convention centers, park systems, museums, and similar facilities. Such board members often spend time raising private funds, recruiting volunteers, and promoting the organizations. This is also true of advisory boards such as beautification commissions and councils on aging.

Public Employees. The state allows local governments to establish civil service systems with hiring, evaluation, and promotion based on merit but does set some minimum qualifications. In the area of public safety, for example, the state requires that peace officers receive 20 hours of training within six months of being hired. Full-time firefighters must complete a 120-hour training course plus 120 hours annually after one year on the job. Police chiefs must complete a 40-hour training program, although this requirement does not apply to sheriffs, who are elected county officials.[19]

The state extensively regulates school system personnel at all levels. There are rules regarding the qualifications, selection, and performance of local superintendents. Teachers must satisfy certification requirements and meet certain standards to advance their careers. Local school personnel also must teach required materials, complete reports mandated by the state, and satisfy regulations regarding student discipline.[20]

Finances

Most financial constraints other than the constitutional limits on debt appear in general laws. The most basic is the requirement that local governments "operate under an annual balanced budget."[21] The state also restricts revenues. Counties and municipalities can use several sources but rely most heavily on sales and property taxes. In the past, most school districts relied on property taxes for the lion's share of their local revenue. However, dissatisfaction with property taxes, particularly among homeowners, prompted the General Assembly to place a constitutional amendment on the November 1996 ballot that would allow schools to use a 1 percent sales tax if approved by local voters. Voters ratified the amendment but did so by only 50.8 percent—just over 28,000 votes out of more than 1,869,000 ballots cast. This narrow margin suggested that local school boards would have difficulty convincing voters to approve an additional sales tax. The tax quickly proved popular, however. In March 1997, for example, voters in sixty-three of the sixty-seven school districts with sales tax referenda on the ballot approved the measure.[22] More recently, some observers have proposed funding schools with state sales taxes.[23]

User fees are especially important to special districts and authorities, as with the payments made to hospitals, fares paid to transit systems, and landing fees paid by aircraft owners to airport authorities. Cities and counties have increasingly turned to user fees as a revenue source, however, especially for utility services such as water.

Georgia, like most states, limits local taxes.[24] In addition to property taxes, counties are allowed to levy a 1 percent sales tax on top of the 4 percent state tax. Counties cannot levy the tax without voters' approval, however. Disputes occasionally arise over the agreements a county and its cities must reach over their respective shares of the taxes collected. Since 1985, counties also have been permitted to use a 1 percent special purpose local option sales tax (SPLOST). This special tax is temporary, must be approved in a referendum, and must finance a list of specific projects. It has proven quite popular with local voters. State law allows local governments to employ an income tax, but referendum requirements are so severe that it has not been used.

The state also restricts how taxes are administered. For example, the property tax applies to 40 percent of a residential property's market value, not 100 percent. Related requirements deal with standards for determining the market value of property, the training of assessors, and certification of each county's tax digest (overall valuation of taxable property). In addition, general law prevents the taxation of property owned by various charitable, religious, nonprofit, and governmental organizations. State law reduces the tax burden of agricultural, timber, conservation, and historic property. It also forbids application of the sales tax to services, certain transactions involving government agencies and nonprofit organizations, and a list of consumer goods that includes water sold through mains, animals used for breeding, and Bibles. In 1996 the General Assembly passed a law to phase out the state sales tax on groceries, which remain subject to local sales taxes.

Finally, general law regulates budgetary practices.[25] Local governing bodies are required to adopt an annual budget detailing revenue sources and expenditures for a specified fiscal year. They must hold budget hearings after publishing notices announcing the hearings. Most transfers of funds within departments can be done administratively, but changes in amounts appropriated in the budget can be made only by the governing body. Most local governments must submit to audits by state agencies, make an annual report on their finances to the Georgia Department of Community Affairs, and have an annual audit of their finances. The most important function of such audits is to verify that funds have been collected and spent in accordance with legal requirements and accounting standards.

Procedures

The legislature has passed a number of general laws that can be viewed as attempts to promote fairness in public decision making. Many apply to all governments in Georgia, not just those at the local level. Like many states, Georgia mandates that elected and appointed bodies conduct their business in meetings open to the public. The exceptions to such "government in the sunshine" include discussions of future real estate acquisitions and hirings, evaluations, and dismissals of employees. Even then, officials must first meet with a quorum in a public session and vote (with each member's vote recorded) to meet behind closed doors. Still, disputes arise over unofficial gatherings and retreats by elected officials. Likewise, the state requires notification and public hearings before certain actions are taken, as when cities and counties buy land and consider rezoning property.[26]

State law also limits officials' ability to withhold information from the press or the public. Citizens are guaranteed the right to inspect public records and to make copies for no more than twenty-five cents per page. Certain items are exempt from the law, and a great deal of litigation has occurred to determine whether specific documents and computer records are "public."[27]

Other statutes require disclosure of information related to the use of political influence. Candidates are required to disclose all campaign contributions and expenditures of $101 or more. Also, all candidates must submit financial disclosure statements during campaigns, and elected county, municipal, and school officials must submit such statements each year.[28]

Similar requirements cover policy making. City council members, county commissioners, and those appointed to planning and zoning commissions are required to disclose interests in property affected by rezoning proposals and must disqualify themselves from voting on matters in which they have an interest. Those applying for a rezoning must disclose certain gifts and campaign contributions to local officials considering the rezoning application.[29] Ironically, the committees required by state law to advise cities and counties on impact fees for development must have a minimum of 40 percent of their members from "the development, building, or real estate industries."[30]

The General Assembly has also adopted other laws dealing with the issue of biased decision making. To avoid conflicts of interest, city council members are "ineligible to hold any other municipal office" during their terms.[31] Appointed board members of certain types of authorities are not to participate in decisions in which they have "substantial interest or involvement." They also are required to disclose such interests.[32]

Local Government Structure

Local government organization has been especially controversial during two periods in U.S. history. The first occurred in the early twentieth century—the Progressive Era—when reformers sought to eliminate the power of political machines. Reformers tried to weaken these local political party organizations with procedural changes such as the nonpartisan ballot, at-large elections, majority vote requirements, laws designed to eliminate voting fraud, the development of the civil service, and the council-manager form of government. Among other effects, these reforms are associated with lower turnout in local elections.[33]

The second effort began with the civil rights movement of the 1960s and sought to reverse many Progressive Era changes. Critics argued that at-large elections and majority vote requirements were biased against nontraditional candidates. The problem, they asserted, involved more than a lack of resources. People's tendency to vote along racial lines meant that whites would control at-large governing bodies of communities where they out-numbered minorities. Majority vote requirements, their detractors claimed, meant that candidates such as minorities and women could get a plurality in the first election but lose a seat after powerful and traditional groups united to defeat minorities in the runoff.

Research supports some of these claims. Most studies indicate that blacks clearly win seats closer to their share of a community's population when elections are conducted by district rather than at large. The evidence regard-ing the fate of Hispanics and women under at-large systems is less convinc-ing. Results are also ambiguous concerning runoffs. Activists of the second reform era frequently found an ally in the U.S. Department of Justice, which used the provisions of the Voting Rights Act to force changes in local electoral systems. When such changes are made, minority candidates generally see major improvements in the proportion of seats they hold on local governing bodies. Both waves of reform, along with other factors, have left an imprint on Georgia's local government structure.[34]

Counties

It is difficult to speak of administering county government in Georgia. First, an elected commission in each county has "governing authority" to enact ordinances, adopt a budget, and the like. These legislative bodies range in size from one to twelve members, but the structure often has no clearly iden-tified executive. Second, voters choose several department heads—called constitutional officers—even though the county commission approves their budgets and is legally liable for their actions. Their position is comparable to the plural executive at the state level. These officials include a sheriff, tax commissioner, superior court clerk, and judge of the probate court. They can include a treasurer, coroner, and surveyor, although under certain con-ditions these offices can be abolished. Elected department heads and court officials deal directly with the county commission rather than reporting to an executive. Critics argue that such jobs are administrative and should be filled by hiring the best-qualified person rather than electing someone to the position.[35]

Georgia's 159 counties utilize five forms of government (see figure 10.1). The first exists only in Georgia and combines legislative and administrative

Figure 10.1. Structure of County Governments in Georgia

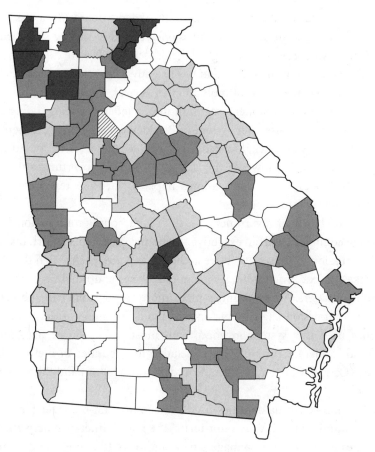

Note: The data below indicate the total number of counties for each form of government:

	Commission / Administrator	63
	Traditional Commission	57
	Commission / Manager	28
	Sole Commissioner	10
	Elected Executive	1

Source: Compiled by authors from Georgia Department of Community Affairs county profiles at http: //www.dca.state.ga.us/CountySnapshotsNet/. Barrow County was reclassified by the authors as having a Traditional Commission form of government.

power in a single county commissioner rather than a board. As late as 1988, Georgia had twenty-four sole-commissioner counties, mostly small, rural jurisdictions where supporters argued that larger boards were expensive and unnecessary. Citizens in several counties recently have voted to abandon the sole commissioner in favor of multimember boards. Lawsuits also have attacked the sole-commissioner system. In 1992, a federal appeals court ruled that the single-commissioner system in Bleckley County, where 22 percent of the residents were black, violated the Voting Rights Act. In a five-to-four decision in June 1994, however, the U.S. Supreme Court overturned this decision, which left the sole commissioner in place.[36] In 2006, ten counties retained the sole commission form.

The second form of government, the traditional county commission, lacks a chain of command with an executive to whom departments report. Instead, the commission exercises executive authority as a group, although the chair may take the lead in coordinating county services and building consensus on policy matters. Some counties place more responsibility in the hands of their commission chair by making the job a full-time position. Fifty-six counties used this system in 2006, with most having fewer than thirty thousand residents. The remainder included five counties in metropolitan Atlanta (Carroll, Clayton, Newton, Rockdale, and Walton) and Bibb County (Macon).

In 2003, 28 Georgia counties used the commission-manager form and 64 the commission-administrator form. The major difference between the two types is that county managers have authority to appoint and remove key department heads, prepare and propose the budget for the commission, and are responsible to the full commission. Most county administrators come up short on one or more of these key characteristics. Still, both types of officials generally can be fired whenever the county board of commissioners chooses to do so.[37] The number of counties using these two forms of professional administration is more than double the total of ten years earlier. Most of this change represents a shift from the traditional county commission, which was used in 93 counties in 1993.

The final form of county government in Georgia is the elected executive, which exists only in DeKalb County, where the executive has authority to appoint department heads, prepare the annual budget, and veto ordinances adopted by the county commission. The consolidated government implemented in 1991 by Athens–Clarke County is somewhat of a hybrid. It is a manager-commission system, but the elected mayor has veto power and prepares a budget with the hired manager.[38]

Municipalities

Georgia's municipalities essentially use four forms of government, although they are organized very differently from counties.[39] In the early 1990s, about 85 percent of Georgia cities used a mayor-council form of government, which has two variants. The strong mayor form comes closest to a separation of legislative and executive powers. Policy making is the responsibility of the city council. The mayor is elected separately and usually prepares the budget and appoints and removes department heads. The weak mayor has fewer distinctions between the powers of the council and those of the mayor. The mayor normally presides over city council meetings but has limited budgetary power, no veto, and limited control over the selection of department heads.

A handful of Georgia municipalities use a commission form of government in which voters elect a mayor and other members who frequently are designated to head specific departments. This system effectively merges executive and legislative responsibilities. Another 13 percent of Georgia cities in the early 1990s utilized the council-manager form of government. This system vests policy making with the city council. The mayor normally presides over the council, which hires a professionally trained manager to run the city on a day-to-day basis. City managers generally have authority to hire and fire most department heads. This system resembles the structure of a corporation, with voters akin to shareholders and the council like a board of directors.

Special Districts

The structure of special districts in Georgia varies widely. Local school boards bear responsibility for educational policy making, while the superintendent oversees administration. With the ratification of a constitutional amendment in November 1992, Article 8, Section 5 of the Georgia Constitution now requires that all members of Georgia's local school boards be elected and all superintendents be hired by the school boards. Previously, two-thirds of the county superintendents and 85 percent of the boards had been elected; elected superintendents in office on January 1, 1993, were allowed to serve out their terms. Surprisingly, at that time, eighteen systems had elected superintendents but appointed school boards. School boards appointed by grand juries date back to the end of Reconstruction and were quite numerous at one time.[40]

Special districts exist to provide such services as public hospitals, water, public housing, downtown development, and airports. Others, often called tax allocation districts, provide a range of services to assist the development of certain sections of cities and counties. Special districts often appear more like private firms than local governments because their boards are generally appointed for fixed terms by the governing bodies of the cities or counties in which they operate. Most of Georgia's special districts lack the power to levy property taxes; instead, they tend to rely on sales taxes, fees charged for services, and revenue from the sale of bonds. In part because of the indirect selection of special district boards and executives, some observers have expressed concern that special districts are less accountable to the public or less well managed than the traditional city and county departments whose heads report directly to a chief executive and elected governing body.[41]

Participation in Local Politics

Political participation in the United States, especially voting, tends to be lower at the local level than it is for state or national governments. This may seem surprising since political participation should be easier at the local level because the time, effort, and other costs of getting involved can be relatively low. Local politics can also be more informal and personal because officials are more readily accessible.

Several factors might explain limited participation in local politics. Virtually all city elections are nonpartisan, which means that political parties are not very active in mobilizing voters. Voter interest and knowledge may be low because media attention to local campaigns is less extensive than coverage of national and state elections. Unlike the emotional and economic issues that dominate national politics, local governments devote much of their effort to very basic services. Research does suggest that even though citizens do not vote often in local elections, they frequently contact local government agencies with service complaints and requests.[42] Moreover, issues such as crime, drugs, traffic, schools, land use, and pollution always have the potential to activate citizens locally, either at the ballot box or in other ways.

Elections

Local elections in the United States are notorious for low voter turnout. Historically, turnout generally ranges between 30 and 40 percent of registered voters. Turnout has tended to be higher in mayor-council than in council-manager cities and is higher when the mayor's office is on the ballot. Turnout exceeds 50 percent when city elections are held at the same time as state or national races but drops below 30 percent for city elections held independently of all other races. Also, turnout is higher in more affluent cities and in smaller communities.[43]

Local Campaigns. Local elections in Georgia vary extensively. At one end of the scale are at-large offices in large cities and counties. There, campaigns for mayor, county executive or commission chair, sheriff, and similar offices are often expensive, media-driven efforts that focus on candidates' personal characteristics and management style as much as their positions on issues. District elections in large places can also be competitive and expensive.

In Atlanta's October 1989 city elections, 38 percent of the nearly 200,000 registered voters went to the polls, although turnout varied from under 2 percent in two precincts to more than 50 percent in thirty others. Maynard Jackson raised almost $2 million to regain the mayor's seat he had given up in 1982, when he was ineligible to serve a third consecutive term. The incumbent city council president, who ran unopposed for his at-large office, raised $122,500 in donations. The eighteen winners of city council seats received a combined $762,350 in money and in-kind contributions, including $305,370 donated to eight candidates who ran unopposed. Donations to council candidates ranged from a few dollars to a $38,000 contribution from one development firm. Of the $3.3 million in donations greater than $100 to all candidates in 1989, only 51 percent came from contributors in Atlanta. Twenty-six percent came from suburban donors, and 22 percent originated outside Georgia.[44] Such patterns have continued. In 2005, Mayor Shirley Franklin and City Council President Lisa Borders cruised to reelection. A few weeks ahead of the November 8 election, Franklin had received almost $1.2 million in contributions, while Borders had raised more than $700,000. Two unopposed candidates for at-large city council seats had raised a combined $580,000.[45]

Suburban campaigns have also become expensive. In 2004, for example, Gwinnett County experienced a heated race for county commission chair. Gwinnett has more than 700,000 residents and is heavily Republican, which means that major contests usually take place in GOP primaries. Each of the three candidates received more than 30 percent of the vote in the July Republican primary, leading to an August runoff. The incumbent, who lost the runoff, raised more than $587,000. The victorious challenger received almost $498,000 in contributions, including $8,000 in October and November, when he received 70 percent of the vote against a Democrat who had raised less than $5,000.[46]

At the other extreme lie small municipalities and counties, where it is often difficult to attract candidates for office, campaigns can be personal, and little money is spent to win elections. In 1991, the candidates for mayor and two council seats in Watkinsville, a small city just outside Athens, were chosen without opposition and spent no money on campaigns. In September 1992, the remaining three council seats appeared on the ballot. Two of the seats went uncontested, and none of the candidates spent any money. Only 12.1 percent of those registered voted, a stark contrast with the 78.7 percent turnout figure for the presidential election two months later. In 1995, eight cities in Gwinnett County had contested races in the November municipal elections, but five others canceled elections when only one person qualified to run for each city council seat. Jonesboro, in Clayton County, had a different quandary: three city council seats but only two candidates. Local contests for judgeships and district attorneys are also notorious for their lack of competition.[47] However, Oconee County demonstrates how the rise of a contentious issue can change local turnout. Statewide voter turnout in the July 1996 primary election was 27 percent. It reached 44 percent in Oconee County, however, as candidates in the Republican primary for school board chair debated the role of religion in the schools.[48]

Voting Patterns. Elections in Georgia changed significantly when the rights of black voters were expanded in 1946, following the elimination of the white primary, and in 1965, when Congress passed the Voting Rights Act. This was especially true in Atlanta, where the white business leaders who dominated local politics in the 1940s and 1950s forged an alliance with moderate black leaders to promote incremental and peaceful racial change along with the city's growth.[49] This coalition essentially wrote off poor whites, who formed a solid bloc favoring racial segregation. Voting during the 1960s and 1970s was polarized along racial and class lines. In municipal and Democratic primary contests, where candidates were not differentiated by party, blacks and higher-status whites tended to vote together for moderate or liberal candidates. In presidential elections, higher-status whites shifted some of their votes to the Republican nominee, while less-affluent whites were more likely to join with blacks in support of the Democrat. Racial polarization tended to be higher for more visible local offices, such as mayor of Atlanta, than for lesser positions or when a black candidate was running.

Atlanta voting patterns also changed over time. Racial polarization jumped after passage of the 1965 federal Voting Rights Act but declined by the mid-1970s. Moreover, polls indicated that after the election of Atlanta's first black mayor in 1973, blacks maintained their level of trust in local government, while whites' modest decline in trust resembled general nationwide trends. A 1981 poll suggested that voters rarely supported someone of their own race who disagreed with them on issues. When Jackson was returned to the mayor's office with 79 percent of the vote in 1989, however, he won by building a coalition that cut across racial and class lines. As Atlanta's demographic makeup shifted during the 1990s, class differences became more pronounced, particularly in elections with major candidates of the same race, and gay and lesbian voters became an important voting bloc citywide and an even more significant force in certain city council districts.

Elected Officials. One of the most notable changes in local politics in Georgia has been the increased presence of black, female, and Republican officeholders. In 1971, 26 blacks held elected city and county offices in Georgia, a number that grew to 371 in 1993 and 395 in 2001, when only Alabama and Mississippi had more.[50]

In 1981, women held 183 city council and mayoral positions in Georgia, while another 22 women served as county commissioners. By 1985, Georgia had 251 female mayors or city council members, and 24 women held county commission seats. The share of women on county commissions rose from 5.1 percent in 1981 to 7.4 percent in 1991. Over the same period, the share of women on school boards grew from 15.5 to 22.7 percent.[51]

Republicans, too, have made significant inroads at the local level, although the degree of partisan change is difficult to measure because many

local elections are nonpartisan. In 1991, 87.6 percent of county commissioners were Democrats, 10.3 percent were Republicans, and 2.1 percent were independents; in 1981, those figures were 96 percent, 3.8 percent, and 0.2 percent, respectively. The GOP experienced somewhat smaller gains in elected
administrative offices, such as sheriff, during the same ten years. Republican gains were especially pronounced in metropolitan areas. In the Atlanta
area, Republicans held 45.1 percent of the commission seats by 1991, a sharp
rise from 12.3 percent ten years earlier. In Georgia's other metropolitan areas, Republicans made up 12.8 percent of county commissioners in 1989 and
15.8 percent in 1991. Outside Georgia's metropolitan areas, however, Republicans comprised fewer than 5 percent of all county commission seats during
the 1980s and early 1990s.[52]

A nationwide survey by the National Association of Counties in 2006 found
that most county officeholders are male (85 percent) and white (87 percent).
Many come from professions that allow some schedule flexibility, and 61 percent hold other jobs in addition to their elected office. They generally have
higher levels of education than the general public; 76 percent have completed
some college, and 45 percent have a college degree. In the survey, 46 percent
self-identified as Republican, 41 percent as Democrat, and 13 percent as independent. Many of these officeholders may run in nonpartisan elections.[53]

Referenda. Citizens vote for more than candidates. In a referendum, they are
asked to vote yes or no on a public policy question. Some of these elections
are required by general law, as with the sale of general obligation bonds.
Other referenda are held under local acts passed by the General Assembly.
Between 1953 and 2004, Georgians voted on nearly eighteen hundred measures that were on the ballot in specific cities or counties as a result of local
bills passed by the General Assembly.[54] Still others are held at the behest of
city or county officials as advisory rather than binding.

Referenda generally attract few voters. In the first thirty-two counties voting on a special purpose local option sales tax in 1985, nineteen had turnouts
of 25 percent or less and only three exceeded 40 percent.[55] Low turnout can be
attributed at times to the scheduling and low-key nature of referendum elections. Indeed, some public officials have been accused of holding tax referenda
on dates when voters are likely to pay attention to—and oppose—new taxes. In
September 2005, for example, only 12 percent of Cobb County voters cast ballots in a special election that ratified an increase in the local sales tax from 5 to

6 percent.[56] Local voters are often asked to decide referenda on controversial issues such as alcohol. Support for Sunday sales and liquor by the drink often comes from business and political leaders who tout alcohol sales as a way to attract hotel and restaurant chains and to generate sales tax revenues. In some cases, communities feel forced to approve alcohol sales because their neighbors already permit such sales and thus enjoy business and tax benefits.[57]

Recall Elections. Similar to a referendum is a recall, which permits citizens to vote on whether to remove an elected official from office. Georgia permits the recall of anyone holding an elective state or local office. For a recall vote to be held, a valid petition must be filed, with the required number of petition sponsors, number of signatures, and time limit varying. The major hurdle is quickly getting signatures equal to 30 percent of the total number of registered voters at the last election when the office appeared on the ballot.

Petition sponsors also must demonstrate that the official they want to remove committed misconduct or some other serious breach of responsibility. In 1988, the courts declared unconstitutional a state law that permitted the recall of an official if citizens were unhappy with his or her judgment or performance. If a petition is valid, citizens vote yes or no on removing the official named. If more than half of those voting cast their ballots in favor, the official is removed immediately and a special election is held to fill the vacancy. Since it took effect in April 1989, Georgia's new recall statute has been used sparingly, although recall efforts have occurred somewhat regularly in smaller Atlanta suburbs, where elected officials do not serve full time and professional staff support is limited.[58]

Interest Groups in Local Politics

Like their state and national counterparts, local groups lobby, endorse candidates, make campaign contributions, try to influence public opinion, and use other tactics. Many national and state groups, such as chambers of commerce, unions, teachers groups, and environmental organizations, have local affiliates. Nonetheless, local interest groups operate on a smaller scale, both in terms of geographical area and number of members. Unlike groups operating in a state capital or Washington, D.C., those at the local level often have few resources except the ability to mobilize large numbers of people. As a result, groups arise and disappear over specific issues.

Among the most prominent and effective local interest groups are those in the business community. In small communities, business leadership is often concentrated in the local chamber of commerce and among executives of major local firms, which have the staff to monitor and deal with local government. For example, one study found that officials of chambers of commerce and banks were among the most likely to attend economic development meetings in Georgia's rural counties and small towns.[59] Local chambers of commerce often promote their communities to outside investors and tourists, sometimes with subsidies from city and county governments. Local lodges and service organizations also provide a means for bringing together leaders from business, government, and nonprofit groups.[60]

Larger communities can have numerous business organizations with substantial budgets and full-time staffs. These groups can even compete with one another. The Atlanta area, for example, has multiple chambers of commerce with thousands of member firms. In the city of Atlanta, other organizations have long promoted downtown, conventions and tourism, and the Midtown and Buckhead areas.[61] Politicians often respond to such economic power by helping to promote a wide range of development plans promoted by business leaders. Individual companies (especially large ones) can also have political clout because they pay substantial taxes, employ many workers, and can move. Local officials also worry as the number of locally headquartered companies decreases because of bankruptcy and outside buyouts. Perhaps especially crucial are developers, whose projects can transform entire neighborhoods and add substantial value to a community's property tax base. However, many neighborhood and historic preservation groups see developers as the enemy.[62]

Government employees also can comprise powerful interest groups in local politics. In many small counties in particular, a substantial percentage of jobs are located in local government.[63] In larger places, police officers, firefighters, public school teachers, and health care workers can be politically important groups.

Perhaps the most unusual interest groups at the local level are neighborhood organizations, which tend to be all-volunteer and lack permanent structure, staff, and financial resources. Even though membership and activity can fluctuate, neighborhood organizations can exert substantial political clout, especially when development can affect an area's property values and quality of life. In established parts of metropolitan Atlanta, groups representing middle-class and affluent homeowners testify and appear in large numbers at planning commission rezoning hearings, attend meetings of city councils and county commissions, contact elected officials, endorse candidates, picket, and even file lawsuits. For example, action by neighborhood groups forced almost a decade's worth of delays and changes in a highway that the state built between downtown Atlanta and the Carter Presidential Center. Homeowners' organizations also are cropping up in newer suburban areas to fight commercial development, traffic, and apartments.[64]

Local Policies

Many factors influence policies adopted by local governments, including constitutional and legal constraints imposed by the state, the structure of local government, and political participation. Many key decisions revolve around government services, taxing and spending, a community's physical characteristics and quality of life, and related issues.

Services

Service decisions are complicated and often controversial. Local leaders must make important choices about the types and level of services they provide. They must decide who should produce the services—government, the private sector, nonprofit organizations, or volunteer groups—as well as how services should be funded.

The Georgia Department of Community Affairs conducts an annual and exhaustive survey of services provided by local governments (see table 10.4). The surveys ask only whether local governments provide a service but do not ask how widely available a service is, how much is spent on it, or otherwise measure performance. For example, the counties that provide public transit do not necessarily have big fleets of buses—this category includes narrower services such as paratransit (vans for the disabled or elderly).

Cities are more likely to provide the wide range of water and solid waste services one might expect in built-up, more densely populated settlements. Such services are less necessary in rural areas. Counties must serve as administrative arms of the state in providing courts, public records, a variety of social services, and other functions. Thus, jails are essentially a county function. Because counties administer a number of social welfare programs for

Table 10.4. Services Provided by Georgia Cities and Counties, 2004

	Percentage Providing Service	
Service	Cities	Counties
Animal Control	25	49
Building Inspection	45	67
Building Permits	65	81
Construction and Code Enforcement	48	77
Emergency Medical Services (EMS)	7	56
Emergency 911	6	78
Fire Protection	62	72
Health Screening Services	1	22
Jail	7	92
Law Enforcement	70	99
Planning	60	69
Public Hospital	1	5
Public Transit	2	37
Senior Citizens' Programs	13	52
Wastewater Collection	56	15
Wastewater Treatment	52	12
Water Distribution	79	26
Water Supply	75	20
Water Treatment	72	17

Note: Number of responding governments = 495 cities, 156 counties. The completed questionnaires cover 156 of Georgia's 159 counties and 495 of the 529 city governments surveyed.

Source: Georgia Department of Community Affairs 2004a, 2004b.

the state, it should not be surprising that they are more likely than cities to run health and senior programs. The substantial county role in emergency services could be a function of their greater geographical size and economies of scale.

Some services differ substantially by the size of the local government. For example, a majority of counties with populations of less than 25,000 do not provide animal control, whereas all but one of the thirty-five counties with more than 50,000 residents do so. This finding reflects in part the power counties received in 1972 to provide urban services, which means that citizens do not need to live inside a city to get garbage pickup, police protection, water distribution and treatment, zoning, animal control, health screening, and similar services. Comparable differences exist between larger and smaller cities. In Southwest Georgia, Albany (more than 76,000 residents) provides eleven of the nineteen services in table 10.4. It relies on an independent authority for hospital and emergency medical services and on other governments for the remaining six services. In nearby Morgan, the county seat of Calhoun County, which had a 2003 population of 1,457, the city government provided seven of the nineteen services, including all five related to water. Four other services simply were not available, while the remainder came from the county or from other providers.[65]

Beyond the simple decision to provide certain services, local officials must deal with the needs and demands of different neighborhoods. Savannah addressed this problem with a program that began in the 1970s to provide higher service levels to neighborhoods in greater need. By taking this approach rather than furnishing every area with the same level of street paving, inspections, flood control, and other services, officials attempted to promote equality of conditions.[66]

Local Government Finances

A substantial part of local policy making involves finances. As might be expected, government decisions about how to raise and spend money can be controversial. As with services, local budgets highlight differences between Georgia's cities and counties (see table 10.5). On the revenue side, counties depend more heavily on property and sales taxes. In contrast, city revenues are tied to enterprise funds, which are restricted to specific utility-type services such as water and sewer systems, solid waste, electric and gas supply systems, and airports. Enterprise funds operate almost as if they were businesses and generate revenue by charging for their services (for example, monthly water bills, airport parking and landing fees). They are normally separated from the general revenues a local government spends on services such as police, fire, and libraries. Counties also receive a higher share of their funds from other governments, in large part because of their roles in building and maintaining highways and in providing social services.

On the spending side, as one would expect from the revenue patterns, cities devote a significant proportion of their funds to services operated through enterprise funds. Looking only at general expenditures, both types

Table 10.5. Georgia City and County Finances, 2004

	Cities	Counties*
TOTAL REVENUES	$5.64 billion	$7.37 billion
Percentage of Total		
General Revenue	42.8%	87.5%
Property Taxes	11.2	37.5
General Sales Taxes	6.8	9.1
Special Purpose Local Option Sales Taxes	2.4	11.2
Excise/Special Use Taxes	8.0	4.7
Licenses/Permits/Fees	2.8	2.6
Intergovernmental Revenue	4.4	9.5
Service Charges/Other	7.1	12.9
Enterprise Fund Revenues	57.2	12.5
TOTAL EXPENDITURES	$6.44 billion	$7.98 billion
Percentage of Total		
General Expenditures	35.1%	76.8%
Administration	5.3	12.6
Courts	0.8	6.2
Public Safety	13.5	21.2
Community Development	1.6	2.1
Health and Human Services	0.3	8.9
Leisure Services	2.5	3.6
Public Works	0.7	0.7
Highways/Streets/Drainage	3.1	5.1
Capital Expenditures	4.2	13.0
Other	3.1	3.5
Enterprise Fund Expenditures	60.7	20.4
Debt Service (interest)	4.2	2.8

* Includes consolidated city-county governments.

Source: Georgia Department of Community Affairs 2005b.

of government devote the largest share to public safety, which includes police and fire protection. Counties also devote substantial resources to courts as well as health and human services, a reflection of the tasks counties perform on behalf of the state.

Table 10.5 does not include local school systems, which are independent of Georgia's city and county governments, or independent authorities, which many cities and counties set up to oversee public hospitals, industrial development, airports, downtown development, and similar services. Public schools depend heavily on state revenues. Participation by citizens and interest groups can influence these patterns, but so can other factors, including state and federal mandates.

Regulation

Local governments' most important actions include regulation. Cities and counties license a variety of businesses, inspect restaurants and other establishments in the interest of public health and safety, and regulate taxi, trash collection, cable television, and similar services sold to the public.

Perhaps the most controversial type of local regulation concerns land use. Georgia's cities and counties have the power to adopt subdivision regulations, which control the way in which large tracts of land may be divided into smaller parcels. Cities and counties also perform zoning, which includes several elements. The most important are the adoption of a map specifying the land use permitted for each piece of property and an ordinance spelling out zoning procedures. At a minimum, communities are divided into agricultural, residential, commercial, and industrial zones, although most places have more detailed categories. Local ordinances also generally control the size and location of buildings in each type of zone. The types of land use are arranged in a hierarchy with farmland and open space, which have the most restrictions, at the upper end and heavy industry at the bottom.

Landowners seeking to use their property for a different use may apply to have it rezoned—for example, from single-family residential to commercial. Following public notices of the requested change and reviews by the city or county planning staff, a planning commission made up of appointed citizens holds a public hearing and makes a recommendation to the city council or county commission, which has the final authority to reclassify the property by amending the zoning ordinance. Zoning and subdivision regulation can be extremely controversial because of their effects on density, economic development, neighborhood characteristics, traffic, and property values.

In the city of Atlanta, citizen participation in rezoning increased and had greater effect during the 1970s after the city established a system of formal neighborhood involvement, another example of the effects of government structure. In the mid-1980s, most rezoning requests in the Atlanta metropolitan area involved only the applicant and local government officials. Substantial citizen opposition arose in some cases, mainly in established neighborhoods. Still, only 21 percent of all applications were denied, while another 7 percent were tabled or withdrawn. The rest were approved, most with some compromises. In the end, planning commissions reached unanimous decisions more than 75 percent of the time, as did city councils and county commissions, which adopted two-thirds of the recommendations made by their staff and 75 percent of those from planning commissions. Thus, by the time a rezoning application reached elected officials, compromise was often the result, although some decisions still led to lawsuits.[67]

Economic Development

Planning, zoning, and regulation obviously affect a community's physical development. Local leaders also dedicate significant effort to promoting economic development, often by trying to attract new employers and helping existing companies expand. Such efforts involve a variety of individuals, organizations, and groups, frequently in cooperation with the state, who use tax breaks, loans, provision of land and buildings, marketing assistance, job training, and improvements to infrastructure, such as roads, water, sewers, and traffic lights. Economic development involves more than manufacturing, however. Some communities use highway access as a selling point for warehouse and distribution facilities. Others use facilities, natural resources, and amenities to promote retirement, recreation, or tourism. These efforts mean, of course, that Georgia communities often compete with one another.

Economic development generally requires close collaboration between political and business leaders. In many communities, the local chamber of commerce takes a leading role. Some areas also have specialized organizations such as convention and visitors bureaus.[68] Many communities have also relied on semiautonomous authorities to promote development. In 2005, for example, the state Department of Community Affairs found roughly three hundred authorities created for industrial or economic development, with many of them representing multiple governments.[69] Examples of cooperative efforts include Augusta, where the local government and several private firms have developed an area along the Savannah River as a center for tourism, conventions, and the arts. Albany's political and business leaders have emphasized redevelopment of the city's downtown as a way to deal with the community's economic problems. Along the coast, the city of Savannah, Chatham County, and the Georgia Ports Authority work with the Savannah Economic Development Authority to promote use of the port, tourism, and the expansion and recruitment of businesses throughout the region.

Intergovernmental Relations

Local Competition and Cooperation

Competition among local governments is fairly common, including efforts to outdo other communities in attracting new businesses, securing state and federal grant money, or just creating a better image. For example, leaders from several cities and counties in metropolitan Atlanta used a variety of tactics to attract the headquarters of United Parcel Service when the company relocated to Georgia from Connecticut.

Relations among local governments are not necessarily competitive or antagonistic. In fact, several factors promote cooperation, including institutions designed to coordinate the activities of governments within an area or to promote their shared interests. The state has established regional development centers whose functions include assisting local governments and playing a key role in long-term planning. Each of these agencies is governed by a board composed largely of officials from the cities and counties within its region.

A second stimulus for intergovernmental cooperation is the work of professional organizations. Groups such as the Georgia Municipal Association (GMA), the Association County Commissioners of Georgia (ACCG), the Georgia City-County Managers Association, organizations representing other types of officials (clerks, zoning administrators, and so forth), and units of the University System of Georgia facilitate information sharing and professional development among local government officials.

A third basis for cooperation is a desire either to improve the quality and cost of services or to address problems that are regional in scope. Such cooperative efforts can be particularly important in cases involving large-scale projects. For example, Athens–Clarke County joined with Barrow, Jackson, and Oconee Counties to form the Upper Oconee Water Basin Authority, which developed the Bear Creek Reservoir to supply all four counties with water. Macon and Bibb County have combined some operations, including planning, to improve efficiency and effectiveness in service delivery.[70]

Finally, higher-level governments can force lower-level governments to cooperate. For example, with the state facing the threat of losing federal highway money because of Atlanta's pollution levels, the legislature created the Georgia Regional Transportation Authority to promote policies that improved transportation and air quality. The legislature also adopted a 1997 law forcing all governments in a county to agree on plans for providing services to reduce duplication and competition.[71]

Dealing with the State

Local leaders promote their interests and those of their communities in several ways. Most cities and counties have an annual agenda and ask their local legislators to promote it in the General Assembly. Most local governments also maintain regular contact with state agencies such as the Department of Community Affairs and Department of Transportation as well as with various regional bodies.

Local interests also get represented in professional organizations. These include the GMA and the ACCG. Other groups represent the interests of employees and officials such as sheriffs, teachers, school superintendents, and police officers. These groups publish newsletters, issue reports, hold conferences for their members, and pass policy recommendations that are forwarded to the General Assembly. In 2006, for example, ACCG listed seven priorities—and even more recommendations—for the annual legislative session. The organization also updated its members regularly on the status of bills in the General Assembly.[72] The ACCG and comparable organizations also lobby on behalf of their recommendations. During 2004, for example, the ACCG spent more than $11,000 on lobbying, more than $8,500 of that amount for a reception held during the legislative session. For its part, the GMA reported spending more than $15,600 on lobbying during 2004, ranging from upward of $8,000 for a reception to under $10 for lunch or dinner for a legislator.[73]

The Future of Local Government in Georgia

Like much of Georgia, local government and politics have changed dramatically during the past generation. One of the most visible changes is the increased number of cities and special districts. Another is the growth in local government responsibilities and budgets, especially among Georgia's urban counties. More startling during the past fifty years are the declining influence of white "courthouse gangs" in rural areas and the growing clout of black voters and local officials. Many observers also would be surprised by the partisan changes that have occurred at the local level, including large numbers of consistently "red" (Republican) and "blue" (Democratic) communities.

Despite significant changes, local government in Georgia faces major challenges in the twenty-first century. Many of these issues relate to land use and natural resources, particularly transportation, water supply, and waste disposal; others deal with human resource problems such as education. Many rural and central city areas face problems of economic decline, while suburban communities must contend with rapid growth.

One view of the future argues that Georgia's communities must have more flexibility to organize and operate their local governments. That was the primary message touted in 1992 by the Governor's Local Governance Commission, which called for the removal of constitutional limitations on local government and a reduction in the General Assembly's involvement in local concerns. Little change resulted from the commission's recommendations, however. Even with reform, the state's local officials still face many difficult problems.

Public Policy

This chapter draws from the rest of the book and other research to provide an overview of the policy process in Georgia state government and to analyze several major policy areas. It also makes comparisons to earlier periods and contrasts Georgia with the federal government and other states before concluding with a discussion of the future of Georgia politics.

Policy Making in Georgia

Policy can be considered a government's course of action in response to a perceived problem. Policies may be contradictory: perhaps the most obvious example is the federal government subsidizing tobacco growers yet trying to discourage people from smoking. Government inaction also constitutes a policy, as with the federal government's nonresponse to AIDS in the mid-1980s and lack of action in the face of genocide in Rwanda during the 1990s.

Descriptions of the policy process typically include several steps (see figure 11.1). The earliest stages include identifying a problem and formulating alternative responses. Together, these are called agenda setting. The next step is the adoption of a policy, which can involve any combination of the executive, legislative, and judicial branches. With the policy in place, it still must

Figure 11.1. The Policy Process

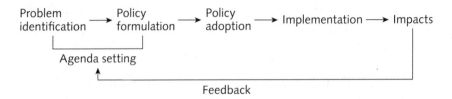

be implemented. Once implemented, policies have impacts, not all of which may have been intended or anticipated. The impacts may prompt action by those dissatisfied enough to try modifying or eliminating an existing policy, thereby starting the process all over again.[1]

This general description of policy making applies to Georgia, although the process differs in some ways from what occurs in the national government and in other states. Policy making today also departs from earlier periods in Georgia politics, when different participants and rules dominated.

Agenda Setting

Setting the political agenda—either by determining which issues are considered important or by narrowing the options to take in response to a problem—can be critical in shaping public policies. Most studies of policy making argue that interest groups, the governor, agencies, legislative leaders, and the media influence agenda setting. Events, especially if seen as crises, can also shape the policy agenda.[2]

In Georgia, the formal powers of the office and the ability to use the media give the governor the preeminent role in setting the agenda. The governor's agenda-setting capacity may be diminished, however, by the plural executive. During agenda setting, Georgia's legislative leaders, particularly the presiding officers in the two chambers, are more powerful than their counterparts in Congress and more professionalized legislatures. Indeed, for many years, critics berated leaders for their control over committee assignments and the flow of legislation, their use of behind-the-scenes deals, and their "punishment" of legislators who disagreed with their leaders.[3]

The media role in agenda setting also differs between Georgia and other locales. Television and radio networks, interest group publications, and

Washington reporters working for a wide range of big-city newspapers and television stations cover the federal government. Full-time legislatures in larger states may receive more thorough coverage, as with New York City newspapers and television stations covering state government in Albany and the Los Angeles and San Francisco media reporting regularly on events in Sacramento.

In Georgia, the legislative session is short, and the media can seldom afford to have staff who specialize in the legislative process or specific policy areas. The premier media players probably are Atlanta's television stations and daily newspaper. One measure of their influence in agenda setting was the passage of ethics legislation by the General Assembly in 1992 under what may have seemed a barrage of newspaper stories and editorials.

Outside of Atlanta, local broadcast media can now easily use satellite and other technology to broadcast reports from the Capitol. Some of the larger daily newspapers also send reporters to the Capitol during the legislative session or for major events hosted by the governor. Even those newspapers, like smaller ones, rely on news services such as the Associated Press or the Morris News Service, which is based in Atlanta and can supplement reporting by the daily newspapers that Morris owns in Athens, Augusta, Savannah, and Jacksonville (where the newspaper provides extensive coverage of Southeast Georgia).[4] At the start of the 2006 legislative session, for example, while the *Macon Telegraph* had a reporter at the Capitol, the Morris newspapers relied on their Atlanta bureau, and the *Rome News-Tribune* did its own story on local legislators and relied for other news on the Associated Press, which also served as a major source for stories in the *Columbus Ledger-Enquirer, Gainesville Times,* and *Marietta Daily Journal.*[5]

The final participants usually cited as influential in agenda setting are interest groups. Not all groups are created equal, however. As chapter 5 argues, Georgia's lack of a professional legislature and long history of limited party competition have heightened the influence of organized interests, particularly several professions and major Atlanta firms. Unlike national politics, in Georgia the influence of citizen groups (for example, seniors and women) is seldom felt compared to that of more numerous and resource-laden business lobbyists. Georgia incorporates local interests in policy making in part through the large volume of local bills and legislative allocation of grants to their districts—what many observers describe as providing pork to the folks back home.

Policy Adoption

Observers consider legislatures, courts, and agencies most influential during the policy adoption stage; however, the procedures of these institutions vary significantly.

Georgia's method of policy adoption differs somewhat from general descriptions of the policy process. Georgia's legislative committees and their chairs seem less powerful than those in Congress, in part because of the control over committee assignments by party leaders in the Georgia House and Senate. Perhaps the major exception is the House Rules Committee, which is as powerful in killing bills as was the comparable congressional committee a generation ago. As in some other states, the brevity of the sessions, legislative rules, the part-time nature of the job, and the lack of staff support heighten the presiding officers' influence. These features of an "amateur" legislature also give the governor and interest groups a prominent role in policy adoption. Preparation of the budget, use of administration floor leaders in each chamber, and the threat or use of the veto also enhance the governor's power.[6]

Courts also serve as key players in the adoption of policies. In particular, the appellate courts' decisions provide guidance to lower courts and often target the policies of other government officials. For example, landmark cases decided by the U.S. Supreme Court have reshaped legislative representation, racial segregation, and the use of the death penalty (among other policies) in Georgia. State courts, especially the Georgia Supreme Court, can also adopt important policies.[7]

Policy Implementation

Finally, state agencies usually bear responsibility for seeing that policies are carried out, although this task can be turned over to lower-level governments or the private sector. Implementation can also be influenced by legislative oversight of agencies as well as court decisions. As with policy formulation, implementation in Georgia can be complicated by the plural executive. In addition, state laws placing additional burdens on cities, counties, and school districts have become an especially sore point with local officials, who frequently object to such "unfunded mandates."[8] The state also uses private firms and nonprofit organizations to carry out policies through contracting, grants, subsidies, vouchers to clients, and several related approaches.[9]

Policy Change and Stability in Georgia

The extent to which V. O. Key Jr. would recognize the policy process in Georgia today is unclear. He probably would not be completely surprised, having noted more than fifty years ago that the South's "rate of evolution may seem glacial, but fundamental shifts in the conditions underlying its politics are taking place."[10] The formal rules of politics have changed significantly since his astute observations; so have the participants. The same can be said if one looks back to the Georgia of the 1960s and probably even the 1980s.

Perhaps the most noticeable difference is the policy agenda itself. In both the 1940s and 1960s, politics in Georgia (like the rest of the Deep South) was almost exclusively the politics of race. Racial conflict of course has not disappeared from Georgia, but the policy agenda increasingly has focused on economic development, education, and a range of new issues.[11]

Participants and procedures have changed, too, most significantly in the area of Georgia's relationship with the national government. Federal grants and laws have affected every state, but change in Georgia was undeniably hastened by federal action beginning in the 1960s, particularly the Civil Rights Act and the Voting Rights Act. The battles among factions in a state dominated by Democrats in Key's day have given way to an increasingly vibrant two-party system, although competition is often complicated by the two parties' racial and geographic bases. Unlike the 1940s and 1960s, the policy process includes organized ideological, social, and religious groups. Moreover, these changes have occurred after the death of the county-unit system and the shift of electoral power from rural to suburban areas. Politics has also become somewhat more open—or at least better reported—following reform drives in the 1970s and 1990s. Perhaps most startling to Key would be Republican control of state government at the start of the twenty-first century.

Policy making in Georgia is not entirely a story of change from twenty, forty, or sixty years ago, however. Policies are still enacted within a system characterized by low levels of voter turnout. Money and the influence of lobbyists remain important components of elections and policy making. Localism remains alive and well in the General Assembly. Still, although observers do not often think of the state as a policy innovator, Georgia has adapted to change and is constantly pressured to keep pace with other states, especially in the Southeast.[12] The remainder of this chapter will examine developments in several major policy areas.

Politics, Policy, and the State Budget

There are several ways to examine policy change. One involves the state budget—particularly its overall growth and the relative distribution of its expenditures and revenue sources. Adopting a budget is a complex task, and the successes and failures of those involved in the process relate directly to political power within the State Capitol. Budgets themselves constitute statements of both policy and political priorities.

The budget is probably the most important piece of legislation the Georgia General Assembly considers during its annual session. Budgets generally begin with the agencies in which funds eventually will be spent. The agencies predict coming expenditures based on a number of factors: past expenditures, new projects, changes in the number or circumstances of clients being served, one-time-only expenditures (for example, outlays for buildings or new equipment), revenue from other sources, and changes in inflation or other economic trends. The agencies' budgetary requests are often quite detailed, listing expenditures in areas such as salaries, equipment, travel, supplies, and capital improvements.

The various departments that house the agencies collect their requests for the upcoming fiscal year and send them to the Office of Planning and Budget in the governor's office every year by September 1.[13] The governor then submits the budget the following January and the fiscal year starts on July 1. The Office of Planning and Budget often serves as a budget cutter, closely scrutinizing requests. Some observers argue that agencies pad their budgets to diminish the effects of this process. Those programs that have the full support of the governor are less likely to feel the budget ax, but officials at all agencies know that cuts take place at this stage. For example, the budget submitted to the legislature by Governor Zell Miller for fiscal 1997 asked for appropriations of $11.3 billion: departments had requested $12 billion. Governor Sonny Perdue's proposed budget for fiscal year 2007, which he submitted in January 2006, included a combination of cuts and increases to agency requests that reflected both the governor's priorities and improvements in Georgia's economy. Perdue recommended spending more than $18.6 billion in state funds; with federal and other monies added in, total proposed spending exceeded $34 billion. Six departments were expected to spend more than $1 billion each from state and other sources. The governor recommended retaining the Department of Community Health's request for more than $2.3 billion in state funds. He reduced the Board of Regents' request for $1.9 billion by almost $6 million while slashing the Department of Transportation's proposed $702 million in state funds by more than $38 million. In contrast, the State Board of Education's request for $6.45 billion was enlarged by more than $768 million, the $1.4 billion sought by Human Resources grew by $7 million, and Corrections saw its request grow from $958 million to $997 million.[14]

The purpose of the Office of Planning and Budget is to make sure that the governor's priorities are reflected in the appropriations that will be forwarded to the General Assembly. The OPB consists of 75 employees and is responsible for planning based upon estimates of revenue, past expenditure, and budget requests.[15] The OPB maintains a staff of policy specialists and budget analysts to accomplish this goal, although politics is at the core of any budget process.

After the Office of Planning and Budget has revised the budget to reflect the governor's political priorities, it is introduced in the legislature as a bill. The budget generally will take up the entire legislative session after being introduced in January. Each chamber has an appropriations committee, which will conduct debate and determine the wording of the final bill. Because many groups are interested in the continued funding of government programs or in money for new policy areas, lobbying the House and Senate Appropriations Committees is common. Moreover, the task of drafting the legislative budget is so important politically that members compete fiercely for seats on both chambers' appropriations committees.

The legislative role in the budgetary process is to modify and ultimately adopt the budget. The legislature has the final say in how much is appropriated to each agency and for what purpose. The legislature may support items that the Office of Planning and Budget reduced or deleted from agency requests. Cuts are also possible but less likely at this stage. The governor stands relatively removed from the budgetary process at this juncture, at least in formal terms. Governors may influence the legislature's activities or try to sway public opinion and thereby to influence the budget indirectly as it weaves its way through the General Assembly. Interest groups also will attempt to affect the budget both directly, by testifying at public hearings, and indirectly, by manipulating public opinion and by mobilizing their members. Many lobbyists who engage in these formal methods note that they are ineffective without established ties to legislators. For example, the Medical Association of Georgia maintains a list of doctors who have personal friendships with legislators and could intercede in the policy process.[16] For the 2007 fiscal year, the General Assembly held close to the budget submitted by Governor Perdue, deviating less than 10 percent from the total budgets recommended by the Office of Planning and Budget.

The budget is a piece of legislation and must be passed like any other bill. House and Senate versions of the budget must be identical before they can be sent to the governor. Because the process examines expenditures in such detail, it is quite time-consuming. The budget is often not completed until the final days of the legislative session. In many cases, the budget is the final bill passed.

The last-minute passage of the budget would make it difficult for the legislature to override a veto, since the legislature often passes the budget and immediately goes home. Georgia's governor is not likely to veto the budget as a whole but is likely to use the item veto. In so doing, the governor may not add to the budget but may merely delete from it.

The budget process of course has winners and losers. Those interests that represent large groups of mobilized voters are likely to succeed, as are major firms and business organizations that make important campaign contributions. Many agencies are also protected by the presence of earmarked (dedicated) funds. The Georgia Department of Transportation (GDOT), for example, is protected to some degree because taxes collected on motor fuel throughout the state must be spent on roads, thereby providing GDOT with somewhat greater freedom from the whims of the legislature than other departments that must fight for a piece of the budgetary pie. Still, more than $1.1 billion of the agency's nearly $1.8 billion in 2006 came from federal funds. More than $600 million came from state motor fuel taxes, and the legislature added another $14 million from general revenues.[17]

The budget process thus has many twists and turns in which a variety of political players may have input. The result often seems to be a budget that is too complicated for average citizens to understand, and no one person has total control over the process. In Georgia, as in many other states, however, the governor has more formal control over budget outcomes than any other single individual. In recent years, when Georgia faced tight budgets and increased demands for services, the legislature has supported most governors' requests for cuts and new sources of funding.

Georgia's Spending Patterns

One common way to examine policy change is to consider the ways that governments allocate their resources. The state budget has grown substantially over the years. The first billion-dollar budget occurred in 1967. The budget for fiscal year 1996 reached almost $10.7 billion, while the one for fiscal 2006 totaled $17.6 billion. With the state emerging from an economic slowdown, the governor proposed a 2007 budget of $18.6 billion.[18]

State expenditures rose somewhat steadily until the 1970s, after which growth accelerated (see figure 11.2), in part because of increased federal aid and efforts to keep pace with inflation. Budgetary growth seems less steep when adjusted for inflation. Much of the expansion of the budget during the 1980s can be attributed to the rapid growth of Georgia's economy, although changes in spending parallel the economy's rise and decline.

Although Georgia's budget grew after World War II, few shifts occurred in the relative allocations to major functions (see figure 11.3). Education has commanded more than 40 percent of state spending since 1964, while interest

Figure 11.2. State General Expenditures in Current and Constant Dollars, 1970–2002

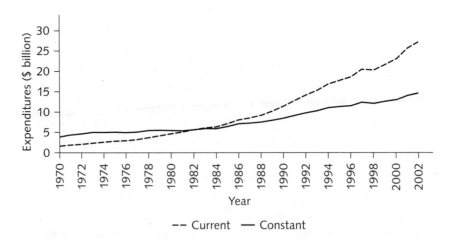

Note: Constant dollars calculated from the Consumer Price Index with 1982 = $1.00. For the calculator used to convert current to constant dollars, see http://minneapolisfed.org/research/data/us/calc/.

Source: Akioka 2004.

Figure 11.3. Percentage of State Expenditures Spent on Different Functions, 1970–2002

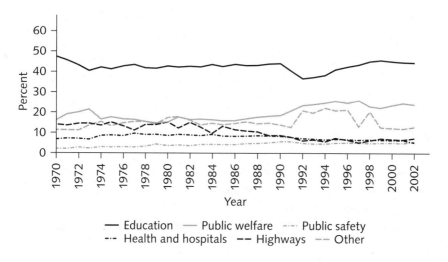

Source: Akioka 2004.

on debt has remained around 2 percent. The major changes in allocation are represented by the declining share of spending on highways and natural resources and increasing proportions spent on health care and hospitals, public welfare, and public safety. Some of these changes reflect the shifting political priorities of governors and legislative leaders; others reflect pressures from interest groups and the requirements of existing or new federal programs.

Georgia's Revenue Sources

In addition to the annual decisions about spending on programs, questions about revenue sources can have significant long-term consequences. In raising revenues, Georgia's state government relies on taxes, fees, revenues from other governments, and borrowing (debt). In developing tax policies, states must consider what to tax as well as how to tax it and at what rate. Like most states, Georgia relied heavily during earlier eras on property taxes, but the General Assembly adopted individual and corporate income taxes in 1929 and a general sales tax in 1951. These decisions made Georgia among the earliest states to use an income tax but one of the latest to adopt a general sales tax. State revenue systems vary, however. In 2005, five states (Alaska, Delaware, Montana, New Hampshire, and Oregon) did not have general sales taxes; most state sales taxes exempted food and prescription drugs. Another nine states did not use an individual income tax, although two taxed dividends and interest.[19]

Georgia's tax system has been regarded as somewhat regressive—that is, as taking a greater percentage from those with low incomes than from those with higher incomes. Progressive tax systems do just the opposite. This lack of progressivity resulted in large part from the application of the sales tax to necessities, particularly groceries, and the flat rate applied to income beyond a certain level (tax of $5,810 plus 6 percent of taxable income over $100,000 in 2005). This regressivity, along with pressure from Governor Zell Miller, prompted the General Assembly to pass a 1996 law that phased out the tax on food over the next two years, although the decision obviously resulted in a loss of revenue for the state.[20]

Today, Georgia derives the lion's share of its revenues from the income tax and the general sales tax (see figure 11.4), which grew from 3 to 4 percent in

Figure 11.4. Percentage of State Revenue from Different Sources

—— General sales taxes   —— Income taxes   ···· Selective sales taxes
–·· Intergovernmental revenue   – – Licenses, charges, and miscellaneous

Source: Akioka 2004.

1989. Local governments also have several options for adopting sales taxes with voter approval.

The relative distribution of revenue shows some variation over time. This phenomenon may be most apparent in swings in federal aid, the changing position of sales taxes and income taxes during the 1980s, and the larger share contributed by sales taxes after the rate increase in 1989. Changes in the relative importance of income tax revenues result from individual rather than corporate returns.

Critics have lodged several other complaints about Georgia's tax system in addition to its lack of progressivity. One is the degree to which it has been built on an ad hoc basis, sometimes as a result of short-term political considerations. Another target is the limited coverage of the sales tax, which applies to commodities but to few of the personal and professional services that comprise a significant share of today's economy.

The property tax has also come under attack on at least three grounds: first, critics argue that using the property tax to fund schools is both inefficient and unfair, particularly to those with no children in local public schools; second, many observers complain that people wind up paying excessive taxes because their property increases in value even if the tax rate does not change; third, homeowners and businesses criticize the performance of the officials who determine the value of property being taxed. Increasing taxes can be especially burdensome for homeowners with fixed incomes, particularly seniors. Some local governments have responded to this dilemma by freezing homeowners' tax bills until they sell their property. Other criticisms are directed at tax breaks for certain activities or groups (for example, kaolin mining, senior citizens). A related issue is the degree to which the state has a diverse enough revenue base to weather a recession. Together, these issues pose potential problems for the state, although whether governors and legislators are prepared systematically and carefully to consider these problems remains unclear.[21]

Economic Development

Promoting the economy is often viewed as a critical function of a state's government. The major players in shaping development policy in most states are business groups and governors.[22] Policies to boost the private economy are often sold as essential to a state government's fiscal soundness. Critics question the effectiveness of such efforts, with some even wondering whether the main beneficiaries are politicians seeking reelection.

States compete intensively for new jobs and businesses, particularly in the South, which many decades ago pioneered the idea of using financial incentives to lure manufacturers. These incentives include a variety of tax breaks, methods to reduce companies' loan costs, and a range of improvements to infrastructure such as sewer and water, streets, and buildings. In general, the South has sold itself as a place of cheap labor and land, few labor unions, low levels of regulation, and generous government financial support—what many observers simply call a "good business climate." The trouble is that many states with such business climates also have low education and income levels. Moreover, rankings of states and localities often tell only part of a region's economic story.[23]

Adopting incentives has often been compared to an arms race in which states try to outbid their neighbors in the incentives game. Indeed, states have tended to copy their neighbors' policies.[24] Georgia has actively sought to promote economic growth (see table 11.1). In addition to incentives, these efforts have included the symbolism of renaming its lead agency the Department of Economic Development in 2004. Like most states, Georgia has long sought to lure outside investment. More recently, the state has increasingly emphasized both helping existing businesses and promoting Georgia products overseas. By the mid-1990s, for example, Georgia had provided training for more than 165,000 workers at twenty-three hundred companies during the previous thirty years, including employees of a large credit card processing facility in Columbus. The state also added infrastructure such as improvements to the port at Savannah.[25] By 2006, Georgia maintained trade offices in Brazil, Canada, Chile, Europe (London and Munich), Japan, Korea, Mexico, and the Middle East (Jerusalem).[26]

The state of Georgia has avoided some riskier strategies for luring businesses, such as making or guaranteeing loans for buildings and equipment and using general obligation bonds (debt guaranteed by tax revenue). In contrast, Georgia uses revenue bonds, which are paid off with revenue from the company benefiting from the state aid. However, many activities not supported with direct aid from the state do benefit from tax breaks, and businesses can also receive financial support from local governments. Some policies provide benefits that vary geographically, as with Georgia's tax credit (reduction in income taxes) for companies that create jobs: the size of

Table 11.1. State Economic Development Policies, 2005

Type of Policy	Number of States Using Policy	Used in Georgia?
Financial Assistance		
State Industrial Development Authority	42	Yes
Private Development Credit Corporation	39	Yes
State Revenue Bond Financing	45	Yes
State General Obligation Bond Financing	24	No
State Loans for Building Construction	42	No
State Loans for Equipment/Machinery	43	No
State Loan Guarantees for Building Construction	30	No
State Loan Guarantees for Equipment/Machinery	34	No
State Financing for Existing Plant Expansion	44	No
State Incentives for High Unemployment Areas	43	Yes
Tax Incentives		
Corporate Income Tax Exemption	41	No
Personal Income Tax Exemption	37	No
Excise Tax Exemption	28	No
Exemption/Moratorium on Land/Capital Improvements	40	Yes
Exemption/Moratorium on Equipment/Machinery	44	Yes
Exemption/Moratorium on Goods in Transit	49	Yes
Exemption on Manufacturers' Inventory	47	Yes
Exemption on New Equipment	49	Yes
Exemption on Raw Materials for Manufacturing	50	Yes
Tax Incentives for Creation of Jobs	45	Yes
Tax Incentives for Industrial Investment	45	Yes
Tax Credits for Use of Specified State Products	8	No
Tax Stabilization Agreements for Certain Industries	12	No
Tax Exemptions for Research and Development	42	Yes
Accelerated Depreciation of Industrial Equipment	41	Yes

Note: Excludes eight types of financial assistance offered by local governments. Georgia local governments offer five of these eight economic development programs, mainly bonds and loans.

Source: Site Selection magazine, November 2005 (http://www.siteselection.com/issues/2005/nov/p704/pdf/Chart1.pdf).

the credit depends on the economic condition of the county where the firm is located.

Many economic development efforts involve multiple incentives, especially in cases involving large firms. For example, Georgia's unsuccessful efforts to persuade DaimlerChrysler to build an automobile manufacturing plant near Savannah involved land, tax breaks, job training, highway improvements, and other benefits.[27] In 2006, Korean auto manufacturer Kia Motors chose Georgia for its first U.S. facility. The plant was projected to cost $1.2 billion, employ roughly twenty-five hundred workers at its Troup County site, and stimulate growth in related businesses. Newspapers estimated the value of state and local government incentives for Kia at roughly $400 million, including state purchase of the site, road and other infrastructure improvements, a railroad spur, property tax abatements, tax credits for job creation, and job training. All told, the package was thought to cost $160,000 in incentives per new job, with workers' earnings averaging about $50,000 annually plus benefits.[28]

In addition to using incentives, local governments and business organizations market their areas as locations for manufacturing, transportation, tourism, retirement, and other industries. However, a dilemma arises if communities compete by offering deals to firms that might have located or expanded in Georgia anyway. In addition, research suggests that financial incentives have limited effects on firms' location decisions, which are based primarily on market factors. Thus, neighboring states or communities may end up competing on a level playing field, but each of them may have given away more financially than was necessary to attract a firm. Indeed, one research organization has raised concerns that Georgia is giving away too much tax revenue in exchange for questionable economic gains, a trade-off the group dubbed "Don't tax and they will come?"[29] Moreover, it is unclear that economic development policies can exert much influence on states' economic conditions.[30]

Transportation

Georgia has a complicated transportation system that includes almost 450 airports (107 of which are public-use airports), 5,000 miles of railways, more than 113,000 miles of public highways, and 4 major ports.[31] There are twelve public transportation systems, which include Fulton and DeKalb Counties' MARTA system and commuter bus systems such as the CCT in Cobb County. Finally, the state has 2,943 miles of bicycle and pedestrian trails.[32] For most Georgians, discussions of transportation center on the time it takes to journey to work. In this respect, Georgia does not compare well to other states. In 2004, the average Georgian spent 26.8 minutes per day traveling to work, more than 2 minutes higher than the nationwide average of 24.7 minutes. Georgia ranked as the seventh-worst state for commuting to work. These long commutes result in part from the fact that the vast majority of Georgians travel to work alone rather than in carpools or by using transportation systems—79.9 percent in 2004, compared to a U.S. average of 77 percent.[33]

Another aspect of transportation that sets Georgia apart from other states is its major airport. Located ten miles from the center of Atlanta's business district, Hartsfield-Jackson serves more passengers than any other airport in the world. In 2004, 6.8 million people traveled through the airport, almost 500,000 of them traveling internationally. The airport serviced sixty-nine metric tons of cargo and eight thousand metric tons of mail in that year. It is Georgia's largest single work location, with 53,000 workers and a total payroll of $2.4 billion. The airport's economic impact is estimated at $18.7 billion.[34] The airport clearly represents a significant contribution to transportation in the state and is likely to become more of a factor in the years to come, as the airport is currently expanding its runway, retail, and other facilities.

Georgia's railroads are dominated by two large private companies, CSX and Norfolk Southern. Rail passenger service in the state is provided by Amtrak, with stations located in Atlanta, Gainesville, Jesup, Savannah, and Toccoa.

The Georgia Department of Transportation

GDOT has authority to plan, construct, and maintain highways and bridges. It also has some planning and financial responsibilities for airports, ports, railways, public transportation systems, and even bike paths and trails.[35] As currently organized, GDOT was established by Governor Jimmy Carter in 1972, and the department's mission is to make transportation safe and efficient throughout the state.

GDOT's most visible activity is maintaining and upgrading Georgia's highways. The department maintains a database of traffic patterns across the

state and records specific information on almost twenty-two thousand intersections and roadways for planning use.[36] The department uses the Internet
to provide the public with information on traffic congestion and construction delays.

GDOT's governing board is elected by a caucus of the membership of the
Georgia General Assembly for each of the state's thirteen congressional districts. Board members are elected in staggered five-year terms, with two or
three members up for election each year. The board is assisted by a commissioner, who oversees GDOT's nine divisions.

GDOT maintains seven district offices throughout the state, has six thousand employees, and operates with a $1.6 million annual budget (as of 2006).
In addition to in-house employees, the GDOT contracts with private companies to do much of the work of planning, constructing, and maintaining
highways. Unlike some of Georgia's other departments, which rely predominantly on state appropriations, the GDOT has a strong supplemental revenue base, provided by the federal government, the state's motor fuel tax, and
other highway-use taxes and fees. The motor fuel tax is collected from individual drivers as a portion of the amount paid for fuel at regular gas retailers.
In addition, the GDOT often receives U.S. Department of Transportation
funds earmarked for special projects (discussed later in the chapter). Competition among private vendors for DOT contracts is intense, and a system
of sealed bids determines which vendors receive contracts.

This system has not eliminated the concerns of critics who believe that
contracts often go to vendors with strong political ties.[37] One recent study
noted that much of the $626 million in contracts GDOT awarded between
1999 and 2005 went to companies that hired former department employees.
A proposed contract to rebuild the Interstate 85–Highway 316 interchange
produced multiple bids, all of which surpassed the department's estimates of
the project's cost.[38]

GDOT Projects

Perhaps no GDOT project created more controversy than the 211-mile Outer
Perimeter Expressway around metro Atlanta. The debate over this project
produced rampant allegations of misconduct regarding the planning and
contracting process. In addition, residents along the road's proposed path

expressed strong objections, nonprofit (especially environmental) groups voiced opinions, and municipal and county governments entered the debate. GDOT argued that the new perimeter was necessary to alleviate traffic congestion, especially along the highway's "Northern Arc" through Bartow, Forsyth, Gwinnett, and Cherokee Counties. State officials estimate a 308 percent increase in traffic in those areas by 2025; however, estimates for that portion of the perimeter totaled $2.4 billion for 59 miles of road. Other portions of the proposal have generated less controversy, although they are further behind in the planning process. However, the fact that they have been less controversial does not necessarily mean that they are inexpensive. By 2002, $35 million had been spent to acquire the about half of the right-of-way for the eastern section of the road.[39] Governor Roy Barnes's support of the road pushed planning forward during his tenure, while his successor, Sonny Perdue, has publicly stated that the Northern Arc will not be built, although he has also acknowledged the need for traffic congestion relief in the proposed area. At this point, the future of the Northern Arc is unclear, and some commentators have called for the conversion of land already acquired to park space.[40]

GDOT's more popular projects and programs include the NaviGAtor system, which allows residents to plan trips by viewing real-time video of traffic conditions on Georgia's interstates. Electronic message signs warn drivers of congestion or construction ahead and HERO (Highway Emergency Response Operator) units assist drivers who experience difficulty while traveling on interstates. GDOT also promotes Perdue's Fast Forward Program, designed to streamline the process of road improvement, as a means of dealing with growing congestion problems across the state and especially in metro Atlanta. Other projects include vegetation control on highways and wildflower medians.

Coordination of Transportation Policy

In most cases, even GDOT is required to coordinate transportation planning with a multitude of other agencies and departments. For example, the Georgia Ports Authority operates all Georgia ports, and the National Transportation Safety Board and the National Highway Traffic Safety Administration of the U.S. Department of Transportation are stakeholders in establishing transportation policy in the state. Although some observers argue that GDOT has too much power, the fragmentation of policy in this area clearly contributes to the state's sometimes slow reaction to transportation problems.

Particularly during Governor Barnes's tenure, Georgia attempted more systematic transportation planning. The Georgia Regional Transportation Authority coordinates transportation planning in the thirteen counties designated as not in compliance with federal clean-air statutes regarding ozone.[41] The Regional Transportation Authority functions as an advisory and planning partner for other state agencies. Many critics argue that the agency has little if any authority, and without strong support from Governor Perdue, its major impact has been to provide commuter busing information and options. In late 2005, another attempt to coordinate transportation policy in the Atlanta region was made with the creation of the Regional Transit Planning Board. Some observers express optimism that the new board will be more fiscally accountable and therefore better able to acquire funding from sources critical of the financial practices of MARTA and other transit boards. It is too soon to assess the Regional Transit Board's impact, but many people are encouraged by the fact that regional solutions are being sought for problems that cross political jurisdictions.[42] However, GDOT dominates the statewide planning process, and any attempts to coordinate transportation regionally must include the department.

Environmental Policy

Discussions of economic development and transportation in Georgia often extend to questions related to environmental quality. Environmental policies impact all residents. They also result from a variety of influences from the private sector and from government at all levels. Nonprofit and nongovernmental organizations also seek to make themselves heard in environmental debate, making it one of the most contentious policy areas. Recent controversies focus on whether market solutions may be a good way to address some environmental problems and to what degree property rights permit land use that may not be in the best interests of communities as a whole.

States have taken an increasingly active role in environmental policy, as is evidenced by their increased spending over time. In 1986, states spent $8.7 billion on the environment. By 2003 that total had increased to $15.1 billion, and states were spending $51 per capita on environmental programs. The states are the primary sources of environmental data, collecting information on water, air, and land quality. Much of the states' natural resources budgets go toward data collection and monitoring of the environment, often in collaboration with federal agencies, universities, and nonprofit organizations. According to some estimates, only one-third of all spending on the environment comes from federal sources. However, environmental policies and agencies are often the first to be cut back in times of budgetary scarcity, as has been the case since 2000.[43]

Air Quality

Many metropolitan areas, including Atlanta, are not in compliance with federal air quality standards set forth in the Clean Air Acts of 1990 and 1997. Areas of noncompliance are often referred to as "nonattainment zones." Federal law requires policies in these jurisdictions to have no negative impact on ozone, carbon monoxide, lead, or other particulate levels. For residents, the best known policy is auto emission standards, which vary according to the area of the state in which cars are registered. These standards also affect corporations. Air permits are issued, and new companies must explain how their businesses will control emissions to comply with the standards. One recent controversy was the potential opening of a coal-burning electrical production facility in mid-Georgia. Although such a facility could add one hundred new jobs, some residents, concerned about the air emissions from the proposed plant, aimed to block its opening.

Land Quality and Property Rights

One challenge facing Georgia's environmental future is the growth in population and corresponding demand for development. In 1989, the General Assembly required that all counties regulate land use, with provisions regarding the development of wetlands, water basins, and mountains. The Georgia Land Conservation Council (formerly the Georgia Community Greenspace Program) requires that rapidly growing counties set aside 20 percent of all undeveloped land to be preserved. This program is funded in part through state allocations and in part through donations from individuals and nonprofit organizations.

The state also has a number of other programs for land conservation, including a Solid Waste Trust Fund, which is financed by a one dollar fee imposed on the purchase of tires. The monies are supposed to be spent on cleaning up illegal dump areas; however, state officials have used the fund for other purposes in recent years: observers estimate that other agencies have raided more than $12 million from the fund.[44] Other recent initiatives include the reclamation of unused rail lines to provide park space or walking/biking trails, such as the highly popular Silver Comet Trail in Cobb County and Atlanta's proposed Beltline Park.[45]

One controversial issue related to land regulation is eminent domain. Federal, state, and local governments are permitted to condemn property and take ownership for public use. Property owners are supposed to receive just compensation for the taking of their land, usually determined by market analyses of property values. In some instances, property owners have also been compensated when nearby public use facilities, such as landfills or airports, cause property values to drop. The debate over just compensation is generally limited to property owners in specific disputes, and the courts generally settle each case individually. Recent controversies over eminent domain in Georgia focus on whether governments can take property from homeowners to use for economic development. In some cases, local governments have attempted to take property for development by private interests rather than for more general public purposes such as roads, parks, or schools. Hostility to such actions intensified after a June 2005 U.S. Supreme Court decision upheld such a condemnation in Connecticut.[46] Georgia legislators took up the issue in 2006 and curtailed private land takings for economic development in the state.[47] The issue was finally settled by an amendment to the Georgia Constitution prohibiting such takings.

Water Quality

Water quality is the most important issue of environmental policy in the state in terms of dollars spent, legislative debate, and judicial intervention. Georgia, Florida, and Alabama have a long-standing dispute over the Chattahoochee River, in terms of both water quality and the use of water from the river. In addition, the Flint River Basin has been the subject of much study and controversy for more than twenty years. Other divisive issues on water policy deal with the extent to which northern sections of the state, especially communities in metropolitan Atlanta, take water from the Chattahoochee and return waste or runoff water to the river. The debate on the Chattahoochee appears to involve both quantity and quality of river water.

Some uses of the river require that water levels remain adequate to produce electricity at downstream facilities and to make the river navigable for barge traffic. Other Georgians are concerned about the quality rather than the quantity of water in the river for recreational use and to maintain wildlife ecosystems. As one might expect, these issues have involved litigation, including a major suit that forced the city of Atlanta to undertake a $2 billion overhaul of its sewer system paid for in part by a sales tax increase.[48] Complicating planning for the Chattahoochee is the fact that the Flint River empties into the Chattahoochee just north of the Florida state line. Some attempts to coordinate water use have been made, notably the Metro Atlanta Water District and the newly formed Middle Chattahoochee Water Coalition. Coastal areas of the state have different concerns, including saltwater intrusion, while farming areas are more focused on agricultural runoff. In urban areas, wastewater and construction runoff are additional topics of concern. Statewide water planning is also under way and will be crucial to the success of any water plan.

One suggested policy for water quality is trading water rights. Persons or organizations that have water use permits can sell all or portions of their rights to other parties. Many observers argue that such a system would create market efficiencies and would better define water use limitations; others believe that this approach would result in reduced regulation of water quality and overuse of water resources.[49] Another controversial issue related to transfer of water rights is the transfer of water from one basin to another. Water basins are defined naturally by the direction of water runoff and groundwater flow. So-called interbasin transfers allow areas of high use to take water from other basins that have lower demand. Interbasin transfers often result when one community pumps water from a nearby basin into its water system. Proponents of interbasin transfer note that such water use encourages more uniform growth and land development and makes efficient use of water resources.[50] Critics argue that interbasin transfers adversely affect downstream water use for natural and human communities.[51] This debate is complicated by the fact that many communities are located in more than one basin. Many metro Atlanta counties use in-terbasin transfers, but new provisions for such use are certain to generate debate.

The Future of Environmental Policy

In the years ahead, environmental policy in Georgia will rely on new tech-nologies for air, water, and land quality. Proposals for monitors that can test emissions from passing cars are already being discussed, and new methods for passive water- and air-quality testing are in use and are proposed for the future.[52] The state legislature, which in the past has deferred to regulatory agencies, will likely become more involved in environmental planning. Water-planning districts are being institutionalized, and the General Assembly has begun to provide state fiscal resources for planning.

Essential to success are more statewide coordination and regional plan-ning with neighboring states. The "water wars" involving Alabama, Georgia, and Florida are nonproductive, slowing all three states' efforts to control pol-lution. Market approaches may also be an important trend for the future of environmental policy in Georgia.[53]

Education

Funding for Georgia's public schools and colleges remains the big-ticket item in the state budget. Funding for education is shared among levels of govern-ment. Federal funds account for 5–10 percent of the education budgets of the fifty states. In the past twenty years, state governments have assumed a larger role for education funding than in the more distant past. One scholar evaluated the degree to which funding levels in the states were dominated by state rather than local funds and ranked Georgia in the middle in terms of state funding responsibility.[54] Georgia spends slightly less per pupil ($8,866) than the U.S. average of $8,900, ranking it twenty-second among the states in per-pupil spending. Georgia's public schools receive just under 7 percent of their funding from federal sources, just under 50 percent from the state, and about 44 percent from local sources (see figure 11.5).[55]

Controversies have recently arisen in Georgia over funding disparities in public education. Kenneth K. Wong examined the gap in spending between school districts in Georgia and other states to assess the difference between

Figure 11.5. Public Education Revenue Sources for Georgia and the United States, 2002

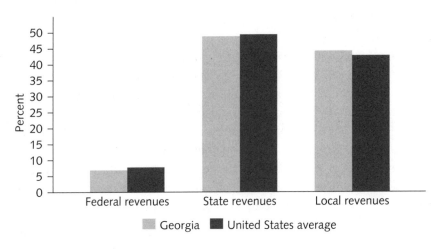

Source: U.S. Census Bureau 2002a.

the highest- and lowest-spending districts. Georgia's gap was .35 (35 percent), higher than the average gap for the nation as a whole (29 percent).[56] Over the past few years, the General Assembly has discussed several proposals to decrease reliance on local funding, generally provided through local property taxes, and increase the state's proportion of public educational revenues. Some legislators have proposed raising the state sales taxes to cover educational expenses and cutting and/or eliminating local property taxes. Such a change would be dramatic and might shift tax burdens to populations with lower incomes. Local school districts, especially in areas where family incomes are low, favor this proposal and have initiated court action to try to force the state to adopt this policy. Other school districts oppose additional state funding assistance. They have also made legislative proposals to prevent school districts from seeking additional state assistance until local property taxes reach the maximum permitted by Georgia law.[57] At the heart of the debate lies the fact that more affluent school districts do not want to subsidize education in poorer school districts, while poor school districts are increasingly looking to the state for supplemental sources of income.

These issues have surfaced in other states and in the federal courts. Despite a 1973 U.S. Supreme Court ruling that states can permit local school districts independently to address their financial needs, residents of eighteen states have successfully sued to even out disparities in school district funding. Courts have recognized the needs of disadvantaged students, and in some cases, the threat of court action has prompted states to enact policies that address inequities.[58]

Education also numbers among the perennial issues that governors and legislatures must address.[59] It has remained a major issue for most of the period since World War II, although the controversies sparking debate have varied. Until the early 1970s, political conflict over education was part of the larger debate over segregation. Controversies over the racial composition of school systems have subsided, although they remain salient in many school systems.[60] Recent debates over education policy have also concentrated on the performance of teachers and students. Such "reform" initiatives were not limited to Georgia but were quite visible throughout the South.[61] Curriculum and symbolic issues such as school prayer also spark controversy in some areas.

Much of the impetus for reform is reflected in Georgia's history of poor performance on several indicators, although measures of educational quality are frequently topics of debate themselves. In 1992 Georgia's average SAT verbal score was 398, compared to the national average of 423; Georgia's math scores averaged 444, below the national average of 476. Although SAT scoring has changed in recent years, the new scores reflect similar results. In 2004 Georgia students averaged 981 on the reasoning portions of the SAT, lower than the national average, 1,026. The percentage of students proficient in eighth-grade mathematics amounted to 17 percent in 1990 and was virtually unchanged in 1992 at 16 percent; over that same period, the national level grew from 20 to 25 percent.[62] Data for 2004 indicate that Georgia high school students fall below the national average in all areas of ACT testing (see figure 11.6).

New accountability standards place strong pressure on improving test scores, and Georgia frequently tests its students, especially in elementary grades, when tests are administered each year.[63] State testing requires that students perform at grade level on the Criterion-Referenced Competency Test in the third, fifth, and eighth grades to be promoted to the next grade. Critics argue that evaluating students on the basis of a single test is inappropriate and causes students to feel too much pressure. Other critics of the state policy argue that holding students in the same grade may discourage

Figure 11.6. Average ACT Scores (Composite and Subtest) for All Students at State and National Levels

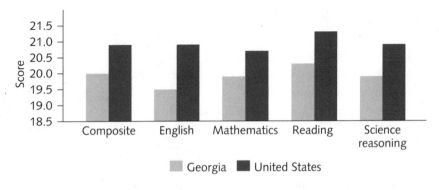

Source: Georgia Department of Education, *Report Card 2004* (http://reportcard.gaosa.org/yr2004/k12/Reports.aspx?TestType=ST9&10=ALL:ALL).

students and increase the chances that they will later drop out. In 2006, 18 percent of third-graders, 15 percent of fifth-graders, and 13 percent of eighth-graders did not perform well enough in reading to receive promotion. Math scores had failure rates of 9, 11, and 23 percent, respectively, for those grades. Statewide, seventy-five thousand students faced grade retention. Most students attended summer school and attempted the test again before school began in the fall of 2006.[64]

Almost half of the state's public school students are poor enough to qualify for reduced-price or free meals at school; in some districts, that rate reaches nearly 100 percent. Dropout rates have also caused concern: approximately one in five Georgians over the age of twenty-five lacks a high school diploma.[65] Recent trends indicate that Georgia schools will have increasing numbers of Latino/Hispanic students. In 2004, more than 9,000 students qualified for services under the federal government's Migrant Education Program, and almost 40,000 of the state's 1.4 million students were enrolled in programs teaching English as a second language.[66]

The election of the first Republican state superintendents of schools heightened debate over the state's role in education. Superintendent Linda Schrenko cut the size of the state Department of Education but ran into considerable trouble in achieving other policy goals. Governor Zell Miller, a Democrat, supported many of her initiatives, including higher salaries for classroom teachers. She had difficulty working with the state school board, and her mismanagement of state and federal funds resulted in an indictment and conviction. Schrenko's successor, Cathy Cox, has taken a more consensus-building approach and has received strong support from Governor Sonny Perdue.

Proceeds from the Georgia Lottery are dedicated by law to scholarships and student loans, voluntary pre-kindergarten (pre-K), and capital improvements for education. In his 2006 proposals, Perdue advocated the elimination of capital funding projects using lottery funds in favor of a focus on other programs. According to the governor, this adjustment will help the lottery remain solvent while continuing to meet the increasing demands for pre-K and scholarship programs.

Georgia's leading educational program is the HOPE (Helping Outstanding Pupils Educationally) scholarship, which finances college for all students who maintain B averages and pays tuition for all students in good standing at the state's technical schools. The 2006 costs for this program are estimated at $509 million. Proponents of the program note that finances no longer prevent any student who is academically prepared from attending college. Another frequently cited benefit is the rising quality of students attending university system schools, in part because scholarships entice these students away from private or out-of-state institutions. Critics of the program focus on the students who fail to maintain the required standards as well as on the lack of an income limit for scholarship recipients, which means that lower-income lottery players may be subsidizing college for affluent students.

Pre-kindergarten programs will also continue to receive funding. In 2006, an estimated $290 million in lottery funds will provide voluntary pre-kindergarten programs to four-year-olds across the state, helping to better prepare children for their subsequent schooling. When Governor Miller first proposed the HOPE scholarship and the statewide pre-K programs, they generated some controversy, but they are now highly popular, and no Georgia politician would oppose them in the current political environment. Indeed, protection of these programs has become standard in most political rhetoric.

Another issue working through local school districts is the continuing debate over teaching values and promoting ideas rooted in religious beliefs. Such controversies are not limited to Georgia, however.[67] Court cases in Georgia include a successful suit to eliminate prayer at high school football games and controversy over student clubs that support gay and lesbian students. A recent controversy in Cobb County schools illustrates the degree to which parents, teachers, and school districts quickly become involved in this debate over values. In this case, a parent petitioned the school board to have stickers placed on science textbooks indicating that evolution was a "theory," not a "fact." Other parents filed suit to have the stickers removed, and a federal district court agreed that the stickers unconstitutionally endorsed religion.[68] In 2006 parents and the school board reached an agreement and the stickers were removed, but the case illustrates Georgia's continuing controversies over religion in public schools.

In recent years, Georgia's teachers have constituted a growing political force. Many observers of the 2002 gubernatorial election noted that teachers, unhappy with incumbent Roy Barnes's lack of responsiveness to their needs, voted for his opponent, Sonny Perdue, who won. In his 2006 reelection bid, Perdue worked to retain the teachers' support.

One review of teacher salaries nationwide places teachers in Georgia at an average salary of $45,848 per year, the highest rate in the Southeast and fifteenth nationally.[69] The state improved teacher pay between 1993 and 2003 by over 17 percent, making it the state with the most improvement over that period. Georgia's relatively modest national ranking in salary may in part reflect its low proportion (third lowest in the nation) of male K–12 teachers because male faculty make higher salaries overall. Teachers will continue to be in high demand in the state, as Georgia has the nation's fifth highest growth rate of student-aged population (1.8 percent in 2004).[70]

Tackling education problems is seldom easy. Future policy debates will focus on funding, particularly local school systems' reliance on property taxes, differences between rich and poor districts, and the link between education and the state lottery. Debates also have grown heated over curriculum, including graduation requirements, tracking, achievement tests, and the teaching of values. None of these questions seems likely to go away, which could make for contentious sessions in the General Assembly, within the state education department, and at local school board meetings.

Social Welfare Policies

Policies dealing with poverty seldom seem to lack controversy—in Georgia, the other forty-nine states, or nationally. Although the states are heavily involved in poverty programs, policy tends to be made at the national level. Congress has adopted a range of programs to combat poverty, beginning with the Social Security Act of 1935. Some of these programs are

Figure 11.7. Rates of Poverty in the United States and Georgia, 2004

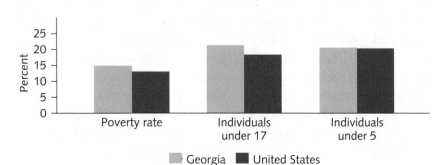

Source: U.S. Census Bureau 2004a.

administered by the states with a combination of federal and state funds. Most of these programs experienced changes in the 1990s. The most dramatic of these changes was the Personal Responsibility and Work Opportunity Reconciliation Act of 1996 (often known as Workfare), which set limits on the number of years that able-bodied adults may receive benefits. All social welfare policies seek to provide a safety net for citizens who are "needy," but definition of who is needy and how long assistance is provided remain open to debate. Some programs are entitlements based on factors other than individual financial need: people qualify for Social Security and Medicare, for example, based on age or disability.

The federal government uses several measures to determine poverty. These measures establish who is eligible for some forms of government assistance at the state and federal level. The poverty rate is calculated using annual income for individuals and families. In 2004, the poverty threshold for a family of four was set at $18,850 and for individuals at $9,310.[71] U.S. poverty rates fluctuate. In 2000, the overall rate of poverty for all fifty states stood at 11.3 percent, a significant decline from the 15.1 percent rate in 1993. Since 1975, the poverty rate has remained between 11 and 16 percent, although it tends to rise during economic recessions, as it did following 2001.[72]

States in the South tend to have higher overall rates of poverty than the rest of the nation. Mississippi, Alabama, Louisiana, the Carolinas, and Arkansas rank consistently as the poorest states, although Oklahoma and New Mexico also have high poverty rates. In Georgia, 14.8 percent of the population (1.2 million persons) stood below the poverty threshold in 2004 (see figure 11.7). The rate was higher for children under seventeen, with 19.1 percent of that age group living in poverty, and higher still for children under five, at 20.6 percent. In 2004, Georgia residents' median family income totaled $43,037. The overall poverty rate for the United States amounted to 13.3 percent in that year. Georgia consistently ranks with its southern neighbors among the poorer states, with the thirteenth-highest poverty level in 2004.[73]

Income represents one measure of poverty. Other indicators also place Georgia among the states with the highest percentages of needy persons. As the previous data indicate, younger Georgians are more likely to experience poverty than other residents of the state. One estimate places Georgia forty-first in overall child well-being, a measure that includes child poverty rates, school dropout rates, teen pregnancy, child death rates, and low birth weights.[74]

A number of programs provide help for eligible needy Georgians (see table 11.2). Most of these social welfare programs are funded by the federal government and administered by the state using federal funds. For example, the Child Care and Development Fund subsidizes child care for families with children under thirteen years of age. The federal government provides a broad set of rules for eligibility of families, but states may set eligibility standards at up to 85 percent of the median income for all families within

Table 11.2. Expenditures in Georgia for Social Welfare Programs, 2001–2004

Program	Spending Criteria	Amount
Medicaid Health Insurance for Children	Per Child	$1,134
Child Care Subsidies	Per Family	$6,452
Child Care Subsidies	Per Child	$3,568
Head Start	Per Student	$7,724
Public Health Insurance for Parents	Per Adult	$2,046
TANF Cash Assistance	Per Family	$3,052
TANF Cash Assistance	Per Individual	$1,307
Food Stamps	Per Household	$2,486
Earned Income Tax Credit	Per Tax Filer	$1,979

Source: National Center for Children in Poverty, Columbia University, State Data, Cross Policy, 2001, 2003, 2004 (http://nccp.org/state_detail_GA.html).

the state. In addition, participants in some states (including Georgia) receive free child care while attending school, although some states provide child care only for working parents. Other programs to provide assistance include food stamps, which offer eligible recipients subsidies for groceries, and Head Start, a federally funded program to prepare young children for school. The Earned Income Tax Credit can be thought of as a "negative income tax," providing eligible federal income tax filers with additional tax refunds over the amounts withheld by employers in the previous year. Some states (but not Georgia) provide Earned Income Tax Credits for state income taxes as well. Several programs—most notably Medicaid and PeachCare—provide Georgians with health insurance. Medicaid, which provides health care for uninsured persons below the poverty level, is a particularly expensive program, taking up more than $2.1 billion in Georgia's 2007 budget.[75]

The program most often associated with welfare assistance provides cash payments to families with children. Originally a section of the Social Security network of the 1930s, Aid to Families with Dependent Children (AFDC) provided monthly payments to families in poverty in all states. In 1993, monthly payments averaged $381 for all fifty states and $255 in Georgia. In 1996, the Personal Responsibility and Work Opportunity Reconciliation Act replaced AFDC with a program called Temporary Assistance for Needy Families (TANF). TANF sets income eligibility rules similar to AFDC but caps the total number of years that families can qualify for aid and requires recipients to be working and/or attending school to qualify. In 2004, monthly payments under TANF averaged $439 per family nationwide, compared to $290 monthly in Georgia. These figures average $2,195 per person annually nationwide and $1,307 per person in Georgia.[76] By fiscal 2005, the maximum monthly benefit for a family of three in Georgia was $280.[77]

Social Security, which provides cash payments to elderly individuals, and Medicare, which provides medical subsidies for the elderly, are fully funded by the federal government and do not affect Georgia's state budgets. These programs also do not vary among states—that is, recipients may move from one state to another without benefit interruption or change. While debate on the criteria for eligibility for Social Security benefits has taken place, it occurs at the federal level, and Georgia's policy makers are not likely to voice their opinions about highly popular yet increasingly expensive programs.

The arguments over welfare focus on several issues, particularly individual incentives, social effects, and program costs. Variation among the states constitutes one point of contention, with some concern that higher benefit levels may encourage people to move to other states and that competition among states keeps benefit levels low.[78] The passage of the Personal Responsibility Act resulted from changes in policy direction aimed at encouraging people to use welfare benefits for short-term assistance. The debates on "dependency" led to this shift, as many citizens and policy makers believed that AFDC discouraged recipients from giving up government support to enter the labor market.

In Georgia, the legislature set a lifetime limit of forty-eight months of TANF support, lower than the congressional limit of sixty months. States also have flexibility in setting other eligibility and benefit levels. Between 1997 and 2005, the average number of people receiving monthly cash assistance in Georgia has dropped from more than 302,000 to 99,730. Not all of this drop can be attributed to policy change, however, as economic conditions also have an impact. Still, by October 2005, 12,358 people had reached their lifetime TANF limits.[79]

Social welfare policy debates also focus on the total costs of such programs. In 1993, AFDC spending reached $24.9 billion nationally, with the federal government picking up 54 percent of the tab. Since 1996, the federal government has mandated that states spend funds at a level equal to 80 percent of 1994 levels, although some states (including Georgia) lowered their spending mandates to 75 percent by meeting work participation rates among recipients. While meeting this mandate was easier for states during the economically robust years following the passage of the 1996 act, they have had more difficulty since 2000. Georgia's population growth and the corresponding increase in the number of persons eligible for social welfare assistance, combined with mandates and declining federal funds, have caused social welfare costs to reach crisis levels. Medicaid continues to increase as a percentage of state expenditures, from 9 percent in 1991 to 12.6 percent in the governor's proposed budget for fiscal 2007, second only to education spending. Georgia legislators have also focused on ensuring that illegal immigrants do not receive social welfare benefits. Estimates put Georgia's illegal immigrant population at nearly 250,000. These residents are not eligible for food stamps, Social Security, or TANF, although they have access to public education and to emergency medical treatment, as federal law mandates. Medicaid spending on illegal immigrants in Georgia was estimated at $111 million in 2005 (about 2 percent of Medicaid expenditures); $67 million of that sum came from the federal government. One study suggested that an average undocumented family contributes between \$2,340 and \$2,470 in state and local taxes, adding between \$215 and \$252 million to state and local government revenues.[80] Emotional debates and questions about entitlements lie behind much of the state's social welfare policy making.[81]

Nationally, critics also argue that welfare programs hinder deficit reduction. Such claims have increasingly focused on "middle-class" welfare such as Social Security, mortgage subsidies, and even veterans' benefits, which are awarded without considering whether recipients are needy. Neither the welfare debate nor more general discussions of government benefits seem likely to abate soon either at the Georgia Capitol or in Washington, D.C. Georgia's main dilemma may be deciding how to respond to national program changes and budget cuts.

Public Safety and Security

States, along with their local governments, have long been the cornerstone in protecting the public on a daily basis through law enforcement, prosecution, corrections systems, and related efforts. Since the 2001 terrorist attacks on the United States and the 2005 Gulf Coast hurricanes, traditional means of promoting public safety have been broadened, primarily through state emergency management agencies. Some observers have expressed concern, however, that increases in state and local resources for homeland security could come at the expense of traditional funding for basic public safety.[82]

Crime

Although some crimes fall strictly under the jurisdiction of the federal government, most authority for dealing with crime rests with states and localities. In some instances, crimes fall under dual jurisdictions, and defendants may face charges in both federal and state courts. The states differ from each other and the federal government in identifying crimes and setting penalties. In many instances, various states define similar crimes in different ways. Differences in what constitutes criminal behavior may also vary within a state, as with myriad local laws governing alcohol purchase and consumption. Local variation can also occur when different district attorneys emphasize the prosecution of certain types of crimes over others. Local governments usually provide citizens with police protection and can maintain jails for the short-term confinement of suspects and prisoners. States generally provide longer-term prisons, although the federal government also operates such facilities.

Public attitudes toward crime vacillate. For example, as the United States emerged from the recession of the early 1990s, the Gallup Poll found that people believed that crime had replaced the economy as the most important issue facing the country. In January 1994, 37 percent of Americans chose crime as most important, compared to 9 percent a year earlier, and another 9 percent identified drugs as the most important issue. More than 20 percent of Americans continued to rank crime as the most important issue through 1998, but in May 1999 it was edged out as the most important issue by ethics—not surprising given the impeachment trial of President Bill Clinton. Crime continued to recede as an important issue after that, especially in comparison to international concerns and the economy after 2001.[83] Americans continue to worry about crime, however: for most of the 1980s and 1990s, at least 40 percent of respondents reported being afraid to walk at night within a mile of their home. By 2005, however, 60 percent of those asked said that they were not afraid.[84]

Similar swings in attitudes have occurred in Georgia (see chapter 4). Somewhat surprisingly, public fears about crime remained high during the mid-1990s while crime rates dropped. Some of this dissonance may have resulted from media coverage. Indeed, 42 percent of Georgians surveyed in 1996 thought that television and radio exaggerated crime in the Atlanta area; 52 percent thought coverage was accurate. A review of four Atlanta television stations during one week in June 1996 examined the content between the start of evening news broadcasts and the first weather segment, including commercials. Coverage of violent crime varied between 2 and 63 percent among the broadcasts. Among the stations, the average time devoted to violent crime ranged from 19 to 47 percent of each broadcast.[85]

The Federal Bureau of Investigation issues reports on crime based on reports submitted voluntarily from local police agencies around the country. The reports concentrate on seven major violent (murder and nonnegligent manslaughter, forcible rape, robbery, aggravated assault) and property (burglary, larceny, motor vehicle theft) offenses. Because comparing total crimes for different places can be misleading, the rate at which these crimes are reported is standardized, normally as a ratio of the total reported per 100,000 population.

For the nation as a whole in 2004, the rate for violent crime was 465.5 offenses per 100,000 population, a drop of 2.2 percent from 2003. Georgia's violent crime rate was slightly lower, at 455.5, and rose 0.2 percent from 2003 to 2004. Eighteen states had higher violent crime rates, including the neighboring states of Florida, South Carolina, and Tennessee. Georgia's property crime rate in 2004 stood at 4,265.9 per 100,000 population, a rise of just 0.1 percent from 2003 and well above the national rate of 3,517.1. Georgia's rate was higher than those in Florida, North Carolina, and Alabama but below those in Tennessee and South Carolina. Just as crime varies among states, it differs across Georgia. In 2004, for example, the state reported more than 40,000 violent crimes, including 613 cases of murder or manslaughter. Nearly 8,000 of these violent crimes occurred in Atlanta, with another 1,105 in Savannah, 904 in Columbus, and 690 in Macon. While the totals for Atlanta might seem high, the rest of its metropolitan area had more than twice as many violent crimes, including an estimated 266 murders/manslaughters compared to 112 in Atlanta proper. Of Georgia's more than 376,000 property crimes in 2004, just over 33,000 were reported in Atlanta, with more than 165,000 others in Atlanta's suburbs.[86]

Perceptions of high levels of crime can prompt public officials to devote substantial resources to the criminal justice system. In many ways, looking tough on crime and spending tax money provides politicians with a no-lose proposition. In fiscal 2002, state governments allocated 3.7 percent of their expenditures to corrections and police protection, virtually the same as back in 1990. In addition, U.S. local governments devoted 7.4 percent of their general expenditures—more than $73 billion—to police protection and corrections.[87]

Law Enforcement in Georgia

Georgia's counties, municipalities, state agencies, and colleges employ peace officers. All persons who become officers must be at least eighteen years old, hold a high school diploma, and complete a training course at a police academy.[88]

State Agencies. Several state agencies come under the supervision of the Board of Public Safety, which is chaired by the governor. The Georgia State Patrol is the best known of the state's policing agencies. A division of the Georgia Department of Public Safety, the State Patrol enforces laws on Georgia highways. During 2003, troopers logged 1.4 million duty hours, patrolled almost 20 million miles of roadways, issued more than 200,000 speeding tickets and 8,610 citations for driving under the influence of drugs or alcohol, and gave more than 371,000 warnings.[89] The Department of Public Safety at one time bore responsibility for issuing driver's licenses; after shifting among agencies with various titles, that task finally settled in 2005 with the new Department of Driver Services. Other agencies bear responsibility for some related services—for example, the Department of Revenue has charge of issuing vehicle titles and tags.

Founded in 1937, the Georgia Bureau of Investigation (GBI) received its current name in 1940. During fiscal 2004, GBI had 806 positions, including 389 handling investigations and 235 assigned to forensics. The GBI operates in cooperation with local agencies and is divided into regional investigative offices, drug enforcement offices, and crime laboratories. The GBI primarily works with drug and narcotics enforcement, forensic investigations, and the Georgia Crime Information Center, which reports crimes within the state. During fiscal 2004, GBI labs handled more than 88,000 cases, including a growing number of cases associated with the production of methamphetamines.[90]

Other agencies with enforcement powers are the Game and Fish Division of the Georgia Department of Natural Resources, which deals with water and boating safety in addition to wildlife; the Department of Revenue's Alcohol and Tobacco unit, which deals with taxes on these specific goods; the state examining boards, which deal with licensing regulations; the State Ethics Commission, which monitors elections and lobbying; the state Fire Marshal's Office; and the Securities Investigation Unit. More recently, the state has expanded the role of the Georgia Emergency Management Agency and its Office of Homeland Security.

Local Agencies. In 2002, Georgia's local governments spent $1.8 billion on police and corrections plus another $736 million on inspections and fire protection. Almost 75,000 people held jobs in police protection, more than 85 percent of them as sworn officers.[91]

Probably the most visible local law enforcement officials are county sheriffs, Georgia's only elected officials with the power to arrest people. The Georgia Constitution requires each county to elect a sheriff, but the state sets few qualifications beyond a minimum age, a high school diploma or its equivalent, the lack of criminal record, and mandatory training after assuming office. Georgia's sheriffs have jurisdiction only within the boundaries of their counties, although they may execute warrants statewide. Sheriffs hire deputies to assist in their duties. This system has at times become the target for charges of corruption, favoritism, and incompetence.[92] Unlike judges, sheriffs are elected on a partisan ballot. Campaigns can be heated, especially when incumbents are challenged by other law enforcement officials, such as one of their deputies.

Clarke, Cobb, Gwinnett, and other counties maintain police departments, thereby reducing the power of their sheriffs. In these instances, the county police are responsible for most law enforcement activities, and the sheriff maintains jurisdiction over courts and detention.[93] Also at the local level, public college and university police departments have criminal arrest jurisdiction within limited distance of campuses. They also enforce traffic and property laws.

Corrections

At the end of 2003, Georgia had just over 533,000 people under correctional supervision, with 87,000 of that total in prisons or jails and the remainder on probation or parole. By January 2006, Georgia also had 109 prisoners under sentences of death. The state executed 36 convicts between 1977 and the end of 2004, the sixth-highest total among the states.[94]

At the end of fiscal year 2004, the Georgia Department of Corrections had roughly 14,000 employees and more than 48,000 prisoners. The number of employees had dropped by about 500 from five years earlier, while the number of inmates had increased by about 9,000. The department maintained 37 prisons, 23 of which held more than 1,000 prisoners each. Corrections also ran transitional, diversion, and detention centers as well as two probation boot camps. As in other states, prison conditions have been a source of controversy in Georgia as well as the subject of extended litigation in the federal courts.[95] Policy makers have also debated turning over corrections to private companies.

Georgia's counties and cities also operate correctional facilities. Local jails are often forced to hold people who have not been convicted but are awaiting trial and cannot afford bail. Inmates at county facilities are required to work on maintenance projects while detained. Those in detention centers, while generally only short-term inmates convicted of driving under the influence or probation offenses, also work on community service projects. Diversion centers hold inmates only at night, permitting them to hold jobs during the day. Transition centers (halfway houses) are designed to assist former prisoners in returning to normal life. Like state prisons, local facilities have become the subject of litigation by inmates and the federal government. Complaints concentrate on inadequate security, access to legal help, and medical treatment.

Future Issues

Several debates will undoubtedly continue over public safety in Georgia. Some of these relate to law enforcement and corrections, including how to keep offenders from committing additional crimes. Much of the focus here is on types and levels of punishment, the quality of personnel and technology, the workload of probation and parole officials, and the adequacy of rehabilitation programs. There is also no reason to think that the death penalty will fade away as a controversial issue.[96]

The Future of Georgia Politics

What might Georgians expect from their political system as the state moves further into the twenty-first century? Two key factors may affect the types and rate of change. One is the nature of external shocks to Georgia politics. Perhaps the most significant would be changes in the federal system, which would provide states with fewer resources, impose more requirements, or perhaps grant them more autonomy.

The second fundamental question is how economic and population changes, particularly migration from states outside the South, will mesh with Georgia's traditionalistic political culture. One scenario is that as Georgia becomes more diverse, it will become more like the rest of the United States. Greater diversity could also bring more competition—and more conflict—among political parties and interest groups. Perhaps ironically, growing conflict could spur increased citizen participation in politics, including elections.

Given the rise of Georgia's Republican Party, it is unclear whether the state is facing a new form of one-party control or whether the two political parties will compete regularly for statewide offices and a majority of the seats in the General Assembly. While one or the other party is often viewed as having a lock on certain areas, their geographical presence around Georgia could shift with population changes. Moreover, if Earl Black and Merle Black are right that southern politics will be shaped by efforts to gain the support of the white middle class, party competition in Georgia could have heavy racial and religious symbolism. Within this context, public policy debates and election campaigns could take on a rough-edged tone that Key would recognize. The exact future effects of these trends remain unclear, but they undoubtedly will not produce a complete break with Georgia's past.

NOTES

Abbreviations

ABH   *Athens Banner-Herald*
AC   *Atlanta Constitution*
AJC   *Atlanta Journal-Constitution*
NYT   *New York Times*
OCGA   *Official Code of Georgia Annotated*

Chapter One. States and Local Governments in the Federal System

1. Council of State Governments 2003, 550.
2. U.S. Census Bureau, Governments Division 2005.
3. For detailed examples of local government cooperation, see Pastor et al. 2000.
4. Rubin 2000, 66–68.
5. U.S. Census Bureau 2002b.
6. U.S. Census Bureau 2006c, tables 427, 459; U.S. Office of Management and Budget 2001.
7. U.S. Census Bureau 2004b.
8. U.S. Census Bureau 2001b, table 596; U.S. Census Bureau 2006c, table 608.
9. U.S. Census Bureau 2005d, table 602.
10. U.S. Census Bureau 2006c, table 654.
11. U.S. Department of Agriculture 2004.
12. The U.S. Office of Management and Budget defines a metropolitan area as an urban area with a central city of fifty thousand or more residents, its county, and any surrounding counties tied to the central city economically and socially.
13. The ten largest cities and their rates of population change from 1990 to 2000 are New York (+9.4 percent), Los Angeles (+6 percent), Chicago (+4 percent),

Houston (+15.1 percent), Philadelphia (−4.3 percent), Phoenix (+33.6 percent), San Diego (+10.1 percent), Dallas (+18.1 percent), San Antonio (+14.8 percent), and Detroit (−7.5 percent). For more analysis of urbanization during the 1990s, see B. Katz and Lang 2003; Florida 2005; Berube, Katz, and Lang 2005, 2006.

14. U.S. Census Bureau 2001a, table 3; U.S. Census Bureau 2006c, tables 18, 20. Despite popular images of the nation's various "belts," scholars have criticized use of such terminology as oversimplified (e.g., Weinstein and Gross 1988).

15. U.S. Census Bureau 2001b, tables 30, 31, 34.

16. U.S. Census Bureau 2001b, tables 31, 34; Shaila Dewan, "Gentrification Changing Face of New Atlanta," *NYT,* March 11, 2006, A1.

17. On the problems of urban education, see Stone et al. 2001.

18. U.S. Census Bureau 2006c, tables 692, 693.

19. For a description of trends in federalism, see Wright 2003.

20. Berman 2001.

21. Robin Toner, "GOP Blitz of First 100 Days Now Brings the Heavy Combat," *NYT,* April 9, 1995, 1; see also Sclar 2000.

22. Krugman 2005; Bob Dart, "Farm Subsidies to Be Plowed Under," *AJC,* June 18, 1995, A10; "A Fine Crop of Reforms" (editorial), *AC,* June 21, 1995, A10.

23. The southern electoral votes are Texas (34), Florida (27), Georgia (15), North Carolina (15), Virginia (13), Tennessee (11), Maryland (10), Alabama (9), Louisiana (9), Kentucky (8), South Carolina (8), Arkansas (6), Mississippi (6), West Virginia (5), and Washington, D.C. (3).

24. See Lublin 2004; Black and Black 2002.

25. See Mitau 1966, 93–110.

26. Schneider 1992.

27. See Heilig and Mundt 1984; Welch 1990; Welch and Bledsoe 1988; Davidson and Grofman 1994.

28. Thomas and Hrebenar 1996, 129–131, 139–143.

29. Abney and Lauth 1986, 195–212; Berry, Portney, and Thomson 1993.

30. Warner 2001.

31. See Eisinger 1988; Altshuler and Luberoff 2003; Blakely and Bradshaw 2002.

32. For an overview of these policies, see Bowman and Kearney 2002.

33. U.S. Census Bureau 2006c, table 427. See also Chubb and Moe 1990; Henig 1994.

34. U.S. Census Bureau 2006c, table 438; U.S. Census Bureau 1983, table 482.

35. U.S. Census Bureau 2006c, table 426.

36. See Robert Pear, "Republican Governors Working with Congress to Shift Medicaid Authority to States," *NYT,* April 2, 1995, 12; Milt Freudenheim, "States Shelving Ambitious Plans on Health Care," *NYT,* July 2, 1995, 1.

37. Robert Frank, "Proposed Block Grants Seem Unlikely to Cure Management Problems," *Wall Street Journal,* May 1, 1995, A1.

38. U.S. Census Bureau 2006c, tables 451, 455.

39. For some critical views on the state role in dealing with local issues, see Rusk 2003; M. Orfield 2002.

40. For a leading argument for this approach, see Osborne and Gaebler 1992.

41. Key 1949, chap. 6.

Chapter Two. The Setting for Contemporary Georgia Politics

1. On studying the context of state politics, see Gray 2003.

2. See Spalding 1991.

3. For a detailed account of Georgia during this period, see Coleman 1991, 71–88.

4. Evans 1972, 90–127.

5. Coleman 1991, 89–116.

6. Evans 1972, 139–140.

7. Coleman 1991, 110–113.

8. For a detailed description of antebellum Georgia, see Boney 1991.

9. On the war in Georgia, see Boney 1991.

10. On Reconstruction, see Wynes 1991, 208–224.

11. Evans 1972, 304–305.

12. See Wynes 1991, 225–237.

13. See W. Holmes 1991, 257–276.

14. See W. Holmes 1991, 319–336.

15. For a detailed account of Watson's life on which much of the following discussion is based, see Woodward 1963. See also W. Holmes 1991, 295–308.

16. For an overview of this period, see W. Holmes 1991, 309–318.

17. For a complete review of Russell's life, see Fite 1991.

18. See Key 1949, 119–122; Hill 1994, 224–225; Henderson and Roberts 1988, 49–62.

19. On this period, see Bartley 1991.

20. On Allen's mayoral administration, see Pomerantz 1996. For another view, see Kruse 2005.

21. See Fite 1991.

22. On opposition to civil rights, see Bartley 1997.

23. For a good synopsis of postwar racial change, see Bartley 1970; Bartley 1991, 361–374.

24. U.S. 621 (1965).

25. U.S. 368 (1963).

26. U.S. 1 (1964).

27. See Hill 1994, 225.

28. Linda Greenhouse, "Justices, in 5–4 Vote, Reject Districts Drawn with Race the 'Predominant Factor,'" *NYT,* June 30, 1995, A1, A3.

29. A more detailed discussion of the controversy over districts drawn using the 2000 census appears in chapter 4.

30. On the three-governors controversy, see Henderson and Roberts 1988, 49–62. For further reading on the recent history of Georgia, see Bartley 1990.

31. For more detail on this topic, see chapter 6.

32. See chapter 7.

33. Bachtel and Boatright 1992; U.S. Census Bureau 2006b.

34. Bachtel and Boatright 1992. Recent estimates are available through the American FactFinder menu at the U.S. Census Bureau Web site (http://factfinder.census .gov/home/saff/main.html?_lang=en).

35. Bartley 1991, 351.

36. Fite 1991, 235, 244–245.

37. Stone 1989; G. Orfield and Ashkinaze 1991, 103–148; Stone et al. 2001; Kruse 2005.

38. Shaila Dewan, "Gentrification Changing Face of New Atlanta," *NYT,* March 11, 2006, A1.

39. U.S. Census Bureau 2005b, 2004a.

40. Data in this paragraph are taken from results available for Georgia in the U.S. Census Bureau's American FactFinder "Fact Sheet" search option (http://factfinder .census.gov/home/saff/main.html?_lang=en). The data are estimates included in the American Community Survey, which is conducted annually by the Census Bureau.

41. Detailed data for cities and counties are available through the "Data Sets" search option available at the U.S. Census Bureau's American FactFinder site (http:// factfinder.census.gov/home/saff/main.html?_lang=en). Data are estimates made annually by the Census Bureau as part of the American Community Survey.

42. U.S. Census Bureau 1963, table 41. Rates of poverty are also calculated for households and vary among regions/counties within the state. The bureau uses "income thresholds that vary by family size and composition to determine who is in poverty. If a family's total income is less than the family's threshold, then that family and every individual in it is considered in poverty. The official poverty thresholds do not vary geographically, but they are updated for inflation using Consumer Price Index (CPI-U). The official poverty definition uses money income before taxes and does not include capital gains or noncash benefits (such as public housing, Medicaid, and food stamps)." This explanation is available from the "Overview" link on the bureau's Poverty Web site (http://www.census.gov/hhes/www/poverty/overview.html). For data on poverty rates in the states, see U.S. Census Bureau 2005c, table 21.

43. U.S. Census Bureau 2006c, table 218; U.S. Census Bureau 1963, table 154.

44. Akioka 2004, 93.

45. U.S. Census Bureau 2006a.

46. Maria Saporta, "Losses Sting, as Leaders Reflect," *AJC,* March 8, 2006, C1; "Turner Loyal to Time Warner, but Divestitures Bother Him," *AJC,* February 28, 2006, C1.

47. Key 1949, 664.

48. See Black and Black 2002; Lublin 2004.

49. Thomas Stinson, John Kessler, Andrea Jones, Mary Macdonald, Matt Kempner, Michelle Hiskey, Gayle White, John Blake, Bo Emerson, Dave Hirschman, "Reddest of the Red: State Bucks National Trend, Remains Republican Fortress," *AJC,* November 12, 2006, A1; James Salzer, "GOP Secures Georgia," *AJC,* November 8, 2006, D1.

50. http://www.sos.state.ga.us/elections/election_results/2006_1107/default.htm.

51. See Key 1949; see also chapters 7, 10.

52. Key 1949, 491–508.

53. U.S. Census Bureau 1995, 291; Lucy Soto, "Turnout Matches '92, but Percentage Down," *AC*, November 7, 1996, C8.

54. Carlos Campos, "78 Percent Registered in Georgia Cast Votes," *AJC*, November 10, 2004, B5.

55. Key 1949, 123.

56. The number of lobbyists is reported and updated at the Georgia State Ethics Commission's Web site (http://www.ethics.state.ga.us/gaethics/Reports/Lobbyist/Lobbyist_Menu.aspx).The number of interests represented by lobbyists is calculated from the spreadsheet available at the same site.

57. Thomas and Hrebenar 2003; Jeanne Cummings, "Ethics Rules Are Few and Far Between," *AJC*, February 23, 1992, D1; Rhonda Cook, "Georgia's Hidden Persuaders," *AJC*, February 23, 1992, A1; Michael Hinkelman, "Developers Dole Out Dough," *AJC*, February 26, 1990, A1; "Our Opinions: Ethics Not Optional" (editorial), *AJC*, May 4, 2005, A18; Cynthia Tucker, "No Cash? No Love from GOP" (editorial), *AJC*, March 8, 2006, A13; Ann Hardie, "The $1 Million Lobby: Largesse Up 30% during GOP Control," *AJC*, February 2, 2006, F1.

Chapter Three. Georgia's Constitution

1. See Segers and Byrnes 1995.

2. On the police power in Georgia, see Hill 1994, 31–32, 59–60, 70, 85–90.

3. Hill 1994, 152–155.

4. Hill 1994, 110.

5. *Goldrush II v. City of Marietta*, 276 Ga. 683, 482 S.E.2d 347 (1997).

6. Hill 1994, 56–59.

7. Hill 1994, 194–195.

8. Hill 1994, 99.

9. See Hill 1994; R. Katz 1986; Coleman 1991.

10. For a thorough account, see Henderson 1991, 77–96.

11. Hill 1994, 20–22.

12. Hill 1994, 14–15.

13. Fleischmann and Custer 2004.

14. Bill Montgomery, "New Constitution in Hands of Voters," *AC*, November 2, 1982, A9; Hill 1994, 21.

15. Hill 1994, 15–17.

16. Bill Shipp, "Adopting a New Constitution and Dancing with a Grizzly Bear," *AC*, January 1, 1981, B2.

17. "A Constitutional Mess," *AC*, August 28, 1981, A4.

18. Rosenthal 1990, 87.

19. Bill Shipp, "Do the State a Favor: Forget the New Constitution," *AC*, August 15, 1981, B2; Henderson and Roberts 1988, 267–269.

20. "Streamlined State Constitution," *AC*, June 30, 1983, A22; "New State Constitution Deserves Ratification" (editorial), *AC*, October 24, 1982, C2.

21. Duane Stafford, "Voters Left Some Blanks Unfilled," *AJC*, November 7, 2004, JJ6.

22. Hill 1994, 70.

23. On ratification procedures and recent efforts in other states, see Council of State Governments 2005, 3–18.

24. Hill 1994, 30–33.

25. *Suber v. Bulloch County Board of Education*, 722 F.Supp. 736 (S.D. Ga., 1989).

26. *Stephens v. State*, 265 Ga. 356, 456 S.E.2d 560, cert. denied, 516 U.S. 849 (1995).

27. *Bowers v. Fulton County*, 221 Ga. 731, 146 S.E.2d 884 (1966). See also Altman, Bolster, and Bross 1986; Hill 1994, 194–195.

28. *Kelo v. New London*, no. 04-108 (2005). On one response in Georgia, see Christopher Quinn, "Legislature 2006: House OKs Land Seizure Legislation," *AJC*, March 10, 2006, D10.

29. Hill 1994, 33–36.

30. *Grissom v. Gleason*, 262 Ga. 374, 418 S.E.2d 27 (1992).

31. *Tolbert v. Mitchell*, 253 Ga. 566, 322 S.E.2d 487 (1984).

32. *American Subcontractors Association v. City of Atlanta*, 259 Ga. 14, 376 S.E.2d 662 (1989).

33. Douglas A. Blackmon and Holly Morris, "Court Gives Split Ruling on Gay Rights," *AC*, March 15, 1995, E1.

34. For example, City of Atlanta Code of Ordinances, chapter 94.

35. Cameron McWhirter, "Atlanta Halts Effort to Fine Club," *AJC*, November 6, 2005, E4.

36. On the right to vote, see McDonald, Binford, and Johnson 1994.

37. *Nixon v. Herndon*, 273 U.S. 536 (1927).

38. *Smith v. Allwright*, 321 U.S. 649 (1944).

39. 154 F.2d 450 (1946).

40. For a thorough discussion, see Stone 1989.

41. W. Holmes 1991, 280.

42. For a good synopsis of postwar racial change, see Bartley 1991.

43. *Stell v. Savannah–Chatham County Board of Education*, 333 F.2d 55 (1964).

44. *Gratz v. Bollinger*, 539 U.S. 244 (2003); *Grutter v. Bollinger*, 539 U.S. 306 (2003). On the University of Georgia's admissions policies, see Doug Cumming, "Applicants Nervously Await Decisions," *AC*, March 25, 1998, C5; *Wooden v. Board of Regents*, 247 U.S. F 3d 1262 (2001).

45. 379 U.S. 241 (1964).

46. 527 U.S. 581 (1999).

47. 372 U.S. 368 (1963).

48. *Wesberry v. Sanders*, 376 U.S. 1 (1964).

49. 379 U.S. 621 (1965).

50. See Hill 1994, 225.

51. 515 U.S. 900 (1995); Linda Greenhouse, "Justices, in 5–4 Vote, Reject Districts Drawn with Race the 'Predominant Factor,'" *NYT,* June 30, 1995, A1.

52. 539 U.S. 461 (2003).

53. Hill 1994, 36–38.

54. *Coleman v. City of Griffin,* 55 Ga. App. 123, 189 S.E. 427 (1936).

55. *Spillers v. State,* 145 Ga. App. 809, 245 S.E.2d 54 (1978).

56. See, for example, Doug Cumming, "Bowers: Education on Origin Theories Must Avoid Religion," *AC,* March 13, 1996, C1; Kristina Torres, "Final Plea Heard in Evolution Case," *AJC,* November 13, 2004, B1.

57. Hill 1994, 38–40.

58. *K. Gordon Murray Productions, Inc. v. Floyd,* 217 Ga. 784, 125 S.E.2d 207 (1962).

59. *State v. Café Erotica,* 269 Ga. 486, 500 S.E.2d 547 (1998).

60. *Hirsch v. City of Atlanta,* 261 Ga. 22, 401 S.E.2d 530 (1991).

61. *Ellis v. Parks,* 212 Ga. 540, 93 S.E.2d 708 (1956).

62. *State v. Miller,* 260 Ga. 669, 398 S.E.2d 547 (1990).

63. *Vaughn v. State,* 259 Ga. 325, 381 S.E.2d 30 (1989).

64. See *OCGA,* title 24, chap. 9, sec. 30.

65. *Statesboro Publishing Co. v. City of Sylvania,* 271 Ga. 92, 516 S.E.2d 926 (1999).

66. *Cunningham v. State,* 260 Ga. 827, 400 S.E.2d 916 (1991).

67. *Harris v. Entertainment Systems,* 259 Ga. 701, 386 S.E.2d 140 (1989).

68. *Goldrush II v. City of Marietta,* 267 Ga. 683, 482 S.E.2d 347 (1997).

69. 394 U.S. 557 (1969).

70. 413 U.S. 49 (1973).

71. 505 U.S. 123 (1992).

72. 420 U.S. 469 (1975).

73. Hill 1994, 42–51.

74. *Bergman v. McCullough,* 218 Ga. App. 353, 461 S.E.2d 544 (1995), cert. denied, 517 U.S. 1141 (1996).

75. *Crutchfield v. State,* 218 Ga. App. 360, 461 S.E.2d 555 (1995).

76. *Fleming v. Zant,* 259 Ga. 687, 386 S.E.2d 339 (1989).

77. *Atkins v. Virginia,* 536 U.S. 304 (2002).

78. Sandra Eckstein, "Ruling: Prosecutors Bear Racial Onus in Drug Cases," *AJC,* March 18, 1995, C4; "Supreme Court's Flip Flop" (editorial), *AC,* April 3, 1995, A6.

79. 520 U.S. 305 (1997).

80. No. 04-1067 (2006).

81. 435 U.S. 223 (1978).

82. 408 U.S. 238 (1972).

83. 428 U.S. 153 (1976).

84. 433 U.S. 584 (1977).

85. 481 U.S. 279 (1987).

86. *Pavesich v. New England Life Insurance Co.,* 122 Ga. 190, 50 S.E. 68 (1904).

87. *Zant v. Prevatte*, 248 Ga. 832, 286 S.E.2d 715 (1982).

88. *State v. McAfee*, 259 Ga. 579, 385 S.E.2d 651 (1989)

89. *Doe v. Bolton*, 410 U.S. 179 (1973); *Roe v. Wade*, 419 U.S. 113 (1973). In a decision that divided the justices among several viewpoints, the U.S. Supreme Court first recognized a right to privacy in *Griswold v. Connecticut* (381 U.S. 479 [1965]).

90. 478 U.S. 186 (1986).

91. *Christensen v. State*, 266 Ga. 474, 464 S.E.2d 188 (1996).

92. *Powell v. State*, 270 Ga. 327, 510 S.E.2d 18 (1998).

93. *Morrison v. State*, 272 Ga. 129, 526 S.E.2d 336 (2000).

94. *Lawrence v. Texas*, 539 U.S. 558 (2003).

95. For the U.S. Supreme Court's view of assisted suicide and the right to privacy, see *Washington v. Glucksberg* (521 U.S. 702 [1997]); *Vacco v. Quill* (521 U.S. 793 [1997]). On the Oregon conflict, see *Gonzales v. Oregon* (no. 04-623 [2006]).

96. See Mark Curriden, "Is Naming Judges Serving Justice?" *AJC*, November 29, 1992, G1; Andrew Kull, "The Slow Death of Colorblind Justice," *AJC*, November 29, 1992, H1; Mark Curriden, "Road to a Judicial Appointment Not Clear—Even to State's Judges," *AC*, December 21, 1992, C3.

97. Nancy Badertscher and Sonji Jacobs, "Some Bills Made It; Others Didn't," *AJC*, March 15, 2006, B4; "School Funding Shouldn't Become Political Football" (editorial), *ABH*, March 15, 2006.

Chapter Four. Public Opinion

1. See Segers and Byrnes 1995. Much of the information on public opinion in Georgia presented in this chapter is taken from three statewide polling organizations. The Survey Research Center at the University of Georgia produces a semi-annual Georgia Poll; the Applied Research Center at Georgia State University produced the quarterly Georgia State Poll until 2003; the University of Georgia's Carl Vinson Institute of Government produces the Peach State Poll. The *Atlanta Journal-Constitution* also produces polls on issues of importance to Georgians.

2. Flanigan and Zingale 2002, 117.

3. Flanigan and Zingale 2002, 117.

4. All data in this section are taken from the American National Election Studies polls at the University of Michigan (www.umich.edu/~nes/nesguide/nesguide .htm).

5. Data from the Georgia Poll are stored at the Odum Institute at the University of North Carolina (http://152.2.32.107/odum/jsp/home.jsp).

6. Question wording for moderates was "middle of the road" for the 2004 Georgia State Poll from which these data are taken.

7. Erikson, Wright, and McIver 1993, 13–19, 30–35.

8. Brace et al. 2004.

9. Gray 2003.

10. Erikson, Wright, and McIver 1993, 73–95.

11. Erikson, Wright, and McIver 1993, 96–140.

12. For a summary of these cultures, see Erikson, Wright, and McIver 1993, 150–176.

13. Erikson, Wright, and McIver 1993, 47–72, 150–176.

14. Erikson, Wright, and McIver 1993, 195–196.

15. Lieske 1993.

16. For a more elaborate image, see Gastner, Shalizi, and Newman 2004. See also Fiorina with Pope and Abrams 2005.

17. Vinson Institute of Government 2004.

18. Vinson Institute of Government 2005b.

19. Data for various years of the Georgia Poll may be accessed at www.src.uga .edu/surveys/GA-Poll/index.html.

20. Tom Opdyke, "History Unfurled," *AJC*, August 2, 1992, F1.

21. Mark Sherman, "Miller's Approval Rating below 50 Percent," *AJC*, May 2, 1993, D1.

22. For a review of all Georgia's flags, see Jackson 2006.

23. Ben Smith, "Supporters of the 1956 Flag Still Seek Legislative Sponsor," *AJC*, January 21, 2004, B4.

24. Polling data were made available from the Applied Research Center at Georgia State University.

25. Georgia State University Applied Research Center, Georgia State Poll, Winter 2003 (http://aysps.gsu.edu/srp/georgiastatepoll/gastatepoll_winter03.pdf).

26. An additional 32 percent indicated that the shortfall should be addressed by a combination of factors, and 6 percent indicated that they did not know how the state legislature should address budgetary imbalances.

27. This discussion is summarized from three documents: Peter Blustone and Sally Wallace, "What Georgians Are Thinking about Taxes I," *Policy Brief* 101 (March 2005), Andrew Young School of Policy Studies, Georgia State University (http://frc.gsu.edu/frpreports/brief101/index.htm); Peter Blustone, "What Georgians Are Thinking about Taxes II," *Policy Brief* 104 (April 2005), Andrew Young School of Policy Studies, Georgia State University (http://frc.gsu.edu/frpreports/brief104/ index.htm); Peter Blustone, "What Georgians Are Thinking about Taxes III," *Policy Brief* 105 (April 2005), Andrew Young School of Policy Studies, Georgia State University (http://frc.gsu.edu/frpreports/brief105/index.htm).

28. John Blake, "Poll: Georgians More Optimistic about Race Relations," *AC*, March 17, 1995, H1.

29. John Blake, "Affirmative Action Perplexes Blacks, Whites," *AC*, May 11, 1995, A1.

30. John Blake, "Affirmative Action: Can Policies Right Past? Races Differ," *AC*, May 11, 1995, C2.

31. These data are compiled by the authors from the Georgia State Poll conducted by Kennesaw State University on behalf of Georgia State University.

32. Vinson Institute of Government 2005a.

33. Richard Morin and Dan Balz, "Bush's Popularity Reaches New Low," *Washington Post*, November 4, 2005, A1.

34. The Georgia Poll is conducted by the University of Georgia's Survey Research Center. The data may be accessed at www.src.uga.edu/surveys/GA-Poll/index.html.

35. The Georgia Poll phrases approval ratings questions in the following format: "Some people approve of [name's] performance as [office]. How about you? Do you strongly approve, approve, disapprove or strongly disapprove of [name's] performance as [office]?" The data presented are sums of the percentages of respondents who approve or strongly approve of officeholders' performance.

36. Georgia State University Applied Research Center, Georgia State Poll, winter 2004 (http://aysps.gsu.edu/srp/georgiastatepoll/gastatepoll_winter03.pdf).

37. Vinson Institute of Government 2005c, 10.

Chapter Five. Voting and Elections

1. See Bibby and Holbrook 2003.

2. Bibby and Holbrook 2003, 81–86.

3. In 2004, one other item, a referendum on the Georgia flag, appeared on ballots statewide.

4. Data on turnout in Georgia elections can be found at www.gwu.edu/~action/2004/states/ga.htm.

5. *OCGA*, title 21, chap. 2, secs. 195, 196.

6. The other states with runoffs are Alabama, Arkansas, Florida, Kentucky, Mississippi, North Carolina, Oklahoma, South Carolina, South Dakota, and Texas.

7. McDonald, Binford, and Johnson 1994, 72–74.

8. Bullock and Johnson 1992, 1–8, 93–118.

9. Bullock and Johnson 1992, 135–177; Haeberle 1993.

10. *Brooks v. Miller*, 158 F.3d 1230 (1998); *Brooks v. Barnes*, no. 98-1521, cert. denied, May 24, 1999; Kathey Pruitt, "Majority Vote Still Needed in Primaries," *AC*, May 25, 1999, B3.

11. Bullock and Johnson 1992, 38–39, 51–53, 115–117.

12. These data compiled by the authors from a survey conducted by the Burruss Institute of Public Service, Kennesaw State University, 2005.

13. "Political Notebook: Runoff Law May Come into Play in House Race," *AJC*, October 29, 2000, JJ2.

14. Bowler and Donovan 2003.

15. Charles Walston, "Public Initiative on Hold for Now," *AJC*, March 4, 1995, C2.

16. Council of State Governments 2004, 307–322.

17. *OCGA*, title 21, chap. 4.

18. Cox and Rosenfeld 2001, 39–46, 202–204.

19. Coleman 1991, 306–307, 392; Henderson 1991, 55–60.

20. *Baker v. Carr,* 296 U.S. 186 (1962).

21. For an interesting account of a Georgia campaign in the early days of "one person, one vote," see Carter 1992.

22. See *Perdue v. Baker,* 277 Ga. 1; 586 S.E.2d 606 (2003).

23. Gary Hendricks, "House Divided Will Be Boon to Blacks, GOP," *AJC,* August 4, 1991, C1.

24. Doug Nurse, "Redistricting: New Maps Yield Tight, Single-Member Units," *AJC,* April 1, 2004, JJ5.

25. "Redistricting Proposal Just a Political Move" (editorial), *ABH,* January 15, 2006.

26. See "Legislature 2005: In Brief," *AJC,* March 16, 2005, B3; Tom Baxter, "Changing the Map," *AJC,* March 7, 2005, D8.

27. Care should be taken when interpreting voting turnout. In many instances, turnout is calculated as a percentage of registered voters. Unless otherwise noted, data throughout this chapter reflect voter turnout as a percentage of a jurisdiction's voting-age population.

28. U.S. Census Bureau 2006c, table 407. Debates about measuring turnout continue to flare, including questions regarding biases in surveys and whether to use total voting-age population in calculations even though some residents are not eligible to register. See reports of the U.S. Election Project at George Mason University (http://elections.gmu.edu).

29. Atkeson and Partin 1995; Squire and Fastnow 1994.

30. Wood 2002; Hajnal and Lewis 2003.

31. More information on these differences is available from the U.S. Election Assistance Commission (www.eac.gov).

32. Council of State Governments 2005, 361–362.

33. Council of State Governments 1996, 162–163; Lewis 2005. See also the activities and reports of the National Association of Election Officials (www .electioncenter.org).

34. Carlos Campos, "Voter ID Bill Approved; Opponents Vow to Continue Fight," *AJC,* January 26, 2006, A1; Nancy Badertscher and Sonji Jacobs, "Legislature 2006: Voter ID Costs Still Debated," *AJC,* January 28, 2006, E1.

35. Georgia Secretary of State, press release, November 18, 2004 (http://www.sos .state.ga.us/pressrel/111804.htm).

36. Cathy Cox, "Elections System's Safeguards Effective," *AJC,* March 10, 2005, A23; Bullock, Hood, and Clark 2005.

37. Bill Osinski, "Voting Irregularities Alleged," *AC,* August 7, 1992, D3; Bill Osinski, "Early-Ballot System May Replace Ga. Absentee Voting," *AJC,* October 17, 1993, F7; Alan Judd, "Absentee Voter Fraud Untouched by ID Law," *AJC,* January 29, 2006, A1; Carlos Campos, "Election 2004: Early Voting Was Big, Officials Confirm," *AJC,* November 2, 2004, B5.

38. U.S. Census Bureau 1995, 290; Mark Sherman, "Motor Voter Law Pulls in 250,000," *AJC,* May 20, 1995, C1; Lucy Soto, "A Million New Eligible Voters," *AJC,*

October 6, 1996, H4; Lucy Soto, "Motor Voter System Stalls on Occasion," *AC*, November 6, 1996, B2.

39. U.S. Election Assistance Commission 2000.

40. Key 1949, 491–508.

41. Black and Black 1987, 175–179.

42. U.S. Census Bureau 2006c, tables 406–408.

43. Holbrook and Van Dunk 1993; Bibby and Holbrook 2003.

44. On primaries, see Flanigan and Zingale 2002, 40–47, 81–82, 171–176; see also James Salzer and Nancy Badertscher, "Parties Spin Vote Their Way; Perdue's Coattails Run Short, but Democrats Outnumbered," *AJC*, July 22, 2004, A1.

45. Bullock and Johnson 1992, 193–194.

46. Scammon and McGillivray 1993, 159–164.

47. Jill Vejnoska, "Prediction of Low Voter Turnout Becomes Reality across Georgia," *AC*, August 17, 1996, B4. See also Richard Whitt and Eric Stirgus, "Election 2004: Runoff to Test Voters' Mettle," *AJC*, August 1, 2004, C1.

48. See Key 1949, 107–127; W. Holmes 1991, 296–305, 311–318; Anderson 1975; Carter 1992.

49. Beyle 1996, 213–218.

50. All data on campaign expenditures in this section are from the Office of the Georgia Secretary of State (www.sos.state.ga.us). However, the responsibility for maintaining such data was transferred to the State Ethics Commission in January 2006.

51. Institute on Money in State Politics 2006.

52. Jim Galloway, "Perdue Raises More Than Rivals Combined," *AJC*, January 11, 2006, B5.

53. Calculated by the authors from filing reports for each of the candidates, found at www.ethics.state.ga.us.

54. See summaries of campaign spending for Georgia candidates at http://www .followthemoney.org/database/state_overview.phtml?si-200610.

55. Beyle 2003, 198–199.

56. State Ethics Commission, *Contribution Limits* (http://ethics.georgia.gov/oo/ article/0,2086,26886019_27007652_27760091,00.html).

57. James Salzer, "Who's Got the Political Money? PACs: In Georgia, Attorneys Top the List for Special-Interest Campaign Contributions," *AJC*, October 30, 2004, B1.

58. Frances Schwartzkopff, "Skirting New Ethics," *AC*, April 6, 1992, D1; Ben Smith, "Homemakers Generous Campaign Givers," *AJC*, June 5, 2005, C1.

59. Mark Sherman, "Critics Say Ethics Law Has Loophole Big Enough to Drive Lots of Cash Through," *AJC*, January 23, 1993, B1.

60. Alan Judd, "2 Speaker Candidates Funnel Bucks to Legislators," *AJC*, January 12, 2003, A1.

61. Jeanne Cummings, "Candidates for Governor Pour Money into Major Markets," *AC*, May 23, 1990, A6.

62. Berkovitz 1996.

63. Jim Tharpe, "Negative Ads Dog Senate Race: Candidates Spend Millions to Sully Each Other's Name," *AJC*, October 26, 2002, E6.

64. Swint 1998.

65. Mark Sherman, "Bowers' Ruling Draws Fire," *AJC*, June 3, 1995, C1.

66. Calculated by the authors from press releases by the Georgia secretary of state (http://www.sos.state.ga.us/pressrel/2004_press.htm).

67. Dan Chapman, "Georgia Vote for President Highest Ever, but Percentage of Electorate Was Second in History," *AJC*, November 14, 2000, D1; "Meet the Electorate: Voters in Last Week's Presidential Race," *AJC*, November 12, 2000, C4.

68. "@Issue," *AJC*, November 12, 2000, C4.

69. Ben Smith, "Black Voters: Turnout Apparently Cut Bush's Coattails," *AJC*, November 9, 2000, D10.

70. Carlos Campos, "Election 2004: Vote Exceeds 3.2 Million in Georgia," *AJC*, November 4, 2004, D6; Andrea Jones, "Election 2004: New Voters: First Timers Eager to Have Say," *AJC*, November 3, 2004, EX2; Mary McDonald, "Election 2004: Republican Gains; GOP Has Sewn Up Georgia's Capitol: Rural Vote Shifts from Democrats," *AJC*, November 3, 2004, EX2.

71. Tom Baxter, "Election 2004: America Votes: Exit Polls: Morality, War, Money Split Voters," *AJC*, November 3, 2004, EX3; "Election 2004: President: By County: How Georgians Voted for President," *AJC*, November 4, 2004, B5.

72. Brian Feagins, "Election 2004: Democrats Disappointed with Results," *AJC*, November 4, 2004, JJ7; Moni Basu, "The Voices of Bush Country," *AJC*, January 5, 2005, A15.

73. Tom Baxter, "Election 2004: America Votes: Exit Polls: Morality, War, Money Split Voters," *AJC*, November 3, 2004, EX3.

74. Vinson Institute of Government, 2005b.

75. For 2006 election results in Georgia see, http://www.sos.state.ga.us/elections/election_results/default.htm.

Chapter Six. Political Parties and Interest Groups

1. Hershey and Beck 2003.

2. For post-1970 changes in the South as an example of such variation, see Black and Black 2002.

3. Georgia's 1990 U.S. Senate race between Wyche Fowler and Paul Coverdell, in which a Libertarian candidate's portion of the vote forced a runoff and changed the outcome of the election. See also Elliott, Gryski, and Reed 1990.

4. Black and Black 1992, 141–210.

5. Key 1964, 315.

6. W. Holmes 1991, 295–308.

7. For more on Grady, see Bartley 1990, 82–85.

8. Key 1949, 106–107; Henderson 1991.

9. See Rae 1992; Black and Black 1987, 3–22, 232–256.

10. Black and Black 1992, 243.

11. Black and Black 2002; Lublin 2004.

12. James Salzer and Sonji Jacobs, "Candidates Emphasize Black Vote; Democrats Look for Governorship Backing," *AJC*, December 2, 2005, E1.

13. Ben Smith, "GOP Woos Black Voters to Little Avail," *AJC*, December 28, 2005, B1.

14. Abramowitz and Saunders 1998.

15. Moni Basu and Gayle White, "Election 2004: Democratic Georgia Grew into a GOP Peach," *AJC*, October 17, 2004, A1.

16. Bill Osinski, "Modest-Sized but Enthusiastic Crowd Turns in Petitions at Capitol," *AJC*, June 28, 1992, A3.

17. See Henderson and Roberts 1988, 193–200; Bass and DeVries 1976, 141–143.

18. Jeremy Redmon, "Georgia 2006: Cox, Taylor Trade Jabs Over Minority Appointments, Tax Issues," *AJC*, July 16, 2006, D7.

19. Associated Press, "Poll Suggests Perdue Vulnerable Against Taylor, Cox in 2006," http://www.firstcoastnews.com/news/georgia/news-article.aspx?storyid=26061.

20. James Salzer, "Cox Seen As Rising Star in Politics Despite Loss," *AJC*, July 20, 2006, D8.

21. Jim Galloway, "Reed Loses GOP Race," *AJC*, July 19, 2006, A1.

22. See election results for 2006 statewide races at http://www.sos.state.ga.us/elections/election_results/2006_1107/default.htm.

23. Jim Galloway, Carlos Campos, Mark Davis, Jill Young Miller, "Statewide Races to Watch," *AJC*, November 7, 2006, A10.

24. Scher 1992.

25. Nancy Badertscher, "More Democrats Hitch a Ride on Republican Tide," *AJC*, November 13, 2004, A1; Nancy Badertscher, "Another House Democrat Joins GOP," *AJC*, November 10, 2004, B4.

26 Council of State Governments 1990, 1995.

27. Council of State Governments 2004, 82.

28. James Salzer, "Stripped of Power, Caucus Aims to Pull Party to the Middle," *AJC*, December 23, 2004, A1; Jim Tharpe, "Parties Take Stock: Flattened Democrats Seek to Regain Footing," *AJC*, November 7, 2004, E12.

29. Talmadge suffered from scandals relating to his addiction to alcohol and financial mismanagement.

30. Mike Christensen, "Anti-Talmadge Vote Was Gone—and So Was Mack Mattingly," *AJC*, November 9, 1986, A1; Lamis 1990, 101–103.

31. See election results at http://www.sos.state.ga.us/elections/election_results/2006_1107/swfed.htm.

32. Bullock 1993.

33. Tom Baxter and Jim Galloway, "Legislature 2005: More Blacks Register to Vote," *AJC*, February 10, 2005, C5.

34. Lockerbie and Clark 1995, 127–132.

35. Aldrich 2000.

36. U.S. Advisory Commission on Intergovernmental Relations 1986, 120–121.

37. Lockerbie and Clark 1995, 132–133.

38. Lockerbie and Clark 1995, 134–135.

39. Lockerbie and Clark 1995, 137–142.

40. See Clark and Bruce 1995.

41. See election results at http://www.sos.state.ga.us/elections/election_results/2006_1107/swfed.htm.

42. Mark Sherman, "Religious Right's Strength Could Be GOP's Weakness," *AJC*, July 25, 1993, G1; Lockerbie and Clark 1995, 131–132, 140–141.

43. Hrebenar and Scott 1990, 29–35.

44. Hrebenar and Scott 1990, 10–29.

45. For a discussion of the many forms that lobbying takes and the different types of lobbyists, see Hrebenar and Scott 1990, 69–165, 214–239; Hrebenar and Thomas 1992, 10–12.

46. Hrebenar and Scott 1990, 166–192; Council of State Governments 1996, 167–184.

47. Epstein 1994.

48. Thomas and Hrebenar 1996.

49. Thomas and Hrebenar 2003.

50. Hrebenar and Thomas 1992, 17–26.

51. Key 1949, 123–124, 467–468, 475.

52. Main, Epstein, and Elovich 1992, 231–248.

53. Main, Epstein, and Elovich 1992, 235–248.

54. Hayes 1992. For the states as a whole, see Hunter, Wilson, and Brunk 1991.

55. State Ethics Commission (http://www.ethics.state.ga.us/gaethics/Reports/Lobbyist/LobbyistbyName.aspx).

56. Main, Epstein, and Elovich 1992, 238–243; Institute on Money in State Politics 2006.

57. For a comparative analysis, see Opheim 1991; Newmark 2005.

58. Jeanne Cummings, "Ethic Rules Few and Far Between in Georgia," *AJC*, June 23, 1991, D1; Mark Sherman, "Cleland Panel Finalizes Tough Ethics Proposals," *AC*, December 6, 1991, A1.

59. *OCGA*, title 21, chap. 5, secs. 71–73.

60. Rhonda Cook, "Reports Don't Tell Lobbying Secrets," *AJC*, April 25, 1993, D1.

61. The figures are taken from the Institute on Money in State Politics 2006, which provides summaries from the databases of the Georgia Secretary of State and the State Ethics Commission. These data are for all donations and contributions reported for elections held in 2004. These data do not include local races.

62. Main, Epstein, and Elovich 1992, 236–240.

63. Ann Hardie, "Lobbyists Stand Ground," *AJC*, January 19, 2006, A1.

64. Ann Hardie, "The $1 Million Lobby," *AJC*, February 2, 2006, F1.

65. Frank LoMonte, "Lobbyists Play, Pay Power Game," *Athens Daily News/Banner Herald,* March 10, 1991, D1; Rhonda Cook, "Oink If You Know the Secret Menu for Legislature's Wild Hog Supper," *AJC,* January 10, 1993, A1; Melissa Turner, "More Than 200 Politicians Take Olympic Ticket Offer," *AJC,* August 5, 1995, A1; Ben Smith III, "Who Leases Ga. Power's Lots? Not Just Anyone," *AJC,* May 5, 1991, A1; Rhonda Cook, "Legislators Being Feted in Daytona," *AJC,* February 13, 1993, A1; Mark Sherman, "Lobbyists Ply Lawmakers with Food," *AC,* August 9, 1995, E3; Mark Sherman, "Lobbyist-Paid Trips Are Common," *AC,* August 9, 1995, B1; Jill Young Miller, "Free Doctoring a Legislative Perk," *AJC,* February 19, 2006, E1.

66. The figures are calculated by the authors from the database of the State Ethics Commission (www.ethics.state.ga.us) as of January 2006.

67. Mark Sherman, "How NRA's Allies Outflanked Foes," *AC,* March 16, 1995, B4; Ben Smith III, " 'Christian Right' Grows in Influence," *AJC,* October 9, 1994, D1.

68. Jill Vejnoska, "Interest-Cap Unlikely to Get to Ga. Senate Floor," *AJC,* February 14, 1993, A1.

69. Abney 1988.

70. Steve Janus, letter to the editor, *AC,* August 11, 1995, A16.

71. Betsy White, "Schrenko Gives Priority to Contributors," *AJC,* February 24, 1996, C4.

72. Rhonda Cook, "Firms Gave Thousands to Ryles in '92," *AJC,* January 30, 1993, C1; Mark Sherman, "Politicians Cash in on Campaign Leftovers," *AC,* August 5, 1993, D1; Institute of Money in State Politics 2006.

73. Alan Judd, "Unregulated Donations Build Richardson Fund," *AJC,* February 24, 2006, A1; Jim Galloway, "GOP Not First with Lobby Fund," *AJC,* February 25, 2006, B1.

74. Richard Whitt, " '90 Timber Tax Cut Goes Awry," *AJC,* December 27, 1992, A1.

75. James Salzer, "Christian Coalition Touches All Bases; Coalition Asks State Candidates 82 Questions," *AJC,* September 2, 2004, D1; Jim Galloway, "Election 2004: Coalition Spotlights 2 Judicial Hopefuls; the Candidates Were the Only Individuals Who Did Not Boycott the Christian Group's Survey," *AJC,* July 7, 2004, B1.

76. Jim Tharpe, "Gay Union Battle Brews: Same Sex Marriage; Proposed Ban's Friends, Foes Prepare Campaigns," *AJC,* May 12, 2004, B1.

77. Bartley 1991.

78. *Jaeger v. Douglas County,* 862 F.2d 824, 831 (1989); *Chandler v. Miller,* 529 U.S. 305 (1997).

79. Scott Bronstein, "Ga.'s Workers' Comp Law Protested," *AC,* March 3, 1992, C4.

80. On split-party control in the states, see Fiorina 1996, 24–43, 132–140.

Chapter Seven. The Legislature

1. Comparisons in this section are based on Council of State Governments 2005, vol. 37, chap. 3. For important historical comparisons, see Squire 2006.

2. For a discussion of the different types of legislatures, see Hamm and Moncrief 2003, 157–160; Squire 1988; Squire 2000. For data on legislative compensation, see Council of State Governments 2005, 37:140–156.

3. Squire 1988, 1992.

4. Maddox 2004.

5. Data available from "About State Legislators" search option available from the National Conference of State Legislatures (www.ncsl.org/programs/legman/legman.htm).

6. See Jackson, Stakes, and Hardy 2001, 1–9.

7. *Georgia v. Ashcroft,* 539 U.S. 461 (2003).

8. *Larios v. Cox,* 314 F.Supp.2d 1214 (2004).

9. Rhonda Cook, "Attorney General's Authority Upheld," *AJC,* September 5, 2003, A1.

10. *Chandler v. Miller,* 520 U.S. 305 (1997).

11. Council of State Governments 2004, 36:92–93.

12. National Conference of State Legislatures 2006c.

13. National Conference of State Legislatures, *Current Number of Legislators, Terms of Office, and Next Election Year,* http://www.ncsl.org/programs/legman/about/numoflegis.htm.

14. Moncrief et al. 1992.

15. Eleven of ninety-nine chambers did not have seats up for election in 2002. National Conference of State Legislatures 2006a, 2006d, 2004b.

16. National Conference of State Legislatures 2006b.

17. Moncrief et al. 1992.

18. James Salzer, "2002 Georgia Legislature: Boundaries Put Careers on the Line," *AJC,* April 15, 2002, B1; James Salzar, "Rookies Aim for Seats In Legislature," *AJC,* May 2, 2004, D1.

19. National Conference of State Legislatures 2005.

20. Calculated by the authors from candidate Web sites and House and Senate Information Offices of the Georgia General Assembly.

21. Georgia Senate Public Information Office and Clerk's Office 2006, 142–144 (this directory is commonly known as the "picture book" because it includes photos and biographies of all members of the legislature); C-SPAN.org 2006.

22. Nancy Badertscher and James Salzer, "GOP Flexes Muscle," *AJC,* November 11, 2004, B1.

23. Thomas Stinson, John Kessler, Andrea Jones, Mary Macdonald, Matt Kempner, Michelle Hiskey, Gayle White, John Blake, Bo Emerson, Dave Hirschman, "Reddest of the Red: State Bucks National Trend, Remains Republican Fortress," *AJC,* November 12, 2006, A1; James Salzer, "GOP Secures Georgia," *AJC,* November 8, 2006, D1.

24. Hurst 2004.

25. Jewell and Whicker 1994, 63–76.

26. James Salzer and Rhonda Cook, "Rural Leadership Chosen," *AJC*, November 13, 2002, B1; James Salzer, "Johnson: Partisan Days Are Ending," *AJC*, November 17, 2002, F4; Jim Galloway, "Coleman: Change of Direction Is Needed," *AJC*, November 17, 2002, F4.

27. Rhonda Cook, "'A New Day in Georgia': Coleman Wins Speaker's Race; in Senate, GOP Strips Taylor of Most Power," *AJC*, January 14, 2003, D1; Tom Baxter and Jim Galloway, "Legislature 2005: Democrat Denied Ceremonial Role," *AJC*, January 13, 2005, C8.

28. Council of State Governments 2004, 36:124–127; National Conference of State Legislatures 2004a.

29. National Conference of State Legislatures 2004a; Rhonda Cook and Nancy Badertscher, "General Assembly Leaders Add Staff," *AJC*, September 28, 2003, C1.

30. Council of State Governments 2005, 37:176–177.

31. On the committee system, see Jackson, Stakes, and Hardy 2001, 73–81.

32. Georgia House of Representatives 2005, rules 11.1, 11.3, 11.8; Nancy Badertscher, "GOP's 'Hawks' Ruffle Democratic Feathers," *AJC*, January 17, 2005, B1.

33. Georgia Senate 2005, sec. 2, pt. 1.1.

34. Information on the membership of House and Senate committees as well as biographies and district maps for individual members is available at the General Assembly's Web site (http://www.legis.state.ga.us/). On HOPE allocations, see Georgia Student Finance Commission 2006.

35. See Jackson, Stakes, and Hardy 2001, 101–110.

36. For the constitutional requirements on lawmaking, see Constitution of the State of Georgia, art. 3, sec. 5.

37. Council of State Governments 2004, 36:120–121.

38. Georgia House of Representatives 2005, rule 59.

39. Gary Pomerantz, "The State Capitol's Wily Wizard of Oz," *AC*, March 8, 1992, A1.

40. Georgia Senate 2005, rule 3-1.2b. See also Georgia House of Representatives 2005, 143; Sonji Jacobs and Nancy Badertscher, "Bills Race Clock for Today's Deadline: Republicans Expect Smooth 'Crossover,'" *AJC*, March 13, 2006, C1.

41. Council of State Governments 2004, 36:162–163.

42. Steve Harvey, "Georgia Funds Allocated Secretly," *AC*, May 9, 1992, A1.

43. Mark Sherman, "Governor OKs Strict Ethics Law," *AC*, April 7, 1992, A1.

44. Main et al. 1992.

45. Abney 1988.

46. Jim Tharpe and Nancy Badertscher, "Legislature '05: Lobbies Spend a Million in 2004," *AJC*, February 2, 2005, B1; James Salzer, "Legislature 2005: On the House: Lobbyist for Stores Dispenses Goodies to Lawmakers," *AJC*, March 26, 2005, F5; Nancy Badertscher and Sonji Jacobs, "Legislature '05: The Big Issues: Open Season for Lobbying at Gold Dome," *AJC*, December 20, 2004, D1; Sonji Jacobs, "Legislature '05: The Big Issues: Abortion Foes to Push Limits," *AJC*, December 12, 2004, D1.

47. Mark Sherman, "Cleland Panel Finalizes Tough Ethics Proposals," *AC*, December 6, 1991, A1; Peter Mantius, "BCCI Tied to Change in State Law," *AC*, September 27, 1991, A1; Mark Sherman, "Governor OKs Strict Ethics Law," *AC*, April 7, 1992, A1.

48. Newmark 2005.

49. James Salzer, "Legislature '05: Lobbyists May Face New Rules," *AJC*, February 13, 2005, A1; James Salzer, "Lobbyists Cozy Up to Party in Power," *AJC*, January 14, 2005, A1.

50. See Jackson, Stakes, and Hardy 2001, 175–181, 199–218.

51. Steve Harvey, "Two Who Bucked Murphy Lose Committee Posts," *AJC*, December 22, 1992, C5.

Chapter Eight. The Executive Branch

1. Beyle 2005, 201.

2. Council of State Governments 2005, 37:231–238.

3. See Teaford 2002.

4. See Beyle 2004, 205–219.

5. Beyle 2005, 200–201.

6. Council of State Governments 2005, 37:215–216.

7. For a brief history of Georgia's governorship, see Jackson and Stakes 1988, 38–45.

8. Beyle 2003, 215–217. On differences in veto power among the states, see Council of State Governments 2005, 37:220–221.

9. Beyle 2003, 212–215; Constitution of the State of Georgia, art. 3, sec. 9; Lauth 1986.

10. Beyle 2003, 210–214.

11. Perdue 2003a.

12. Stacy Shelton, "Perdue Swears in 24 Environmental Advisers," *AJC*, June 9, 2005, C3.

13. Bill Rankin, "Perdue's Court Pick Historic," *AJC*, June 9, 2005, A1.

14. See Key 1949, chap. 6.

15. Beyle 1996, 235–236; Storey 2005. Updates on party control of the fifty governorships and forty-nine partisan legislatures (Nebraska legislators are officially nonpartisan) are generally available from the Council of State Governments (www.csg.org) and National Conference of State Legislatures (www.ncsl.org).

16. Beyle 2003, 205–210.

17. Dilger 1995.

18. Fisher and Nice 2005.

19. There is no established list of gubernatorial roles, although scholars tend to compare the importance of many of the same activities. For comparison, see Rosenthal 1990; Beyle 2003, 218–227; Bowman and Kearney 2002, 176–201.

20. See Beyle 2003, 219–226; Bowman and Kearney 2002, 177–178.

21. Lauth 1990.

22. Beyle 2003, 218–221.

23. See Eisinger 1988; Brace 1993; Saiz and Clarke 2003.

24. On agenda setting and the media generally, see Beyle 2003, 224–226; DiLeo 2001.

25. David Beasley, "Land-Use Plan May Change Face of Rural Georgia," *AJC*, October 30, 1988, 1C; David Beasley, "State Land-Use Plan: Hardest Part Is Yet to Come," *AC*, April 17, 1989, 3E.

26. Ken Foskett, "State Privatization Moving Too Fast, Critics Say," *AJC*, November 25, 1995, B6; Shelly Emling and Ken Foskett, "Privatization Proposals Win OK," *AC*, February 16, 1996, B4.

27. Nancy Badertscher, "Task Force to Evaluate Topics: Governor Names Pair to Co-Chair New Board," *AJC*, May 28, 2003, B3; Georgia Governor's Commission for a New Georgia 2006.

28. Georgia Governor's Local Governance Commission 1992; *OCGA*, title 36, chap. 86; Don Melvin, "Who Needs a Charter?" *AJC*, July 1, 1995, C2.

29. Rosenthal 1990, 5–38.

30. T. Hall 2002.

31. Council of State Governments 2005, 37:168–169.

32. Thompson and Boyd 1994.

33. Rosenthal 1990, 20.

34. Beyle 1996, 209–213.

35. See Henderson and Roberts 1988; Henderson 1991.

36. See Rosenthal 1990, 22–24.

37. Rosenthal 1990, 13–17.

38. See, for example, Dick Pettys, "Miller Isn't Shy in Touting Grants of $4 Million-Plus," *AC*, July 13, 1993, B3.

39. King and Cohen 2005.

40. Ken Foskett, "Plan Spreads Lotto Green across State," *AC*, January 5, 1994, D1; Ben Smith III, "Miller Tax Plan Hailed as a Good Political Move," *AJC*, December 18, 1993, B1; Ken Foskett, "Lawmakers Give Miller Agenda Cooler Reception," *AC*, March 20, 1995, B1.

41. Rosenthal 1990, 35–36.

42. See Bowman and Kearney 2002, 181–183, 194–195.

43. Conant 1992. On the power of reorganization in the states, see Council of State Governments 2005, 37:220–221.

44. Council of State Governments 2005, 37:218–219.

45. Betsy White, "Battle Weary," *AC*, October 3, 1996, B4; James Salzer, "Perdue Asks Resignations of 4 on State School Board," *AJC*, January 10, 2003, C3; Joey Ledford, "DOT's Reynolds: Perdue Forced Exit," *AJC*, August 22, 2003, C1; Nancy Badertscher and Jim Galloway, "Perdue Ousts DHR's Chief," *AJC*, September 17, 2003, A1.

46. Bartley 1991, 361–370; Stone 1989, 25–76.

47. "Carter Plans Trip to Latin America," *AC*, February 19, 1972, 6B; "Carter Leaves Desk for 9-City Air Tour," *AC*, December 9, 1972, 12B; "Carter Flies from Paris to Israel," *AC*, May 25, 1973, 7A; "Busbee Arrives in South Korea," *AC*, October 27, 1975; Beau Cutts, "Ga. Leaders to Go to NYC to Lure Business, Tourism," *Atlanta Journal*, March 21, 1983, 7B; Elizabeth Kurylo, "Miller Going to Russia, May Talk with Yeltsin," *AC*, December 5, 1991, A4; James Salzer, "'Growing Jobs' No Snap: Perdue Finds Task Easier Said Than Done," *AJC*, August 10, 2005, C1.

48. *OCGA*, title 45, chap. 15; Jackson and Stakes 1988, 63–69.

49. Rhonda Cook, "Oink If You Know the Secret Menu for Legislature's Wild Hog Supper," *AJC*, January 10, 1993, A1.

50. Peter Mantius, "Weak Regulatory Setup Lets Insurers Call the Shots," *AJC*, November 20, 1988, 1A; Rhonda Cook, "Firms Gave Thousands to Ryles in '92," *AJC*, January 30, 1993, C1.

51. Data are taken from the campaign contributions report available at the Georgia secretary of state's Web site (http://www.sos.state.ga.us/elections). The General Assembly transferred supervision of campaign finance reporting to the State Ethics Commission effective January 1, 2006 (www.ethics.georgia.gov).

52. Shelley Emling, "Insurance Chief Agrees to Collect Tax," *AC*, August 18, 1995, C2.

53. Georgia Governor's Office of Planning and Budget, *Fiscal 2005 Budget-as-Passed (Conference Committee Substitute to H.B. 1181)* (http://www.legis.state.ga.us/legis/budget/GEN05.htm).

54. See Anderson 1975, 195–204.

55. Jackson and Stakes 1988, 96–99.

56. Hal Strauss, "Work of State Licensing Boards Limited," *AJC*, September 2, 1984, A1; Frank LoMonte, "Consultants Costing Ga. Big Bucks," *ABH*, August 25, 1991, 1A; Mark Sherman, "DOT Board Had $88,000 in Expenses," *AC*, August 12, 1993, C1; "DNR Board Out of Balance" (editorial), *AC*, August 31, 1993, A18; Carrie Teegardin and Ann Hardie, "Auto Deal Gone Sour? Don't Count on Help from State's Consumer Agencies," *AJC*, October 24, 2005, A1.

57. Walters 1997.

58. The Census Bureau converts part-time positions into full-time equivalents to produce its final employment totals. See U.S. Census Bureau 2005d, table 458.

59. Bullard and Wright 1993; Richard Whitt, "Whites and Males at the Top," *AJC*, September 24, 1995, H6.

60. Georgia Governor's Commission on Effectiveness and Economy in Government 1992, 48.

61. For detail on the budget, see Georgia Governor's Office of Planning and Budget 2005.

62. Jackson and Stakes 1988.

63. Andy Miller, "PeachCare for Kids Kicks Off Blitz for New Health Insurance," *AJC*, July 15, 1998, C3; Andy Miller, "Legislators OK New Agency," *AJC*, March 21, 1999, D6; Peter Mantius, "Health Agency Created as Barnes Combines Divisions,"

AJC, April 20, 1999, C2; Kathey Pruitt, "New Czar for Health Dismisses 19 Staffers," *AJC,* July 15, 1999, E2; Andy Miller, "Barnes Names Members of New Health Department's Board," *AJC,* August 5, 1999, G2.

64. On the problems of assessing the work of government, see Jones 1982; Osborne and Gaebler 1992.

65. See Abney and Lauth 1986.

66. Betsy White, "Miller to Nix School-Grant Allocations," *AC,* February 8, 1994, C1; James Salzer, "Legislature '05: House Serves Up 'Pork' for Suburbia," *AJC,* March 19, 2005, C1; James Salzer, "Legislature 2005: Pork Clogs Budget Path," *AJC,* March 29, 2005, B3.

67. See Osborne and Gaebler 1992.

68. Campbell Public Affairs Institute 2001, 2002. See also Barrett and Greens 1999.

69. Burke and Wright 2002.

70. Wilson 1989, 376.

Chapter Nine. The Legal System

1. See Glick 2003.

2. See Jacob 1995, 26–36.

3. U.S. Census Bureau 2005d, tables 338, 429, 457.

4. This description is based on Constitution of the State of Georgia, art. 6; Judicial Council of Georgia and Administrative Office of the Courts 2005.

5. Peter Mantius, "9-Member Court Appealing for More Judges," *AJC,* December 2, 1995, D1; Georgia Court of Appeals n.d.

6. Georgia Court of Appeals n.d.

7. Judicial Council of Georgia and Administrative Office of the Courts 2004, 11–15.

8. Judicial Council of Georgia and Administrative Office of the Courts 2005, 4–5.

9. Sentell 2004, 106–113.

10. Sentell 2004, 82–84.

11. Sentell 2004, 53–59.

12. Songer, Kuersten, and Kaheny 2000.

13. See Glick 1993, 214–218.

14. Sandra Eckstein, "Ruling: Prosecutors Bear Racial Onus in Drug Cases," *AJC,* March 18, 1995, C4; Bill Rankin, "Justice Explains Reversal on Rulings," *AJC,* March 18, 1995, D9; Georgia Supreme Court Commission on Racial and Ethnic Bias in the Court System 1995, 158–167; Ken Foskett and Bill Rankin, "Sentencing: Judges Get Choices for Two-Time Drug Offenders," *AC,* March 20, 1996, B2.

15. Georgia General Assembly 2005. For the text of HB 170, see http://www.legis .state.ga.us/legis/2005_06/pdf/hb170.pdf. See also Jim Tharpe, "Parents' Grief Leads to a Victory," *AJC,* April 6, 2005, B1.

16. Eaton and Talarico 1996.

17. U.S. Bureau of Justice Statistics, *Sourcebook of Criminal Justice Statistics 2004*, table 6.84.2004 (http://www.albany.edu/sourcebook/pdf/t6842004.pdf); U.S. Bureau of Justice Statistics, *Sourcebook of Criminal Justice Statistics 2006*, table 6.80.2006 (http://www.albany.edu/sourcebook/pdf/t6802006.pdf).

18. Mark Silk, "Juries Prefer Alternatives to Death Penalty," AC, July 3, 1996, B2.

19. For more detail, see the Web site of the Judicial Branch of Georgia, Administrative Office of the Courts (http://www.georgiacourts.org/aoc).

20. *Gideon v. Wainwright*, 372 U.S. 335 (1963).

21. Judicial Branch of Georgia, Administrative Office of the Courts n.d.; Bill Rankin, "Three Systems: Is One Superior?" AJC, April 21, 2002, A21; Bill Rankin, "A Cheap Dose of Due Process in Dodge," AJC, April 22, 2002, A1; Bill Rankin, "Other States Offer Lessons in Reform," AJC, April 23, 2002, A1.

22. Nancy Badertscher, "Indigent Defense Measure Now Law," AJC, June 16, 2004, D1; Bill Rankin, "Counties' Legal Plans Rejected; Indigent Protection Cited," AJC, October 30, 2004, B1; Bill Rankin, "Legislature '05: Defender System Gets Early Praise; State Indigent Program Off to Quiet Start," AJC, February 6, 2005, F1.

23. Council of State Governments 2005, 37:318–321; American Judicature Society n.d.

24. Glick 1993, 131.

25. Bratton and Spill 2002.

26. M. Hall 2001.

27. M. Holmes et al. 1993.

28. Steffensmeier and Britt 2001.

29. Gorton and Boies 1999.

30. M. Hall 1992; M. Hall and Brace 1994.

31. William Glaberson, "A Spirited Campaign for Ohio Court Puts Judges in New Terrain," NYT, July 7, 2000, A11; William Glaberson, "States Taking Steps to Rein in Excesses of Judicial Politicking," NYT, June 15, 2001, A1; Adam Liptak, "Judicial Races in Several States Become Partisan Battlegrounds," NYT, October 24, 2004, 1; Rothman and Schotland 2005.

32. Bonneau 2005.

33. The Web site of the Administrative Office of the Courts also lists qualifications for each type of court (http://www.georgiacourts.org/courts/index.html; see links for specific types of courts).

34. Peter Mantius, "Campaign Ad Draws Official Rebuke," AC, July 3, 1996, C5; Judicial Qualifications Commission of Georgia 1984.

35. Don Plummer, "DA Raises Cash for Judge's Foe," AJC, July 2, 2004, B1; Jim Galloway, "Election 2004: Coalition Spotlights 2 Judicial Hopefuls," AJC, July 7, 2004, B1; Jim Wooten, "Groups' Picks Speak Volumes" (editorial), AJC, July 18, 2004, F8; Jim Galloway, "Election 2004: Sears Fends Off GOP Attack," AJC, July 21, 2004, A1; Jennifer Brett, "Election 2004: Candidates for State Court Beef Up Coffers," AJC, July 24, 2004, JJ1; Bill Rankin, "Court of Appeals Race Very Low-Profile," AJC, November 12, 2004, E8.

36. Perdue 2003b.

37. Georgia Supreme Court Commission on Racial and Ethnic Bias in the Court System 1995, 52–54.

38. Alan Judd, "Judgeships Often Go to Donors to Barnes," *AJC,* October 13, 2002, A1.

39. Randy Evans, "Newest Justice Sure to Make a Difference," *AJC,* June 13, 2005, A9.

40. *OCGA,* title 15, chap. 12, art. 40.

41. *Smith v. the State,* 275 Ga. 715, 571 S.E.2d 740 (2002).

42. Glick 1993, 252–261, 265–269.

43. *Duncan v. Louisiana,* 391 U.S. 145 (1968).

44. Glick 1993, 270–271; *Williams v. Florida,* 399 U.S. 78 (1970); *Ballew v. Georgia,* 435 U.S. 223 (1978); *Apodaca v. Oregon,* 406 U.S. 404 (1972); *Burch v. Louisiana,* 441 U.S. 130 (1979).

45. See *OCGA,* title 15, chap. 12, art. 5.

46. Glick 1993, 255–261, 266–269; *Batson v. Kentucky,* 476 U.S. 79 (1986); *J.E.B. v. Alabama,* 511 U.S. 127 (1994); Georgia Supreme Court Commission on Racial and Ethnic Bias in the Court System 1995, 182–188.

47. Jim Tharpe, "Parents' Grief Leads to a Victory," *AJC,* April 6, 2005, B1.

48. See Glick 1993, 222–223.

49. See McDonald, Binford, and Johnson 1994, 68.

50. On the selection and responsibilities of grand juries, see *OCGA,* title 15, chap. 12, art. 4.

51. U.S. Census Bureau 2006c, tables 291, 604.

52. See Glick 1993, 86–91; Harward 2003.

53. Glick 1993, 102.

54. The State Bar of Georgia provides information on mandatory continuing legal education (see State Bar of Georgia 2006). For more on the Institute of Continuing Legal Education, see http://www.iclega.org/index.html.

55. Glick 1993, 83.

56. Glick 1993, 83–84.

57. State Bar of Georgia, Office of the General Counsel 2006, 4–6, 9.

58. U.S. Bureau of Justice Statistics, *Sourcebook of Criminal Justice Statistics 2005,* table 2.10.2005 (http://www.albany.edu/sourcebook/pdf/t2102005.pdf).

Chapter Ten. Local Government and Politics

1. *OCGA,* title 36, chap. 86; Georgia Department of Community Affairs 1993; Bill Osinski, "Law Has Towns Fighting Oblivion," *AC,* March 28, 1994, B1; Don Melvin, "Who Needs a Charter?" *AJC,* July 1, 1995, C2.

2. See Nice 1987, 137–145.

3. See Hill 1994, 184–200.

4. U.S. Advisory Commission on Intergovernmental Relations 1993, 7–9, 17–22.

5. See Jackson, Stakes, and Hardy 2001, 104–115.

6. Jim Galloway, "Counties Have Grown Like Kudzu during Georgia's History," *AJC*, April 28, 1985, 13A; Lucy Soto, "Paying Up . . . and Up," *AC*, May 17, 1996, D9.

7. See *OCGA*, title 36, chaps. 31, 35.

8. Special districts are covered very briefly in art. 9, sec. 2, para. 6. For additional information, see Constitution of the State of Georgia, secs. 6, 7; *OCGA*, title 36, chaps. 41–43, 62, 63.

9. *OCGA*, title 36, chap. 36; Diefenbacher and Sumner 2004; Anne Rochell, "Cities to Pocket Islands," *AC*, August 17, 1992, C1.

10. *OCGA*, title 36, chap. 68; Donna Williams Lewis, "Conyers Voters Kill Rockdale Merger," *AC*, November 15, 1989, B2.

11. See Leland and Thurmaier 2004, especially chaps. 3, 6, 10; Fleischmann 2000.

12. Carr and Feiock 2004; Fleischmann 1986; Wayne Partridge, "Merger Could Put Augusta on the Map," *Augusta Chronicle*, June 23, 1995, 1A; "A Brighter Future" (editorial), *Augusta Chronicle*, June 22, 1995, 4A; Susan Laccetti, "Panel: N. Fulton Should Incorporate," *AJC*, December 16, 1995, F1; Carlos Campos, "Government Consolidation Plan Shelved," *AC*, November 15, 1996, F1; Eva C. Galambos, "Sandy Springs, Birth of a City: Inaugural Address," *AJC*, December 1, 2005, JH2; Doug Nurse, "New City Bets Millions on Privatization," *AJC*, November 12, 2005, B1.

13. *OCGA*, title 21, chaps. 2, 3.

14. See *OCGA*, title 36, chaps. 20, 45.

15. *OCGA*, title 45, chap. 16.

16. *OCGA*, title 36, chap. 1, sec. 24, chap. 45, sec. 20.

17. *OCGA*, title 36, chap. 32.

18. On zoning in metropolitan Atlanta, see Fleischmann 1989; Fleischmann and Pierannunzi 1990.

19. *OCGA*, title 35, chap. 8, title 25, chap. 4.

20. *OCGA*, title 17, chap. 2.

21. *OCGA*, title 36, chap. 81, sec. 3b.

22. Shelley Emling and Lucy Soto, "November Ballot Will Have 5 Amendments," *AJC*, March 24, 1996, H5; Doug Cumming and Marcus Franklin, "Ready, Set, Build: 63 School Districts Plan Construction," *AC*, March 20, 1997, C4.

23. James Salzer and Nancy Badertscher, "Sales Tax May Fund Schools," *AJC*, August 28, 2005, A1.

24. *OCGA*, title 36, chaps. 5, 7, 8.

25. See *OCGA*, title 36, chap. 81; Hudson and Hardy 2002, 2005.

26. *OCGA*, title 50, chap. 14, title 36, chap. 66, sec. 4; Charmagne Helton, "Retreats Often Stray into Illegal Territory," *AC*, August 15, 1995, C3; Duane D. Stanford, "Gwinnett Ends Secret Land Deals," *AJC*, November 1, 2005, B1; "Let Sun Shine on Gwinnett Schools" (editorial), *AJC*, November 2, 2005, A14.

27. *OCGA*, title 50, chap. 18, art. 4.

28. *OCGA*, title 21, chap. 5, art. 3.

29. *OCGA*, title 35, chap. 67A.

30. *OCGA*, title 36, chap. 71, sec. 5B.

31. *OCGA*, title 36, chap. 30, sec. 4.

32. *OCGA*, title 36, chap. 62, sec. 5, chap. 62A, sec. 1.

33. See Judd and Swanstrom 2004, chaps. 3, 4; Bridges and Kronick 1999; Wood 2002.

34. See Welch 1990; McDonald, Binford, and Johnson 1994; Bullock and Johnson 1992; Fleischmann and Stein 1987.

35. Ken Foskett, "The Privileges of the Powerful," *AJC*, April 26, 1992, F1; "Deadwood on the Ballot" (editorial), *AC*, November 11, 1996, A12.

36. Association County Commissioners of Georgia 2003; Steve Goldberg, "One-Man Rule: Power Is Enormous," *AC*, July 5, 1990, C2; Bill Torpy, "Sole Commissioners Fading: Lawsuit against Bleckley County Threatens 10 of 19 Left in State," *AJC*, July 5, 1992, A1; *Holder v. Hall*, 512 U.S. 874 (1994); Dan Chapman, "The Heart and 'Sole' of Running a County," *AJC*, November 25, 2000, G1; Clint Williams, "Solo Rule Cool in Bartow," *AJC*, July 16, 2000, C5; "Bartow Treads on People's Rights" (editorial), April 13, 2004, A10; Cameron McWhirter, "Can One Man Run a County? Yes, but It's Not Easy," *AJC*, January 22, 2006, A1.

37. On the difference between county administrators and county managers, see Ammons and Campbell 1992. For an overview of each county governmental form, see http://www.dca.state.ga.us/CountySnapshotsNet/.

38. DeKalb voters approved this form of government in 1982, with the first officials elected in 1984; see Georgia General Assembly 1981, 4304–4331. On Athens, see Charter of the Unified Government of Athens–Clarke County, art. 3 (http://www.municode.com/resources/gateway.asp?sid=10&pid=12400).

39. This overview is based on Hudson and Hardy 2005.

40. Bachtel and Boatright 1992, 66–70; McDonald, Binford, and Johnson 1994, 68.

41. See Wells and Scheff 1992; Steve Visser, "A Taxing Decision: Property-Owner Organizations Could Be Key to Controlling Sprawl," *AJC*, June 14, 1999, E7; Janet Frankston, "Self-Taxing Districts Gain Traction," *AJC*, January 13, 2003, E1; David Pendered, "Beltline on Fast Forward," *AJC*, December 22, 2005, A1.

42. For a good overview of citizen contacting, see Hirlinger 1992. On other participation at the local level, see Hajnal and Lewis 2003; Gerber and Phillips 2003.

43. Wood 2002; Hajnal and Lewis 2003; Kelleher and Lowery 2004; Oliver 2001.

44. Fleischmann and Stein 1998; official disclosure reports of Atlantans for Maynard Jackson, October 17, 1989, January 3, 1990, City of Atlanta, Office of Municipal Clerk, Atlanta City Hall; "Incumbency Provides Big Boost to Lomax's Campaign Financing," *AJC*, April 29, 1989, A1; Mark Sherman, "Ethics of Council Donations Questioned," *AJC*, April 15, 1990, A1.

45. Ernie Suggs, "Watchdog Group Calls War Chests Excessive," *AJC*, October 20, 2005, C1.

46. Data are from campaign finance reports filed with the Gwinnett County Board of Registration and Elections and can be accessed from the Elections icon in the Departments menu of the county's Web site (http://www.co.gwinnett.ga.us).

47. This discussion is based in part on reports filed with city and county election officials. See also Lucy Soto, "More Seats Than Candidates," *AJC*, September 25, 1995, c1; Don Plummer, "'No Contest' at Polls for District Attorneys," *AC*, November 8, 1996, e5.

48. Laura Kinsler, "It's Horton over Hunter in Oconee BOE," *ABH*, July 10, 1996, 1.

49. This discussion of Atlanta is based on Murray and Vedlitz 1978; Bullock and Campbell 1984; Bullock 1985; Abney and Hutcheson 1981; Stone 1989; Pierannunzi and Hutcheson 1991; Tankersley and Custer 2004; Fleischmann 2004; Fleischmann and Hardman 2004; Kruse 2005.

50. U.S. Census Bureau 1971, table 565; U.S. Census Bureau 1994, table 443; U.S. Census Bureau 2006c, table 403.

51. U.S. Census Bureau 1983, table 800; U.S. Census Bureau 1987, table 416; Bullock 1993, 3–5.

52. Bullock 1993, 3–7.

53. Richard Clark, "Opinions in County Government: A National Survey of County Elected Officials, 2006," National Center for the Study of Counties, Vinson Institute of Government, University of Georgia, www.naco.org/ContentManagement/ContentDisplay.cfm?ContentID=21068.

54. Georgia General Assembly 2005b, 3:174A–291A.

55. "Sales Tax Sustains 75% Success Rate," *Georgia County Government*, December 1985, 10–11.

56. Richard Whitt, "Cobb Drivers See Relief in Tax Hike: Penny Increase per Dollar Barely Squeaks Through," *AJC*, September 22, 2005, A1; Mike King, "End Tax Votes in Special Elections" (editorial), *AJC*, September 29, 2005, A15. On controversies over tax elections in Fayette County, see Kevin Duffy, "County OKs First 5-year Tax Increase: Slim Margin to Fund Roads," *AJC*, November 11, 2004, JM1.

57. Peter Scott, "A Wet Tide Pouring over the State," *AJC*, November 2, 1996, D6; Peter Scott, "Drys Put Cork in More Liquor Sales," *AC*, November 7, 1996, C10; Clint Williams, "Election 2005: Sunday Liquor Sales in Canton," *AJC*, November 17, 2005, JQ1.

58. *OCGA*, title 21, chap. 4. See also Charles Yoo, "East Point Group Will Rethink Recall," *AJC*, November 13, 2003, JD1; Jeffrey Scott, "Recall of Lithonia Mayor Sought: Group Submits Petition to County," *AJC*, July 29, 2004, JA1.

59. Cox, Daily, and Pajari 1991.

60. "Civic Leaders in Macon Set to Stay in All-Male Rotary," *AC*, April 6, 1993, D5.

61. Maria Saporta, "The Myriad Business Voices," *AC*, January 9, 1989, 1B.

62. Ben Smith, "Show Me the Money: Beaudreau Did Accept Money from Developers," *AJC*, May 20, 2005, JJ1; "Our Opinions: Uncloak NASCAR Museum Bid" (editorial), *AJC*, November 9, 2005, A18; Ben Smith and Duane D. Stafford, "King of the Deal," *AJC*, November 13, 2005, A1; Maria Saporta, "Worries Emerge about the Future of G-P's Community Involvement," *AJC*, November 16, 2005, C3.

63. Robin Toner and Jim Galloway, "Pride Thwarts County Mergers," *AJC*, April 28, 1985, 1A.

64. Shelley Emling, "DeKalb Homeowners Unite for Political Clout," *AJC*, November 27, 1992, D12; Frances Schwartzkopff, "No Place Like a Homeowners' Group to Take on Government," *AJC*, February 9, 1991, A1; Lucy Soto, "Discovering Strength in Numbers," *AJC*, June 18, 1995, G1; Chandler Brown, "Homeowners Groups Wield Clout: More Than Zoning on Their Plates," *AJC*, December 2, 2004, JF2.

65. Georgia Department of Community Affairs 2004a, 2004b.

66. Toulmin 1988.

67. Hutcheson and Prather 1988; Fleischmann 1989; Fleischmann and Pierannunzi 1990.

68. See, for example, the Web site of the Athens Convention and Visitors Bureau (http://www.visitathensga.com/).

69. See Georgia Department of Community Affairs 2005a.

70. On regional cooperation, see Fleischmann 2000.

71. On the Georgia Regional Transportation Authority, see http://www.grta.org/default.asp. See also Georgia Department of Community Affairs 2004–2005; D. L. Bennett, "Cities, Counties Go Toe-to-Toe in Talks," *AC*, November 15, 1999, D4.

72. Association County Commissioners of Georgia 2006.

73. On lobbying expenditures, see data from the State Ethics Commission Web site (http://www.ethics.state.ga.us/gaethics/Reports/Search_LobExp.aspx).

Chapter Eleven. Public Policy

1. For descriptions of this process, see Kingdon 1995; Baumgartner and Jones 1993; Peters 1993, 39–112.

2. For a discussion of the "problem environment," see Nice 1994, 20–25.

3. See Squire 1992; Ben Smith III, "Political Tremors at the Capitol," *AJC*, March 27, 1994, G3.

4. For more detail on Morris Communications in Georgia, see www.morris.com.

5. See the following Morris News Service stories: Audrey Goodson, "Lawmaking Is No Easy Task," *Savannah Morning News*, January 8, 2006; Walter C. Jones, "Are Tax Breaks Political Gimmicks?" *Augusta Chronicle*, January 8, 2006; Walter C. Jones, "Governor Proposes Pay Hikes," *ABH*, January 11, 2006. Comparable or nearly identical stories on the legislature appear in all three papers during the legislative session. See also Diane Wagner, "Delegates Taking Own Goals to Capitol," *Rome News-Tribune*, January 9, 2006; Mike Billups, "Legislature Opens in a Hurry; House GOP Jumps into Controversy on First Day," *Macon Telegraph*, January 9, 2006; and typical stories drawn from the Associated Press: Greg Bluestein, "Perdue Looks to Court Teachers Again," *Marietta Daily Journal*, January 9, 2006; Doug Gross, "Legislature's Session Opens with Quick Start," *Columbus Ledger-Enquirer*, January 9, 2006; Harris Blackwood, "Wild Hog Supper Kicks Off Session," *Gainesville Times*, January 9, 2006.

6. For a general discussion, see Hamm and Moncrief 2003, 188–189.

7. For a general discussion of courts as policy makers, see Glick 2003, 250–258.

8. See Georgia Governor's Local Governance Commission 1992; "National Unfunded Mandates Day a Success," *Georgia's Cities*, November 30, 1993, 1; Association County Commissioners of Georgia 2006.

9. For a discussion of alternatives to government provision of services, see Osborne and Gaebler 1992.

10. Key 1949, 664.

11. See Key 1949, 671–675; Black and Black 1987; Black and Black 2002.

12. On policy innovation and Georgia's relatively low rank on several indicators, see Nice 1994; Walker 1969; Gray 1973.

13. An overview of the process used to develop the governor's annual budget request to the General Assembly is available from the Office of Planning and Budget (www.opb.state.ga.us).

14. Georgia Governor's Office of Planning and Budget 2006, 27, 36–37, 90, 101, 141, 184, 279, 338. See also Lauth 1986.

15. For an overview of the OPB, see http://opb.georgia.gov.

16. See Main, Epstein, and Elovich 1992, 237; Lauth 1990.

17. Georgia Governor's Office of Planning and Budget 2006, 336–338.

18. Georgia Governor's Office of Planning and Budget 2006, 23.

19. Council of State Governments 2005, 37:445–449.

20. Ken Foskett, "'96 Georgia Legislature: Time May Be Ripe for Lifting Food Sales Tax," *AJC*, January 8, 1996, C1; Ken Foskett, "Miller Savors Food Tax Cut," *AJC*, January 12, 1996, A1; Ken Foskett, "'96 Georgia Legislature: State Looks to Replace Lost Taxes," *AJC*, February 4, 1996, G1.

21. Steve Harvey, "Panel Says State Must Revise Taxes," *AJC*, July 25, 1992, A1; Richard Whitt, "Study: Eliminating Sales Tax on Food Would Require Increase in Tax Rate," *AJC*, September 18, 1993, D5; Charles Seabrook and Richard Whitt, "Georgia's Untaxed Mineral Wealth," *AJC*, November 7, 1993, A1; Frank LoMonte, "Economists Question the Wisdom of Zell Miller's Tax Relief Plans," *ABH*, February 20, 1994, 1A; "Gwinnett Opinions: What Do You Think? About Those Property Taxes . . ." *AJC*, July 31, 2005, JJ9; James Salzer and Nancy Badertscher, "Sales Taxes May Fund Schools," *AJC*, August 28, 2005, A1; Melody Harrison, "Small Business Backs Sales Tax," *AJC*, October 7, 2005, A19; Patti Bond, "The Great Georgia Land Grab," December 18, 2005, A1; D. L. Bennett, "How Assessments Work—or Don't—on One Block," *AJC*, July 2, 2006, D1; Georgia Budget and Policy Institute 2005b. In addition, a series of careful studies on fiscal issues affecting the state is available from the Fiscal Research Center at Georgia State University's Andrew Young School of Policy Studies (http://frp.aysps.gsu.edu/frp/frpreports/index.html).

22. Witko and Newmark 2005.

23. Cobb 1993; Eisinger 1988; Cortright and Mayer 2004. For differences in one major state program, see Dalehite, Mikesell, and Zorn 2005.

24. Grady 1987.

25. Nancy Nethery, "Quick Start Gets Companies Up and Running," *AC*, October 20, 1992, C1; Matthew C. Quinn, "QuickStart: Job Program Helps Bring in the Business," *AC*, April 9, 1996, E2; Maria Saporta, "Commitment to Columbus," *AC*, March 8, 1996, H1; Matthew C. Quinn, "Major Improvements Boost Savannah's Port," *AC*, June 27, 1995, D1.

26. For updates on activities of the Georgia Department of Economic Development, see www.georgia.org/business. On the role of foreign investment in state economies, see Torau and Gross 2004.

27. Walter Woods, "Daimler Talks: 2 Sides Apart by $22 Million," *AJC*, April 16, 2005, F1.

28. Walter Woods, "$160,000 per Job to Land Kia," *AJC*, March 14, 2006, A1.

29. Georgia Budget and Policy Institute 2005a.

30. Grady 1987; Eisinger 1988, 220–224; Skoro 1988; Brace 1993.

31. Georgia's major ports are located in Bainbridge, Columbus, Brunswick, and Savannah.

32. Toon 2004.

33. Information taken from U.S. Census Bureau, *2004 American Community Survey* (http://factfinder.census.gov/home/saff/main.html?_lang=en).

34. *Hartsfield-Jackson News* (www.atlanta-airport.com/default.asp?url=http://www.atlanta-airport.com/sitemap/sitemap.htm).

35. The Georgia Ports Authority operates state ports, but the DOT is charged with much of the planning and financial oversight of these facilities. Local boards also have jurisdiction over public transportation systems, such as the MARTA board in Fulton and DeKalb Counties.

36. Data on intersections showing the average number of vehicles are available on the DOT Web site (www.dot.state.ga.us/DOT/plan-prog/transportation_data/TrafficCD/index.shtml). Collecting such information is part of the Georgia State Traffic and Report System (STARS) of the GDOT.

37. As chapter 6 indicates, highway construction PACs are among the groups with the highest reported campaign contributions in Georgia.

38. Ariel Hart, "DOT Ties Aid Firms; Ex-Staffers Know Ropes, Win Jobs," *AJC*, December 14, 2005, A1; Ariel Hart, "Bids for Project Top Estimate, $147 Million Price Will Be Closely Evaluated by DOT," *AJC*, October 22, 2005, B1.

39. Julie B. Hairston. "Explosive Growth Makes Arc Necessary, GDOT Says Road Needed to Alleviate Congestion, Reduce Fatalities, According to Officials," *AJC*, April 22, 2002, E6; Julie B. Hairston, "Eastern Arc on Fast Track, Western Segment Expected to Be Placed on Back Burner," *AJC*, July 1, 2002, E1.

40. Maria Saporta, "Transform Northern Arc Land into Green Acres," *AJC*, April 28, 2003, E3.

41. The thirteen counties are Cherokee, Clayton, Cobb, Coweta, DeKalb, Douglas, Fayette, Forsyth, Fulton, Gwinnett, Henry, Paulding, and Rockdale.

42. Paul Donsky, "Transit Agencies May Join Forces: Vote Today Could Lead to Metro Plan," *AJC*, December 15, 2005, E1.

43. Brown 2002.

44. Stacy Shelton, "Perdue Swears in 24 Environmental Advisors," *AJC,* June 9, 2005, C3.

45. David Pendered and Ty Tagami, "Park Could Bloom in Urban Wasteland: City Moves Beltline Vision Quickly Ahead," *AJC,* January 15, 2006, D1.

46. *Kelo v. New London,* no. 04-108 (2005).

47. Sonji Jacobs and Nancy Badertscher, "Legislature 2006: In Brief," *AJC,* January 26, 2006, C4; Christopher Quinn, "Cities Defend Land Condemnation," *AJC,* September 27, 2005, B1; Christopher Quinn, "Perdue to Guide Eminent Domain," *AJC,* January 30, 2006, B1.

48. The city also increased water rates and undertook several major construction projects; for more information, see http://www.cleanwateratlanta.org/default.htm. The major party bringing the lawsuit was the Upper Chattahoochee Riverkeeper; for more information, see http://www.ucriverkeeper.org/programs5.htm.

49. The Georgia Water Planning and Policy Center has several working papers on this issue, including Rowles and Thompson 2005.

50. Harold Reheis, "Equal Time: Water Transfers Prove Useful and Cost Effective" (editorial), *AJC,* July 10, 2003, A15.

51. Bob Hanner, "Water Resource Management: Critics of House Bill Lob Many False Claims" (editorial), *AJC,* April 9, 2003, A23.

52. *Growing Old and Polluting the Air* 1999.

53. McCutchen 1994.

54. Wong 2003.

55. U.S. Census Bureau 2004c, 5, 11.

56. Wong 2003.

57. Mary MacDonald, "School Funding No. 1 Priority: School Board Favors Fairer Formula to Divvy Taxes," *AJC,* December 22, 2005, JN1; Kristina Torres, "Schools May Help Sue State," *AJC,* January 12, 2006, JH7.

58. See Wong 2003, 365–374.

59. See Herzik 1991.

60. See Henig 1994.

61. Bartley 1990, 194–232; Henig et al. 1999.

62. SchoolMatters 2006. Data for SchoolMatters reports were supplied by the Georgia Department of Education, Public Information and Publications Division.

63. In 2001, Georgia students in grades one through six took ten standardized tests in English and math. Only sixteen states test more often than Georgia in the elementary grades.

64. Patti Ghezzi, "Thousands Fail Portions of CRCT," *AJC,* June 12, 2006, B1; "CRCT Failure Rates, 2004–2006," *AJC,* June 6, 2006, A6.

65. U.S. Census Bureau 2004a.

66. Georgia Department of Education 2004.

67. See Gibson 2004.

68. Bill Rankin, "Petitions Key in Cobb Sticker Case: School Board's Attorney Doubts Documents Exist," *AJC*, January 5, 2006, C1.

69. Data from the American Federation of Teachers (http://www.aft.org/salary/ 2004/download/releases/SalarySurvey-Ga.pdf).

70. National Education Association, "Rankings of the States 2004 and Estimates of School Statistics 2005," http://www.nea.org/edstats/ images/05rankings-update.pdf.

71. *Federal Register,* vol. 69, no. 30, February 13, 2004, 7336–7338.

72. U.S. Census Bureau 2005c.

73. U.S. Census Bureau 2003; Fronczek 2005.

74. Family Connection Partnership, Georgia KIDS COUNT data (http://www .gafcp.org/kidscount/kidscountregfm.html).

75. Summaries of the 2007 Georgia budget can be accessed at http://www.gbgi .org/pubs/gabudget/20060407.pdf. The full document is available at http://sao .georgia.gov/00/channel_createdate/0,2095,39779022_54620664,00.html.

76. Figures calculated from data available from the National Center for Children in Poverty, Columbia University (http://nccp.org/wizard/wizard.cgi?action= x&page=pol_1).

77. Georgia Department of Human Resources 2003.

78. See, for example, Becker 1996, 22.

79. Georgia Department of Health and Human Services 1997; Georgia Department of Human Resources 2003.

80. Coffey 2006.

81. Coffey 2006.

82. Sheets 2005.

83. U.S. Bureau of Justice Statistics, *Sourcebook of Criminal Justice Statistics 2006,* table 2.1.2006 (http://www.albany.edu/sourcebook/pdf/t212006.pdf).

84. U.S. Bureau of Justice Statistics, *Sourcebook of Criminal Justice Statistics 2005,* table 2.37.2005 (http://www.albany.edu/sourcebook/pdf/t2372005.pdf).

85. Gary M. Pomerantz and Denise Prodigo-Herrmann, "Crime, Competition, and Ratings," *AJC*, June 23, 1996, B2.

86. U.S. Federal Bureau of Investigation 2005a, sec. 2, "Offenses Reported," 76–84, 98, 147–148.

87. U.S. Census Bureau 2006c, 291, 299–300.

88. On mandatory training, see *OCGA*, title 35, chap. 8, secs. 8–10.

89. Georgia Department of Public Safety 2003, 24, 33–34.

90. Georgia Bureau of Investigation n.d.

91. U.S. Census Bureau 2005a, 2004c.

92. For one interesting account of a sheriff and his constituents, see Greene 1991. See also Jingle Davis, "Sheriff Faces Felony Count in Camden," *AJC*, July 18, 1992, B3; Corey Dade and Mae Gentry, "Brown Case Verdicts Welcomed by County," *AJC*, August 11, 2005, JB1 (and many more articles related to the conviction of former DeKalb sheriff Sidney Dorsey for murdering the man who had defeated him); D. L. Bennett, "Fulton Salvages Barrett's Sour Deal," *AJC*, September 23, 2005, A1;

Rhonda Cook, "Fulton Sheriff Dogged by Critics," *AJC*, January 29, 2006, D1; as well as many more *AJC* articles on the problems in the Fulton County Sheriff's Office during 2003–2005.

93. On county police departments, see *OCGA*, title 36, chap. 8.

94. U.S. Bureau of Justice Statistics, *Sourcebook of Criminal Justice Statistics 2003*, table 6.2 (http://www.albany.edu/sourcebook/pdf/t62.pdf); U.S. Bureau of Justice Statistics, *Sourcebook of Criminal Justice Statistics 2006*, table 6.80.2006 (http://www.albany.edu/sourcebook/pdf/t6802006.pdf); U.S. Bureau of Justice Statistics, *Sourcebook of Criminal Justice Statistics 2004*, table 6.84.2004 (http://www.albany.edu/sourcebook/pdf/t6842004.pdf).

95. Georgia Department of Corrections 2005, 33, 41–42; Chilton 1991.

96. Bill Rankin and Cameron McWhirter, "Georgia Death Penalty Bashed," *AJC*, January 29, 2006, A1.

REFERENCES

Abney, Glenn. 1988. "Lobbying by the Insiders: Parallels of State Agencies and Interest Groups." *Public Administration Review* 48 (September–October): 911–917.

Abney, Glenn, and John D. Hutcheson Jr. 1981. "Race, Representation, and Trust: Changes in Attitudes after the Election of a Black Mayor." *Public Opinion Quarterly* 45 (Spring): 91–100.

Abney, Glenn, and Thomas P. Lauth. 1986. *The Politics of State and City Administration*. Albany: State University of New York Press.

Abramowitz, Alan I., and Kyle L. Saunders. 1998. "Ideological Realignment in the U.S. Electorate." *Journal of Politics* 60 (August): 634–652.

Akioka, Lorena M. 2004. *Georgia Statistical Abstract, 2004–2005*. Athens: Selig Center for Economic Growth, Terry College of Business, University of Georgia.

Aldrich, John. 2000. "Southern Parties in State and Nation." *Journal of Politics* 62 (August): 643–670.

Altman, James S., Paul Bolster, and James L. Bross. 1986. "Judicial Review of Georgia Zoning: Cyclones and Doldrums in the Windmills of the Mind." *Georgia State University Law Review* 2 (Spring–Summer): 97–129.

Altshuler, Alan, and David Luberoff. 2003. *Mega-Projects: The Changing Politics of Urban Public Investment*. Washington, D.C.: Brookings Institution Press.

American Judicature Society. N.d. *Judicial Selection in the States: Appellate and General Jurisdiction Courts: Summary of Initial Selection Methods*. http://www.ajs.org/js/SummaryInitialSelection.pdf.

Ammons, David N., and Richard W. Campbell. 1992. "Does Your County Have Professional Management . . . or Just Limited Professional Assistance?" *Georgia County Government*, July, 24–27.

Anderson, William. 1975. *The Wild Man from Sugar Creek: The Political Career of Eugene Talmadge*. Baton Rouge: Louisiana State University Press.

Association County Commissioners of Georgia. 2006. *2006 Legislative Priorities*. http://www.accg.org/static/policy_priorities_2006.pdf.

———. 2003. *Characteristics of Georgia County Government 2003.* http://www.accg
.org/static/formofgov.pdf.

Atkeson, Lonna Rae, and Randall W. Partin. 1995. "Economic and Referendum Voting: A Comparison of Gubernatorial and Senatorial Elections." *American Political
Science Review* 89 (March): 99–107.

Bachtel, Douglas C., and Laura Boatright, eds. 1992. *The Georgia County Guide.*
Athens: Cooperative Extension Service, University of Georgia.

Barrett, Katherine, and Richard Greens. 1999. "Grading the States." *Governing,*
February, 17–28.

Bartley, Numan V. 1997. *The Rise of Massive Resistance: Race and Politics in the South
during the 1950s.* Baton Rouge: Louisiana State University Press.

———. 1991. "Part Six: 1940 to the Present." In *A History of Georgia,* 2nd ed., edited
by Kenneth Coleman, 337–407. Athens: University of Georgia Press.

———. 1990. *The Creation of Modern Georgia.* 2nd ed. Athens: University of Georgia
Press.

———. 1970. *From Thurmond to Wallace: Political Tendencies in Georgia, 1948–1968.*
Baltimore: Johns Hopkins University Press.

Bass, Jack, and Walter DeVries. 1976. *The Transformation of Southern Politics: Social
Change and Political Consequence since 1945.* New York: Basic Books.

Baumgartner, Frank R., and Bryan D. Jones. 1993. *Agendas and Instability in American Politics.* Chicago: University of Chicago Press.

Becker, Gary S. 1996. "How to End Welfare as We Know It" (editorial). *Business
Week,* June 3, 22.

Berkovitz, Tobe. 1996. *Political Media Buying: A Brief Guide.* www.ksg.harvard.edu/
case/3pt/berkovitz.html#anchor572218.

Berman, David. 2001. "State-Local Relations: Authority, Finances, Partnerships." In
Municipal Yearbook 2001, 61–76. Washington, D.C.: International City/County
Management Association.

Berry, Jeffrey M., Kent E. Portney, and Ken Thomson. 1993. *The Rebirth of Urban
Democracy.* Washington, D.C.: Brookings Institution Press.

Berube, Alan, Bruce Katz, and Robert E. Lang, eds. 2006. *Redefining Urban and Suburban America: Evidence from Census 2000.* Vol. 3. Washington, D.C.: Brookings
Institution Press.

———, eds. 2005. *Redefining Urban and Suburban America: Evidence from Census
2000.* Vol. 2. Washington, D.C.: Brookings Institution Press.

Beyle, Thad. 2005. "Governors: Elections, Campaign Costs and Powers." In *The Book
of the States,* 37:191–202. Lexington, Ky.: Council of State Governments.

———. 2003. "The Governors." In *Politics in the American States: A Comparative
Analysis,* 8th ed., edited by Virginia Gray and Russell L. Hanson, 194–231. Washington, D.C.: CQ Press.

———. 1996. "Governors: The Middlemen and Women in Our Political System." In
Politics in the American States: A Comparative Analysis, 6th ed., edited by Virginia
Gray and Herbert Jacob, 207–252. Washington, D.C.: CQ Press.

Bibby, John F., and Thomas M. Holbrook. 2003. "Parties and Elections." In *Politics in the American States: A Comparative Analysis*, 8th ed., edited by Virginia Gray and Russell L. Hanson, 62–99. Washington, D.C.: CQ Press.

Black, Earl, and Merle Black. 2002. *The Rise of Southern Republicans*. Cambridge: Belknap Press of Harvard University Press.

———. 1992. *The Vital South: How Presidents Are Elected*. Cambridge: Harvard University Press.

———. 1987. *Politics and Society in the South*. Cambridge: Harvard University Press.

Blakely, Edward J., and Ted K. Bradshaw. 2002. *Planning Local Economic Development: Theory and Practice*. 3rd ed. Thousand Oaks, Calif.: Sage.

Boney, F. N. 1991. "Part Three: 1820–1865." In *A History of Georgia*, 2nd ed., edited by Kenneth Coleman, 127–204. Athens: University of Georgia Press.

Bonneau, Chris W. 2005. "What Price Justice(s)? Understanding Campaign Spending in State Supreme Court Elections." *State Politics and Policy Quarterly* 5 (Summer): 107–125.

Bowler, Shaun, and Todd Donovan. 2003. "The Initiative Process." In *Politics in the American States: A Comparative Analysis*, 8th ed., edited by Virginia Gray and Russell L. Hanson, 129–156. Washington, D.C.: CQ Press.

Bowman, Ann O'M., and Richard C. Kearney. 2002. *State and Local Government*. 5th ed. Boston: Houghton Mifflin.

Brace, Paul. 1993. *State Government and Economic Performance*. Baltimore: Johns Hopkins University Press.

Brace, Paul, Kevin Arceneaux, Martin Johnson, and Stacy G. Ulbig. 2004. "Does State Political Ideology Change over Time?" *Political Research Quarterly* 57 (December): 529–540.

Bratton, Kathleen, and Rorie L. Spill. 2002. "Existing Diversity and Judicial Selection: The Role of the Appointment Method in Establishing Gender Diversity in State Supreme Courts." *Social Science Quarterly* 83 (June): 504–518.

Bridges, Amy, and Richard Kronick. 1999. "Writing the Rules to Win the Game: The Middle-Class Regimes of Municipal Reformers." *Urban Affairs Review* 34 (May): 691–706.

Brown, R. Steven. 2002. *Coping with the Budget Crunch*. www.ecos.org/files/685_file-brown_pdf.

Bullard, Angela M., and Deil S. Wright. 1993. "Circumventing the Glass Ceiling: Women Executives in American State Governments." *Public Administration Review* 53 (May–June): 189–202.

Bullock, Charles S., III. 1993. *The Partisan, Racial, and Gender Makeup of Georgia County Offices*. Athens: Vinson Institute of Government, University of Georgia.

———. 1985. "Aftermath of the Voting Rights Act: Racial Voting Patterns in the Atlanta-Area Elections." In *The Voting Rights Act: Consequences and Implications*, edited by Lorn S. Foster, 185–208. New York: Praeger.

Bullock, Charles S., III, and Bruce A. Campbell. 1984. "Racist or Racial Voting in the 1981 Municipal Elections." *Urban Affairs Quarterly* 20 (December): 149–64.

Bullock, Charles S., III, M. V. Hood III, and Richard Clark. 2005. "Punch Cards, Jim Crow, and Al Gore: Explaining Voter Trust in the Electoral System in Georgia, 2000." *State Politics and Policy Quarterly* 5 (Fall): 283–294.

Bullock, Charles S., III, and Loch K. Johnson. 1992. *Runoff Elections in the United States*. Chapel Hill: University of North Carolina Press.

Bullock, Charles S., III, and Charles M. Lamb, eds. 1984. *Implementation of Civil Rights Policy*. Monterey, Calif.: Brooks/Cole.

Burke, Brendan F., and Deil S. Wright. 2002. "Reassessing and Reconciling Reinvention in the American States: Exploring State Administrative Performance." *State and Local Government Review* 34 (Winter): 7–19.

Campbell Public Affairs Institute, Maxwell School of Public Affairs, Syracuse University. 2002. *Paths to Performance in State and Local Government: A Final Assessment from the Maxwell School of Citizenship and Public Affairs*. http://www.maxwell.syr.edu/gpp/grade/2002full.asp.

———. 2001. *The Government Performance Project: 2001 State Grade Report*. http://www.maxwell.syr.edu/gpp/grade/state_2001/index.asp?id=2.

Carr, Jered B., and Richard C. Feiock, eds. 2004. *City-County Consolidation and Its Alternatives: Reshaping the Local Government Landscape*. Armonk, N.Y.: Sharpe.

Carter, Jimmy. 1992. *Turning Point: A Candidate, a State, and a Nation Come of Age*. New York: Times Books.

Chilton, Bradley. 1991. *Prisons under the Gavel: The Federal Takeover of Georgia Prisons*. Columbus: Ohio State University Press.

Chubb, John E., and Terry M. Moe. 1990. *Politics, Markets, and America's Schools*. Washington, D.C.: Brookings Institution Press.

Clark, John A., and John M. Bruce. 1995. "Checkbooks and Grassroots: Comparing Political Activists in Georgia." Paper presented at the annual meeting of the Midwest Political Science Association, Chicago, April 6–8.

Clark, John A., and Charles L. Prysby, eds. 2004. *Southern Political Party Activists: Patterns of Conflict and Change, 1991–2001*. Lexington: University Press of Kentucky.

Cobb, James C. 1993. *The Selling of the South: The Southern Crusade for Industrial Development, 1936–1990*. 2nd ed. Urbana: University of Illinois Press.

Cobb, James C., and William Stueck, eds. 2005. *Globalization and the American South*. Athens: University of Georgia Press.

Coffey, Sarah Beth. 2006. "Undocumented Immigrants in Georgia: Tax Contribution and Fiscal Concerns." *Georgia Budget and Policy Institute: Georgia Revenue Analysis*. www.gbpi.org/pubs/garevenue/20060119.pdf.

Coleman, Kenneth. 1991. "Part Two: 1775–1820." In *A History of Georgia*, 2nd ed., edited by Kenneth Coleman, 69–126. Athens: University of Georgia Press.

Conant, James K. 1992. "Executive Branch Reorganization: Can It Be an Effective Antidote for Fiscal Stress in the States?" *State and Local Government Review* 24 (Winter): 3–11.

Cortright, Joseph, and Heike Mayer. 2004. "Increasingly Rank: The Use and Misuse of Rankings in Economic Development." *Economic Development Quarterly* 18 (February): 34–39.

Council of State Governments. 1996, 2003, 2004, 2005. *The Book of the States.* Vols. 31, 35, 36, 37. Lexington, Ky.: Council of State Governments.

Cox, George H., John H. Daily, and Roger N. Pajari. 1991. "Local Government Support of Economic Development." *Public Administration Quarterly* 15 (Fall): 304–327.

Cox, George H., and Raymond A. Rosenfeld. 2001. *State and Local Government: Public Life in America.* Belmont, Calif.: Wadsworth/Thomson Learning.

C-SPAN.org. 2006. *109th Congress: A Profile.* www.c-span.org/congress/109congress .asp.

Dalehite, Esteban G., John L. Mikesell, and C. Kurt Zorn. 2005. "Variation in Property Tax Abatement Programs among States." *Economic Development Quarterly* 19 (May): 157–173.

Davidson, Chandler, and Bernard Grofman. 1994. *Quiet Revolution in the South.* Princeton: Princeton University Press.

Diefenbacher, Jennifer G. S., and W. Edwin Sumner. 2004. *Annexation: Putting the Pieces Together.* 4th ed. Atlanta: Georgia Municipal Association.

DiLeo, Daniel. 2001. "To Develop or to Redistribute: An Analysis of the Content of Governors' Agendas." *State and Local Government Review* 33 (Winter): 52–59.

Dilger, Robert Jay. 1995. "A Comparative Analysis of Gubernatorial Enabling Resources." *State and Local Government Review* 27 (Spring): 118–126.

Dye, Thomas R. 2005. *Understanding Public Policy.* 11th ed. Upper Saddle River, N.J.: Pearson Education.

Eaton, Thomas A., and Susette M. Talarico. 1996. "A Profile of Tort Litigation in Georgia and Reflections on Tort Reform." *Georgia Law Review* 30 (Spring): 627–729.

Eisinger, Peter K. 1988. *The Rise of the Entrepreneurial State: State and Local Economic Development Policy in the United States.* Madison: University of Wisconsin Press.

Elling, Richard C. 1996. "Bureaucracy: Maligned yet Essential." In *Politics in the American States,* 6th ed., edited by Virginia Gray and Herbert Jacob, 286–318. Washington, D.C.: CQ Press.

Elliott, Euel, Gerald S. Gryski, and Bruce Reed. 1990. "Minor Party Support in State Legislative Elections." *State and Local Government Review* 22 (Fall): 123–131.

Epstein, Lee. 1994. "Exploring the Participation of Organized Interests in State Court Litigation." *Political Research Quarterly* 47 (June): 335–351.

Erikson, Robert S., Norman L. Luttbeg, and Kent L. Tedin. 1991. *American Public Opinion: Its Origins, Content, and Impact.* 4th ed. New York: Macmillan.

Erikson, Robert S., Gerald C. Wright, and John P. McIver. 1993. *Statehouse Democracy: Public Opinion and Policy in the American States.* Cambridge: Cambridge University Press.

Evans, Lawton B. 1972 (1898). *History of Georgia.* New York: American Book.

Fiorina, Morris P. 1996. *Divided Government.* 2nd ed. Boston: Allyn and Bacon.

Fiorina, Morris P., with Jeremy C. Pope and Samuel J. Abrams. 2005. *Culture War? The Myth of a Polarized America.* New York: Pearson.

Fisher, Patrick, and David Nice. 2005. "Staffing the Governor's Office: A Comparative Analysis." In *The Book of the States,* 37:203–207. Lexington, Ky.: Council of State Governments.

Fite, Gilbert Courtland. 1991. *Richard B. Russell, Jr., Senator from Georgia.* Chapel Hill: University of North Carolina Press.

Flanigan, William, and Nancy H. Zingale. 2002. *Political Behavior of the American Electorate.* 10th ed. Washington, D.C.: CQ Press.

Fleischmann, Arnold. 2004. "All the Ingredients: Race, Class, Gender, and Sexuality in the 2001 Election for Atlanta City Council President." Paper presented at the annual meeting of the Western Political Science Association, Portland, Oreg., March 11–13.

———. 2000. "Regionalism and City-County Consolidation in Small Metro Areas." *State and Local Government Review* 32 (Fall): 213–226.

———. 1989. "Politics, Administration, and Local Land-Use Regulation: Analyzing Zoning as a Policy Process." *Public Administration Review* 49 (July–August): 337–344.

———. 1986. "The Goals and Strategies of Local Boundary Changes: Government Organization or Private Gain?" *Journal of Urban Affairs* 8 (Fall): 63–76.

Fleischmann, Arnold, and Jennifer Custer. 2004. "Goodbye, Columbus." In *Case Studies of City-County Consolidation: Reshaping the Local Government Landscape,* edited by Suzanne M. Leland and Kurt Thurmaier, 46–59. Armonk, N.Y.: Sharpe.

Fleischmann, Arnold, and Jason Hardman. 2004. "Hitting Below the Bible Belt: The Development of the Gay Rights Movement in Atlanta." *Journal of Urban Affairs* 26 (2004): 407–426.

Fleischmann, Arnold, and Carol Pierannunzi. 1990. "Citizens, Development Interests, and Local Land-Use Regulations." *Journal of Politics* 52 (August): 838–853.

Fleischmann, Arnold, and Lana Stein. 1998. "Campaign Contributions in Local Elections." *Political Research Quarterly* 51 (September): 673–689.

———. 1987. "Minority and Female Success in Municipal Runoff Elections." *Social Science Quarterly* 68 (June): 378–385.

Florida, Richard. 2005. *Cities and the Creative Class.* New York: Routledge.

Fronczek, Peter. 2005. *Income, Earnings, and Poverty from the 2004 American Community Survey.* American Community Survey Reports. Washington, D.C.: U.S. Census Bureau. http://www.census.gov/prod/2005pubs/acs-01.pdf.

Gastner, Michael, Cosma Shalizi, and Mark Newman. 2004. *Maps and Cartograms of the 2004 U.S. Presidential Election Results.* http://www-personal.umich .edu/~mejn/election/.

Georgia Budget and Policy Institute. 2005a. *Don't Tax and They Will Come? The Questionable Link between State Corporate Income Taxes and Economic Development.* Atlanta: Georgia Budget and Policy Institute. http://www.gbpi.org/ pubs/20050718report.pdf.

———. 2005b. *Tax Reform and Modernization in Georgia.* Atlanta: Georgia Budget and Policy Institute. http://www.gbpi.org/pubs/specialreport/20050207.pdf.

Georgia Bureau of Investigation. N.d. *2004 Annual Report.* http://www.ganet.org/gbi/Annual_Report.html.

Georgia Court of Appeals. N.d. *History of the Court of Appeals.* http://www.gaappeals.us/history/.

Georgia Department of Archives and History. 2004. *Georgia Official and Statistical Register.* Atlanta: Georgia Department of Archives and History.

Georgia Department of Community Affairs. 2005a. *2005 Directory of Registered Local Government Authorities.* http://www.dca.state.ga.us/development/research/programs/RASearch.asp?SearchYear=2005.

———. 2005b. *Georgia Local Government Finance: 2004 Highlights (December).* Atlanta: Georgia Department of Community Affairs.

———. 2004–2005. *Service Delivery Strategies.* http://www.dca.state.ga.us/development/PlanningQualityGrowth/programs/serviceDeliveryStrategy.asp.

———. 2004a. *2004 County Government Information Catalog (November).* Atlanta: Georgia Department of Community Affairs.

———. 2004b. *2004 Municipal Government Information Catalog (November).* Atlanta: Georgia Department of Community Affairs.

———. 1993. *Local Government Efficiency Grant General Program Guidelines.* Atlanta: Georgia Department of Community Affairs.

Georgia Department of Corrections. 2005. *FY 2004 Annual Report.* http://www.dcor.state.ga.us/pdf/05AnnualReport3.pdf.

Georgia Department of Education. 2004. *Enrollment in Compensatory Programs.* http://reportcard2004.gaosa.org/k12/demographics.aspX?ID=ALL:ALL&TestKey=CompProg&TestType=demographics.

Georgia Department of Health and Human Services. 1997. *Welfare Reform in Georgia: Annual Report 1997.* Atlanta: Georgia Department of Health and Human Services.

Georgia Department of Human Resources. 2003. *TANF in Georgia.* http://dfcs.dhr.georgia.gov/DHR-DFCS/DHR-DFCS_CommonFiles/4922055TANF_in_Georgia.pdf.

Georgia Department of Public Safety. 2003. *2003 Annual Report.* http://dps.georgia.gov/vgn/images/portal/cit_1210/45/36/398136822003_Annual_Report.pdf.

Georgia General Assembly. 2005a. *2005 Summary of General Statutes.* http://www.legis.state.ga.us/legis/2005_06/05sumdocnet.htm.

———. 2005b. *Acts and Resolutions of the General Assembly of the State of Georgia: 2005.* Atlanta: Georgia General Assembly.

———. 1981. *Acts and Resolutions of the Georgia General Assembly: 1981.* Vol. 2, *Local and Special Acts and Resolutions.* Atlanta: Georgia General Assembly.

Georgia Governor's Commission for a New Georgia. 2006. *Task Force Recommendations.* http://www.newgeorgia.org/taskforcerecommendations.shtml.

Georgia Governor's Commission on Effectiveness and Economy in Government. 1992. *Final Report.* Atlanta: Governor's Commission on Effectiveness and Economy in Government.

Georgia Governor's Local Governance Commission. 1992. *A Platform for Local Governance Change.* Atlanta: Governor's Local Governance Commission.

Georgia Governor's Office of Planning and Budget. 2006. *The Governor's Budget Report: FY 2007.* http://www.opb.state.ga.us/Budget/BudgetBook_Final_07.pdf.

Georgia House of Representatives. 2005. *Rules, Ethics, and Decorum of the House of Representatives, 2005 Session.* Atlanta: Georgia House of Representatives.

Georgia Senate. 2005. *Rules of the Georgia State Senate, 2005 Session.* Atlanta: Georgia Senate.

Georgia Senate, Public Information Office and Clerk's Office. 2006. *Members of the General Assembly of Georgia.* http://www.legis.state.ga.us/legis/2005_06/house/downloads/2006pictureBook.pdf.

Georgia Student Finance Commission. 2006. *HOPE Scholarship Program, September 1, 1993–May 20, 2006.* http://www.gsfc.org/Hope/Hope_support/html_summary_grant_all_cov_H.htm.

Georgia Supreme Court Commission on Racial and Ethnic Bias in the Court System. 1995. *Let Justice Be Done: Equally, Fairly, and Impartially.* Atlanta: Georgia Supreme Court Commission on Racial and Ethnic Bias in the Court System.

Gerber, Elizabeth R., and Justin H. Phillips. 2003. "Development Ballot Measures, Interest Group Endorsements, and the Political Geography of Growth Preferences." *American Journal of Political Science* 47 (October): 625–639.

Gibson, M. Troy. 2004. "Culture Wars in State Education Policy: A Look at the Relative Treatment of Evolutionary Theory in State Science Standards." *Social Science Quarterly* 85 (December): 1129–1149.

Gimpel, James G., and Jason E. Schuknecht. 2003. *Patchwork Nation: Sectionalism and Political Change in American Politics.* Ann Arbor: University of Michigan Press.

Glick, Henry R. 2003. "Courts: Politics and the Judicial Process." In *Politics in the American States: A Comparative Analysis,* 8th ed., edited by Virginia Gray and Russell L. Hanson, 232–260. Washington, D.C.: CQ Press.

———. 1993. *Courts, Politics, and Justice.* 3rd ed. New York: McGraw-Hill.

Gorton, Joe, and John L. Boies. 1999. "Sentencing Guidelines and Racial Disparity across Time: Pennsylvania Prison Sentences in 1977, 1983, 1992, and 1993." *Social Science Quarterly* 80 (March): 37–54.

Grady, Dennis O. 1987. "State Economic Development Initiatives: Why Do States Compete?" *State and Local Government Review* 19 (Fall): 86–94.

Gray, Virginia. 2003. "The Socioeconomic and Political Context of States." In *Politics in the American States: A Comparative Analysis,* 8th ed., edited by Virginia Gray and Russell L. Hanson, 1–30. Washington, D.C.: CQ Press.

———. 1973. "Innovations in the States: A Diffusions Study." *American Journal of Political Science* 67 (December): 1174–1185.

Greene, Melissa Fay. 1991. *Praying for Sheetrock: A Work of Nonfiction.* Reading, Mass.: Addison-Wesley.

Growing Old and Polluting the Air: Air Quality Laboratory Monitors Emissions of an Aging Vehicle Fleet (press release). 1999. http://gtresearchnews.gatech.edu/newsrelease/EMISSION.html.

Haeberle, Steven H. 1993. "Divisive Competition in Runoff Primaries." *Southeastern Politics Review* 21 (Winter): 79–98.

Hajnal, Zoltan L., and Paul G. Lewis. 2003. "Municipal Institutions and Voter Turnout in Local Elections." *Urban Affairs Review* 38 (May): 645–668.

Hall, Melinda Gann. 2001. "State Supreme Courts in American Democracy." *American Political Science Review* 95 (June): 315–330.

———. 1992. "Electoral Politics and Strategic Voting in State Supreme Courts." *Journal of Politics* 54 (May): 427–446.

Hall, Melinda Gann, and Paul Brace. 1996. "Justices' Responses to Case Facts: An Interactive Model." *American Politics Quarterly* 24 (April): 237–261.

———. 1994. "The Vicissitudes of Death by Decree: Forces Influencing Capital Punishment Decision Making in State Supreme Courts." *Social Science Quarterly* 75 (March): 136–151.

Hall, Thad E. 2002. "Changes in Legislative Support for the Governors' Program over Time." *Legislative Studies Quarterly* 27 (February): 107–122.

Hamm, Keith, and Gary Moncrief. 2003. "Legislative Politics in the States." In *Politics in the American States: A Comparative Analysis,* 8th ed., edited by Virginia Gray and Russell L. Hanson, 157–193. Washington, D.C.: CQ Press.

Harward, Brian M. 2003. "Legal Services for the Poor in the United States." Ph.D. diss., University of Georgia.

Hayes, Allan J. 1992. "Lobbying in Georgia." Typescript, Department of Political Science, University of Georgia.

Heilig, Peggy, and Robert Mundt. 1994. *Your Voice at City Hall: The Politics, Procedures, and Policies of District Representation.* Albany: State University of New York Press.

Henderson, Harold P. 1991. *The Politics of Change in Georgia: A Political Biography of Ellis Arnall.* Athens: University of Georgia Press.

Henderson, Harold P., and Gary L. Roberts. 1988. *Georgia Governors in an Age of Change: From Ellis Arnall to George Busbee.* Athens: University of Georgia Press.

Henig, Jeffrey. 1994. *Rethinking School Choice: Limits of the Market Metaphor.* Princeton: Princeton University Press.

Henig, Jeffrey, Richard Hula, Marion Orr, and Desiree Pedescleaux. 1999. *The Color of School Reform: Race, Politics, and the Challenge of Urban Education.* Princeton: Princeton University Press.

Hershey, Marjorie Randon, and Paul Allen Beck. 2003. *Party Politics in America.* 10th ed. New York: Longman.

Herzik, Eric B. 1991. "Policy Agendas and Gubernatorial Leadership." In *Gubernatorial Leadership and State Policy,* edited by Eric B. Herzik and Brent W. Brown, 25–37. Westport, Conn.: Greenwood.

Hill, Melvin B., Jr. 1994. *The Georgia State Constitution: A Reference Guide.* Westport, Conn.: Greenwood.

Hirlinger, Michael W. 1992. "Citizen-Initiated Contacting of Local Government Officials: A Multivariate Explanation." *Journal of Politics* 54 (May): 553–564.

Holbrook, Thomas M., and Emily Van Dunk. 1993. "Electoral Competition in the American States." *American Political Science Review* 87 (December): 955–962.

Holmes, Malcolm D., Harmon M. Hosch, Howard C. Daudistel, Dolores A. Perez, and Joseph B. Graves. 1993. "Judges' Ethnicity and Minority Sentencing: Evidence Concerning Hispanics." *Social Science Quarterly* 74 (September): 496–506.

Holmes, William F. 1991. "Part Five: 1890–1940." In *A History of Georgia*, 2nd ed., edited by Kenneth Coleman, 255–336. Athens: University of Georgia Press.

Hrebenar, Ronald J., and Ruth K. Scott. 1990. *Interest Group Politics in America*. 2nd ed. Englewood Cliffs, N.J.: Prentice Hall.

Hrebenar, Ronald J., and Clive S. Thomas, eds. 1992. *Interest Group Politics in the Southern States*. Tuscaloosa: University of Alabama Press.

Hudson, Betty J., and Paul T. Hardy, eds. 2005. *Handbook for Georgia Mayors and Councilmembers*. 4th ed. Athens: Vinson Institute of Government, University of Georgia.

———, eds. 2002. *Handbook for Georgia County Commissioners*. 4th ed. Athens: Vinson Institute of Government, University of Georgia.

Hunter, Kenneth G., Laura Ann Wilson, and Gregory G. Brunk. 1991. "Societal Complexity and Interest-Group Lobbying in the American States." *Journal of Politics* 53 (May): 488–503.

Hurst, Julia Nienaber. 2004. "Lieutenant Governors: Powerful in Two Branches." In *The Book of the States*, 36:187–188. Lexington, Ky.: Council of State Governments.

Hutcheson, John D., and James E. Prather. 1988. "Community Mobilization and Participation in the Zoning Process." *Urban Affairs Quarterly* 23 (March): 346–368.

Institute on Money in State Politics. 2006. *State at a Glance: Georgia 2004*. http://www.followthemoney.org/database/state_overview.phtml?si=200410.

———. 2004. *State Elections Overview, 2004*. Helena, Mont.: Institute on Money in State Politics. http://www.followthemoney.org/press/Reports/200601041.pdf.

Jackson, Edwin L. 2006. *Flags That Have Flown over Georgia*. Athens: Vinson Institute of Government, University of Georgia. http://www.cviog.uga.edu/Projects/gainfo/flagsga.htm.

Jackson, Edwin L., and Mary E. Stakes. 1988. *Handbook for Georgia State Agencies*. 2nd ed. Athens: Vinson Institute of Government, University of Georgia.

Jackson, Edwin J., Mary E. Stakes, and Paul T. Hardy. 2001. *Handbook for Georgia Legislators*. 12th ed. Athens: Vinson Institute of Government, University of Georgia.

Jacob, Herbert. 1995. *Law and Politics in the United States*. 2nd ed. New York: HarperCollins.

Jewell, Malcolm E., and Marcia Lynn Whicker. 1994. *Legislative Leadership in the American States*. Ann Arbor: University of Michigan Press.

Jones, Bryan D. 1982. "Assessing the Products of Government." In *Analyzing Urban-Service Distributions*, edited by Richard C. Rich, 155–169. Lexington, Mass.: Lexington Books.

Judd, Dennis R., and Todd Swanstrom. 2004. *City Politics: Private Power and Public Policy*. 4th ed. New York: Pearson-Longman.

Judicial Branch of Georgia, Administrative Office of the Courts. N.d. *Indigent Defense Reports.* http://www.georgiacourts.com/aoc/press/idc/idc.html.

Judicial Council of Georgia and Administrative Office of the Courts. 2005. *2005 Annual Report: Georgia Courts.* http://www.georgiacourts.org/aoc/publications/ar2005.pdf.

———. 2004. *2004 Annual Report: Georgia Courts.* http://www.georgiacourts.org/aoc/publications/ar2004.pdf.

Judicial Qualifications Commission of Georgia. 1984. *Code of Judicial Conduct, State of Georgia.* http://www.georgiacourts.org/agencies/jqc/Pages/canons.html.

Katz, Bruce, and Robert E. Lang, eds. 2003. *Redefining Urban and Suburban America: Evidence from Census 2000.* Vol. 1. Washington, D.C.: Brookings Institution Press.

Katz, Robert N. 1986. "The History of the Georgia Bill of Rights." *Georgia State University Law Review* 3 (Fall–Winter): 83–142.

Kelleher, Christine, and David Lowery. 2004. "Political Participation and Metropolitan Institutional Contexts." *Urban Affairs Review* 39 (July): 720–757.

Key, V. O., Jr. 1964. *Parties, Politics, and Pressure Groups.* New York: Crowell.

———. 1949. *Southern Politics in State and Nation.* New York: Knopf.

King, James D., and Jeffrey E. Cohen. 2005. "What Determines a Governor's Popularity?" *State Politics and Policy Quarterly* 5 (Fall): 225–247.

Kingdon, John W. 1995. *Agendas, Alternatives, and Public Policies.* 2nd ed. New York: HarperCollins.

Krugman, Paul R. 2005. *The Great Unraveling: Losing Our Way in the New Century.* New York: Norton.

Kruse, Kevin M. 2005. *White Flight: Atlanta and the Making of Modern Conservatism.* Princeton: Princeton University Press.

Lamis, Alexander P. 1990. *The Two-Party South.* 2nd ed. New York: Oxford University Press.

Lauth, Thomas P. 1990. "The Governor and the Conference Committee in Georgia." *Legislative Studies Quarterly* 15 (August): 441–453.

———. 1986. "The Executive Budget in Georgia." *State and Local Government Review* 18 (Spring): 56–64.

Leland, Suzanne, and Kurt Thurmaier, eds. 2004. *Case Studies of City-County Consolidation: Reshaping the Local Government Landscape.* Armonk, N.Y.: Sharpe.

Lewis, R. Doug. 2005. "2004 Election Success and State Initiatives." In *The Book of the States,* 37:346–349. Lexington, Ky.: Council of State Governments.

Lieske, Joel. 1993. "Regional Subcultures of the United States." *Journal of Politics* 55 (November): 888–913.

Lockerbie, Brad, and John A. Clark. 1995. "Georgia: Two-Party Reality?" In *Southern State Party Organizations and Activists,* edited by Charles D. Hadley and Lewis Bowman, 127–143. Westport, Conn.: Praeger.

Lublin, David. 2004. *The Republican South: Democratization and Partisan Change.* Princeton: Princeton University Press.

Maddox, H. W. Jerome. 2004. "Working Outside of the State House (and Senate): Outside Careers as an Indicator of Professionalism in American State Legislatures." *State Politics and Policy Quarterly* 4 (Summer): 211–226.

Main, Eleanor C., Lee Epstein, and Debra L. Elovich. 1992. "Georgia: Business as Usual." In *Interest Group Politics in the Southern States,* edited by Ronald J. Hrebenar and Clive S. Thomas, 231–248. Tuscaloosa: University of Alabama Press.

McCutchen, Kelly. 1994. *Can Environmentalists and Business Agree?* www.gppf.org/article.asp?RT=6&p=pub/Environment/env_bus.htm.

McDonald, Laughlin, Michael B. Binford, and Ken Johnson. 1994. "Georgia." In *Quiet Revolution in the South: The Impact of the Voting Rights Act, 1965–1990,* edited by Chandler Davidson and Bernard Grofman, 67–102. Princeton: Princeton University Press.

Mitau, G. Theodore. 1966. *State and Local Government: Politics and Processes.* New York: Scribner.

Moncrief, Gary F., Joel A. Thompson, Michael Haddon, and Robert Hoyer. 1992. "For Whom the Bell Tolls: Term Limits and State Legislatures." *Legislative Studies Quarterly* 17 (February): 37–47.

Murray, Richard, and Arnold Vedlitz. 1978. "Racial Voting Patterns in the South: An Analysis of Major Elections from 1960 to 1977." *Annals of the American Academy of Political and Social Science* 439 (September): 29–39.

National Conference of State Legislatures. 2006a. *Incumbent Reelection Rates in 1994 State Legislative Elections.* http://www.ncsl.org/programs/legman/elect/incmb1.htm.

———. 2006b. *Legislative Term Limits: An Overview.* www.ncsl.org/programs/legman/about/Termlimit.htm.

———. 2006c. *Legislator Compensation 2005.* www.ncsl.org/programs/legman/about/04salary.htm.

———. 2006d. *Total Legislative Turnover 1994-96.* http://www.ncsl.org/programs/legman/elect/tottrn.htm.

———. 2005. *Women in State Legislatures 2005.* www.ncsl.org/programs/wln/2004electioninfo.htm.

———. 2004a. *50 State Staff Count.* www.ncsl.org/programs/legman/about/staffcount2003.htm.

———. 2004b. *2002 Election Turnover.* http://www.ncsl.org/programs/legman/elect/02Turnover.htm.

Newmark, Adam J. 2005. "Measuring State Legislative Lobbying Regulation, 1990–2003." *State Politics and Policy Quarterly* 5 (Summer): 182–191.

Nice, David C. 1994. *Policy Innovation in State Government.* Ames: Iowa State University Press.

———. 1987. *Federalism: The Politics of Intergovernmental Relations.* New York: St. Martin's.

Oliver, J. Eric. 2001. *Democracy in Suburbia.* Princeton: Princeton University Press.

Opheim, Cynthia. 1991. "Explaining Differences in State Lobby Regulation." *Western Political Quarterly* 44 (June): 405–421.

Orfield, Gary, and Carole Ashkinaze. 1991. *The Closing Door: Conservative Policy and Black Opportunity.* Chicago: University of Chicago Press.

Orfield, Myron. 2002. *American Metropolitics: The New Suburban Reality.* Washington, D.C.: Brookings Institution Press.

Osborne, David, and Ted Gaebler. 1992. *Reinventing Government: How the Entrepreneurial Spirit Is Transforming the Public Sector.* Boston: Addison Wesley.

Pastor, Manuel, Jr., Peter Dreier, J. Eugene Grigsby III, and Marta López-Garza. 2000. *Regions That Work: How Cities and Suburbs Can Grow Together.* Minneapolis: University of Minnesota Press.

Perdue, Sonny. 2003a. *2003 Executive Orders.* www.gov.state.ga.us/2003 exec_orders .shtml.

———. 2003b. *Governor Perdue Announces Formation of the Judicial Nominating Commission* (press release). June 11. http://www.gov.state.ga.us/press/2002_2003/press141.shtml.

Peters, B. Guy. 1993. *American Public Policy: Promise and Performance.* 3rd ed. Chatham, N.J.: Chatham House.

Pierannunzi, Carol, and John D. Hutcheson Jr. 1991. "Deracialization in the Deep South: Mayoral Politics in Atlanta." *Urban Affairs Quarterly* 27 (December): 192–201.

Pomerantz, Gary. 1996. *Where Peachtree Meets Sweet Auburn: The Saga of Two Families and the Making of Atlanta.* New York: Scribner.

Rae, Nicol C. 1992. "The Democrats' 'Southern Problem' in Presidential Politics." *Presidential Studies Quarterly* 22 (Winter): 135–151.

Rosenthal, Alan. 2001. *The Third House: Lobbyists and Lobbying in the United States.* 2nd ed. Washington, D.C.: CQ Press.

———. 1990. *Governors and Legislatures: Contending Powers.* Washington, D.C.: CQ Press.

Rothman, David B., and Roy A. Schotland. 2005. "2004 Judicial Elections." In *Book of the States,* 37:305–308. Lexington, Ky.: Council of State Governments.

Rowles, Kristin, and Ben Thompson. 2005. *Water Quality Trading: Legal Analysis for Georgia Watersheds.* Albany: Georgia Water Planning and Policy Center. www .h2opolicycenter.org/pdf_documents/water_workingpapers/2005-021.pdf.

Rubin, Irene. 2000. *The Politics of Public Budgeting: Getting and Spending, Borrowing and Balancing.* 4th ed. New York: Chatham House.

Rusk, David. 2003. *Cities without Suburbs: A Census 2000 Update.* 3rd ed. Washington, D.C.: Woodrow Wilson Center Press.

Saiz, Martin, and Susan Clarke. 2003. "Economic Development and Infrastructure Policy." In *Politics in the American States: A Comparative Analysis,* 8th ed., edited by Virginia Gray and Russell L. Hanson, 418–447. Washington, D.C.: CQ Press.

Scammon, Richard M., and Alice V. McGillivray, eds. 1993, 1996. *America Votes: A Handbook of Contemporary American Election Statistics.* Washington, D.C.: CQ Press.

Scher, Richard K. 1992. *Politics in the New South: Republicanism, Race, and Leadership in the Twentieth Century.* New York: Paragon House.

Schneider, William. 1992. "The Suburban Century Begins." *Atlantic Monthly,* July, 33–44.

SchoolMatters: Georgia's Public Schools and Districts. 2006. Atlanta: Standard and Poor's. http://www.schoolmatters.com/app/location/q/stid=11/llid=111/stllid=211/locid=11/catid=-1/secid=-1/compid=-1/site=pes.

Sclar, Elliott D. 2000. *You Don't Always Get What You Pay For: The Economics of Privatization.* Ithaca: Cornell University Press.

Segers, Mary C., and Timothy A. Byrnes, eds. 1995. *Abortion Politics in American States.* Armonk, N.Y.: Sharpe.

Sentell, R. Perry, Jr. 2004. *Essays on the Supreme Court of Georgia.* Athens: Vinson Institute of Government, University of Georgia.

Sheets, Trina R. 2005. "State Emergency Management and Homeland Security: A Changing Dynamic." In *The Book of the States,* 37:525–529. Lexington, Ky.: Council of State Governments.

Skoro, Charles L. 1988. "Ranking of State Business Climates: An Evaluation of Their Usefulness in Forecasting." *Economic Development Quarterly* 2 (May): 138–152.

Songer, Donald, Ashlyn Kuersten, and Erin Kaheny. 2000. "Why the Haves Don't Always Come Out Ahead: Repeat Players Meet Amici Curiae for the Disadvantaged." *Political Research Quarterly* 53 (September): 537–556.

Spalding, Phinizy. 1991. "Part One: Colonial Period." In *A History of Georgia,* 2nd ed., edited by Kenneth Coleman, 7–67. Athens: University of Georgia Press.

Squire, Peverill. 2006. "Historical Evolution of Legislatures in the United States." *Annual Review of Political Science* 9 (June): 19–44.

———. 2000. "Uncontested Seats in State Legislative Elections." *Legislative Studies Quarterly* 25 (February): 131–146.

———. 1998. "Membership Turnover and Efficient Processing of Legislation." *Legislative Studies Quarterly* 23 (February): 23–32.

———. 1992. "Legislative Professionalism and Membership Diversity in State Legislatures." *Legislative Studies Quarterly* 17 (February): 69–79.

Squire, Peverill, and Christina Fastnow. 1994. "Comparing Gubernatorial and Senatorial Elections." *Political Research Quarterly* 47 (September): 705–720.

State Bar of Georgia. 2006. *Continuing Legal Education.* http://www.gabar.org/programs/continuing_legal_education/.

State Bar of Georgia, Office of the General Counsel. 2006. *Annual Report for Operational Year 2005–2006.* http://www.gabar.org/public/pdf/ogc/ogc_report.pdf.

Steffensmeier, Darrell, and Chester L. Britt. 2001. "Judges' Race and Judicial Decision Making: Do Black Judges Sentence Differently?" *Social Science Quarterly* 82 (December): 749–764.

Stone, Clarence N. 1989. *Regime Politics: Governing Atlanta, 1946–1988*. Lawrence: University Press of Kansas.

Stone, Clarence N., Jeffrey R. Henig, Bryan D. Jones, and Carol Pierannunzi. 2001. *Building Civic Capacity: The Politics of Reforming Urban Schools*. Lawrence: University Press of Kansas.

Storey, Tim. 2005. "2004 Legislative Elections." *Spectrum: The Journal of State Government* 78 (Winter): 8–11.

Swint, Kerwin C. 1998. *Political Consultants and Negative Campaigning*. Lanham, Md.: University Press of America.

Tankersley, Holley, and Jennifer Custer. 2004. "The End of a Regime? The Election of Shirley Franklin as Atlanta's First Female Mayor." Paper presented at the annual meeting of the Western Political Science Association, Portland, Oreg., March 11–13.

Teaford, Jon C. 2002. *The Rise of the States: The Evolution of American State Government*. Baltimore: Johns Hopkins University Press.

Thomas, Clive S., and Ronald J. Hrebenar. 2003. "Interest Groups in the States." In *Politics in the American States: A Comparative Analysis*, 8th ed., edited by Virginia Gray and Russell L. Hanson, 100–128. Washington, D.C.: CQ Press.

———. 1996. "Interest Groups in the States." In *Politics in the American States: A Comparative Analysis*, 6th ed., edited by Virginia Gray and Herbert Jacob, 122–158. Washington, D.C.: CQ Press.

Thompson, Pat, and Stephen R. Boyd. 1994. "Use of the Item Veto in Texas, 1940–1990." *State and Local Government Review* 26 (Winter): 38–45.

Toon, John D. 2004. "Georgia Department of Transportation." In *New Georgia Encyclopedia*. http://www.georgiaencyclopedia.org/nge/Article.jsp?id=h-2444&sug=y.

Torau, Megan A., and Ernest Gross. 2004. "The Effects of Foreign Capital Investment on State Economic Growth." *Economic Development Quarterly* 18 (August): 255–268.

Toulmin, Llewellyn M. 1988. "Equity as a Decision Rule in Determining the Distribution of Urban Public Services." *Urban Affairs Quarterly* 23 (March): 389–413.

U.S. Advisory Commission on Intergovernmental Relations. 1993. *State Laws Governing Local Government Structure and Administration*. Report M-186. Washington, D.C.: U.S. Government Printing Office.

———. 1982. *State and Local Roles in the Federal System*. Report A-88. Washington, D.C.: U.S. Government Printing Office.

U.S. Census Bureau. 2006a. *Foreign Trade Statistics: State Exports for Georgia*. http://www.census.gov/foreign-trade/statistics/state/index.html.

———. 2006b. *Metropolitan and Micropolitan Statistical Areas*. http://www.census.gov/population/www/estimates/metroarea.html.

———. 2006c. *Statistical Abstract of the United States*. Washington, D.C.: U.S. Census Bureau.

————. 2005a. *2002 Census of Governments*. Vol. 4, Government Finances, no. 5, Compendium of Government Finances: 2002. http://www.census.gov/ prod/2005pubs/gc024x5.pdf.

————. 2005b. Cumulative Estimates of Population Change for the United States, and for Puerto Rico and State Rankings: April 1, 2000 to July 1, 2005. http://www .census.gov/popest/states/tables/NST-EST2005-02.csv.

————. 2005c. *Historical Poverty Tables*. http://www.census.gov/hhes/www/poverty/ histpov/hstpov2.html.

————. 2005d. *Statistical Abstract of the United States*. Washington, D.C.: U.S. Census Bureau.

————. 2004a. *2004 American Community Survey: Data Profile Highlights*. www .factfinder.census.gov/servlet/ACSSAFFFacts.

————. 2004b. *2002 Census of Governments*. Vol. 3, no. 2, *Compendium of Public Employment*. http://www.census.gov/prod/2004pubs/gc023x2.pdf.

————. 2004c. *2002 Census of Governments*. Vol. 4, Government Finances, no. 1, Public Education Finances: 2002. http://www.census.gov/prod/2004pubs/ gc024x1.pdf.

————. 2003. *Small Area Income and Poverty Estimates, 2003*. http://www.census .gov/hhes/www/saipe/index.html.

————. 2002a. *2002 Census of Governments*. Vol. 1, no. 1, *Government Organization*. http://www.census.gov/prod/2003pubs/gc021x1.pdf.

————. 2002b. *2002 Census of Governments: Government Units in 2002*. Report GC02-1(P). Washington, D.C.: U.S. Bureau of the Census. http://ftp2.census.gov/ govs/cog/2002COGprelim_report.pdf.

————. 2001a. *Ranking Tables for States: 1990 and 2000*. http://www.census.gov/ population/cen2000/phc-t2/tab03.pdf.

————. 2001b. *Statistical Abstract of the United States*. Washington, D.C.: U.S. Census Bureau.

————. 1995. *Statistical Abstract of the United States*. Washington, D.C.: U.S. Census Bureau.

————. 1994. *Statistical Abstract of the United States*. Washington, D.C.: U.S. Census Bureau.

————. 1987. *Statistical Abstract of the United States*. Washington, D.C.: U.S. Census Bureau.

————. 1983. *Statistical Abstract of the United States*. Washington, D.C.: U.S. Census Bureau.

————. 1971. *Statistical Abstract of the United States*. Washington, D.C.: U.S. Census Bureau.

————. 1963. *Statistical Abstract of the United States*. Washington, D.C.: U.S. Census Bureau.

U.S. Census Bureau, Governments Division. 2005. *Public Education Finances, 2003*. ftp2.census.gov/govs/school/03f33pub.pdf.

U.S. Department of Agriculture. 2004. *2002 Census of Agriculture.* Vol. 1, *State Level Data.* Table 1. http://www.nass.usda.gov/census/census02/volume1/us/st99_1_001_001.pdf.

U.S. Election Assistance Commission. 2000. *Sources of Voter Registration Applications, 1999–2000.* Washington, D.C.: U.S. Election Assistance Commission. www.eac.gov/election_resources/2000table_2.htm.

U.S. Federal Bureau of Investigation. 2005a. *Crime in the United States, 2004.* Washington, D.C.: U.S. Federal Bureau of Investigation. http://www.fbi.gov/ucr/cius_04/.

———. 2005b. *Uniform Crime Reports: Preliminary Semiannual Reports.* Washington, D.C.: U.S. Federal Bureau of Investigation. http://www.fbi.gov/ucr/2005prelim/table4.htm.

U.S. Office of Management and Budget. 2001. *Budget of the United States Government, FY 2002.* http://www.whitehouse.gov/omb/budget/fy2002/budget.html.

Vinson Institute of Government, University of Georgia. 2005a. "Georgians Say New Residents Benefit the State." *Peach State Poll.* www.cviog.uga.edu/peachpoll/2005-09-26data.php.

———. 2005b. *Peach State Poll.* http://www.cviog.uga.edu/peachpoll/2005-05-24data.php.

———. 2005c. *Trends in Public Opinion and Satisfaction with the State of the State.* www.cviog.uga.edu/peachpoll/2005-08-25.pdf.

———. 2004. *The Peach State Poll Examines the Public's View of Democracy and Sense of Political Efficacy.* www.cviog.uga.edu/peachpoll/2004-08-02.pdf.

Walker, Jack L. 1969. "The Diffusion of Innovations among the American States." *American Journal of Political Science* 63 (September): 880–899.

Walters, Jonathan. 1997. "Who Needs Civil Service?" *Governing,* August, 17–21.

Warner, Mildred. 2001. "Local Government Support for Community-Based Economic Development." In *Municipal Yearbook 2001,* 21–27. Washington, D.C.: International City/County Management Association.

Weinstein, Bernard L., and Harold T. Gross. 1988. "The Rise and Fall of the Sun, Rust, and Frost Belts." *Economic Development Quarterly* 2 (February): 9–18.

Welch, Susan. 1990. "The Impact of at-Large Elections on Black and Hispanic Representation." *Journal of Politics* 52 (November): 1050–1076.

Welch, Susan, and Timothy Bledsoe. 1988. *Urban Reform and Its Consequences: A Study in Representation.* Chicago: University of Chicago Press.

Wells, Donald T., and Richard Scheff. 1992. "Performance Issues for Public Authorities in Georgia." In *Public Authorities and Public Policy: The Business of Government,* edited by Jerry Mitchell, 167–176. New York: Greenwood.

Wilson, James Q. 1989. *Bureaucracy: What Government Agencies Do and Why They Do It.* New York: Basic Books.

Witko, Christopher, and Adam J. Newmark. 2005. "Business Mobilization and Public Policy in the U.S. States." *Social Science Quarterly* 86 (June): 356–367.

Wong, Kenneth K. 2003. "The Politics of Education." In *Politics in the American States: A Comparative Analysis*, 8th ed., edited by Virginia Gray and Russell L. Hanson, 357–388. Washington, D.C.: CQ Press.

Wood, Curtis. 2002. "Voter Turnout in City Elections." *Urban Affairs Review* 38 (November): 209–231.

Woodward, C. Vann. 1963. *Tom Watson: Agrarian Rebel*. New York: Oxford University Press.

Wright, Deil S. 2003. "Federalism and Intergovernmental Relations: Traumas, Tensions and Trends." In *Book of the States*, 35:21–25. Lexington, Ky.: Council of State Governments.

Wynes, Charles E. 1991. "Part Four: 1865–1890." In *A History of Georgia*, 2nd ed., edited by Kenneth Coleman, 205–254. Athens: University of Georgia Press.

INDEX